THE SERVANT LEADER:

What the World Needs Now

BARRY K. WEINHOLD, PHD

CICRCL Press

4820 Topaz Drive
Colorado Springs 80918
(719) 445-0565
www.weinholds.org

WHAT READERS ARE SAYING
ABOUT THIS BOOK

"This book not only inspired me to look for the servant leaders in my community but also inspired me to look for the servant leader within myself. I felt changed by reading this book… as if I somehow chose to step into a more powerful part of myself just by reading it."

—*Elaine K. Wolf, MC/LPC/PhD candidate*

"Trump is talking about implementing "extreme vetting" to make sure incoming immigrants share our values. If we used the values outlined in this book, Trump and most other politicians would not make it in the country, let alone be qualified as leaders. Barry's nine-point definition of what a servant leader is should be what we base our values and votes upon. It would be a very different world, especially, if applied to other countries as well."

—*Michael Holtby, LCSW, BCD*

"As we move closer into the transition from leaders of the masses into shared leadership, we need a resource for taking responsibility for leading with love, compassion and empathy. Barry Weinhold's book, "The Servant Leader" is the resource that we've been waiting for."

—*Sharon River Hansen, MA LPC*

"As I continue to develop as a leader - and struggle to recognize my own long-standing limitations - Dr. Weinhold has shown me a path and process that can work in my life now. The Servant Leader is both an inspiration for me to grow beyond my own selfish agenda, as well as a practical toolkit to put this into action. And in the leadership programs I facilitate for Fortune 500 companies, I regularly witness the struggles to reach the Stage Three and Stage Four development that Barry describes - within the individuals and within their company culture."

—*Bob Berry, Director and Author, ItsTheUsers.com and the Youth Life Excellence Virtual Academy*

"The Servant Leader book was a tolling of a bell. I had heard the call many years ago and tried to apply its principles in specific areas of my life. Barry's book has deepened my understanding of a Servant Leader and has given me additional tools as I feel an urgency to live it more fully."

—*Molly Dooley, LCPC, Licensed Clinical Professional Counselor*

"This book is a manual in how to become and raise an excellent servant leader. By following the steps in this book people can overcome years of negative patterns within their own lives and be ready to lead themselves and others to greatness. Many theories of leadership can be glorified carrot vs. whip strategies. This book, however, brings focus to the difficult but rewarding work of changing the core issues within a leader to help him/her stop negative, self-serving patterns and intuitively know how to inspire those he/she is leading. If you want to become a leader that is remembered for greatness then do the work in this book!"

—*Larry Alwine, MA*

"During these environmentally and politically chaotic days, who among us, at some point, hasn't shaken our fist demanding, "C'mon, we certainly can do better than this!" I find relief in this just-in-the nick-of-time book that spells out, "Yes, in order to survive-we must! And here's what, who, and how we can answer that call."

—*Molly Lord, MA, Director, Tuned-In Productions*

"An encouraging road map to our best selves, our best world. A clear map, complete with check points, wisdom and directions to assist the servant leader along the way. Finally, here is a voice that clarifies the dire situation that the immature human has put us all in. If you have the courage to do the work, Dr. Weinhold has illuminated the path to the solution. The Servant Leader book smartly weaves the perspectives of science, psychology and sociology presenting us with a rope to use to either hang ourselves or climb out of the abyss."

—*Jim Wooden,/Director, The Art of Creativity*
Productions, Santa Monica CA,

"As a public servant I found this book to be not only inspiring but also an invaluable road map to both life and leadership. I now feel I am armed with the knowledge and wisdom one needs to truly be a servant leader in this Me, Me, Me world in which we live."

—*Ryan Bouton, GIS Analyst, City of Colorado Springs*

"TODAY'S LEADER: One who shouts "Do This, Don't Do That." TOMORROW'S SERVANT LEADER: Someone who leads by doing his/her work on himself/herself and leads by setting an example and by leading his/her life in an exemplary fashion. I know Barry well. He has done his work and he leads in this way and it is easy to follow him."

—*Robert Fochler, Herbalist and Astrologer*

DEDICATION

TO WARREN BROWN
(1923-2013)

PROBABLY ABOUT 20 YEARS AGO, Warren and I were sitting and talking about things after playing tennis when suddenly he said to me, "I would like you to speak at my funeral. Would you be willing to do that?" I immediately said, "Yes, I would be delighted to do so." Then I asked him if there is something he hadn't told me that was behind that request. He said, "No, no, I just thought about that recently and I wanted to ask you. I plan to be around for some time."

I met Warren in the spring of 1971 when I came Colorado Springs to interview for a position at UCCS. Warren was the Chair of the Search Committee and The Professor in Charge of the School of Education at UCCS. I was the Director of the Counseling Center at the University of Wisconsin at Green Bay and was an Assistant Professor in the School of Education at UWGB.

I was scheduled to be there for three days of interviews and Warren was in charge of showing me around. Well, back then, UCCS did not have much of a campus, so the first day what Warren did was drive me to Boulder to visit the campus there and meet some of the staff in the School of Education at UC Boulder.

The second day he toured me around the city and hosted a reception at his house, so I could meet some of the UCCS faculty. During our drive around Colorado Springs, he drove me out to Black Forest, a stand of virgin Ponderosa Pine just north of the city. On the way out to Black Forest, a herd of antelope crossed the road in front of us and shortly after getting in the forest we saw a couple of deer grazing in a pasture. I thought, he couldn't have arranged this if he had tried. This is the place where the deer and the antelope play.

I had to leave the next afternoon and it occurred to me that I might not even get to see the campus during my visit. When I asked Warren about that he smiled and said, 'the committee asked me to do things with you that would leave you with the most favorable impression of UCCS and Colorado Springs. So we deliberately kept you from touring our small campus. I will see that we do that in the morning.'

Ultimately, I was offered a position at UCCS and I accepted it. The most significant part of my decision to accept this position at UCCS was a chance to have Warren Brown as my boss. I felt so comfortable around him and I saw how open he was to my ideas. I knew that this was where I wanted to be.

He never disappointed me after that either. He was an ideal boss for me. He was encouraging and positive in all his interactions with me. Soon we became friends. We both liked to play tennis and so we started our friendship on the tennis court. Warren was an athlete and so any sport he played was done with great skill. He challenged me on the court, but we were pretty evenly matched. In all the years of playing singles with Warren, I don't think either one of us ever won straight sets.

Warren was also a devoted husband and father. He demonstrated his great love for his wife, Audrey, and his children, Lynn, Bob, and Julie. He also was a devoted grandfather, who always was involved in his grandchildren's lives. When we would get together, he would always begin by telling me something about his children and grandchildren. He was very proud of all of them.

Now I would like to return to my working relationship with Warren. He was my boss for many years and I would call Warren a servant leader. I define a servant leader as someone whose focus is on assisting those faculty who he was assigned to lead. His eyes were always downward looking for ways he could assist his faculty in doing a better job.

Other qualities of a servant leader that Warren embodied were his ability to listen and not judge. When I was engaged in a conversation with Warren, I always felt I was being heard.

Another quality of a servant leader that Warren had was his ability to have empathy for others. I always felt understood and accepted by Warren. Even when we disagreed about something, which wasn't very often, I always felt he understood where I was coming from.

Warren was also aware of many things that others were not. He was a deep thinker, a true philosopher. As a result, he was very aware of the injustices in the world. Warren had great compassion for the underdog.

Warren had requested that I read the words of Seneca, the Roman Philosopher who lived over 2000 years ago. Seneca wrote: "The first lesson of philosophy is that we cannot be wise about everything. We are fragments in infinity and moments in eternity: for such forked atoms to describe the universe, or for that matter, the Supreme Being, must make the planets tremble with mirth...."

"How does one acquire wisdom? By practicing it daily, in however modest a degree: by examining your conduct each day at its close; by being harsh to your own faults and lenient to those of others; by associating with those who excel in wisdom and virtue; by taking some acknowledged sage as your invisible counselor and judge. Read good books many times, rather than many books; travel slowly, and not too much. The primary sign of a well-ordered mind is a man's ability to remain in one place and linger in his own company."

"Life is not always so joyful as to merit continuance; after life's fitful fever it is well to sleep."

Warren also had the highest integrity. He stood by his beliefs even when others did not agree with him. He believed, for example, in always doing the right thing. I never heard him speak negatively about his other colleagues, even though some of them did not agree with what he stood for.

Finally, Warren had a commitment to the growth of his faculty. He believed that we all had intrinsic value actually beyond just our contributions to the School of Education. Warren recognized that he had a big responsibility to do everything in his power to nurture the personal and professional growth of his faculty.

You might ask, "isn't this what all the UCCS Deans did?" Unfortunately, most administrators I encountered had their eyes "up" not "down." They saw the job of Dean of the School of Education as a stepping-stone to a higher-level position. As a result, their main concern was to do and say things that their superiors approved of. Their goal was to be seen as someone who deserved to get a promotion to the next higher level. Warren never did that. He didn't want to be promoted to a higher-level position.

This got him in trouble at times with his peers and superiors because he did not seem to fit the mold of his fellow administrators. It is probably why Warren eventually resigned his position as Dean and returned to the faculty to teach the course that he loved the most: The Social and Cultural Foundations of Education. He brought fresh ideas to this course and helped count-less teachers broaden their social and cultural lenses.

Warren inspired many of his students, but sometimes his students crit-icized him because they didn't want their social and cultural beliefs chal-lenged or expanded. These students suffered from what I call "premature hardening of the categories."

In closing, I want to say that I am writing a new book on the subject of servant leadership and I intend to dedicate this book to Warren Brown, who was a true servant leader.

I will close my remarks with some words by Marcus Auralius, Warren's favorite philosopher and words that asked me to read at his memorial ser-vice. I quote,"...thou will disappear in that which produced thee...Pass then through this little space of time conformably to nature and end thy journey in content, just as an olive falls when it is ripe: blessing the nature that pro-duced it, and thanking the tree on which it grew...."

Warren you are missed, but not forgotten. You leave a legacy through your family and through your students as well as those faculty members who served under you at UCCS. You made a big difference in the lives of many people. Thank you for all that you did in your lifetime of service.

ACKNOWLEDGEMENTS

Any book written by a single author has had many eyes view the contents of the book. That is true with this book as well. I would like to acknowledge the following people who contributed to this book in numerous ways.

I especially want to thank Elaine Wolf for her editing of the manuscript. Her sharp eye and keen mind were very helpful in helping shape the final product. Larry Alwine also helped with the editing and provided many helpful comments. I want to thank all the reviewers who read the book and made personal comments about its effect on them. This includes Elaine Wolf, Michael Holtby, Sharon River Hansen, Bob Berry, Molly Dooley, Larry Alwine, Molly Lord, Jim Wooten, Ryan Bouton, and Robert Fochler.

I would also like to thank Janae Weinhold, who provided much needed technical support for me. Finally, I want to thank Matt Baldanza from fiveRR for his interior design of the book and for finalizing the cover design.

CONTENTS

PREFACE

"If you feel like you don't fit in in this world, it is
because you are here to help create a new one."

—*Jogelya Daner*

YOU MAY RECEIVE A CALLING to become a servant leader. Listen to this calling. Do you remember? This book is about this new kind of leader: the servant leader. Servant leaders learn to lead from within and are more likely to be "spiritual" rather than religious. The outcome of the inner work of a servant leader is individuation. This means that the servant leader has to create a fully functioning Self in order to be effective. The servant leader has to be able to give and receive unconditional love.

I believe that anyone who wants to be a servant leader has to engage in inner work activities that include therapy. It is unlikely that you will have completed your individuation process as a toddler and you will need to complete it as an adult. From my research, less than one percent of adults completed this process as a toddler. By reading this book, you can determine your path of inner work.

I also believe that all elected leaders need to make their physical and mental health records public. Voters need to know if they are voting for a physically and mentally healthy person. It is time to break down the stigma of having mental health issues. Everybody has them and they need to be honest and not try to hide this part of their background.

There are several specific tasks that you will need to be able to perform as a servant leader. I discuss each of these tasks in detail in this book. Here is a brief summary of the main tasks:

THE SPECIFIC MAIN TASKS OF THE SERVANT LEADER

1. Break free of the Matrix or the simulated reality that you have been programmed to follow. This involves doing your inner work that enables you to change your perceptions of the simulated reality you were programmed to follow and to be able to live effectively outside this reality.

In psychological terms, it means achieving your own individuation, or the birth of the psychological Self. This allows you to reconnect with your ability to give and receive unconditional love or what we have termed LOVevolution. This is how humans evolve.

2. To help others achieve this organic process of individuation. Unless others can transcend the simulated reality that has been programmed into them and be able to give and receive unconditional love, they will remain as stuck as slaves to the limited consciousness and will not evolve.

3. To recognize other potential forms of slavery, like the Human 2.0 that Super Artificial Intelligence researchers plan to introduce in the next five years or less. This means the servant leader must actively resist any human tendencies to escape his/her emotional body. To be "chipped" means giving up your free will and your ability to have any feelings, such as unconditional love. I explain how this works later in this book.

4. To help others resist the temptation to give up their free will and escape their emotional body, by signing up to get a chip implanted in them. It will be tempting for those, who have not achieved individuation and still live in the simulated reality of the Matrix. They will be tempted to sign up for the enhanced simulated reality that comes with becoming chipped.

The role of the servant leader will be to help others understand the consequences of being chipped and help them develop their organic path to individuation. This path allows them to keep their human soul and their heart that can give and receive unconditional love. Super Humans have no heart or soul and no longer can give and receive unconditional love. Servant leader needs to empower others to resist this "Trojan horse."

Everybody has the opportunity to be a servant leader at some point in his or her lives. If you are a parent or grandparent, a coach of a Little League team, the Youth Director at your Church, a supervisor of fellow workers, or an elected official, you can be a servant leader. What it takes, from my perspective, is a willingness to do the inner work required for you to be more conscious of how to better assist those under your care. If you have a desire to be of service to others, this book will show you how best to perform that service.

I for one, am angry and appalled by the behavior of our leaders, starting with fathers who refuse to parent their children, to elected local, state and national officials who are clearly self-serving leaders and act like adolescents. It seems to me, that we have to do better than this if we are going to evolve and survive the craziness that self-serving leaders perpetuate. What the world needs now are leaders who truly are servant leaders, who can truly serve those under their care. Servant leaders are not born, they are made. They usually have to go through four stages of spiritual development.

THE STAGES OF SPIRITUAL DEVELOPMENT OF A SERVANT LEADER

Scott Peck, in his book, *A Different Drum*[1],presents a pattern of progression through identifiable stages in human spiritual life. I myself have passed through them in my own spiritual journey. Scott Peck described them this way:

1. **Stage One: the Chaotic and Antisocial Stage.** In this stage people pretend that they are spiritual or religious covering up their lack of principles. Although they may pretend to be loving (and often think of themselves that way), their relationships are filled with manipulation and self-serving. Being unprincipled, there is nothing that governs their behavior except their own ego. Since their ego can change from moment to moment, there is a lack of integrity to their actions. Some can become quite disciplined in their service to themselves and their ambition and rise to positions of considerable prestige and power, even to become presidents.

2. **Stage Two: The Formal, Institutional Stage.** In this stage, people obey the law, but they do not understand the spirit of the law. Consequently, they are legalistic, parochial and dogmatic. They are threatened by anyone who thinks differently from them and believe they are "right". They then regard it as their responsibility to correct the people who are "wrong." They are "true believers." Their thinking is dominated by right-wrong, good and evil, etc. They have simplistic solutions to every problem and to try to escape the mystery of uncertainty. All those outside of Stage Two are perceived as Stage One people, because they do not understand those who might be in Stage Three or Four.

3. **Stage Three: The Skeptic, The Individual and the Questioner.** These people include the atheists, agnostics and those who are scientifically minded and demand measureable, well-researched and logical explanations. They may threaten those in Stage Two institutions because they ask too many questions. Although a skeptic, they are not antisocial and are often deeply involved in social causes. Despite being individualistic

3

in their thinking, they are on a higher spiritual level than those in Stage Two. This questioning stage is a pre-requisite to entering Stage Four.

4. **Stage Four: The Mystical, Communal Person.** Out of love and compassion for others, this person uses his/her ability to transcend their own psychological background, their culture and limitation with all others, reaching toward a notion of a planetary culture. They seek answers to life's great mysteries. Mystics acknowledge the enormity of the unknown, but rather than being frightened by it, they seek to penetrate deeper into it so that they might better understand these mysteries. They often use meditation, self-reflection and prayer to seek answers to these deep questions. This person regards conventional religion as a movement away from collective consciousness and inner truth to an acceptance of what I would call "The Matrix" or the simulated reality that they were taught in their family, church and schools. They can still be involved in religious practices in a church setting. They enter a religious community in search of answers about the mystery of life while others in the same congregation may be there to escape those same mysteries. This person sees the whole world as one community.

Servant leaders are likely in Stage Three or Stage Four of their spiritual development. If they are doing their inner work, they are uniquely prepared to lead others from an internal perspective.

There are external obstacles in the way of being about to lead from within. For example, with the advent of Super PACs and the Citizen's United ruling by the Supreme Court, the problem has gotten even worse. Now, elected officials are forced to vote for laws that protect and support the wealthy interests of those who secretly contributed money to get them elected.

This book presents an alternative to this self-serving forms of leadership. This model of leadership that provides hope for a better way for leaders of all kinds to behave. This book explores this model of leadership, which is not new. Lao Tsu, the Chinese philosopher, living in the four century B.C. was one of the first to write about the qualities of servant leadership.

As a psychologist who has specialized in treating men, I believe the most important quality of a servant leader is to develop a fully individuated Self. Very few adults living in our modern world have achieved this developmental milestone. When someone is fully individuated from his/her family, religion, culture and other social forces, he/she can make decisions that truly reflect his/her role as a servant leader.

I call it, "going on internal power" and breaking free from the illusions of the simulated reality called more recently, "The Matrix." This means that this person has a well-developed set of values and beliefs as well as a strong trust in his/her own inner guidance and intuition when making decisions. This book helps the reader determine what he/she needs to do to develop a fully individuated Self, if he/she wants to become a servant leader.

This book actually is the second in a series of four books titled the "Real Men Series." The first book, "The Male Mother,"[2] was published in 2014. That book was sub-titled, "The Missing Skill Set For Fathers,"[1] and was written to give support to fathers of all ages and types so they could show up more authentically as a father for their kids. The other books yet to be written in the series are, "The Wise Elder" and "The Open-Hearted Lover."

The theme of each of these four books is to provide men and women with the information and skills to become more fully who they can be: Real Men and Real Women. From my perspective as a licensed psychologist who specializes in counseling men, I see how wounded men are and how they often cope with their wounds by pretending not to have been wounded. Typically, men don't have permission to express their pain directly and instead create a false front and use addictive substances and activities to numb or hide their pain.

This book is also useful to women who wish to extend their ability to be a servant leader. I believe women, if they fully develop their inner feminine, and integrate it with their inner masculine are uniquely equipped to be servant leaders.

Carl Jung stated that all men and women have two sides to their personality: a masculine side and a feminine side. He also said there is an immature and a mature nature to each of these sides. He called them archetypes because he found they are the original you that has been simulated. I see most leaders, both men and women, operating out of their immature archetypes, which are what the culture most accepts.

Our current cultural mythology about what is accepted in "who men are," forces men to stay stuck in their immature masculine archetype and totally ignore their feminine side. The same is true for women who are stuck in playing out their immature feminine archetypes and ignoring their masculine side. This is like walking through life with one arm tied behind your back. An individuated servant leader has integrated both sides of his/her personality.

This book looks at men and women who have not become real men or real women and instead are "faking it until they make it." They create a false self and hope know one will notice. One of the most extreme ways men "fake it" is to became a leader of others. Men and some women with false selves, who decide to become leaders, have been showing up in this world for almost 6600 years.

To say the least, they have been a destructive force that is currently preventing a better type of leader from emerging. Most people have fallen prey to their power and greed and for a variety of reasons, we have decided to let them control the world. I feel the best description of their actions is to call them "life-taking leaders." Their actions have been responsible for countless wars killing and maiming millions of people in this time frame.

The history of the world is filled with countless examples of men and some women who used their leadership role to serve themselves. This includes the Kings of Mesopotamia, who declared themselves as agents of God, to the modern political leaders who sell their soul to the highest bidder.

The self-serving leader has become a predominate fixture at all levels of leadership starting with fathers/mothers who don't know how to be servant leaders for their kids in their families, up to dictators who rule countries and to clergy of major religions who seek power and influence over others.

This book presents an entirely different style of leadership that dates as far back as the sixth century B. C. E. where the keeper of the archives in Loyang, China by the name of Lao Tsu wrote down his teachings for posterity. This was translated into English in 1972 as the Tao Te Ching.[3]These ancient teachings reflect many of the main concepts of servant leadership.

Throughout history, there are leaders who could be considered servant leaders. Certainly, Jesus Christ can be considered one of those. Other more current leaders include Mahatma Gandhi, Nelson Mandela and Martin Luther King. The Old Testament tells of Isaiah who lived a life of servant-based leadership. His inspired book contains four Servant Songs (42:1-9; 49:1-13; 50:4-11; 52:13-53:12) and the word "servant" appears in the Book of Isaiah 40 times.[4]

Robert Greenleaf is considered the founder of the modern servant leadership movement. He wrote five books on the subject. His philosophy can be summed up in a quote from his "Essentials" book: "The servant-leader is servant first... Becoming a servant-leader begins with the natural feeling that one wants to serve, to serve first. Then conscious choice brings one to aspire to lead. That person is sharply different from one who is a leader first...The difference manifests itself in the care taken by the servant first to make sure that other people's highest priority needs are being served. The best test, and the most difficult to administer, is this: Do those served grow as persons? Do they, while being served, become healthier, wiser, freer, more autonomous, more likely themselves to become servants?[5]

Since we are in the middle of a Presidential election cycle in this country, I plan to use a number of examples in this book of the values, beliefs and actions of the current political leaders and candidates for elected office. Clearly, none of the current candidates for the Presidency are servant leaders. In the book, I show why they all fall short of this designation.

I intend to show how these values, beliefs and actions represent either a self-serving leadership style or a servant leadership style. I will also provide examples of current corporate thinking by the leaders of corporations. Most of whom are self-serving leaders. I also focus on what a father or mother would need to do to be considered a servant leader in his/her family.

I hope you enjoy this book and find in it some ideas that help you better understand that leaders are not born to be leaders and what happened to them growing up shaped their values, beliefs and actions. As a developmental clinical psychologist, I am interested in what happened to people growing up in their families that influenced whether or not they became adults with fully integrated masculine and feminine archetypes.

I also intend to show you how you can tell who are the real servant leaders and distinguish them from pseudo-servant leaders. I hope some current leaders or those who aspire to become servant leaders will read this book and draw the strength they need to do their inner work and become a true servant leader.

NOTES

1   Peck, S. (1998). The different drum. New York: Touchstone.

2   Weinhold, B. (2014). The Male Mother: The Missing Skill Set For Fathers. Colorado Springs: CO, CICRCL Press

3   Feng, G. F. and English, J. (1972). Tao Te Ching. New York: NY, Vintage Books.

4   Servant Leadership In Isaiah. http://www.purposequest.com/assets/pdfs/misc/leadership/serveLeadIsaiah.pdf Accessed May 20, 2016.

5   Greenleaf, R, (2002). Servant leadership. Mawhah, NJ: Paulist Press.

INTRODUCTION

"Kindness in words creates confidence. Kindness in thinking creates profoundness. Kindness in giving creates love."

—*Lao Tsu*

THE WORLD IS IN DIRE need of great leaders, ones who inspire people not through words, but by actually serving them. The cutting edge in our leadership discourse is the old fashioned idea that leaders should serve those who elected them. There is a growing awareness that our elected officials are not serving the needs of those who elect them. It has become a major issue in the 2016 presidential campaign.

With secret corporate money flooding to the candidates of both major political parties in this country, this has led to distrust in the whole political process. Republican Party contender, Donald Trump, a Republican candidate, claims to be self-funded as a billionaire. The Democratic Party contender, Bernie Sanders claims he is taking contributions from average citizens and refuses to take and Super PAC money. This is drawing many young and disenfranchised voters to their camps.

This seems to be a major campaign issue. Both Trump and Sanders are getting votes from voters who want to see PAC money removed from political campaigns. Hilary Clinton, is known to take PAC money and money from rich donors that has caused a lack of trust of her ability to do as she says.

Looking more broadly, the whole human race desperately needs servant-leaders. We need leaders who really attend to others and are beacons of hope in our search for a world society where justice, fairness, and care for the most vulnerable members of our communities, and love can flourish. The recent British electorate's decision to leave the European Union is another example of how big money and bureaucracy have turned off voters who see their autonomy being taken away from them by self-serving leaders.

The call for leaders who genuinely serve their people is obvious in social and political communities. We also see the great need for servant leaders in families where men or women have failed to serve their spouses and children. We can also see it in the economic sphere in business organizations or corporations. The high turnover of staff in many work places suggests that people are looking for an environment where they will not simply be cogs in the wheel of production, but can live more full and happy lives.

Overall, there seems to be an increasing awareness of the need for a new and different style of leadership. This awareness is catching on with many people, young and old and I hope this book supports their belief in an emerging leadership style I am calling servant leadership. I will contrast that style with what I am calling the self-serving leadership style.

In my opinion, a change of leadership style had been long overdue. People on this planet have lived too long under the thumb of ruthless, self-serving leaders and rulers, mostly men, who have used either their elected or appointed position to serve themselves more than serve the people who elected or appointed them.

Today, many people have lost trust in political candidates who are supposed to be "public servants." They see these candidates being bought and sold by corporate entities who want to protect their interests. They see the lobbyists, Super PACs and Citizen's United folks replacing the "public servant" label with a "corporate servant" label.

This erodes away the trust that those they elect will work for them to make their lives better. As a result, many voters just stay from the polling place, (only 36 percent of eligible voters even bothered to vote in 2012) become cynical and live lives of quiet desperation. They truly feel their self-serving elected leaders have betrayed them rather than they having betrayed the elected leader.

The term most often used throughout history to describe a self-serving leader is "Patriarch." This includes both men and women who have by their values, belief and actions appear to serve their own interests and needs more than the interests and needs of the people they are supposed to serve.

Both men and women carry masculine and feminine archetypes that influence their actions. An archetype was first defined by Carl Jung. He proposed that all people, men and women, developed a set of values, beliefs and behaviors that could be classified as either masculine or feminine archetypes. His research showed that cultures tend to reinforce or punish either the masculine or feminine archetypes. He said these archetypes show up in the mythology that a particular culture promotes and they show up in people's dreams.

These self-serving "patriarchs" over-utilize their immature masculine archetypes, while often denying that they even have a feminine archetype. They typically will bring that unbalance into their approach to their leadership position. Briefly below is a Table showing the mature and immature masculine archetypes that they typically show up in leaders:

Table 0-1
The Mature and Immature Masculine Archetypes[1]

Mature Masculine Archetypes	Immature Masculine Archetypes
The King (the energy of just and creative ordering)	The Tyrant, The Bigot, The Patriarch or The Weakling
The Sadist or the Masochist) The emerging mature archetype: The Divine Child	The High Chair Tyrant or The Weakling Prince
The Warrior (the energy of self-disciplined, aggressive action)	The Terrorist or The Victim
The emerging mature archetype: The Hero	The Grandstander, Bully or The Coward
The Magician (the energy of initiation and transformation)	The Wall Street Manipulator or The Crooked Politician
The emerging mature archetype: The Precocious Child	The Know-it-all, The Trickster or The Dummy
The Lover (the energy that connects men to others and to the world)	The Sexual Predator or The Impotent Lover
The emerging mature archetype: The Oedipal Child	Mama's Boy or The Dreamer

Leaders often bring to their leadership position a similar set of mature and immature feminine archetypes. Below Table 0.2, the names of the mature and immature feminine archetypes.

Table 0-2
The Mature and Immature Feminine Archetypes[2]

Mature Feminine Archetypes	Immature Feminine Archetypes
The Servant Leader	The Controlling Boss, Micromanager, The Bureaucrat

Mature Feminine Archetypes	Immature Feminine Archetypes
The Male Mother	The Consuming Parent, The Rejecting Parent,
The Martyr	The Terrorist or The Victim
The Wise Elder	The Ideologue, The Rescuer, The Fraud
The Open-Hearted Lover	The Addicted Lover, The Narcissist, The Eternal Youth

UNDERSTANDING THE IMMATURE MASCULINE ARCHETYPE

The immature masculine archetype can be best understood in current culture as the quest for eternal youth. The differences between a boy or girl and a man or woman should be apparent, but in our current cultural climate, we seem to have lost this distinction.

Boyhood and girlhood have come to dominate the male/female population of Western culture, and manhood/womanhood are discarded as dark, destructive, scary, and problematic. The boy or girl has been pushed to occupy the space left behind by the man or woman —something he/she is not ready for— and his values of youth, physical vitality, and beauty come to dominate.

This immature masculine archetype currently is being celebrated through diverse cultural phenomena. This includes the Boy Band; young, rebellious athletes; the irresponsibility and "don't give a damn" attitude proselytized by the advertising industry (look no further than Coca Cola Zero adverts); and the take-what-I-want-and-fuck-you-if-you-try-to-stop-me of parts of the music industry.

It also includes the self-serving ways of young stockbrokers, bankers, hedge fund managers and real estate moguls, etc. Finally, it includes the wave of movies and TV shows in which immature men and women are turned into poster boys or girls, the admiration of heroics, the constant celebration of youth over wisdom etc. The list is endless.

The problem with this is that we end up with a very limited view of masculinity or femininity that shows up in the leaders we elect. It is rooted in insecurity and the desire for sex, fame, money, and power. We become so uprooted in ourselves, separated from our true core, that we define ourselves through these external factors. We must recognize one basic fact: The self-serving leader is the slave of his/her ego. He/she often has little control over his/her nervous system, and fries his/her life energy on pointless mental pursuits and drama. He/she is the guy or gal who can't sit still and can't tolerate silence.

At an every day level, this is the guy/gal who freaks out from prolonged eye contact. This kind of leader becomes guys and gals who are easily insulted, who try very hard to be seen (or equally hard not to be), who fish for love and is easily hurt.

He or she has little structure and integrity in life, and who —despite his/her myriad claims to goodness— won't stand up for a friend in times of need. It's not that he/she doesn't want to do the right thing. It's that he/she is not able to.

His/her life is in disarray and he/she is completely under the spell of the immature feminine, and is happy only as long as mummy is close. This is the subconscious mother, the archetypal mother, and the feminine as a whole —not necessarily the biological mother. The purpose of the Hero/Heroine archetype, the last archetype of boyhood and girlhood psychology, is to break free from this bondage to the immature masculine or feminine archetypes and develop a balance and integration of both mature masculine and feminine archetypes. This is my prescription for the servant leader.

This description of the immature masculine and/or feminine archetypes is also describes a person who has a Disorganized Attachment Style. The research shows that this attachment style forms before the age of one. In addition, the research shows that these people never become completely mature and remain stuck reenacting the early childhood traumas that created their limited way of interacting with other people. From this research, we know that unless some intervention occurs where they finally realize what they are doing, people will not change their relationship style.[3]

They can appear to be "servants of others" because they adopt a way to being in the world where they become a "solicitous caregiver" or a "little general." They try to organize the lives of others instead of organizing their own life. These people generally live "adrenalized lifestyles" where they appear to have boundless energy, but in the process are burning out their endocrine system. I call these people "pseudo-servant leaders." I discuss this concept later in the book.

THE RISE OF THE SPIRITUAL CLASS.

More and more people are looking for effective way to control their own lives and develop themselves spiritually. For instance, among U.S. Christians, there has been an increase of 7 percentage points between 2007 and 2014 in those who say they feel a deep sense of wonder about the universe at least weekly (from 38% to 45%).

There has been a similar rise in the share of religiously unaffiliated people who say the same (from 39% to 47%) —not to mention a 17-point jump among self-described atheists. There is clearly a strong movement toward spiritual ideas.[4] Another recent survey showed that we've now reached a point that the religiously unaffiliated are more numerous than Catholics [21 percent] and mainline Protestants [15 percent]. These are some of the people that are interested in becoming servant leaders.[5]

THE THREAT OF ARTIFICIAL INTELLIGENCE

Although only a few people have understood the threat that Artificial Intelligence presents to human beings. In the next five years or less, we will see a significant increase of the threat to our lives by computerized or simulated reality, created by the self-serving advocates of Artificial Intelligence. Instead of being called the Illuminati, they have the title of the Digerati. At present, we see the self-serving leaders promoting AI in the development of war weapons. The goal is to have computerized weapons doing the fighting for us. For example, we developed the Drone, a pilotless airplane used, to bomb the enemy.

A.I. is playing a significant role in weapons making and how wars will be fought in the future. We are seeing the beginning of a new arms race around developing new weapons designed to kill others. The self-serving military leaders are acting like excited little boys with new toys.

I present the case in this book that the threat of Artificial Intelligence is real and needs to be seen as such to our humanness. They are planning to build robots or Cyborgs that ultimately could replace humans on this planet. Some very smart people who have studied this topic are speaking out about this threat. Stephen Hawking recently said, "The development of full artificial intelligence could spell the end of the human race." Elon Musk, the founder of Tesla and SpaceX said recently that improving artificial intelligence is like "summoning the demons." He said it could become more dangerous that nuclear weapons.

Nick Bostrom director of the Future of Humanity Institute at Oxford is really worried about AI. Bostrom argues that once machines surpass human intellect, they could mobilize and decide to eradicate humans extremely quickly using any number of strategies (deploying unseen pathogens, recruiting humans to their side or by utilizing simple brute force).[6]

EMERGING RESISTANCE TO THE SELF-SERVING LEADERSHIP STYLE

I am writing this part of the book in the middle of the Presidential Primary election scene. It seems as if "leadership style" actually has become a political issue. Donald Trump has the leadership style of a schoolyard bully. Other Republican candidates seem to be mouthing the negative party line. They are against everything and for almost nothing.

On the Democratic Party side, Hilary Clinton is seen by the young voters (male and female) as a member of the patriarchy, Bernie Saunders, who has been a member of the establishment for 25 years is not drawing this projection. He is a self-described Democratic Socialist. He is calling for a political revolution in this country, and that is capturing the attention of those young people who finally realize the vulnerability of those candidates they believe have been bought off by big money.

It is interesting that there is an emerging awareness of the need for a new leadership style in the political campaigns for the Presidency. Recently, Gloria Steinem and Madeline Albright made headlines for condemning young women for not voting for Hillary Clinton.

Gloria said recently on the Bill Maher Show that, "women are supporting Sanders because they are only interested in going where the boys go." Albright was quoted as saying, "There is a special place in hell for women who don't help each other."

In a Blog on Daily KOS, VM Michael commented on Madeline Albright's statement by writing the following and I quote: "Since when has it been the role of the voter to help the 'public servant' rather than the role of the 'public servant' to help the voter? And how could the eternal damnation of a fellow warmongering female patriarch, presented as a feminist icon, who made millions of dollars off of the wars of the first Clinton presidency, was quoted to support the Bush wars, and is endorsing a second Clinton presidency, ever be appropriate?"[7] Ultimately, when millennials refuse to support Hillary Clinton, they are not rejecting feminism.

Rather, they are rejecting the Patriarchy she represents. After all, what can be more patriarchal than the continued dynastic rule of the Bushes and the Clintons? President Obama winning the Democratic Primaries in 2008, may have caused only a brief disruption of this lineage.

Sanders' idea of a political revolution is driving the final nail in the coffin of what should have been the Clinton dynasty —a dynasty that today has not much to offer this young generation. Feminists of Clinton's, Albright's, and Steinem's generation, struggle while facing the difficult decision between their potentially last chance to vote for a woman presidential candidate, or their potentially their last chance to vote for a presidential candidate who embodies the many feminist values. As a result, many women are fighting long and hard for Bernie Sanders.

I intend to show in this book what life on this planet would be like if we had fully developed, authentic servant leaders. I will discuss the shortcomings of the current self-serving leadership style, where it came from and how to topple this breed from crucial leadership positions.

THE ORIGINS OF SELF-SERVING LEADERSHIP STYLES

The reign of self-serving Leader can be traced back to the "Divine Right of Kings." This concept grew out of the Sumerian culture dating back to about 4000 BCE. Though not claiming to be divine themselves, but rather divinely chosen, the kings of ancient Mesopotamia acted as earthly representatives of the gods. As stated in a Sumerian proverb, "Man is the shadow of God, but the king is God's reflection."

The main responsibilities of the kings involved participation in religious rituals, managing the affairs of the state in war and peace, writing laws and guiding the administration and execution of justice. It is often expressed in the phrase "by the Grace of God," attached to the titles of a reigning monarch.[8]

THE DIVINE RIGHT OF KINGS

The divine right of kings, or the divine-right theory of kingship, is a political and religious doctrine to establish royal and political legitimacy. It asserts that a monarch is subject to no earthly authority, deriving his right to rule directly from the will of God. The king is thus not subject to the will of his people, the existing laws, the aristocracy, or any other estate of the realm, including (in the view of some, especially in Protestant countries) the church.

The concept of divine right incorporates, but exaggerates, the ancient Christian concept of "royal God-given rights," that teach that "the right to rule is anointed by God", although this idea is found in many other cultures, including Aryan and Egyptian traditions.

In China and East Asia, rulers justified their rule with the philosophy of the "Mandate of Heaven," which, although similar to the European concept, bore several key differences. While the divine right of kings granted unconditional legitimacy, the Mandate of Heaven was dependent on the behavior of the ruler, the "Son of Heaven." Heaven would bless the authority of a just ruler, but it could be displeased with a despotic ruler and thus withdraw its mandate, transferring it to a more suitable and righteous person. This withdrawal of mandate also afforded the possibility of revolution as a means to remove the errant ruler. However, revolt was never legitimate under the European framework of divine right.

In the Malay Annals, the rajas and sultans of the Malay States (today Malaysia, Brunei and Philippines) as well as their predecessors, such as the Indonesian kingdom of Majapahit, also claimed divine right to rule. The sultan is mandated by God, and thus is expected to lead his country and people in religious matters, ceremonies as well as prayers. This divine right is called Daulat, and although the notion of divine right is obsolete, it is still found in the phrase Daulat Tuanku that is used to publicly acclaim the reigning Yang di-Pertuan Agong and the other sultans of Malaysia.[9]

Kings were understood to be the "agents of God", as they protected the world like God did. This divine right principle put leaders above the law and made it possible for them to become entirely self-serving. After all, they can claim that, "God made me do it."

Although this system of deifying our leaders has lessened, it is still alive and well in the political system in the U. S. The voters want to trust candidates that promise to serve their interests and not the corporate interests, but demand some proof of their loyalty. Bernie Sanders, a Democratic Party nominee, has proposed sweeping changes in the way our government supports its people.

He is proposing Medicare for all, free tuitions to public colleges and universities, a higher minimum wage, paid family leave and an end to privately run prisons. Realistically, it is unlikely that these policies can be enacted due to the concerted opposition by the current Republican Party in charge of Congress. However, his proposals are taken seriously because he takes no

PAC or Wall Street money to fund his campaign. Many young voters are being revitalized by his message.

Likewise, Donald Trump, the Republican nominee, is gaining strength with voters because he claims to be self-funded. This is happening even though his policy statements do not have any servant leadership qualities. They resemble those of a "school yard bully." He seems to be appealing to those voters who feel underserved by their leaders and his "damn the torpedoes" approach seems to offer some hope to these voters. As an apparent political outsider, he is riding the wave of anger and discontent with our current political system.

WHAT IS A SERVANT LEADER?[10]

Here are here some of the distinguishing characteristics that clearly define a servant leader:
1. **Values diverse opinions.** A servant leader values everyone's contributions and regularly seeks out opinions. If you must parrot back the leader's opinion, you are not in a servant-led organization.
2. **Cultivates a culture of trust.** People don't meet at the water cooler to gossip. Pocket vetoes are rejected.
3. **Helps develop other leaders.** Leading from behind is a quality often used to describe a Servant Leader.
4. **Helps people with life issues.** The servant leader reaches out to others to assist them with their personal development.
5. **Encourages.** The hallmark of a servant leader is encouragement. A true servant leader says, "Let's go do it," not, "You go do it."
6. **Sells instead of tells.** A servant leader is the opposite of a dictator. It's a style all about persuading, not commanding.
7. **Thinks "you," not "me."** There's a selfless quality about a servant leader. Someone who is thinking only, "How does this benefit me?" is disqualified.
8. **Thinks long-term.** A servant leader is thinking about the next generation, the next leader, the next opportunity. That means a tradeoff between what's important today versus tomorrow, and making choices to benefit the future.
9. **Acts with humility.** The servant leader doesn't wear a title as a way to show who's in charge, doesn't think he's better than everyone else, and acts in a way to care for others. He/she may, in fact, pick up the trash or

clean up a table. Setting an example of service, the servant leader understands that it is not about the leader, but about others.

A leader who displays the above personal characteristics is someone who can give and receive unconditional love. This is the defining quality of a servant leader. I will describe these and other characteristics later in the book. As you can see from this list, the servant leader cannot be seen as a self-serving leader. The two are as different as day and night.

ARE SERVANT LEADERS BORN OR ARE THEY MADE?

I don't believe that people who become servant leaders are born that way. As a developmental psychologist, I see a developmental pattern that starts in early childhood that helps produce people who can become servant leaders. In this book, I will discuss what I see as the optimal developmental history of a servant leader.

In this book, I describe the myriad of problems in the world that have been caused by ruthless self-serving leaders. The world does not need any more of these people. For the past 6600 years, they have ruled mostly to benefit themselves. Rather than just describing the history of destruction these men and some women have perpetrated on humanity, I show the reader what drastic changes are possible with a new style of leadership.

I want to put forth a vision of a much better world led by servant leaders. One of my teachers once said to me, "If you can articulate a vision of where you want to go, you are already halfway there. The hardest part, however, is the other half."

This book presents a vision of a better world that is possible, if we had more servant-oriented leaders. The rest of the work to get where we want to go is up to all of us. I show the many obstacles that a servant leader needs to overcome. This is not an easy path to leadership in our modern world. I describe the personal/psychological obstacles as well as the social, cultural, political, economic, religious and education obstacles that a servant leader must address and overcome. For each set of obstacles, I present effective strategies for overcoming these obstacles, if you are a servant leader. Take the Self-Quiz below to see how suited you are to become a servant leader.

SELF-QUIZ:
ARE YOU READY TO BECOME A SERVANT LEADER?

Directions: Place the number in front of each item that best represents your experience with that item.
Key: 1 = Not at all; 2 = Occasionally true; 3 = Usually true; 4 = Most of the Time.

_____ 1. I enjoy meeting new people.

_____ 2. I know things without having to figure them out.

_____ 3. I find watching television or most of the mainstream media, including newspapers a waste of time.

_____ 4. Stating something that I know is a lie is impossible for me.

_____ 5. I root for the underdog, those without voices, and those who have been trapped by the Matrix.

_____ 6. I pick up on others symptoms or pain and feel them in myself.

_____ 7. I get tired of taking on other people's emotions.

_____ 8. I turn to drugs or alcohol to try to block myself from feeling the pain of others.

_____ 9. I am interested in becoming a healer.

_____10. I see future possibilities before others do.

_____11. I require more solitude than others do.

_____12. I am a creative person.

_____13. I get easily bored but I am quite good at entertaining myself.

_____14. I have a difficult time doing things that I don't really enjoy.

_____15. I enjoy bringing the truth to light.

_____16. I have trouble keeping track of time and I can get lost in what I am doing.

_____17. I hate routine.

_____18. I disagree with those in authority.

_____19. I am kind to others.

_____20. I do not enjoy being with people who are obsessed with themselves.

_____21. I eat vegan or vegetarian food.

_____22. I wear my emotions of my sleeve and have a hard time pretending to be happy, if I am not feeling that way.

_____23. I enjoy helping others to bring out their unique gifts.

_____24. I regard spirituality as an important part of my life.

_____25. I place my psychological well-being on the same plane as my physical well-being.

_____26. I volunteer for one or more good causes.

_____27. I love nature and spend time and energy trying to take care of my environment.

_____28. I am more optimistic about my future and distrust cynical and pessimistic views of the future.

_____29. I want to be involved in creating new and better ways of living for other people in the world.

_____30. I can see how what happened to me as a child has affected my adult life.

_____   **TOTAL SCORE**

Interpretation of Scores:
30-60 Very few servant leader qualities are present.
61-90 Good servant leader potential
91-120 You are already there. Congratulations

NOTES

1 Weinhold, B. (2014). *The Male Mother: The Missing Skill Set For Fathers. Colorado Springs: CO, CICRCL Press*, pp. 2-3.

2 *Ibid, PP. 3-4.*

3 Main, M. & Solomon, J (1986). "Discovery of a new, insecure-disorganized/disoriented attachment pattern." In M. Yogman & T. B. Brazelton (Eds.) *Affective development in infancy. Norwood: NJ, Ablex.* pp. 95-124..

4 Masci, D. & Lipka, M. (January 21, 2016). *Americans may be getting less religious, but feelings of spirituality are on the rise. Pew Research Center.*

5 Smith, P. (May 15, 1015). *Growing number of Americans don't identify with a religion, survey says. Pittsburg Post-Gazette.* http://www.post-gazette.com/local/region/2015/05/12/Growing-minority-of-Americans-idnetifying-as-religious-nones-survey-says/stories/20150512000

6 Luckerson, V. (Dec. 2 2015=4). *5 Very Smart People Who Think Artificial Intelligence Could Bring the Apocalypse. Time Magazine.* http://time.com/3614349/artificial-intelligence-singularity-stephen-hawking-elon-musk/ Accessed June 24, 2016.

7 Michael, VM (February 10, 2016). *Gloria, Madeleine, and Hillary: When Feminist turns Patriarch in an Increasingly Progressive America. Daily Kos.* http://www.dailykos.com/stories/2016/2/10/1482705/-Gloria-Madeleine-and-Hillary-When-Feminist-turns-Patriarch-in-an-Increasingly-Progressive-America

8 *Divine Right Of Kings.* https://en.wikipedia.org/wiki/Divine_right_of_kings Accessed May 20, 2016.

9   *Malay Annals.* *https://en.wikipedia.org/wiki/Malay_Annals*. *Accessed May 20, 2016.*

10   *http://www.skipprichard.com/9-qualities-of-the-servant-leader/* *Accessed May 20, 2016.*

CHAPTER 1

THE DESTRUCTIVE EFFECTS OF SELF-SERVING LEADERS THROUGHOUT HISTORY

"Under heaven all can see beauty as beauty only because there is ugliness. All can know good as good only because there is evil."

—*Lao Tsu*

THE 25 MOST RUTHLESS SELF-SERVING LEADERS IN HISTORY[1]

I have compiled a list of the twenty-five most ruthless leaders in the past 6600 years of our history. All of whom were self-serving leaders. You may notice that things have actually gotten a lot worse: 15 of the 25 most ruthless, self-serving leaders in history lived in the 20th century.

I warn you as you read the list below, this is not a pretty picture. However, it does show the amount of ruthless acts that these self-serving leaders have committed on their own people and others throughout recorded history. Have we had enough of these ruthless, self-serving rulers?

Idi Amin Dada. One of the most evil rulers ever, Idi Amin Dada was the military dictator and President of Uganda from 1971 to 1979. Amin joined the British colonial regiment, the King's African Rifles in 1946, Amin held the rank of Major General in the post-colonial Ugandan Army and became its Commander before seizing power in the military coup of January 1971, deposing Milton Obote.

He later promoted himself to Field Marshal, while he was the head of state. His rule was characterized by extensive human rights abuses, political repression, ethnic persecution, extra judicial killings and the expulsion of Indians from Uganda. The estimates range of people killed by his orders from

80,000 to 500,000. Amin was eventually overthrown, but until his death, he held that Uganda needed him and he never expressed any remorse or regrets for the abuses of his regime.

Attila The Hun. Attila (Attila the Hun), was the ruler of the Huns from 434 to 453 A.D. He was leader of the Hunnic Empire, which stretched from the Ural River to the Rhine River and from the Danube River to the Baltic Sea. He was considered as one of the history's greatest villains. In much of Western Europe, he is remembered as the epitome of cruelty and rapacity. He destroyed everything in his path. He crossed the Danube twice and plundered the Balkans, but was unable to take Constantinople.

He also attempted to conquer Roman Gaul (France), crossing the Rhine in 451 and marching as far as Orleans before being defeated at the Battle of the Catalaunian Plains. Subsequently, he invaded Italy, devastating the northern provinces, but was unable to take Rome.

Genghis Khan. Genghis Khan was the founder and Great Khan (emperor) of the Mongol Empire, which became the largest contiguous empire in history after his demise. He came to power by uniting many of the nomadic tribes of northeast Asia. After founding the Mongol Empire and being proclaimed "Genghis Khan", he started the Mongol invasions that resulted in the conquest of most of Eurasia. He was a ruthless warrior and evil ruler. Starting from obscure and insignificant beginnings, he brought all the nomadic tribes of Mongolia under his rule in a rigidly disciplined military state.

Pol Pot. Pol Pot was the leader of the Khmer Rouge and the Prime Minister of Cambodia from 1976 to 1979. Pol Pot became leader of Cambodia on April 17, 1975. During his time in power, his radical communist government forced the mass evacuations of cities, killed or displaced millions of people, and left a legacy of disease and starvation. Under his leadership, his government caused the deaths of at least one million people from forced labor, starvation, disease, torture, or execution.

Count Dracula. Vlad III, Prince of Wallachia (Vlad the Impaler) known for executing his enemies by impalement. He ruled mainly from 1456 to 1462, the period of the incipient Ottoman conquest of the Balkans. Vlad is best known for the legends of the exceedingly cruel punishments he imposed during his reign and for serving as the primary inspiration for the vampire.

He was a fan of various forms of torture including disemboweling and rectal and facial impalement. He tortured thousands while he ate and drank among the corpses. He impaled every person in the city of Amlas, nearly

20,000 men, women and children. Vlad tortured the people ordering them to be skinned, boiled, decapitated, blinded, strangled, hanged, burned, roasted, hacked, nailed, buried alive, stabbed, etc. He also liked to cut off noses, ears, sexual organs and limbs.

Ivan IV of Russia. Ivan IV of Russia, also known as Ivan the Terrible, was the Grand Duke of Muscovy from 1533 to 1547 and was the first ruler of Russia and the first to be proclaimed Tsar of Russia (from 1547). Historic sources present disparate accounts of Ivan's complex personality: he was described as intelligent and devout, yet given to rages and prone to episodic outbreaks of mental illness.

He enjoyed burning 1000s of people in frying pans, and was fond of impaling people. Ivan's soldiers built walls around the perimeter of the city in order to prevent the people of the city escaping. Between 500 and 1000 people were gathered every day by the troops, then tortured and killed in front of Ivan and his son. He is also remembered for his paranoiac suspiciousness and cruel persecution of nobility.

Adolph Eichmann. Adolf Eichmann was born in March 19, 1906, in Solingen, a small industrial city in the Rhineland. He was a German and one of the major organizers of the Holocaust. He was hanged by the state of Israel for his part in the Nazi extermination of Jews during World War II. Just before his death he said, "The death of five million Jews on my conscience gives me extraordinary satisfaction."

King Leopold II of Belgium. Leopold II was the King of the Belgians, and is chiefly remembered for the founding and brutal exploitation of the Congo Free State. Born in Brussels the second son of Leopold I and Louise-Marie of Orléans, he succeeded his father to the throne on 17 December 1865 and remained king until his death. Leopold created the Congo Free State, a private project undertaken to extract rubber and ivory in the Congo region of central Africa, relying on forced labor this resulted in the deaths of approximately 3 million Congolese.

Adolf Hitler. Adolf Hitler was an Austrian-born German politician and the leader of the National Socialist German Workers Party. He was chancellor of Germany from 1933 to 1945 and dictator of Nazi Germany from 1934 to 1945. Hitler was at the centre of the founding of Nazism, the start of World War II, and the Holocaust.

By the end of the second world war, Hitler's policies of territorial conquest and racial subjugation had brought death and destruction to tens of millions of people, including the genocide of some six million Jews in what is now known as the Holocaust.

Josef Stalin. Joseph Vissarionovich Stalin was the Premier of the Soviet Union from 6 May 1941 until his death in 5 March 1953. Among the Bolshevik revolutionaries who brought about the Russian Revolution in 1917. Stalin probably exercised greater political power than any other figure in history. In the 1930s, by his orders, millions of peasants were either killed or permitted to starve to death. Stalin brought about the deaths of more than 20 million of his own people while holding the Soviet Union in an iron grip for 29 years.

Mao Zedong. Mao Zedong was dictator of China from 1943 to 1976. Mao's plan was to make China a superpower country. Mao also said he would turn China into a powerful country that could match the United States and the Soviet Union. In the process however, he created the greatest famine and genocide in history. Under Mao's rule, China endured a series of economic disasters and political terrorism. Millions of Chinese died by execution, starvation and suicide. Tens of millions were sent to labor camps.

Five million were executed. Mao turned neighbors against neighbors and sons and daughters against their teachers and parents. Mao used fear to root out every hint of dissent. A criticism uttered in private could lead to public humiliation, torture or death.

The famine he created killed about 30 to 45 million people. Millions died from disease. Another 700,000 committed suicide out of fear of Mao. Mao led two Great Leap Forwards, which were plans to use China's vast population to rapidly transform the country from an rural economy into a modern communist society.

Both plans killed 40 to 50 million people. Millions of children were also killed. If children stole food, they would have their fingers chopped off. People were also beaten up if they said something that made Mao or his men angry. Mao's brutal men had methods of torture like whipping, burning people with incense or with flame of a kerosene lamp and nailing a person's palms to a table and then to insert bamboo splints under fingernails. Overall, Mao killed over 70 million of his own people.

Tomas de Torquemada. Torquemada was the Grand Inquisitor of Spain from 1483 to 1498. He started the Spanish Inquisition, which was established on November 1, 1478 and disbanded in July 15, 1834. The Spanish Inquisition was an ecclesiastical tribunal run by the Spanish monarchy and established to root out heretics and other individuals who threatened the status of Roman Catholic Church in Spain.

Torquemada's spies turned friends against friends and they made sons and daughters testify against their parents. Torquemada without lack of evidence would order Jews to be tortured or killed because of his discrimination towards them. Countless of people were tortured, whipped, subjected to horrific physical punishments, and forced to surrender all of their property. Children sometimes died from starvation. People were often naked when they were tortured.

The Inquisitor would rip off the victim's nipples, tongue, ears, nose, and genitals. Some people were skinned from their head to their waist. About 2,000 to 10,000 Jews suffered death by being burned on stakes and more than 9,000 were punished by other methods. Many Jews died from starvation. By one account, he killed over 30,000 people. Torquemada's hatred of heretics influenced King Ferdinand and Queen Isabella to expel every Jew or Muslim from Spain that had not embraced Christianity, totaling 200,000 to 300,000. Most of them had ancestors that have lived in Spain for centuries. It is said that Torquemada himself had Jewish blood in him.

Caligula. He was Rome's 3rd emperor from AD 37 to AD 41. He was wild, extravagant, with a penchant for sexual adventures. In the first 3 months in his reign of terror, over 160,000 animals were sacrificed in his honor. He later got a brain fever that made him mentally ill. He then believed he was a god. Under Caligula, the law became an instrument of torture.

He believed prisoners should feel a painful death. He began to brutally murder for fun. He would kill his opponents slowly and painfully over hours or days. He decapitated and strangled children. People were beaten with heavy chains. He forced families to attend their children's execution. Many people had their tongues cut off. He fed prisoners to lions, panthers and bears and often killed gladiators.

One gladiator alone was beaten up for 2 full days. He sometimes ordered people to be killed by elephants. His cruelty caused people to commit suicide. He demanded sex with many women including his three sisters. He would force husbands to give up their wives. He exiled his sisters and had his own brother in law put to death.

He caused many to die of starvation. Sawing people in pieces was one of his favorite things to do, which filleted the spine and spinal cord from crotch down to the chest. He liked to chew up the testicles of victims. He killed

27

some of his most important friends and his father-in-law. One time Caligula said, "I wish Rome had but one neck, so that I could cut off all their heads with one blow

Nero. Nero was Rome's 5th emperor from AD 54 to AD 68. He brought the Roman Empire to ruin. He burned entire cities. He murdered thousands of people including his aunt, stepsister, ex-wife, mother, wife and adoptive brother. He systematically murdered every member in his family.

Some were killed in searing hot baths. He poisoned, beheaded, stabbed, burned, boiled, crucified and impaled people. He often raped women and cut off the veins and private parts of both men and women. He is said to have fiddled while Rome was burning. The great fire killed many of Rome's citizens and left hundreds of thousands destitute.

Though Nero was probably responsible for starting the fire, he blamed it on the Christians. Christians were starved to death, burned, torn by dogs, fed to lions, crucified, used as torches and nailed to crosses. He was so bad that many of the Christians thought he was the Antichrist. He even tortured and killed the apostle Paul and the disciple Peter. Paul was beheaded and Peter was crucified upside down.

Emperor Hirohito. He was emperor of Japan from 1926 to 1989. In that time, he and his army committing many war crimes and killed countless numbers of Chinese, Indonesians, Koreans, Filipinos and Indochinese.

He committed the war crime called The Rape of Nanking, which killed 300,000. He ordered every Chinese war prisoner to be killed. About 200,000 women were sexually assaulted. Husbands were sometimes forced to rape their wives and daughters.

A total of 10 million Chinese were forced into slavery, many were tortured and some even eaten. Many people were shot, beheaded, stabbed, burned, boiled, roasted, buried alive, and impaled. People were sometimes killed by gas, aid, military dogs and being hanged by their tongues on iron hooks. People were often used for bayonet practice. Between 4 and 10 million people in Java were forced to work by Japanese military, the majority of which died. People sometimes had their bodies sliced in half by a sword. Women were often stabbed by a bayonet or a long stick of bamboo through private parts. The Japanese disemboweled, decapitated, hacked, nailed, crucified and dismembered men. Men and women sometimes had their private parts sliced open. Thousands were frozen to death. 4 million people in Indonesia died from famine and 2 million in Vietnam.

Thousands were killed by chemical attacks. About 400,000 were killed by diseases. About 580,000 were killed after being human experiments. The Sook Ching massacre killed 50,000 to 90,000 Chinese. Over 100,000 civilians in the Philippines died from the Manila massacre. His men said that it was easy to kill because Hirohito told them that their lives were valueless compared to himself. He told his men to kill, burn, and loot all Chinese people. Over 20 million Chinese, 10 million Asians in other countries, and millions of people in World War II were killed by Hirohito's troops.

Ayatollah Ruhollah Khomeini. He was the religious leader of Iran from 1979 to 1989. He was also the leader of the 1979 Iranian Revolution, which killed 3,000 to 60,000 people. The Shria Islamic Law had many harsh rules for the normal people. Men and women had strict dress codes, citizens lost equal rights and met with very harsh punishments, were brutalized, tortured and killed. People were imprisoned and tortured for listening to music. People were lashed 100 times for kissing in public. People were tortured and killed if they did not believe in Allah. People were shot, hanged, blinded, gassed, stabbed in the chest, stoned to death and burned alive.

People had their hands cut off for stealing. Women had their faces slashed or burnt by acid. People were killed by machine guns, knives, clubs, cutters, and acid. In the 1988 Iranian Massacres, Khomeini ordered that every prisoner that did not repent anti-regime activities should be killed.

About 30,000 people were killed in 5 months while thousands of others were killed for other reasons including children that were hanged from cranes. Saddam Hussein feared the spread of Khomeini's militant brand of Shiism so he attacked Iran, which started the Iran-Iraq War, which caused the deaths of 1 to 2 million people. During the war, Khomeini sent young boys to fight and refused to make peace with Iraq even though there was at least one moment when Saddam offered peace for Iran. Because Khomeini refused to settle peace,

Iran's economy was ruined and 500,000 to 1 million Iranians were killed. His hatred of America and Western society inspired and paved the way for terrorist groups including Al-Qaeda. He paved the way for the Islamic Holy War, which has killed more than 2 million people to date.

Kim Il Sung. He was dictator of North Korea from 1948 to 1972. Kim Il Sung started the Korean War, which killed 3 million people. After the war, he brainwashed the people of North Korea into idolizing him, even though he made the country a lot worse than it was before. He killed all of his officers and rivals. In addition, he exiled or executed 90% of his generals that fought in the war.

More than 200,000 political prisoners were forced into concentration camps. People were forced into concentration camps for something as little as dropping a picture of Kim Sung accidentally on the ground. If someone committed a crime, the person's children and the children's children would also be killed or sentenced to life imprisonment.

Prisoners were starved, tortured or worked to death. Prisoners were sometimes forced to kneel in a box motionless for months until he or she dies. Hundreds of thousands were killed by firing squads and in concentration camps. Of the population of 22 million Koreans, 900,000 to 3.5 million have died in a famine. Kim Il Sung died in 1994 of a heart attack, which was brought on by a row with his son Kim Jong Il, who has proven that he is worse than his father.

Maximilian Robespierre. He was the leader of the French Revolution. Before he became a tyrant, he wanted the people of France to have freedom and rights, but when he gained power, his personality changed and he became obsessed with guillotining people. He began to create a reign of terror, a 10-month period in which mass executions were carried out. He also began to see everyone including friends as enemies.

People were guillotined for not supporting the French Revolution, hoarding, desertion, rebellion, and other things he saw as crimes. He guillotined entire families of aristocrats and ordinary people. He even guillotined his closest friends. Most were killed without trials.

As many as 40,000 were either executed or died in prison including King Louis XVI and Queen Marie Antoinette. He was also responsible for hundreds of thousands that died in battles during the Revolution. Under his orders, his men attacked Vendee, killing well over 100,000 men, women and children. He believed that killing people was better than forgiving people.

Saddam Hussein. Saddam was dictator of Iraq from 1979 to 2003. During that time, about 2 million people died because of his actions. He authorized many attacks on people like the chemical attack on Kurdish village of Halabja, which killed 5,000 people. Saddam's 1987-1988 campaign of terror against the Kurds killed 50,000 to 100,000.

An Amnesty International report said, "victims of torture in Iraq are subjected to a wide range of forms of torture, including the gouging out of eyes, severe beatings, and electric shocks... some victims have died as a result and many have been left with permanent physical and psychological damage." Saddam also had approximately 40 of his own relatives murdered.

He executed over 400,000 Iraqis. Many of them were tortured to death and filmed so he could watch them at his house. In 2006, Saddam was hanged after being found guilty for being convicted of crimes against humanity by the Iraqi Special Tribunal.

Heinrich Himmler. Heinrich Himmler was the head of the SS, the second most powerful Nazi and the architect of the Final Solution. He, more than anyone, encouraged and facilitated Adolf Hitler's decision to implement the Final Solution to the Jewish question, as well as other programs of ethnic cleansing that destroyed millions of lives during World War II. He was responsible for 6 to 7 million deaths of Poles, Russians, communists, and other groups whom the Nazis deemed unworthy to live including people with physical and mental disabilities.

Himmler once said "The decision, therefore, lies here in the East; here must the Russian enemy, this people numbering two hundred million Russians, be killed on the battle field and person by person, and made to bleed to death". His house contained furniture and books made from the bones and skins of his Jewish victims.

Osama bin Laden. Osama bin Laden was an Islamic terrorist leader that led the terrorist organization called the Al-Qaeda. He is responsible for the 9-11 attack, which injured more than 6,000 and killed about 3,000.

He is also responsible for bombing attacks on the United States Embassies in Dares Salaam, Tanzania and Nairobi, Kenya. In this latter attack, 212 people were killed and 4,000 were injured. He sponsored the Luxor massacre in Egypt, which killed almost 70 people.

Osama has caused other Al-Qaeda bombings throughout the world. The 2004 Madrid train bombings killed 191 people and injured 2,050. In October 2002 in Bali, 3 bombs exploded, killing 202 and injuring 209. The 2004 Super Ferry bombing killed 119 people. Thousands of Iraqis have died from Al-Qaeda bombings. In 2007 alone, bombs exploded in Qahtaniya and Jazeera, Iraq, killing 796 and injuring 1,562 people. Osama encouraged other terrorist groups to attack the United States. Osama was killed on May 2, 2011 by U. S. Navy Seals.

Reinhard Heydrich. Reinhard Heydrich was the chief of the Reich Main Security Office, the second most powerful person in the SS and the mastermind of the Final solution. He was one of the highest ranked of all the Nazis and was responsible for many war crimes. His actions caused the deaths of millions of people. He was responsible for the mass murder of Soviet officials and Russian Jews during Germany's invasion of the Soviet Union, which killed over a million people. He forced 60,000 Jew to leave Germany and go into Poland, where they were sent to Ghettos.

As he chaired the Wannsee Conference, he presented a plan of transportation and deportation of 11 million Jews from every country in Europe to be worked to death or killed. Heydrich thought of the pretext to invade Poland, which killed over 80,000 people and started World War II. There was an assassination attempt on him in 1942. He survived the attempt to kill him, but died 9 days later. In response to his death, Nazis killed nearly everyone in the village of Lidice.

Josef Mengele. He was a physician in the concentration camp Auschwitz and the doctor known as the "Angel of Death." He was in charge of selecting Jews to be sent to concentration camps or to be killed. He practiced many experiments on people. One of the most common experiments was on twins. He would find the similarities and differences in the genetics of twins, as well as seeing if the humane body could be manipulated. There were about 3,000 twins, only 200 survived. The twins were arranged by sex and age.

During the experiment, he would pour chemicals into the eyes of the twins to see if it would change their colors into sewing them together in hope to create conjoined twins. He sometimes tried to change the sex of the twins. He sometimes forced parents to kill their children. He tortured children to see how long they could survive. He often beat prisoners to death personally. He sent over 400,000 people to their deaths in the gas chambers.

Mengele escaped with his family to South America and lived there the rest of his life. It is possible that he used 88 twins in his medical experiments there.

Talat Pasha. He was the Grand Vizier of the Sultan in the Ottoman empire from 1917 to 1918. In 1915, Talat ordered his army to wipe out the Armenian race. People were whipped, tortured, robbed, raped and killed. All of the Armenians were forced into concentration camps. People were overloaded with supplies and forced to trudge miles with no food and they were killed if they couldn't continue.

People were naked when they marched. The whole male population of Angora was exterminated. Many were forced to rape family members. People were killed by bayonets, clubs, axes, hammers, spades, scythes, and saws.

Many had their private parts and sexual organs cut off. Tens of thousands were burned, drowned, poisoned, dismembered, crucified, boiled and beaten to death. Out of the population of 2.5 million Armenians, 1 to 1.5 million people were killed.

Elizabeth Bathory. The only woman of the bunch, Elizabeth Bathory, was a countess who lived in the Carpathian Mountains. She was born in 1560 and died in 1614. She was one of the inspirations of the Dracula fears and her nickname was Countess Dracula. She was possibly the most prolific serial killer in history. She believed that blood on her skin made her fresher and younger. She was responsible for the killing of 650 girls; many were tortured for weeks and were often naked when they were tortured. They were forced to eat their own flesh. She sometimes drank the blood of the girls and stabbed them with needles.

Some had their face, hands and private parts burned and she bit their flesh and private parts. Many of them starved to death, but others were burned or froze to death naked. She might have eaten some of her servants. It is possible that she bathed in blood. She was never put on trial, but was forced to stay in one room for the rest of her life.

OTHER EFFECTS OF SELF-SERVING AND EVIL LEADERS.

The above list of evil rulers does not include the leaders who started wars. This includes the U. S. leaders who got us involved in wars in Vietnam, Afghanistan and Iraq. Certainly, these leaders cannot be considered servant leaders and much of the U. S. involvement in these wars should be considered as self-serving (in our national interest).

These leaders manipulated the public with lies about weapons of mass destruction in Iraq (none were ever found) and used the 911 attack as an excuse to invade Iraq when none of the suicide bombers involved in the 911 attack actually were from Iraq

As a result, of this serve-serving act, millions of people were killed and injured. The war in Afghanistan was started to take out the Taliban, who said were hiding Osama Bin Laden. This war has also resulted in millions of people being killed or injured. In addition, wars started by the British since 1945 have resulted in the deaths of over 10 million people.[2]

WHAT IS THE GLOBAL ELITE?[3]

In addition to the murderous despots, most of the modern world lives in economic slavery to a group of billionaires and trillionaires. According to

Oxfam in 2016, the richest 1 percent control over 50 percent of the global wealth.

Who are the Global Elite? They are the members of the Rockefeller and Rothschild families and other corporate moguls that who set up and control the Federal Reserve Banking System, a private corporation, and all the Central Banks around the world.

Five of the most powerful and wealthiest men in the world are members of the Rothschild and Rockefeller families. In addition, the Queen of England is perhaps the wealthiest person on the planet. Nobody actually knows how much wealth she controls because her shareholdings remain secret in Bank of England accounts. They also are referred to as the Illuminati.

Just recently, a whistleblower released previously secret information on the offshore accounts and shell companies of over 200,000 wealthy individuals, some of which belong to the Global Elite. These self-serving maneuvers are designed to avoid having to pay taxes on their wealth. Many of them are leaders of their countries and may be forced to resign as a result of this disclosure.[4]

The Robber Barons. The Global Elite was preceded by the so-called Robber Barons in the 1870s in the U. S. The term "robber baron" is a derogatory term of social criticism originally applied to certain wealthy and powerful 19th-century American businessmen. The term appeared as early as the August 1870 issue of The Atlantic Monthly magazine. By the late 19th century, the term was typically applied to businessmen who used exploitative practices to amass their wealth.

These practices included exerting control over natural resources, influencing high levels of government, paying subsistence wages, squashing competition by acquiring their competitors to create monopolies so they could raise prices, and schemes to sell stock at inflated prices to unsuspecting investors. The term combines the sense of criminal ("robber") and illegitimate aristocracy (a baron is an illegitimate role in a republic). The list includes the following:

1. John Jacob Astor (real estate, fur)
2. Andrew Carnegie (steel)
3. William A Clark (copper)
4. Jay Cooke (finance)
5. Charles Crocker (railroads)
6. Daniel Drew (finance)

7. James Buchanan Duke (tobacco)
8. Marshall Field (retail)
9. James Fisk (finance)
10. Henry Morgan Flagler (railroads, oil)
11. Henry Clay Frick (Steel)
12. John Wayne Gates (barbed wire, oil)
13. Jay Gould (railroads)
14. Edward Henry Harriman (railroads)
15. Charles T. Hinde (railroads, water transport, shipping, hotels)
16. Mark Hopkins (railroads)
17. Collis Potter Huntington (railroads)
18. Andrew W. Mellon (finance, oil)
19. J. P. Morgan (finance, industrial consolidation)
20. John Cleveland Osgood (coal mining, iron)
21. Henry B Plant (railroads)
22. John D. Rockefeller (oil)
23. Charles M. Schwab (steel)
24. Joseph Seligman (banking)
25. John D. Spreckels (banking)
26. Leland Stanford (railroads)
27. Cornelius Vanderbilt (water transport, railroads)
28. and Charles Tyson Yerkes (street railroads)

Currently, the term "robber barons" can be used to describe modern industrialists and media moguls as well. Six men presently control all of the major media outlets in this country.[5]

HOW THE GLOBAL ELITE CAN USE ARTIFICIAL HUMANS TO FURTHER ENSLAVE US ALL

One of the most nefarious agendas of the Global Elite is population reduction. They have stated that our planet would be more sustainable if we limited the population of the world at 500 million. This would mean eliminating 7 billion current residents of the planet. Their means of reducing the world's populations have been to promote the poisoning of our water and our food supply. They have funded terrorist groups and started wars that also reduce the population.

Now they are developing a much more powerful weapon to reduce the human population. They are planning to introduce an artificial human to

35

replace organic humans. Some of their leaders have proclaimed that we are "incomplete humans" and technology will provide the perfect human that completes what God started.

They will have available in about five years or less, a chip that you can insert under your skin that provides you with "super intelligence" and a simulated or virtual reality that is much better than the one you normally encounter. The trade-off is that they cannot create an artificial emotional body or a soul. In order to agree to be "chipped," you would have to give up these precious human qualities that allow us to love others and ourselves.[6] I discuss this real threat in other chapters of this book.

NOTES

1   http://www.wonderslist.com/10-most-cruel-rulers-ever-in-history/
     https://25mostevil.wordpress.com
2   Weinhold, B. (2013). Twisted beliefs: Why people suffer from premature hardening of
     the categories. Asheville, NC: CICRCL Press.
3   http://theglobalelite.org/secrets-of-the-elite-why-forbess-rich-list-doesnt-include-the-
     wealthiest-families-on-the-planet/ Accessed Mar 6, 2016.
4   The Panama papers: A Report of the International Consortium of Investigative
     Journalists. April 3, 2016.
     https://panamapapers.icij.org/20160403-panama-papers-global-overview.html
     Accessed April 6, 2016.
5   http://theglobalelite.org/secrets-of-the-elite-why-forbess-rich-list-doesnt-include-the-
     wealthiest-families-on-the-planet/ Accessed April 14, 2016.
6   Henry, W. (2015). The Skingularity Is Near.
     http://www.williamhenry.net/skingularity/.

CHAPTER 2

WHY SERVANT LEADERS
ARE ESSENTIAL
TO ADVANCE HUMAN EVOLUTION

*"The secret of change is to focus all of your energy
not on fighting the old, but on building the new."*

—Lao Tsu

SERVANT LEADERS ARE NOT BORN, THEY ARE MADE

Some people seem to think leaders are born to lead. I disagree. Servant leaders are the products of secure early attachment and bonding with their parents. They need to have completed their individuation process, mastered their daily living tasks, learned to cooperate with others and learned to negotiating effectively to get their needs met.

Later in the book, I describe the optimum developmental processes that would provide a solid foundation for someone to become a servant leader. Some people appear to have the good fortune of being in the right place at the right time. That may play into this, but the servant leader still has to be able to "seize the day" when the opportunity to lead presents itself.

A DEVELOPMENTAL VIEW OF THE
HISTORY OF THE HUMAN RACE

I have created a comprehensive meta-theory I call Developmental Systems Theory (DST) to help me understand how human development operates in all human systems and how human systems evolve or not. It involves starting with the individual as a system, and continuing up to and including history of the whole human race as a system.

According to this theory, at each level of human system there are essential developmental processes that need to be completed in four consecutive stages of development: the codependent stage (bonding); the counter-dependent stage (separation and individuation); independent stage (mastery of self-care skills); and interdependent stage (conflict resolution and cooperation). If these essential developmental processes are completed, the system will evolve to the next stage without having to drag along any incomplete developmental processes from the previous stage of development. When this happens, it impedes the evolution process. DST provides a map to study how human systems evolve.

The theory describes two tracks of human evolution: The Trauma Track and the LOVEvolution Track. The LOVEvolution Track is characterized by the ability to give and receive unconditional love. This is what causes human system to evolve. The Trauma Track helps identify the obstacles to human evolution and the LOVEvolution Track presents the ideal development necessary for people to be able to give and receive unconditional love and thus evolve.

Our treatment modalities include Developmental Process Workers who help remove the obstacles that impede human evolution at the individual, couple and family systems levels. In addition, Developmental Process Consultants help human macro-systems to remove obstacles that impede the evolution of any larger human system like businesses, schools, churches, military, etc.[1]

WHAT ARE FRACTALS?

This theory is also based on the geometric concept of "fractals." The term "fractal" was coined by Benoit Mandelbrot in 1975. It comes from the Latin fractus, meaning an irregular surface like that of a broken stone. Fractals are non-regular geometric shapes that have the same degree of non-regularity on all scales. Just as a stone at the base of a foothill can resemble in miniature the mountain from which it originally tumbled down, so are fractals self-similar whether you view them from close up or very far away.

Fractals are the kind of shapes we see in nature. We can describe a right triangle by the Pythagorean theorem, but finding a right triangle in nature is a different matter altogether. We find trees, mountains, rocks and cloud formations in nature, but what is the geometrical formula for a cloud?

How can we determine the shape of a dollop of cream in a cup of coffee? Fractal geometry, chaos theory, and complex mathematics attempt to answer questions like these. Science continues to discover an amazingly consistent order behind the universe's most seemingly chaotic phenomena.[2]

Scientists are learning that all natural systems, including all human systems, are created by the immutable laws of fractal geometry. This includes static elements as well as energy flows, all living things, and their behavior patterns. They are all built on self-similar patterns that replicate each other on increasing and decreasing scales, sort of like Russian nesting dolls.

The various levels of scale are not all exactly alike, but they are all self-similar and build one on top of the other based upon a fundamental "code" that reproduces itself on different scales. In both the metaphysical and practical sense, the entire universe is built by fractal geometry

By looking at an individual as a "system," we can see that whatever is operating in the individual shows up as a self-similar pattern that replicates itself in larger and more complex human systems. The next level of system I have studied is the couple relationship system. Then, when children are born, it moves to the level of a family system, and so on up to the whole human race as a system.

Development always is continuous, but it may be disrupted by having to drag along unfinished developmental processes from previous stages. The task is to uncover any incomplete developmental processes and complete them to free up the process of development and evolution. This can be done at any time in your life.

Servant leaders, who have completed their essential developmental processes in each stage of development, can serve as "strange attractors" in human systems to help these systems to change and evolve. According to chaos theory, in any human system, there are people who often serve as strange attractors to help the system complete any incomplete essential developmental processes and facilitate the further evolution of that system.

I describe what I believe to be the developmental history of true servant leaders and why these people are best equipped to become servant leaders. I also help you identify "pseudo-servant leaders" who have incomplete essential developmental processes in the first or codependent stage of development from their first eight months of life. These people have an insecure attachment to their parents and compensate for this by trying to take care of others. This is often called a disorganized attachment style. While their behavior may look as if they are serving others, they are doing this in service of their own ego.

Tables 2-1 and 2-2 below show the essential developmental processes for each stage of development in each of six levels of human systems. Completion of these essential developmental processes insures evolution will proceed uninterrupted.

Table 2-1
The Developmental Evolution of Human Microsystems[3]

Stage of Development / Primary Task	Essential Developmental Processes of an Individual	Essential Developmental Processes of a Couple	Essential Developmental Processes a Family
Codependent Stage: *Bonding & Attachment*	• Mother receives good pre-natal care and support • Experience a nonviolent birth with immediate interventions to heal any shocks or birth trauma • Experience secure bonding/attachment with mother and or other adult caregivers • Build primal trust with both parents through a consistent resonant connection • Learn emotional resiliency skills • Create a secure internal model of self/other • Build healthy emotional communication and social engagement skills with both parents & others • Achieve secure bonding experiences with siblings and extended family	• Create secure and consistent bonding experiences with each other • Establish deep primal trust in each other • Develop ways to quickly repair any disruptions to couple resonance • Establish good communication and social engagement skills with each other • Establish an identity as a couple • Create secure bonding experiences in the family between parents and children • Establish primal trust among family members	• Create secure bonding experiences in the family between parents and children • Establish primal trust of family members with one another • Establish healthy emotional communication and social engagement skills among family members • Initiate a healthy family vision and induct family members into it • Establish a healthy identity as a family

Stage of Development / Primary Task	Essential Developmental Processes of an Individual	Essential Developmental Processes of a Couple	Essential Developmental Processes a Family
Codependent Stage: *Bonding & Attachment* (cont.)	• Promote effective communication and social engagement skills with parents and others	• Establish healthy emotional communication and social engagement skills among family members • Establish an identity as a family.	
Counter-dependent Stage: *Separation*	• Achieve complete psychological separation from both parents • Learn to explore one's environment in safe ways • Learn to trust and regulate one's own thoughts, feelings, behaviors in socially appropriate ways • Internalize appropriate physical & social limits • Develop healthy narcissism • Resolve internal conflicts between oneness & separateness • Bond with self • Continue to build secure internal working model of reality	• Become functionally separate individuals in the relationship • Identify and acceptindividual differences in thoughts, feelings, and behaviors in each other • Resolve internal conflicts between needs of self & other • Develop effective partnership ways to resolve conflicts of wants and needs, and conflicts of values and beliefs	• Parents and children learn to assert their individual needs and have them supported by other family members • Use fair, equitable, and non-shaming methods of limit setting and discipline • Parents are able to set effective limits for themselves and their children • Resolve conflicts effectively between needs of parents and needs of children

Stage of Development / Primary Task	Essential Developmental Processes of an Individual	Essential Developmental Processes of a Couple	Essential Developmental Processes a Family
Counter-dependent Stage: *Separation* (cont.)	• Successfully complete the psychological birth process		
Independent Stage: *Mastery*	• Master basic self-care • Master the process of becoming a functionally autonomous individual separate from parents • Develop object constancy • Develop trust in core values and beliefs •Achieve secure bonding experiences with nature • Learn effective social engagement skills • Develop secure internal working model of self/other • Develop secure internal working model of self/other •Achieve secure bonding with peers	• Listen empathically and non-defensively to each other • Communicate feelings directly and responsibly • Take responsibility for the influence of past shocks, traumas, or stresses on behavior • Master financial, psychological, and professional self-sufficiency within the relationship • Move beyond an idealized, romanticized approach to love and intimacy • Develop core values and beliefs as a couple • Achieve object constancy as a couple • Bond with nature as a couple	• Support development of individual initiative in family members • Develop individual and couple autonomy within the family structure • Set limits on children, selves, extra-family involvement to preserve couple relationship/couple autonomy within the family structure • Develop core values and beliefs as a family • Achieve object constancy as a family • Bond with nature as a family

Stage of Development / Primary Task	Essential Developmental Processes of an Individual	Essential Developmental Processes of a Couple	Essential Developmental Processes a Family
Inter-dependent Stage: *Cooperation*	• Learn how to co-operate with others • Learn how to ne-gotiate with others to get needs met • Learn to accept responsibility for personal behaviors and life experiences • Experience secure bonding with peers & other adults • Develop a social conscience • Achieve a secure bonding experienc-es with the main culture • Develop a secure bonding experienc-es with the planet • Live out of an authentic adult self • Achieve secure bonding with own children • Understand the influence of in-complete develop-mental processes on own life and the how to heal own developmental shocks, traumas, or stresses successfully	• Create a well-differentiated and clearly defined sense of self • Support part-ner's develop-ment • Learn to coop-erate with each other in getting impor-tant needs met in the relationship • Experience the deepest human connection pos-sible with each other • Develop equality in the relationship • Cooperate to help each other heal developmen-tal shocks, trau-mas, or stresses • Cooperate to develop each person's fullest human potential	• Build consensus in decision-mak-ing skills among family members • Teach family members to co-operate with each other so all get important needs met. • Create rituals that sustain the spiritual dimen-sion of the family • Create divisions of labor based on individual inter-ests and abilities • Help family members cooper-ate to help each other to heal their develop-mental shocks, traumas, or stresses • Teach family members how to cooperate to develop each member's fullest potential as hu-man being.

Table 2-2
The Developmental Evolution of Human Macro-systems[4]

Stage of Development/ Primary Task	Essential Developmental Processes of an Organization	Essential Developmental Processes of Cultures & Nation–states	Essential Developmental Processes of the Human Race
Codependent Stage: *Attachment & Bonding*	• Create bonding experiences for employees • Build trust between employers and employees • Create an organizational identity • Provide for basic needs of employees and managers • Foster healthy emotional communication and social engagement skills with employees and employers • Build organizational esprit de corps	• Create bonding experiences that unify all sub-cultures around common values and practices • Build trust between leaders and citizens • Create healthy national identity • Establish healthy emotional communication and social engagement skills for all citizens • Provide opportunities for all citizens to get their basic needs met • Understand the true history of the nation • Build national esprit de corps	• Establish secure bonding with the world of Nature • Create a respect for the supernatural and spiritual elements of human life • Establish a unique identify as a species • Promote the development of right-brain functions within the individual • Understand the true history of the human race

Stage of Development/ Primary Task	Essential Developmental Processes of an Organization	Essential Developmental Processes of Cultures & Nation–states	Essential Developmental Processes of the Human Race
Counter-dependent Stage: *Separation*	• Support employees to assert their needs and have them taken seriously by employers • Identify and promote unique contributions of each employee to the organization • Identify and promote unique contributions of each employee to the organization • Use fair, equitable, and non-shaming methods of limit-setting with employees • Establishing rules and policies in equitable ways. • Resolving internal conflicts between the needs of employees and the needs of employers in partnership ways	• Encourage all citizens to assert their needs and insist they are taken seriously by leaders • Guarantee freedom of expression and protect minority and cultural rights • Identify and promote unique contributions of every citizen to the nation • Establish fair, equitable, and non-discriminating laws and national policies • Use rule of law to provide equal justice for all citizens. • Identify unique strengths of cultures and nations • Develop effective ways to resolve conflicts of needs between cultural groups and between nations	• Explore ways to become functionally separate from Nature • Establish and respect diversity in the species • Develop left-brain functions within the individual • Create separate nation–states • Create religions based on beliefs in the supernatural and separate from Nature • Resolve conflicts between nations and religions in partnership ways • Understand how incomplete developmental processes influence human development and provide ways to heal developmental shocks, traumas, or stresses of all humans

Stage of Development/ Primary Task	Essential Developmental Processes of an Organization	Essential Developmental Processes of Cultures & Nation-states	Essential Developmental Processes of the Human Race
Counter-dependent Stage: *Separation* *(cont.)*	• Understand the influence of incomplete developmental processes on work performance and provide ways to heal developmental shocks, traumas, or stresses that show up at work	• Understand how incomplete developmental processes influence national health and provide ways to heal developmental shocks, traumas, or stresses of all citizens	
Independent Stage: *Mastery*	• Create an organizational culture with mutually determined values and beliefs • Support individual autonomy within the organizational structure • Give employees responsibility for self-regulation of emotion and self-care. • Support employees' achievement of true pride in their work	• Create a national culture that honors and protects diversity of all cultures. • Create economic/social safety net for those in need • Ensure that voting rights of all citizens are guaranteed • Teach citizens how to take responsibility for self-regulation of emotion and self-care • Help citizens develop true cultural and national pride	• Reunite with the world of Nature as partners • Develop whole-brain thinking functions including both/and thinking • Create & support individual cultures • Celebrate diversity among all cultures • Resolve conflicts of needs between cultures in partnership ways • Provide for the basic needs of all citizens

Stage of Development/ Primary Task	Essential Developmental Processes of an Organization	Essential Developmental Processes of Cultures & Nation–states	Essential Developmental Processes of the Human Race
Independent Stage: *Mastery* *(cont.)*	• Providing specialized training and development for each employee to enhance individual contributions to the organization		• Utilize systemic thinking in making major decisions
Inter-dependent Stage: *Cooperation*	• Create organizations run cooperatively by employees and employers • Utilize cooperative team-building activities• Promote cooperation- building among teams • Create rituals that build and sustain employee morale • Creating divisions of labor based on individual interests and abilities • Foster cooperation that helps each employee develop his or her fullest potential as a human being	• Citizens and their representatives cooperate to create three interdependent and balancing branches of government with equal power to govern • Leaders cooperate to build consensus policies to handle relations between cultural groups and between nations • Leaders cooperate to create meaningful national rituals that build and sustain citizen morale • Create equal opportunities for all citizens to develop their fullest potential	• Establish a planetary partnership culture based on cooperation and respect for differences • Develop the global brain and utilize global thinking in major decision-making bodies • Develop trans-systemic thinking

CHARACTERISTICS OF A SERVANT LEADER[5]

After carefully considering Greenleaf's original writings, I have identified a set of fourteen characteristics of the servant leader that I view as being of critical importance—central to the development of servant-leaders. These characteristics all emanate from an individuated Self and they contribute to the meaningful practice of servant leadership. These fourteen characteristics include:

Being Self-Reflective. It is very important that the servant leader is able to self-reflect. This skill is vital for the servant leader to be able to be in touch with his/her own inner guidance. By reflecting on what the task at the moment is and then going inside to find the inner resources to effectively handle the task is invaluable to a servant leader. A traditional leader will be forced to look to his/her advisors and other around him/her in order to decide what to do and how to best handle any task.

Using Self-Correction Skills. In addition to self-reflection, the servant leader has to be able self-correct. This means he/she has to take in feedback and reflect on what happened in previous situations. Then he/she has to apply what he/she learned from these previous situations to the current one. He/she will have to correct his/her responses to make wiser and more effective decisions.

Employing Listening Skills. Leaders have traditionally been valued for their communication and decision- making skills. Although these are also important skills for the servant leader, they need to be reinforced by a deep commitment to listening intently to others. The servant leader seeks to identify the will of a group and helps to clarify that will. He or she listens receptively to what is being said and unsaid. Listening also encompasses hearing one's own inner voice. Listening, coupled with periods of reflection, is essential to the growth and wellbeing of the servant leader.

Having Empathy. The servant leader strives to understand and empathize with others. People need to be accepted and recognized for their special and unique spirits. One assumes the good intentions of co-workers and colleagues and does not reject them as people, even when one may be forced to refuse to accept certain behaviors or performance. The most successful servant leaders are those who have become skilled empathetic listeners.

Healing of Self and Others. The healing of relationships is a powerful force for transformation and integration. One of the great strengths of servant leadership is the potential for healing one's self and one's relationship to others.

Many people have broken spirits and have suffered from a variety of emotional hurts and traumas. Although this is a part of being human, servant leaders recognize that they have an opportunity to help make whole those with whom they come in contact. In his essay, The Servant as Leader, Greenleaf writes, "There is something subtle communicated to one who is being served and led if, implicit in the compact between servant-leader and led, is the understanding that the search for wholeness is something they share."

Being Aware. General awareness, and especially self-awareness, strengthens the servant-leader. Awareness helps one in understanding issues involving ethics, power, and values. It lends itself to being able to view most situations from a more integrated, holistic position. As Greenleaf (1977/2002) observed: "Awareness is not a giver of solace—it is just the opposite. It is a disturber and an awakener. Able leaders are usually sharply awake and reasonably disturbed. They are not seekers after solace. They have their own inner serenity."

Being Persuasive. Another characteristic of servant leaders is reliance on persuasion, rather than on one's positional authority, in making decisions within an organization. The servant leader seeks to convince others, rather than coerce compliance. This particular element offers one of the clearest distinctions between the traditional authoritarian model and that of servant leadership. The servant leader is effective at building consensus within groups. This emphasis on persuasion over coercion finds its roots in the beliefs of the Religious Society of Friends (Quakers)—the denominational body to which Robert Greenleaf belonged.

Utilizing Conceptualization Skills. Servant leaders seek to nurture their abilities to dream great dreams. The ability to look at a problem or an organization from a conceptualizing perspective means that one must think beyond day-to-day realities. For many leaders, this is a characteristic that requires discipline and practice. The traditional leader is consumed by the need to achieve short-term operational goals. The leader who wishes to also be a servant leader must stretch his or her thinking to encompass broader-based conceptual thinking.

Within organizations, conceptualization is, by its very nature, a key role of boards of trustees or directors. Unfortunately, boards can sometimes become involved in the day-to-day operations—something that should be discouraged—and, thus, fail to provide the visionary concept for an institution.

Trustees need to be mostly conceptual in their orientation, staffs need to be mostly operational in their perspective, and the most effective executive leaders probably need to develop both perspectives within themselves. Servant leaders are called to seek a delicate balance between conceptual thinking and a day-to-day operational approach.

Displaying Foresight. Closely related to conceptualization, the ability to foresee the likely outcome of a situation is hard to define, but easier to identify. One knows foresight when one experiences it.

Foresight is a characteristic that enables the servant leader to understand the lessons from the past, the realities of the present, and the likely consequence of a decision for the future. It is also deeply rooted within the intuitive mind. Foresight remains a largely unexplored area in leadership studies, but one most deserving of careful attention.

Having Stewardship. Peter Block, the author of Stewardship and The Empowered Manager has defined stewardship as "holding something in trust for another." Robert Greenleaf's view of all institutions was one in which CEO's, staffs, and trustees all played significant roles in holding their institutions in trust for the greater good of society. Servant leadership, like stewardship, assumes primarily a commitment to serving the needs of others. It also emphasizes the use of openness and persuasion, rather than control. Committing to the Growth of People. Servant leaders believe that people have an intrinsic value beyond their tangible contributions as workers. As such, the servant leader is deeply committed to the growth of each individual within his or her organization.

The servant leader recognizes the tremendous responsibility to do everything in his or her power to nurture the personal and professional growth of the people who are under their care. In practice, this can include (but is not limited to) concrete actions such as making funds available for personal and professional development, taking a personal interest in the ideas and suggestions from everyone, encouraging worker involvement in decision-making, and actively assisting laid-off employees to find other positions.

Giving And Receiving Unconditional Love. The key characteristic of servant leaders is that they are able to give and receive unconditional love. This enables them to grow and evolve and it allows them stand above the fray and see things from a higher or spiritual plane. They can accept differences in people without getting afraid or judging them. They can see the pure essence of people and know that they are doing the best they can. They accept people as they are and do not have to try to change them.[6]

Using Restorative Justice Discipline Methods. Most organizations and leaders use retributive justice methods to discipline their employees. First, they find out what someone has done wrong or what mistake they have made. Then they administer some punishment for the mistake.

The servant leader uses a different process called restorative justice. It is a process that fosters for a restoration of any breeches in trust with the organization or other co-workers that result from a mistake or some poor performance by an employee.

This may mean gaining an understanding of the reasons why this incident happened and getting everybody's perceptions of what happened. It is important that everybody involved express their feelings directly to the offending employee. Finally, the process involves asking the offending employee to suggest ways he/she can restore the organization's trust in him/her. This person also may be asked to make some form of restitution for the cost of the mistake. The key is that there is a restoration of trust among the relationships involved in any dispute.

Building Community. The servant leader senses that much has been lost in recent human history as a result of the shift from local communities to large institutions as the primary shaper of human lives. This awareness causes the servant leader to seek to identify some means for building community among those who work within a given institution. Servant leadership suggests that true community can be created among those who work in businesses and other institutions.

Greenleaf said: "All that is needed to rebuild community as a viable life form for large numbers of people is for enough servant-leaders to show the way, not by mass movements, but by each servant-leader demonstrating his or her unlimited liability for a quite specific community-related group.[7]

Conclusion. These fourteen characteristics of servant leadership are by no means exhaustive. However, they do serve to communicate the power and promise that this leadership concept offers to those who are open to its invitation and challenges. I see people with these characteristics need to show up at all levels of leadership. Starting in your family by using these skills to raise your children up to serving as President of the U.S.

WHO ARE SOME OF THE MOST FAMOUS SERVANT LEADERS IN HISTORY?

Servant leadership is an ancient philosophy, one that existed long before Robert Greenleaf coined the phrase in modern times. There is a long history of individuals who by their actions can be considered servant leaders.

Lao-Tsu. There are passages that relate to servant leadership in the book, Tao Te Ching, attributed to Lao-Tsu. He is believed to have lived in China sometime between 570 BCE and 490 BCE. He was an older contemporary of Confucius and served as the keeper of the imperial archives in the province of Honan is the sixth century B. C. Late in his life, according to an ancient legend, he was riding off into the desert to die. He was literally sick at heart because of what he observed as "the ways of men." However, he was persuaded by a gatekeeper in northwestern China to write down his teachings for posterity. His book, roughly 5,000 pages in eighty-one chapters, became the foundation of Taoism.

Here are some quotes on servant leadership from Lao-Tsu:

"The highest type of ruler is one of whose existence the people are barely aware. Next comes one whom they love and praise. Next comes one whom they fear. Next comes one whom they despise and defy."

"To lead people, walk behind them."

"When you are lacking in faith, Others will be unfaithful to you."

"He who controls others may be powerful, but he who has mastered himself is mightier still."

"If you want to awaken all of humanity then awaken all of yourself. If you want to eliminate the suffering of the world, then eliminate all that is dark and negative in yourself. Truly, the greatest gift you have to give is that of your own self-transformation."

"The Sage is self-effacing and scanty of words. When his task is accomplished and things have been completed, All the people say, 'We ourselves have achieved it!'"

Servant Leadership Principles Show Up in All Five Major Religions. Kriger and Seng[8] posed a contingency theory in servant leadership based upon the worldview of five religions that together represent over 82% of the world's population. They compared the worldviews of Buddhism, Christianity, Hinduism, Islam, and Judaism in relation to factors such as the nature and exemplars of leadership, core vision, basis for moral leadership, source of wisdom for leaders, levels of being, and the role of community.

They defined eight servant leadership principles found in these five major religions: human dignity, personal responsibility, character, community, the use of power, compassion, stewardship, and justice. Some of these components were drawn from an examination of the Old and New Testament teachings related to how individuals should be treated and the essential values associated with what the Scriptures teach that a healthy society should embody. Many find their roots in Old Testament instructions from God to the nation of Israel regarding how their leaders should structure the Hebrew society.

Jesus, the Model Servant Leader. Jesus committed his own life to sacrificial service under the will of God (Luke 22:42), and he sacrificed his life freely out of service for others (John 10:30). He came to serve the people (Matthew 20:28) although he, according to scripture, was God's son and was thus more powerful than any other leader in the world. He healed the sick (Mark 7:31-37), drove out demons (Mark 5:1-20), was recognized as Teacher and Lord (John 13:13), and had power over the wind and the sea and even over death (Mark 4:35-41; Matthew 9:18-26).

Here are some quotes from The New Testament that show Jesus as a servant leader:

"Jesus called them together and said, "You know that those who are regarded as rulers of the Gentiles lord it over them, and their high officials exercise authority over them. Not so with you. Instead, whoever wants to become great among you must be your servant, and whoever wants to be first must be servant of all. For even the Son of Man did not come to be served, but to serve, and to give his life as a ransom for many." Mark 10:42-45

"When he had washed their feet and put on his outer garments and resumed his place, he said to them, "Do you understand what I have done to you? You call me Teacher and Lord, and you are right, for so I am. If I then, your Lord and Teacher, have washed your feet, you also ought to wash one another's feet. For I have given you an example, that you also should do just as I have done to you." John 13:12-15

"But not so with you. Rather, let the greatest among you become as the youngest, and the leader as one who serves." Luke 22:26

"It shall not be so among you. But whoever would be great among you must be your servant." Matthew 20:26

"Do nothing from rivalry or conceit, but in humility count others more significant than yourselves. Let each of you look not only to his own interests, but also to the interests of others. Have this mind among yourselves, which is yours in Christ Jesus, who, though he was in the form of God, did not count equality with God a thing to be grasped, but made himself nothing, taking the form of a servant, being born in the likeness of men." Philippians 2:3-8

Islam ("the leader of a people is their servant") and other world religions have long embraced the philosophy of servant leadership. A servant to these people is seen in the following: "He should always conduct himself with great humility." In Judaism: "There is none greater than Moses, our teacher. Yet, he said: 'What are we? Your complaints are not against us.'" "He should bear the nation's difficulties, burdens, complaints and anger as a nurse carries an infant."

Below is a description of some of the greatest secular servant leaders in history:

Abraham Lincoln as a Servant Leader. Abraham Lincoln is a good example of a servant leader. Lincoln's actions during the US Civil War are often cited as prime examples of servant leadership behavior. In particular, many scholars look to his attempts to preserve of the Union during this conflict and the freeing of the Southern slaves. Why do these particular actions qualify as servant leadership? The simplest reason is that it would have been much easier for Lincoln to let the Union dissolve and/or simply let slavery remain intact. Rather than taking the easy road, however, Lincoln chose the harder road because it would be more beneficial to the people he was serving in the long run, even if they did not realize it at the time.

Albert Schweitzer as a Servant Leader. For example, Albert Schweitzer was a late 19th and early 20th century German physician and priest who could have had a very easy and profitable life for himself. Instead, he focused most of his skills and energies on helping others. His personal philosophy is summed up in the expression, "reverence for life." He believed that no one should ever destroy life unless it was absolutely necessary. He founded a hospital in Lambarene, Gabon, a French colony at the time. He is quoted as saying, "The only ones among you who will be really happy are those who will have sought and found how to serve." Dr. Schweitzer lived to a ripe old age.

Mahatma Gandhi as a Servant Leader. Many consider Mahatma Gandhi one of the greatest servant leaders of the twentieth century. His great leadership can be attributed to different leadership theories and approaches. However, the servant leadership theory should be on or near the top of any list of theories or approaches describing Gandhi's leadership, throughout his life, Gandhi the displayed of the ten characteristics of servant leadership from Robert K. Greenleaf's work on the subject.

Gandhi showed great awareness of what was going on around him in South Africa and he considered different courses of actions in dealing with oppression that Hindus and Muslims were faced with. While sitting on a train platform after being forcibly removed from a train, he considered his options to deal with the oppression he and the other Hindus and Muslims were facing. Instead of just accepting the oppression, mounting attacks against the ruling class, or just returning to India. Gandhi chose to organize the Hindus and Muslims to resist the oppression by non-violent means.

Gandhi was able to use his influence to keep his followers from resorting to violence even in the light of the Amritsar massacre of 1919, where thousands of his followers were killed by order of the British government. He also was able to stop the fighting between the Hindus and Muslims by going on hunger strike until the two stopped fighting.

The way that Gandhi conducted his salt march of 1930 showed his ability to conceptualize and it also showed the foresight that he had. He took his time, only covering 10 miles a day for 24 days, allowing time for the world press time to arrive and cover the event. He knew this would bring the British oppression of the India people to the world stage and garner support for their cause throughout the world. This slow pace of his march also allowed him time to stop in each village along the way and listen to what the villagers had to say and treated each of them as an individual, valuing what they had to say.

Gandhi showed his empathy for his followers by remaining to reside in his modest home and wearing the same simple clothing of his Hindu followers, even though, he had risen to the champion of the fight for freedom from British rule.

Gandhi never wavered from his community building efforts. His last effort, which resulted in his death, was a walk from village to village along the border between India and Pakistan trying to unite the Hindus and Muslins and stop the border violence.

Mother Teresa as a Servant Leader. Mother Teresa did so many incredible things in her life. She dedicated her life to making the lives of others better. Through starting "The Missionaries of Charity" she saved many lives. She also taught us many things such as how to put others before we think of ourselves. She brought societies together because of the work she did.

She won many awards including the Noble Peace Prize in 1971. The money that she won from those awards went to help funding her shelters. Mother Theresa took her initial vows as a nun on May 24th, 1931. After severing for over 45 years, she passed away on September 5th 1997. Mother Theresa is an excellent example of putting unconditional love into action.

Nelson Mandela As A Servant Leader. Nelson Mandela can also be described as adopting the servant leadership role. The desire for his own freedom was soon overcome by the need for all to have freedom. Nelson Mandela lived to serve others. His achievements were not only to benefit himself or his own goals, but also to achieve goals of the fellow man. Consider the following from the extraordinary lesson on servant leadership that is Nelson Mandela:

Despite the personal cost, he stayed true to his conviction that South Africa should be a democracy with one-person, one-vote equality for all of its citizens.

He worked with those who had imprisoned him at Robben Island to bring about a peaceful transition of power.

He sought opportunities to bring South Africans together as he did by embracing the South African Rugby team (as dramatized in the movie Invictus).

Like our own George Washington, he walked away from power leaving the example for South Africa that dictatorships and royal families are poor governing models.

Martin Luther King as a Servant Leader. Another modern example of a modern servant leader is Dr. Martin Luther King. Dr. King certainly did not choose the easy road when he assumed a leadership role in the Civil Rights Movement and chose to champion the non-violent approach. He knew that approach would be more difficult, but he also knew it would ultimately be more beneficial to those he was trying to serve. Even more servant-like was Dr. King's well-known desire to not be remembered for the prizes and accolades he won in life, but for his role in driving towards social justice. In other words, he cared more about how he helped others than about any recognition he could ever receive.

Martin wrote the following: "Leadership is not bestowed, rather, You must earn it. True greatness comes not by favoritism but by fitness...If you want to be important—wonderful. If you want to be recognized—wonderful. If you want to be great—wonderful. However, recognize that he who is greatest among you shall be your servant. That's your new definition of greatness. Moreover, this morning, the thing that I like about it by giving that definition of greatness, it means that everybody can be great.

Not everybody can serve. You don't have to have a college degree to serve. You don't have to make your subject and your verb agree to serve. You don't have to know about Plato and Aristotle to serve. You don't have to know Einstein's theory of relativity to serve. You don't have to know the second theory of thermodynamics in physics to serve. You only need a heart full of grace. A soul generated by love. And you can be that servant."

Robert Greenleaf, The Founder of Modern Servant Leadership. Robert Greenleaf is considered the most famous modern advocate of servant leadership. He spent five decades challenging organizations in the fields of business, education, health care, and religion to become servant in nature, because he believed this would fundamentally change society for the better. He conjectured that because servant leaders take care of their followers' greatest needs first, followers "become healthier, wiser, freer, more autonomous, more likely themselves to become servants." He later reasoned that cultural forces, such as the questioning of power and authority, would eventually lead to the emergence of cooperation and support as more productive, interactional modes of interpersonal behavior.

According to his essay, "Essentials of Servant Leadership," Greenleaf's philosophy had its roots from reading a work of fiction in 1958: "The idea of the servant as leader came out of reading Hermann Hesse's Journey to the East. In this story, we see a band of men on a mythical journey.

The central figure of the story is Leo, who accompanies the party as the servant who does their menial chores, but who also sustains them with his spirit and his song. He is a person of extraordinary presence. All goes well until Leo disappears. Then the group falls into disarray and the journey is abandoned. They cannot make it without the servant Leo. The narrator, one of the party, after some years of wandering, finds Leo and is taken into the Order that had sponsored the journey. There he discovers that Leo, whom he had known first as servant, was in fact the titular head of the Order, its guiding spirit, a great and noble leader.

His essay "Servant as Leader" inspired people all over the world. He saw the servant leader characteristics as not simply traits or skills possessed by the leader. Rather, he saw servant-leadership is an ethical perspective on leadership that identifies key moral behaviors that leaders must continuously demonstrate in order to make progress on Greenleaf's "best test." The "best test," which gives us the ethical ends for action, combined with his list of traits that identified the means, create a powerful framework for a review of the literature that furthers the conceptual framework for servant-leadership.

He also applied the principles of servant leadership to organizations. He wrote "The Institution as Servant". For educators, he wrote "The Leadership Crisis: A Message for College and University Faculty" and "Teacher as Servant." His other writings targeted seminaries, personal growth, religious leaders, and trustees, among others.

Servant Leadership In the Military. One of the leading places where leadership is taught in this country is in the military. Serving your country is the main reason people join the military. That is the mission. So how does the military rate in its ability to train servant leaders? It is sort of a mixed bag and I believe it still goes back to the personal/psychological history of the soldier who is asked to be a servant leader.

In the U. S. Army, the rank of sergeant literally means "servant." As long as the sergeant can keep one eye on the needs of the mission and another eye on the needs of troops he is assigned to serve, it should work really well. This is also true of the Commissioned Officers. They are all asked to practically memorize the Army's values: Loyalty, Duty, Respect, Selfless-Service, Honor, Integrity, and Personal Courage. The acronym is LDRSHIP. Certainly, these sound like characteristics of servant leadership. In addition, the "Warrior Ethos" is, "I will always place the mission first. I will never accept defeat. I will never quit. I will never leave a fallen comrade." What can go wrong in this picture?

However, in a hierarchical system like the military, an NCO sergeant or any commissioned officer is also concerned about his/her promotion to the next rank that would give him or her more money and privileges. If these leaders have their eyes cast upward too much, trying to please or meet the needs of their superiors so they can get promoted, then servant leadership breaks down.

In any hierarchical system, be it military, educational or corporate, there is a hidden reversal system going on. In these hierarchical systems, leaders always have their eyes focused upward and are constantly trying to take care of the needs of their bosses so they can get promoted. Being a good servant leader usually is not one of the criteria for promotion.

I believe this pattern of behavior, that I call the "reversal process," stems from early attachment problems in the first year of life. Infants either develop a secure attachment style or an insecure attachment style. The secure attachment style is developed over the first year by having regular, consistent bonding experiences with a stable parent. It is a 24/7 job and not all parents are ready for that kind of "servant leadership." If that parent is suffering from a lack of sleep, depression or anxiety, they often dissociate and do not regularly pay attention to the needs of their infant child in providing consistent bonding/attachment experiences.

What the child learns from this experience is that they cannot depend on this parent and cannot trust that they will be able to meet their needs for bonding and attachment. They begin to deny their own needs and focus their attention on meeting the needs of the parent. By age six, they have perfected this care-taking attachment style and as research shows, will continue to be a care-taker the rest of their lives, if not intervention is done to change that style.

Military leaders, who are good at being a servant leader for their troops, likely had secure bonding/attachment experiences as an infant. Those who did not can easily fall into the reversal process and pay more attention to the needs of their superiors than those of their troops they are assigned to serve. It can also distort their attempts to serve the mission. In any hierarchal system, who is more likely to get promoted, the servant leader or the self-serving leader?

NOTES

1   Weinhold, J. & Weinhold, B. (2011). *Healing developmental trauma.* Denver, CO: Love publishing Co. pp. 23-61.

2   http://whatis.techtarget.com/definition/fractal Accessed April 2, 2016.

3   Weinhold, J & Weinhold, B. (2011). *Healing developmental trauma.* Denver, Co: Love Publishing Co. pp. 37-39.

4   Ibid. pp. 40-42.

5   Spears, LC (2010). *Character and servant leadership: Ten characteristics of effective, caring leaders. The Journal of Virtues & Leadership,* Vol. 1 Issue 1, 2010, pp. 25-30. School of Global Leadership & Entrepreneurship, Regent University.

6   Weinhold, B & Weinhold, J. (2015). Developmental trauma: The game changer in the
     mental health profession. Colorado Springs, CO: CICRCL Press/CreateSpace.

7   Greenleaf, R. & Spears, L. (2002). Servant leadership: A journey into the nature of
     legitimate power and greatness 25th Anniversary Edition. Mahwah, NJ: Paulist Press,
     p. 53.

8   http://online.ben.edu/blog/leadership/who-are-these-servant-leaders Accessed April
     23, 2016.

CHAPTER 3

THE ROLE OF THE SERVANT LEADER IN HELPING OTHERS ACHIEVE SECURE BONDING AND ATTACHMENT

"Secure attachment has been linked to a child's ability to successfully recover and prove resilient in the presence of a traumatic event."

—*Asa Don Brown*

WHAT MY CLINICAL RESEARCH TAUGHT ME

My clinical research indicates that most children experience developmental traumas very early in life without anyone ever noticing that they happened. Most of these traumas are caused by a form of parental neglect. Parents may be depressed, dissociated, distracted or "checked out," fail to understand the needs of infants and how to effectively meet them.

If you are married or in a committed relationship where you have children, you need to use your servant leadership skills to help raise your children. This will allow them to grow up and either become servant leaders themselves or be able to identify and support true servant leaders that show up in their life.

The next four chapters provide information on what the ideal development of a servant leader should be in each of four developmental stages as outlined in my Developmental Systems Theory described earlier. This is a description of the LOVEvolution Track of development. This, in my opinion, is the ideal foundation for the development of a servant leader. In addition, these chapters show parents how to utilize servant leader skills to effectively parent their children or grandchildren utilizing unconditional love.

However, no one that I know has been able to complete all the essential developmental processes outlined in this book on schedule. I would estimate that only 1-2 percent of adults have completed all these developmental processes in childhood. This means you as a potential servant leader likely will have to complete them as an adult. The most common reason why you didn't complete these essential developmental processes in early childhood is the presence of hidden and unhealed developmental trauma caused by either abuse or neglect of your needs. Some of the reasons they are still incomplete are listed below:

1. Something happened to you where you could not safely express how you were feeling or what you were thinking at the time.
2. You were afraid of your parents because they verbally, physically or emotionally abused you.
3. You wanted your parents to tell you it was not your fault.
4. You had to take care of your parents more than they took care of you.
5. Your parent(s) never admitted they were wrong or apologized to you for the way they treated you.
6. Your parents didn't pay much attention to you or give you enough guidance.
7. Your mother was "checked out" most of the time.
8. Your mother or father paid more attention to their addictions than they did to you.
9. Your father was working all the time. He never had time to do anything with you.
10. You wanted your parent to tell you more positive things about yourself.
11. Your parents severely criticized your actions.
12. Your parents set limits by shaming you.
13. Your needs were neglected by busy or overwhelmed parents.

In these next four chapters, I discuss how the Trauma Track might interfere with the completion of these essential developmental processes in each stage. This provides the servant leader with ideas of what they might do to heal their developmental traumas. These then become important self-development tasks for someone wanting to be a servant leader.

Table 3-1 contains a map of the essential developmental processes that ideally are completed during the first eight months of life. The child particularly needs a constant caregiver during this period, and the caregivers need support so that they can provide this constancy.

Mothers often suffer from postpartum depression triggered by their own unresolved developmental traumas. Drugs or alcohol use can distract a parent who has an addiction. Economic stresses can also take their toll on parents trying to care for the child as best they know how. In other words, many things can interfere with a parent being able to provide the constant care an infant needs.

Table 3-1
The Essential Developmental Processes of
the Codependent or Bonding/Attachment Stage[1]

Developmental Stage & Primary Task	Essential Developmental Processes of This Stage	Suggested Experiences for Completing the Essential Developmental Processes of This Stage
Co-dependent (conception to 6-8 months) *Bonding & Attachment*	• Mother receives good pre-natal care and support • Experience a non-violent birth with immediate interventions to heal any shocks or birth trauma • Experience secure bonding/ attachment with mother and father and other adult caregivers • Build primal trust with both parents through a consistent resonant connection • Learn emotional resiliency skills from both parents • Create a secure internal model of self/other • Build healthy emotional communication and social engagement skills with both parents & others	•Both parents regularly talk to the child in the womb • Mother maintains a high quality diet and reduces environmental stressors to prevent the risk of shock and excessive cortisol production during pregnancy • Parents build prenatal relationship with the child • Parents use non-violent birthing practices/ with father assisting in the birth • Mothers nurse and room-in with her child at the hospital; prolonged skin-to-skin contact with both parents in first 12-24 hours following birth • Family leave policies allow both parents to stay home without financial stress • Mother receives effective post-natal emotional & physical support. Father shares in early care of child

Developmental Stage & Primary Task	Essential Developmental Processes of This Stage	Suggested Experiences for Completing the Essential Developmental Processes of This Stage
Co-dependent (conception to 6-8 months) *Bonding & Attachment* *(cont.)*	• Achieve secure bonding experiences with siblings and extended family • Promote effective communication and social engagement skills with both parents and others	• Mother and father provide nurturing, respectful touch; eye contact & gazing, singing & speaking in loving ways • Child gets timely emotional and tactile comfort to help heal developmental traumas caused by disruptions in resonant connection to both parents • Child receives unconditional love from both parents • Child is mirrored and validated for his/her essence by both parents • Immediate & extended family members provide consistent, nurturing, and empathic contact with the child • Parents provide comfortable and protective environment to meet child's needs for safety and survival as he/she begins to crawl or walk

Children build their lives on the foundation of secure bonding and attachment with both parents. If this process happens effectively, the rest of life will be a lot easier for them. I believe that the parent-child bonding and attachment process actually begins during the pre-conception and prenatal development period.

Pre-Conception Bonding and Attachment. The parent-child bonding and attachment process ideally begins prior to conception. The prospective parents need information about the essential developmental processes related to conception, gestation, birth, and the first eight months of life that are listed in Table 3.1. Conscious conception is a practice that couples can use as a part of prenatal bonding. In this little-known body of knowledge, the mother pays particular attention to her diet and nutritional state prior to conception. While making love, a couple can tune in to the yet unborn child and invite him/her to join their family.

Pre- and perinatal psychology pioneer, William Emerson, reports working with clients who had problems with aggression and violence. When regressed in therapy, they discovered memories from the time of their conception that involved traumatic issues in their family or immediate surroundings.

The most frequently mentioned memories involved forced sex, including manipulated sex; date rape, and rape; substance abuse; physical abuse; dismal familial, social, or cultural conditions; and personal or cultural shame, such as having been conceived out of wedlock.

Some of Emerson's regressed clients reported biological memories related to conception involving encounters as sperm and/or eggs that contained intense aggression, annihilation, death, power, and/or rejection.[2] This suggests that a couple should strive to conceive a child with as much unconditional love present as possible.

Emerson also reports having clients with memories related to the implantation of the egg with the sperm, the biological process whereby the conceptus attaches itself to the uterine wall. This is critical stage of embryological development where the soul of the incoming child can choose to stay or go. A couple can actually verbally invite the embryo to choose to stay and become part of their family.

Prior to and during implantation, regressed patients report that they experienced the terror of being near death. Some reported feeling unwanted and that they had no place to go, no place to belong. Most importantly, many "decided" at that moment that the world is a hostile and unsafe place for them.

A mother wanting to get pregnant needs to avoid alcohol; drugs of all kinds; and chaotic, conflictual, or stressful environments that activate her Adrenal Stress Response (ASR). The ASR pumps cortisol and other stress-related hormones into her bloodstream and into the bloodstream of the unborn child. The servant leader father supports his partner by taking some of the normal burdens off her to reduce her stress by sharing the cooking, cleaning or shopping as she prepares her body for pregnancy.

Prenatal Bonding. Thomas Verny's pioneering research[3] in pre-and perinatal psychology indicates that babies remember everything and are deeply impacted by the events around them from the very beginning of life.

Unfortunately, babies are only able to communicate this telepathically, a phenomenon not yet widely understood or accepted.

Mom and dads need to talk and sing to their child while in womb. Even playing music supports the prenatal bonding process.

Research from pre- and perinatal psychology also indicates that memory and interactive response patterns begin by the third month of gestation. It is important for both parents to consciously tune in and attempt to make contact with the growing embryo.

Once the pregnancy begins, the mother needs to focus as much of her time as possible on her thoughts and attention on uplifting things that keep her body producing a constant state of endorphins, oxytocin and other pleasure-related hormones. Again, the servant leader father can support his partner in this effort by providing her with expressions of his love that produce these endorphins and oxytocin.

This helps both her and the gestating baby experience harmony and wellbeing. Again, the father can also do this after the first trimester begins, as the child can experience the loving thoughts and feelings they are communicating. As the gestating baby grows larger, both parents naturally draw their attention away from the outer world and attune more deeply to their child.

The womb is the "first school" for the child. Gestating babies are very alert, aware, and attentive to social cues that involve voice, touch, and music. Ideally, the parents should sing and talk to their baby, fill their home with beautiful and inspiring music, rub the baby's body through the mother's belly, and observe his or her cycles of waking and sleeping. They should also talk with the baby about the upcoming transition to the outer world and share their excitement and anticipation about his or her arrival in their family.

Later in the pregnancy, the fetus will kick to respond to this contact. It is a thrill for parents to begin the lifetime relationship with their child at this early age.

Pre- and perinatal experiences are significant not only in forming the personality, but also contribute to the development of the child's attachment and creating their internal working model of reality. Prenates, for example, who are exposed to environmental toxins like nicotine, alcohol, and prescription or illicit drugs through the mother's blood stream via the placenta, can be born with the same addictions as their mothers.

Birth Bonding. Ideally, both parents should wait for their baby to signal his or her readiness to be born, understanding that his or her brain will secrete the hormones that trigger the labor process. They empower their child to direct the birth process, and follow his or her lead in each moment of the final stages of gestation into the birthing process.

They may choose to ignore the well-meaning advice from grandparents or medically trained people who may recommend "inducing" birth, using anesthesia, and other invasive birth practices. These should be avoided, unless it is absolutely necessary. Instead, both parents need to use the tools learned in their natural birthing classes to help them relax and surrender deeply to the birth experience.

If the parents have cleared their own birth traumas, they are free to follow their child's natural birth journey without becoming fearful or being emotionally triggered during the birthing process. They also strive to trust those who are assisting them through the birthing experience.

To reassure the grandparents and close friends, the parents can choose birth facilitators or midwives who have access to medical support for backup, should it be needed. The parents accept the possibility that their child might have karmic needs for an experience of a breech or cesarean birth and make arrangements for those possibilities should they become birthing options. At each step in the birth process, the parents and birth facilitators must stay in energetic attunement with each other and the baby, and quickly refocus their attention if they go out of harmony.

A recent study analyzed the umbilical cord blood from 10 randomly selected newborns in U.S. hospitals collected by the Red Cross after the cord was cut. They found chemicals in this blood from stains and oil repellents used in fast food packaging, clothes and textiles.

Other chemicals found are used in flame-retardants and pesticides. They found a total of 287 toxic chemicals. The researchers concluded, "of the 287 chemicals we detected…we know that 180 cause cancer in humans or animals, 217 are toxic to the brain and nervous system, and 208 cause birth defects or abnormal development in animal tests."[4] We can only imagine what effects these chemicals have on the brain of the fetus.

The infant's developing brain perceives these substances as dangers, and begins creating neural wiring to anticipate danger into his or her cellular defenses. One of the important findings from a cross-section of pre- and perinatal research is the correlation between birth trauma and difficulties later in sustaining adult relationships.

I have found that most birth trauma is the result of the mother being triggered by her own or her partner's unhealed birth trauma. More on that later in the book.

My own Breathwork Therapy and the experiences of many of my clients support this research. Many of my clients reported having birth memories in which they heard exact conversations between the adults who were present at their birth, while others said they knew what the adults who were present were thinking.

After completing their Breathwork Therapy, several clients were able to verify the accuracy of these birth memories with their parents. This anecdotal information helped me validate that newborns are able to tune into the thoughts and feelings of those around them.

THE FOUR INITIATIONS THAT A SERVANT LEADER FATHER MUST PERFORM FOR HIS CHILDREN[5]

I see fathers with servant leader skills being involved in performing four separate essential initiation processes for their children (both boys and girls):

The First Initiation Process: Cutting The Cord and Bonding With Your Child. Cutting the cord occurs shortly after your child's birth. If you, as the servant leader father, can perform this function, it symbolically severs the biological connection the child had with its mother during gestation. This allows you as the father to begin to build your own separate biological bonding process with your child.

This also marks the beginning of the "divine family triangle" (mother, father and child). Bonding with your child is an initiation process that you as a father have to perform during the first 6-8 months of your child's life. It is essential that you be present as much as possible in the everyday life of your infant child during this time of bonding.

The Second Initiation Process: Facilitating The Psychological Birth Of Your Children. The psychological birth of you as a separate human being usually is completed between ages two and three. Here servant leader fathers have an important initiation to perform. From about 8 months until about two to three years, you need to support your child in his/her process of becoming emotionally and psychologically separate from his/her mother.

This allows your child to be birthed psychologically as a fully functioning human being emotionally separate from the symbiotic bonding with his/her mother and with you by age two. Your child cannot complete this psychological birth or individuation process without your full participation where you make good use of your male mother skills.

The Third Initiation Process: Helping Your Children Achieve Mastery. You as a father with servant leader skills needs to provide an emotional and mental structure to help your child master the tasks of everyday life and understand how the world works. You teach your children how to master their everyday skills both inside and outside the home. Most of this initiation occurs by transmission, as your child observes what you do and say and then imitates it. This happens between ages 3-6.

The Fourth Initiation Process: Helping Your Children Learn Negotiation Skills. Negotiation skills are critical in helping your child get his/her needs met and learning to cooperate with others. Much of the "teaching" involved with initiating your child occurs through everyday modeling. As your child watches you negotiate to get your needs met and cooperates with others, he or she learns how to do it for him/herself. This should be completed before your child's 18th birthday.

Your servant leader skills in conducting these four initiations, will enable your children to grow up being able to rely on their own "internal power." As a servant leader, you can teach your children to trust their own inner resources as a guide for their life. Then your children will have the foundation they need to naturally grow into mature, fully individuated adults.

The Divine Family Triangle. The divine family triangle ideally is a tightly woven relational structure in which two bonded parents actively create a secure triangular bond. This insures that your child will complete the essential developmental processes at each stage of his/her development. This Divine Family Triangle crucible, created prenatally, needs to be nurtured and maintained consciously by both parents throughout the child's life.

A much deeper bond can form when the father with servant leader skills initiates the child into the divine family triangle by cutting the umbilical cord. When possible, invite friends and family to surround the couple and infant after the birth with a field of unconditional love and support. The extended family and community of friends can give the parents their first experience of being in a village that helps them raise their child.

If anyone in the support circle is triggered during the birthing process, they can quietly leave and remove their stressful energy from the group while they work on themselves.

Ideally, all in the birthing area should focus on holding the field of unconditional love to support the couple, child, and those assisting with the birth. This helps the child not "file" any birth trauma that might have occurred as a result of any twists and turns of the birthing process.

Both parents should talk to the child during this process and acknowledge the cutting of the cord as the child's first separation from the mother. There will be a second "cutting of the cord" when the servant leader father helps the child complete his/her psychological birth around the age of three.

After the birth, both parents continue to talk to the baby to reassure him or her of their support while adjusting to entering a new and strange environment. They do everything to make sure their child is fully welcomed into the world outside the womb.

Ideally, the parents and birth helpers give the newborn time to crawl up the mother's belly to her breasts for the first feeding. Videos of this process are amazing, as they show very clearly that the child knows exactly what to do if given the time and opportunity.

Marshall found that babies who were placed on their mother's chest and received extended eye contact from their mother, could find their mother's breast and begin nursing naturally within minutes. Skeptics quickly become believers when they see videos of a newborn using his/her sense of smell to guide him/her as he/she slowly climbs his/her mother's belly to her breast.

This process of rejoining with the mother for nurturing and sustenance completes a circuit of connection that moves the child from his/her internal experience of bonding to his/her external experience of bonding with her.

More recent research by Klaus & Klaus and his colleagues[6] found that the optimal conditions for maternal and paternal–infant-bonding calls for extended skin-to-skin contact between the newborn and both parents during the first 36 hours after birth. This should also involve you as the father being in bed with your partner and your baby being passed baby back and forth. Klaus and Klaus define this as the optimal time for bonding with your child.

The Klaus's recommend suckling during the first hour following birth, and room arrangements that allow the parents and child to be together during this extended period. After the child is born, both need to focus on maintaining this state of emotional synchrony with their child.

The developmental process of secure bonding and attachment is more achievable when both parents avoid excessive stress about their jobs, finances, and obligations to other children or family members. Stressors like these can distract them from this critical first parenting experience and can cause fluctuations in the energy connection between them and their child. If possible, both parents should seek to stay at home full-time with the baby for at least the first 12 weeks.

Unfortunately, not nearly enough parents have financial and social resources that allow them to withdraw from the outside world and focus totally on parenting their child during the first few months. This is why national family leave policies are extremely important. They permit the mother and father to stay at home for an extended period of time while their jobs are being held for them and they receive pay.

Extended family leave time for both parents would, in our estimation, have a huge impact on advancing human evolution. In 2015, both Netflix and Microsoft extended their parental leave policies, with Netflix employees receiving unlimited leave during their child's first year.

Most fathers, unfortunately, must return to work within a few days and mothers often within a few weeks or months. It is very difficult for children to handle these rapid transitions in caregiving without it causing them some developmental shock, trauma, and stress. Even though newborn babies cannot speak, they are aware of everything that is happening around them, including parents' thoughts, feelings and activities.

The Perinatal Bonding Cycle. During the first days, weeks, and months after birth, newborns go through many cycles of waking and sleeping that are driven primarily by hunger, the need for pleasure and nurturing, and the need for relief from discomfort and pain.

Their extremely sensitive nervous systems respond to even subtle sensations and energy. This is very visible in something known as the "startle reflex" in which the infant suddenly brings its legs and arms together towards its chest.

These cycles of waking and sleeping are regulated by the baby's need to relieve tension in its nervous system. When babies feel the first pangs of hunger, they begin making small noises and movements.

As the internal tension grows, so do their noises and movements. Eventually the escalating internal tension reaches a point where they release a very clear cry indicating a need. This cry tells the parents to provide comfort, protection, nurturing and safety. Because infants' nervous systems are still developing, a newborn's cry does not provide parents with much information. At this point, caregiving consists of a series of trial-and-error interventions.

As they attune to the child more deeply, they learn to recognize nuances in the child's cries. This allows them to meet the baby's needs more quickly and effectively. Therefore, the child is able to relax more quickly and go into a deep state of equilibrium. Then the cycle starts all over again.

Newborns' sleep and waking cycles can be very short, particularly if they are small—sometimes only two hours long. This short caregiving cycle disrupts parents regular sleep cycles so that they often do not get the amount of REM sleep they need in order to maintain their energy and sense of wellbeing.

Outside respite support for the parents during this time is very important. It can prevent you from becoming overly fatigued, cranky, depressed, or emotionally unavailable during this important period of development.

Bonding not only involves the ability of each of you to reestablish emotional synchronization after a disturbing event, it also involves the ability to create positive play states. This stimulates the child's endocrine system to secrete "upper" hormones such as oxytocin and dopamine.

Periods of positive emotional stimulation create a sense of safety for infants. It helps them develop positively charged curiosity that supports the exploration of novel emotional and physical experiences.

One of the recognized causes of the Shaken Baby Syndrome is angry or frustrated parents or care givers who are triggered by their own unhealed early traumas. They are unable to cope with the feelings that are evoked by a baby's persistent crying. Many newborns cry because they are releasing tension related to birth trauma and may actually be suffering from birth-caused dislocated shoulders, necks, and hips.

Dr. G. Gutmann, a German medical researcher who specializes in the treatment of Traumatic Birth Syndrome, discovered that over 80% of the infants he examined shortly after birth were suffering from an injury to the cervical spine and the neck that occurred during the birthing process. Babies are more difficult to attach or bond to when they suffer a traumatic birth.

If you are unable to provide comfort and stop the child's pain, you will feel frustrated. This may trigger memories of when you previously felt this help-less. It is important for you to stay calm and centered during these episodes and reregulate your feelings that get dysregulated in the birth process or in parenting your infant.

After extended periods of unsuccessful comforting and you trying to cope with your emotional dysregulation, you may have to temporarily dis-engage from the child. Take a "time out" if you can.

You might even see your child as rejecting you because you are unable to quiet him/her. It can bring up insecurities about your ability to care for an infant who is so dependent on you. Your own reactions disturbs the process of emotional attunement and may cause some developmental shock, trauma, or stress for the child. Once you have calmed down and reregulated your emotions you can again safely reengage with your child. Most "shaken baby syndrome" incidents are caused by a parent being triggered by his/her in-ability to get a crying child to stop.

SCHORE'S MODEL OF BONDING/ATTACHMENT

Dr. Allan Schore's research provides a comprehensive lens for under-standing the complex nature of human bonding and attachment, and how developmental shock, trauma, and stress might affect this process. While Schore and some other developmental psychologists use the term attach-ment, we prefer the term "bonding." In this book we use these terms inter-changeably.

In his three books on Regulation Theory[789] Schore uses the language of quantum physics to describe the nuances of parent–child interactions. He identifies the subtle interactions between both parents and the infant that, over time, facilitate children's experiences to move them toward either "growth" or "protection" responses.

His research also helps validate my two-track model of development: the LOVEvolution track and the Trauma Track. Growth takes place when the child perceives its environment as safe. If the child perceives its environment as unsafe, it automatically goes into a protective, trauma-response mode. The body then secretes adrenal hormones to help activate fight, flight or freeze responses. According to Schore, this pattern is set in place before the age of two, which also fits our emphasis on the importance of both parents' active engagement in the early bonding process.

Schore's regulation theory defines attachment as a "biological synchronicity between organisms." This term can be applied not only to behaviors, but also to the cells in all human beings, says cell biologist, Bruce Lipton.

According to Lipton, our cells respond to the perceived safety of their environment. If they perceive it to be safe, they take in the nutrients available in the immediate environment. If they perceive the environment as unsafe, the cells close to protect against whatever is perceive as unsafe.

Schore's theory describes how the exchange of positive emotions between infants and their caregivers creates a safe emotional environment for the child. According to Schore, this environment stimulates the development of the orbito-frontal portion of right prefrontal cortex of the brain. [10]

The orbito-frontal regions of the brain are not functional at birth, but develop gradually through a process of energetic imprinting. They are also involved in emotional control, and reach a critical period of maturation by the ages of 10 to 12 months. This is also the age where Ainsworth and Main were able to identify a child's internal working model and attachment style.

This is critical information for parents, as it affirms the importance of the long-term effects of their conscious parenting during your child's first year. If this part of the brain does not develop during this early sensitive period, children grow up with difficulties in regulating their emotions. This loss is the most acute long-term effect of unhealed early developmental shock, trauma, and stress.[11]

Eckhard Hess' research also indicates that age two months marks a critical developmental milestone in the occipital cortex of infants' brain, one that dramatically increases its social and emotional capacities.[12] For the first time, it can fully see its parents and make direct eye contact.[13]

The mother's and father's emotionally expressive face becomes the most potent visual stimulus in an infant's environment, and the intense interest in its mother's or father's face, especially their eyes, leads the baby to track them and to engage in periods of intense mutual gazing.

The large pupils in infants' eyes serve as a nonverbal communication device that provokes caregiving responses in you. Schore believes [14]that by the age of 2 months, you and your baby are already exchanging high levels of cognitive and social information through your face-to-face interactions. These intense periods of mutual gazing are part of Schore's model of attachment and affect regulation.[15]

The Importance of Right-Brain Synchrony. Schore's research suggests that bonding/attachment involves a right-brain regulation of biological synchronicity between caregivers and children. The right hemisphere, which matures before the left, is specifically impacted by early social experiences with both parents, particularly during experiences of intense excitement. Its development is critical for achieving right-brain synchrony between your child and you as parents. This is how your child develops his/her internal working model of reality.

You can think of your internal working model of reality as a computer program for navigating the world. It contains beliefs and expectations about how others will respond to your needs in certain situations and about the amount of power and influence you have in changing your external reality.

For example, the internal working model of securely bonded children tells them that they are worthy of love and respect; that others are trustworthy and dependable; and that the social world around them is safe, reliable, and consistent. They expect to be loved and cared for and that their caregivers will respond to their expectations respectfully and in a timely manner.

If this doesn't happen, children respond directly by showing how they feel in ways that clearly say something isn't right. This kind of directness by such a young being can be threatening to adults who do not understand how babies communicate.

The right hemisphere stores the internal working model database comprised of children's experiences with their parents. It also contains mechanisms that help your children maintain positive emotions even when experiencing inconsistent care. Schore believes that it is the output from adult caregivers' right brain hemispheres that helps regulate a baby's right brain mechanisms.

This synchrony happens through emotionally synchronized, attuned face-to-face, skin-to-skin, brain-to-brain psychobiological interactions. This energetic system controls your baby's regulatory, homeostatic, and bonding functions.

In the first year of a child's life, the right brain begins its hemispheric specialization for processing emotions. Since its brain is use-dependent, a child's right brain may not learn how to effectively process emotions unless he/she receives proper stimulation. [16]

According to Schore, the orbito-frontal part of the brain also serves as the emotional director or "Senior Executive" of the relational brain. It controls the functions of the entire right hemisphere, which manages unconscious processes.

It also performs, on a moment-to-moment basis, a sorting function that is able to determine whether the incoming information contains pleasure or pain. This valence-tagging function allows a baby's brain to examine every byte of incoming information from its cells to determine its emotional charge.

A child mobilizes itself out of danger when an incoming byte is tagged as "pain." This automatically activates its ASR to produce a protective response. Bytes that are tagged as "pleasure," produce a growth response and open the child to receive and learn.

Schore believes that children's brains are shaped by their earliest experiences. He emphasizes that adult interactions with children throughout the first two years of life determine how the brain's sorting system develops: skewed for growth and learning or skewed for danger and protection.

A child's feelings, cognition, and behavior, he says, only evolve in a growth-facilitating emotional environment.[17] Therefore, the role of parents and early caregivers are crucial in facilitating the development of this very important right-brain function during the first two years of your child's life.

Schore also believes that the right brain is the seat of unconscious emotional regulation. It is critical for learning stress-coping skills and effective interpersonal behavior throughout the lifespan.

He cites a growing body of interdisciplinary studies suggesting that these interpersonal emotional experiences are critical to the early organization of a child's limbic system in the brain. This part of the brain not only processes emotions but is responsible for organizing new learning and adapting to a rapidly changing environment.

Schore also emphasizes that psychology and neuroscience are currently moving away from a long-standing focus on cognitive processes, and towards a focus on the importance of emotions, the Self, and the overall personality. Perhaps the most significant part of his research on infant bonding/attachment is his ability to study and articulate the core psycho-neurobiological processes involved in the emotional synchronization between parents and infants. This means it is important for parents to connect and stay connected to their child during this early period of development.

Schore uses the term "emotional synchronization" to describe the human experience of deep emotional connection, which is based on the developmental principle of reciprocal mutual influence. He recognizes that an adult's right brain and a child's right brain can naturally shift into a pattern of resonance, even when they are not conscious of that process.

This phenomenon is commonly referred to as "being on the same page" or "same wavelength" with someone. Schore says that "the self-organization of the developing brain occurs in the context of a relationship with another self, another brain," usually that of the mother.[18]

As a child you need to have experience repeated face-to-face, skin-to-skin, brain-to-brain synchrony by age two to three months with both parents. If that happens, you will become more sensitive and responsive to this reciprocal attunement. If you did not have this kind of experience, you will struggle with relational reciprocity and social engagement, particularly as you grow older.

Hofer describes how infants' immature internal homeostatic systems are regulated by the caregiver's more mature and differentiated nervous system. In this symbiotic pleasurable state, you and your child's individual homeo-static systems are linked together and provide "mutual regulation of vital endocrine, autonomic, and central nervous systems of both parents and their child by elements of their interaction with each other."[19]

The critical aspect of bonding is adults' conscious ability to use their nervous system as an instrument to attune to their baby, and to create a state of bio-psychological synchronization. This process requires that they to learn to follow very subtle cues coming from their child.

Creating a solid infant–mother and infant-father bond also requires reciprocal interaction. A baby mirrors back any loving gaze from its mother or father, causing the endorphin levels to rise in both parents and the child. This completes a closed loop emotional circuit, a sort of "love loop."

This loop creates a dynamic, interactive system that is less about what you are "doing" to your baby and more about how you are "being" with your baby and how your baby is learning to be with you, according to Schore.[20]

This attunement between adults and children helps them learn to regulate their emotions and their bioenergetic systems, including their hormone production. These attunement experiences are especially important in helping children modulate their production of cortisol and other adrenal hormones, so that they can quiet themselves after an upsetting experience.

Schore gives this example: "Your baby is quietly lying on the floor, happy to take in the sights and sounds of the environment. As you notice the baby looking for stimulation, you respond with a game of peek-a-boo. As you play with your child and she responds with shrieks of glee, you escalate the emotion with bigger and bigger gestures and facial expressions.

Shortly thereafter, you notice your baby turns away. The child's sensory system has reached maximum intake and you sense your child needs you to back off so that she can return briefly to a state of calm and restful inactivity. The synchronization between them is more than between their behavior and thoughts; the synchronization is on a biological level—their brains and nervous systems are linked together."[21]

In this process, you are both teaching and learning. As a result of this moment-by-moment matching of emotion, the emotional connection between each other increases.

In addition, the more you fine-tune your activity level to your child's level during periods of play and interaction, the more you allow your child to disengage and recover quietly during periods of non-play, before initiating actively arousing play again. Again, Schore describes what is happening: "Neuropsychological research now indicates that these cycles of engaged play, disengagement and restful non-play, followed by a return to play behavior are especially helpful for brain growth and the development of cerebral circuits."[22]

This makes sense in light of the fact that future cognitive development depends not on flashcards and videos, but on the attuned, dynamic and emotional interactions between you and your child. Your play periods stimulate your baby's central nervous system to excitation, followed by a restful period of alert inactivity, which allows its developing brain to process the stimulation and the interaction."[23]

Secure bonding with your child requires the optimal functioning of the right hemisphere of the brain of both you and your child. If right brain of your child is not functioning adequately, the impact is not just psychological; it is also biological. The right brain plays a significant role in regulating physiological functions, such as your child's endocrine system, and helps him/her to deal efficiently with life's challenges.[24] Many new studies link early attachment disturbances with chronic and degenerative adult health issues, such as cardiovascular disease and cortisol function.[25]

When in-sync, says Schore[26], adults and babies both experience positive emotions. When they are out-of-sync, both experience negative emotions. If an adult's reaction involves negative emotions, it is likely because they are being triggered by a body memory of their own unhealed developmental shocks, traumas, and stresses.

Having experiences of being out-of-sync with a baby isn't such a bad thing. It can actually be quite valuable. Short-term mis-attunement is not a bio-neurological disaster, if the adult and child can quickly re-attune. The process of falling out of sync and then repairing the disruption actually teaches a child resilience and builds a sense of confidence that the world will respond to his/her need for comfort.

Any mis-attunement becomes a biological crisis only when caregivers do not help a child re-attune. Unfortunately, they may not have a good understanding of the subtleties of parent/baby interactions and do not recognize when they need to reattune with their child.

The lack of understanding about how we bond with each other is, from our perspective, still the biggest problem facing humanity. It is the primary cause of many unintentional developmental shocks, traumas, and stresses that occur during the critical first three years of a child's development.

The human love dialogues described earlier in this chapter, which involve many cycles of appetite, anticipation, and consummation, also contain the first experiences of rationing, frustration, disappointment, disruption, separation, and limitation. It is a mixed bag.

These experiences become interwoven with the desire to relate to others later in life, particularly the sex drive known as libido, which develops in the context of parents' dialogue with their child. For this reason, these early love dialogues have tremendous power—perhaps more than any others.[27]

The Chemistry of Bonding, Unconditional Love and LOVEvolution. Allen Schore's model of attachment includes research findings describing the chemistry of bonding and attachment. It indicates that the intimate contact between adults and children activate both of their hormonal systems. During your mutual gazing interactions, for example, the adult's face activates the production of "upper" hormones, such as dopamine, in the child's brain.

It also helps the child to regulate his/her levels of dopamine and other neurotransmitters. This mutual gazing generates high levels of arousal and elation in a child's behavior that are quieted by the adult caregiver's soothing and calming behaviors. This interaction also helps a child to learn to regulate his/her oxytocin levels.[28]

Oxytocin is known as the "anti-stress hormone" because it counteracts the impact of too much dopamine and high levels of cortisol associated with stress. This factor is critical in understanding how to help your child re-regulate him/herself during any times of mis-synchronization. You just have to restore the mutual gazing process and your child will calm down.

Oxytocin creates feelings of optimism, calmness and connectedness. It also increases curiosity and reduces cravings associated with addictions. It increases your sexual receptivity, facilitates your learning; repairs, heals and restores your wellbeing; encourages your wound healing, diminishes your pain, lowers blood pressure and protects against heart disease. It also plays a key role in pair bonding.[29]

Oxytocin is also released in your brain during social contact, but it is especially pronounced with skin-to-skin contact. This contact promotes bonding between you and your child. When the birth and earliest bonding processes are not disturbed by excessive medical interventions, oxytocin acts as one of nature's chief tools for activating the birth process and bonding instincts of both you and your child.

Roused by the high levels of estrogen ("female hormone") during pregnancy, the number of oxytocin receptors in the expecting mother's brain multiplies dramatically near the end of her pregnancy.[30] This makes the new mother highly responsive to the presence of oxytocin. These receptors increase in the part of her brain that promotes maternal behaviors.

Oxytocin's first important surge is during labor, which helps ensure a final burst of antibodies for the baby through the placenta. Passage through the birth canal further heightens oxytocin levels in both mother and her baby. Oxytocin not only influences maternal behavior, it also stimulates the milk "let down" during nursing. Attempts at nursing during the initial hour after birth cause oxytocin to surge to exceptional levels in both mother and her baby.

Mothers who postpone nursing lose part of the ultimate hormone high that is available immediately after birth. Nature designed this powerful initial imprinting as a fail-safe system that helps mothers and babies find and recognize each other in the hours and days after birth.

Mothers continue to produce elevated levels of oxytocin through nursing and holding their infants, which provides both with a sense of calm and wellbeing. Oxytocin levels are higher in mothers who exclusively breastfeed than in those who use supplementary bottles. Under the early influence of oxytocin, nerve junctions in certain areas of mother's brain actually undergo reorganization, thereby "hard-wiring" her maternal behaviors.

Why Men's "Low T" Is Important In Bonding. Although vasopressin is present and active during bonding between the mother and infant, it plays a much bigger role in the father's physical closeness and touch and promotes bonding between father and mother as well as between father and baby. It also helps fathers recognize and bond to their baby and makes them want to be part of the bonding process rather than be left out. Vasopressin is also known as the "monogamy hormone."

Dr. Theresa Crenshaw, author of The Alchemy of Love and Lust[31], says, "Testosterone wants to prowl, vasopressin wants to stay home." She also describes vasopressin as tempering a man's sexual drive.[32]

When fathers cohabitate with their pregnant partners, vasopressin causes his brain to reorganize in ways that encourage paternal behaviors. They become more dedicated to their mate and express more of their protective behaviors.

Vasopressin reinforces his testosterone-promoted protective inclination regarding his mate and child, but it also tempers his aggression, making him more reasonable and less prone to extreme emotional reactions. In this way, vasopressin helps induce a more sensible view of fatherhood, providing stability as well as vigilance for the family. In short, it promotes "male mother" behavior in him.

Oxytocin, dopamine and vasopressin, which are all involved in the developmental chemistry of parent-child interactions, are co-regulated through the biological and emotional experiences of synchrony. This applies to not only high states of positive and pleasurable exchanges, but also to any moments of emotional dysregulation.

Pleasurable human interactions including birth, breastfeeding, skin-to-skin contact and sexual activity all produce "feel good" chemicals such as oxytocin and phenylethylamine (PEA). This helps soothe, comfort and lift the spirits for those involved. PEA, which is found in cocoa and chocolate, elevates energy, mood and attention. When you fall in love, you become bonded through rising levels of PEA and oxytocin. Much of the desire for intimacy with other humans activates the production of these chemicals and hormones.

The biochemical drive to re-experience the feelings associated with the hormones produced by deep attunement, unconditional love and bonding is so profound and transformative that, once experienced, it becomes a kind of "holy grail" that people will seek for the rest of their lives. This can happen either through intimate relationships or through addictions. The desire to re-experience this state is evident in the almost epidemic use of a drug known as "ecstasy" by teens and adults around the world.[33]

The yearning for a return to the energetic, emotional and chemical experience of deep human communion is the most potent motivator of all of human behaviors. For example, men, who experienced the "hormonal high" that intimacy produces, have an innate desire to connect with their own inner feminine side.

This drive to connect to the more feminine aspects of a man's personality is what leads them to develop their servant leader skills. Most men, however, don't know how to do this, and often settle for a "drug high" instead of the human experience.

The yearning for deep human connection is also anchored at an archetypal level through many images of the Divine Madonna and the Divine Child found in cultures around the world. Perhaps this archetype represents an inner drive for experiences connecting us to the Divine that was imprinted at birth. Our nervous system was flooded with the "upper" hormones associated with birth, and it is normal to seek experiences of it again.

A SUMMARY OF THE RESEARCH ON ATTACHMENT/BONDING

Here is a brief summary of the research on attachment/bonding. Be aware there is an extensive body of research information on this subject and I recommend that you look up some of the studies that relate to attachment/bonding in children and adults. Attachment according to Dan Siegel, "...is an inborn system in the brain that evolves in ways that influence and organize motivational, emotional and memory processes with respect to significant care giving figures."[34]

The attachment system motivates an infant to seek proximity to parents (and other primary caregivers) and to establish communication with them. At the most basic evolutionary level, this behavioral system improves the chances of the infant's survival." Attachment relationships prove the infant with protection against danger and uncertainty of many kinds.

There are two broad categories of attachment: secure and insecure. They can also be classified as organized and disorganized, which is now being seen as a more promising categorization. Generally the more secure and organized your attachment style, the more resilient you are, but bad things can still happen to you that can affect your well-being.

Research showed that about 65 percent of infants had a secure attachment style. About 20 percent had an avoidant style and 15 percent had an ambivalent style. Recent research on the disorganized attachment style suggests that about 35 percent have that style that replaces the other two insecure categories.[35]

The Need For The Servant Leaders To Understand Their Attachment Style. Servant leaders need to understand their attachment style because it difficult to be a true servant leader if you have a Disorganized Attachment Style. Otherwise, you will fail to deliver on your promises as a true servant leader. I call these people, "Pseudo-servant leaders" and I explain below why they might seem like true servant leaders, but likely will fail to deliver.

Research by Mary Main and others have shown that most common attachment style of people who go for psychotherapy is the disorganized style. They also found that the most common attachment style of pseudo-servant leaders is the disorganized attachment style. This causes them to focus their lives on taking care of others, instead of taking care of themselves. This leads people to burnout and utilize dysfunctional ways to get their needs met, through the Drama Triangle.[36]

Do You Know Your Attachment Style? It is also extremely important if you want to be a servant leader that you have a good understanding of your own attachment history and have made sense out of your childhood experiences. If you wish to be effective as a servant leader, you need to know what your attachment style is and how it might interfere with your effectiveness in this role.

I suggest that you read the research of Mary Main and her associates at UC Berkeley and possibly do some personal work to heal any of the early childhood adverse experiences that may have caused you to develop this style. The good news is that once you understand your attachment style, it is possible to change it through therapy or inner work.

Below is a Self-Inventory for you to take to see if you have some of the characteristics of the disorganized attachment style. Take and score the Inventory to help determine how many of the characteristics of a disorganized attachment style you may have.

If your answers on the Self-Inventory show some evidence of a disorganized attachment, suggest you consider some personal therapy or inner work to heal these characteristics before trying to be a servant leader. You are welcome to also give this Self-Inventory to your friends and family to see how much of the disorganized attachment style is present in them.

THE DISORGANIZED ATTACHMENT STYLE SELF-INVENTORY (ADULT FORM)

Directions: Place the number in front of each item that best represents your experience with that item. Key: 1 = Not at all; 2 = Occasionally true; 3 = Usually true; 4 = Most of the Time.

_____ 1. I forget what I am saying in the middle of a sentence.

_____ 2. I get confused when I try to remember any negative experiences from my childhood.

_____ 3. I suffer from momentary lapses in memory while I am talking to others.

_____ 4. I remember times when I was frightened by what one of my parents said or did to me.

_____ 5. When I was growing up one or both of my parents seemed "checked out."

_____ 6. My parents said or did things to me when I was a child that were confusing to me.

_____ 7. I tend to manipulate others to get what I want or need from them.

_____ 8. When I was a child, one of my parents was addicted to alcohol or drugs.

_____ 9. My parents seemed to enjoy saying or doing things to frighten me.

_____10. I find myself "day dreaming."

_____11. My parents seemed to enjoy making growling sounds or frightening gestures toward me.

_____12. When I was a child, my parents seemed more interested in their career than me.

_____13. I tend to assume responsibility for other's feeling and/or behavior.

_____14. I seek out relationships where I feel needed and attempt to keep things that way.

_____15. I am extremely loyal to others, even when that loyalty is unjustified.

_____16. I have a high tolerance for inconsistent and mixed messages.

_____17. I tend to put the needs of others ahead of mine.

_____18. I tend to value the opinions of others more than my own.

_____19. I would describe myself as an anxious person.

_____20. I enjoy being the boss of other people.

_____21. Important people in my life have abandoned me emotionally or physically.

_____22. When I think about my childhood, I draw a big blank.

_____23. I feel empty and alone.

_____24. I have a hard time defining what I need or want.

_____25. I tend to question the motives of others.

_____26. I have a short fuse when I feel frustrated with myself or others.

_____27. I am at my best when I am helping others.

_____28. My thoughts seem to have a life of their own.

_____29. I experience big gaps in my memory about my childhood.

_____30. I have trouble paying attention to what others are saying.

_____   **TOTAL SCORE**

Interpretation:

If your score was between:

40-60   Little evidence of disorganized attachment style.

61-90   Moderate evidence of disorganized attachment style.

91-120   Strong evidence of disorganized attachment style.

Characteristics of People Who Have A Disorganized Attachment Style. Here are some the characteristics you will see in adults who have this attachment style:

1. A childhood history of physical abuse, trauma, emotional abuse, neglect and rejection.

2. A history of pushing away people when they get in close intimate relationships.

3. Under stress, will get confused and dissociate to cope with conflicting inner signals.

4. Had a mother or father who had a disorganized attachment style.

5. Coping mechanisms: "The Little General": They organize their life around taking care of the needs of parents or intimate partners or they become "Solicitous Caregivers" for their partners and friends. They give up their needs to care for others. (FN Game Changer book)

6. Have difficulty identifying their own needs and have poor mechanisms for getting their needs met.

7. Have episodes of anger at others when these people don't reciprocate their caregiving efforts.

8. Get triggered easily by people close to them or situations that remind them of their childhood.
9. Have a hard time trusting others.
10. Suffer from anxiety or depression.

The Attachment Style of Donald Trump and His Followers. Now that Donald Trump has become the GOP nominee for President, to many people's surprise, I decided to apply the above developmental information to him and his followers. It seems from exit pools and interviews, most of his supporters are afraid of something or someone.

Last September, Matthew McWilliams, a political scientist, gathered some striking data while completing his PhD. His findings are drawing considerable attention across social media. He found that the factor most predictive of support for Trump is authoritarianism. The surprise was that this factor cuts across conventional demographic boundaries: education, income, religiosity, age, class, region. McWilliams argues that what binds such diverse people together is authoritarianism.

Authoritarianism is a type of personality profile. It characterizes someone who has a desire for order and a fear of outsiders. Authoritarians look for a strong leader who promises to take action to combat the threats they fear. In short, authoritarians are seeking a sense of safety. Their political choices are driven by unmet attachment needs. Trump makes his supporters feel safe.

That's why Trump supporters hold views that sound extreme to others: Muslims should be banned; Mexico should pay to build a wall; Gays and lesbians should be prevented from marrying. In fact, let's ban them from the country too! Finally, while we're at it, why not critique Abraham Lincoln's decision to free the slaves?

McWilliams' data are compelling because they have proven so predictive. He has conducted several large polls, and the factor that keeps coming up as most predictive of Trump supporters is authoritarianism. The higher a person's score on the Authoritarian Scale, the more likely they said they were to vote for Trump. The slope of that line is so steady it's unnerving. Little wonder, then, that Trump has won most of the primaries so far.

How Is Authoritarianism Measured? It's astoundingly simple. You just ask four straightforward questions:

1. Please tell me which one of the following you think is more important for a child to have: independence or respect for elders?

2. Please tell me which one of the following you think is more important for a child to have: obedience or self-reliance?
3. Please tell me which one of the following you think is more important for a child to have: to be considerate or to be well-behaved?
4. Please tell me which one of the following you think is more important for a child to have: curiosity or good manners?

These four questions were devised by political scientist, Stanley Feldman, in the 1990s. He found that these four questions turned out to be so reliable in assessing authoritarian tendencies that they now form the field's 'industry standard' and are regularly incorporated into all sorts of political or psychological surveys.

Obviously, these questions relate to attachment and parenting styles. Authoritarian parents tend to be rigid and controlling, and focus on external behavior rather than internal experience. They expect a lot from their children, but without offering much warmth or being responsive to the child's emotional needs. Children are expected to do as they are told, without questioning.

Children from authoritarian families report they were afraid of one or both parents as a child. This is a main characteristic of the Disorganized Attachment Style.

The data showed that children raised in environments where they have very little control over their own lives, tend to be unsure of themselves, don't trust easily and have difficulty completing tasks. Fear starts early in life. If the environment often feels scary to you as a baby, then it's very likely going to feel scary to you as an adult.

That continuation happens because your brain and body became wired with enough fear sensors to keep you trapped within the physiological emotional framework your brain set up as an infant. Your brain sees no reason to question that framework. Why question reality?

A parent's style of relating to their child intersects with a child's attachment needs, resulting in a mindset for the child to determine how risky or safe the world is. John Bowlby called this your "internal working model of the world."

Children who develop an insecure or disorganized attachment style report they were afraid of their parents and didn't trust them to provide for their needs. The research shows that whatever attachment style you developed in your first year of life persists into adulthood, if not changed.

Donald Trump is dangerous NOT because he is now the Republican nominee. Donald Trump is dangerous because he legitimizes the myriad of fears of many adults. Leftover infant fears are very powerful, lurking in the dark confines of our neural pathways. That's the whole point of attachment theory. If you're worried about this election, whatever country you live in, don't fight Trump. Fight fear. Find leaders you can trust. That is what a servant leader has to do.[37]

DEVELOPMENTAL TRAUMAS FROM THE CODEPENDENT STAGE

We have identified some of the common "normal" events that cause infants to experience developmental shock, trauma and stress during the codependent stage of development. Here are some of the most common causes:

1. Prolonged illness of a parent or a child causing prolonged breaks in the daily attunement process,
2. Undue stress in the family due to economic conditions, spousal abuse or parents fighting, an absent father or young siblings competing for attention.
3. Addictions that keep the parents from being present to attend to the daily needs of the child.
4. Post-partum depression or emotional overwhelm of the mother.
5. Parents' lack of understanding of infant's needs, causing unintentional neglect.
6. Not comforting an infant who is emotionally dysregulated.
7. Attachment trauma because one or both parents have a Disorganized Attachment Style.

LONG-TERM EFFECTS OF DEVELOPMENTAL TRAUMAS FROM THE CODEPENDENT STAGE

The list below identifies the long-term effects of child behaviors that correlate with developmental traumas during the codependent stage of development.

1. A fear of being alone or of abandonment.
2. Clingy, dependent behaviors.
3. A strong need to take care of people close to you (Solicitous Caregiver).
4. Addictions to foods or drinks to try to fill the empty spaces inside.
5. Manipulating those close to you to take care of you or rescue you.

6. Are easily triggered into emotional dysregulation.
7. Difficulty in reregulating your emotions after being triggered.
8. Inability to trust those close to you.
9. Projecting on others closest to you; blaming them for causing your problems.
10. Angry outbursts at other people when they don't notice your needs or respond to them without you asking.

NOTES

1   Weinhold, J. & Weinhold, B. (2011). Healing developmental trauma. Denver, CO: Love {Publishing Co. pp. 102.

2   Emerson, W. (1996). Points of View. Pre- and Perinatal Psychology Journal, 10(3), Spring, pp. 125-142.

3   Verny, T. (1988). The Secret Life of The Unborn. New York: Delta Books.

4   Klaus, M. (1995). Importance of post-natal relationships. Speech given at the 7th International Congress of the Association for Pre-natal and Perinatal Psychology and Health.

5   Weinhold, B. (2014). The male mother. Colorado Springs, CO: CICRCL Press/ CreateSpace.

6   Gutmann G. (1987). "Blocked Atlantal Nerve Syndrome in Infants and Small Children." Originally published in Manuelle Medizine, Springer-Verlag. English translation published in International Review of Chiropractic, July/Aug 1990.

7   Schore, A. (1999). Affect regulation and the origin of the self: The neurobiology of emotional development. Hillsdale, NJ: Lawrence Erlbaum Associates, Inc

8   Schore, A. (1999). Affect regulation and the origin of the self: The neurobiology of emotional development. Hillsdale, NJ: Lawrence Erlbaum Associates, Inc

9   Schore, A. (1999). Affect regulation and the origin of the self: The neurobiology of emotional development. Hillsdale, NJ:

10 Schore, A. (2003b), p. 39.

11 Schore, 2003a), p. 208.

12 Yamada, et al. (2000). "A milestone for normal development of the infantile brain detected by functional MRI." Neurology, 55, 218-223.

13 Lipari, J. (2000). Cited in Psychology Today, " Raising baby: What you need to know. July/August issue.

14 Hess, E. H. (1975a). "The role of pupil size in communication. Scientific American, 233, 110-119

15 Schore, A. (2003b), p. 41.

16 Schore, A. (2003a), p. 122.

17 Ibid.

18 Schore, A. (1996). "The experience-dependent maturation of a regulatory system in the orbital prefrontal cortex and the origin of developmental psychopathology." Development and Psychopathology, 8, 60.

19 Hofer, M.A. (1990). "Early symbiotic processes: Hard evidence from a soft place." In A. Glick and S. Bone (Eds.), Pleasure beyond the pleasure principle. New Haven: Yale University Press, p.71.

20 Shore, Ibid.

21 Schore, A. cited in Lipari, J. (2004). "Raising baby: What you need to know," Psychology today. https://www.psychologytoday.com/articles/200007/raising-baby-what-you-need-know.

22 Schore (2004). p.3

23 Schore (2004). ibid

24 Wittling, W. (1997). "The right hemisphere and the human stress response." Acta Physiologica Scandanavica, 640 (Supplement). p. 55.

25 Schore, A. (2003a). p. 265.

26 Schore, (2004). ibid.

27 Kaplan, L. (1984). Adolescence: The farewell to childhood. New York: Simon & Schuster, pp. 117–118.

28 Porges, S. (2003). "Social engagement and attachment: A phylogenetic perspective." The Roots of Mental Illness in Children, NY Academy of Sciences, 1008: p. 31

29 Schore, A. (2003b), p. 60.

30 Last, W. (2007). "Sexual energy in health and spirituality," Nexus magazine, Vol. 14:3, May-June, p. 26.

31 Robinson, M. & G. Wilson (2006). "Sex and addiction," http://www.reuniting.info/science/sex_and_addiction news. Vol. 5, No. 2, 2002.

32 Crenshaw, T. (1997). The alchemy of love and lust. New York: Pocket Books, p. 106.

33 Gold, M. S. & Tabrah, H. (2000). "Update on the ecstasy epidemic," Journal of addictions nursing, Vol. 12; Part 3/4, pp. 133.

34 Siegel, D. (2014). The developing mind. (2nd edition). New York: The Guilford Press, p. 91.

35 Weinhold, B. & Weinhold, J. (2015). Developmental trauma: The game changer in the mental health profession. Colorado Springs, CO: CICRCL Press/CreateSpace.

36 Main, M. (1995). "Attachment: Overview, with implications for clinical work." In S Goldberg, R. Muir & J. Kerr (Eds.) Attachment theory: Social, developmental, and clinical perspectives (pp. 407-474. Hillsdale, NJ: Analytic Press.

37 Zeedyk. S (May 6, 2016). How attachment theory explains Trump's success —And Hitler's too. http://kindredmedia.org/2016/05/attachment-theory-explains-trumps-success-hitlers/ Accessed May 7, 2016.

CHAPTER 4

THE ROLE OF THE SERVANT LEADER IN HELPING OTHERS ACHIEVE INDIVIDUATION

"Counter-dependency involves avoiding any dependence on others, being uncomfortable, opening up to or trusting others, pushing others away, appearing overly independent, acting strong, and keeping overly busy. It is common in people with early childhood trauma or abuse. Counter-dependency is a pattern of behavior, not an illness, and can be healed."

—*http://traumadissociation.wordpress.com*

THE COUNTER-DEPENDENT STAGE: A CRITICAL STAGE OF DEVELOPMENT FOR SERVANT LEADERS

In Developmental Systems Theory, the counter-dependent stage of individual development begins around seven months of age when the child's attention gradually shifts away from the oneness of bonding to exploration of the world around him/her and emotional separation. The essential developmental processes for the child during the counter-dependent stage include the completion of psychological separation from both his/her parents. This involves the child's birth as a Self, emotionally separate from his/her parents.

It is also called the "individuation process" and culminates in what researcher Margaret Mahler termed "the psychological birth." During this developmental stage, children learn to experience themselves as emotionally and psychologically separate from their primary caregivers. The successful completion of the essential developmental processes in this stage is critical for those who later want to become servant leaders. This allows them to go on "internal power" and trust their own inner resources in any decisions they have to make.

During this developmental stage, children also develop the cognitive ability for both/and thinking. They also learn to heal the internal split that produces either/or thinking. Your role as a securely bonded father or mother with servant leadership skills becomes increasingly important as this stage unfolds and you have the opportunity to help initiate your son or daughter into Selfhood.

As the counter-dependent stage of development unfolds, from about the eighth or ninth month on, the child ventures further and further from the bonded safety provided by his/her parents during the codependent stage. They develop more and more psychological and emotional separateness. As the child begins to crawl and walk on his/her own, this process accelerates. As the child falls down or gets frightened, he/she quickly returns to his/her parents for comfort. The process of the development of a separate Self goes through several sub-phases. These sub-stages are characteristically punctuated by emotional episodes related to your child's innate emerging sense of self and desire for autonomy.

The latter part of this stage is characterized by utterances of "no" and oppositional behaviors that help your child build boundaries between him/herself and others. This includes not just his/her parents but also siblings, grandparents and other adult childcare providers.

Table 4-1 below describes the essential developmental processes that need to be completed during the counter-dependent stage of individual development. In addition, Table 4-1 suggests ways to help your child complete these essential developmental processes. My research suggests that it takes the cooperation and very conscious effort of two bonded caregivers with servant leadership skills for the child to complete these developmental processes successfully on schedule.

Unfortunately, very few people fully complete these essential developmental processes on schedule. Instead, many children suffer instead from developmental traumas during this stage that interfere with the completion of these essential developmental processes on schedule. These unhealed traumas prevent the psychological birth of the individual from occurring on schedule, thus inhibiting the full development of a fully individuated Self. This can hinder the development of servant leader skills in adults. Later in this chapter and in other parts of this book I show you how, as an adult, you can complete any incomplete developmental processes left over from this early stage of development.

Table 4-1
The Essential Developmental Processes of the
Counter-dependent Stage of Individual Development[1]

Developmental Stage & Primary Task	Essential Developmental Processes in Counter-dependent Stage	Suggested Experiences for Completing the Essential Developmental Processes of Counter-dependent Stage
Co-dependent (8 to thirty-six months) *Separation and Individuation*	• Develops a "love affair" with the world beyond the immediate bonding/connection with parents • Learn to explore one's environment in safe ways • Learn to trust and regulate one's own thoughts, feelings, behaviors in socially-appropriate ways • Internalize appropriate physical & social limits • Develop healthy narcissism • Resolve internal conflicts between oneness & separateness • Bond with self • Continue building secure internal working model of reality • Completing the psychological birth process by age 3.	• Parents offer timely help to heal any narcissistic wounds or developmental traumas in both themselves and the child that disturb resonance • Parents give the child twice as many "yes's" as "no's" as he/she explores the world • Parents arrange environment to provide safety • Adults help the child learn to quickly reestablish the resonance with his/her parents when it is disrupted • Parents use non-shaming responses with the child in setting limits & giving consequences • Caregivers offer empathy & compassion as the child learns to regulate his/her conflicting emotions, thoughts and behaviors • Caregivers authentically mirror the child's essence • Caregivers support the child in becoming a separate individual and trusting his/her internal impulses • Parents give positive support for the child's efforts to develop an autonomous Self

Developmental Stage & Primary Task	Essential Developmental Processes in Counter-dependent Stage	Suggested Experiences for Completing the Essential Developmental Processes of Counter-dependent Stage
Co-dependent (8 to thirty-six months) *Separation and Individuation* *(cont.)*		• Parents help the child internally regulate his/her emotions, especially shame • Parents help the child to identify self-vs.-other needs • Parents model for the child how to effectively meet his/her needs

The Essential Developmental Processes of the Counter-dependent Stage of Individual Development. Only children with secure bonding and attachment in the codependent stage have a solid enough foundation to support them as they attempt to complete the essential developmental processes of the counter-dependent stage of individual development on schedule. They need this secure foundation to gradually move away from the security that being with mother and father brings and venture out into an unknown and often scary world. The more secure your children's bonding and attachment is, the easier it will be for them to complete this emotional separation process during the counter-dependent stage. This natural drive to explore the world, however, requires a different kind of support from their parents than they needed during the bonding and attachment stage.

The separation process requires supervision, limits, consequences and experiences that truly help them learn cause-and-effect thinking, while still protecting them from the possibility of encountering harmful life situations. For example, a child often learns what "hot" means by touching something hot enough to make the appropriate connections in the brain.

Ideally, children should complete this emotional separation process from their parents by about age three. Once individuated, they will have the self-confidence they need to rely on their own internal intuition, knowing and life experiences to help them make age-appropriate day-to-day decisions.

They no longer need to rely solely on others to direct their lives. This is at the heart of the psychological birth. They go on "internal power". At this point, they will have a healthy sense of Self that helps them to accept responsibility for their actions, share and cooperate. They will be able to cope with frustration and stress in appropriate ways, respond effectively to the authority of others, and express their feelings in healthy ways.

As I stated earlier, children need secure bonding and attachment experiences with their mother and father or other adult caregivers during the codependent stage. This provides the foundation to enable children to fully individuate and complete their psychological birth during the counter-dependent stage.

Margaret Mahler,[2] a researcher and child psychologist, did extensive observational research with mothers and their babies to better understand how they can complete the essential developmental processes of the first three years.

She found that holding, singing and talking to the child, mirroring back the child's essence, patient attention to the child's needs and nurturing touch were essential for strong maternal and paternal-infant bonding and attachment during the codependent stage. She described this bonding/attachment experience as "symbiosis."

The innate drive for both mother/father and child to enter a deep state of emotional attunement with each other is at the core of symbiosis. Mahler and others found that there are degrees of symbiosis, depending on the quality of the bonding/attachment experience between mother/father and child.

She found that the stronger the emotional attunement during the codependent stage, the more likely that children will have the foundation they need to complete the psychological birth and become emotionally separate human beings during the counter-dependent stage. Mahler says that with proper guidance from parents, the psychological birth should occur between ages two and three.

She also believes that the separation stage is motivated by children's innate drive to explore the world and to become an autonomous human being. This drive also creates an internal conflict for the toddler. They may want to continue the comfort and warmth of the oneness with their parents, but at the same time they have an innate desire to explore the world around them.[3]

When children start to separate emotionally, the quality of the bonding and attachment relationship with both parents is crucial. If, for example, the mother is depressed, tired, or not available emotionally because she is unable to cope with the demands of parenting, or is anxious because the father is unavailable, this will affect the success of the separation process.

In the presence of such obstacles, children often delay their first moves toward separateness. This delay usually indicates they need more secure bonding and attachment experiences before they can venture out any further on their own.

If this need for further bonding and attachment is not completely met, children will eventually move on physically, but without developing the inner security they need to complete the essential developmental processes of this stage of development. This is the first stage of constructing a narcissistic False Self focused on performing "as if" in their exchanges with the outer world. According to the natural laws of development, physical development continues forward to the next stage, while their social and emotional development may lag behind.

Children then learn to fake their independence with an attitude of "I'm strong and can take care of myself. I'll show you I don't need you." In addition, some children attempt to separate unusually early because of developmental shock or trauma. Perhaps there was intense birth trauma or a milk allergy, or a mother or father who clung too tightly, was overly intrusive, or tried to control every facet of their lives. I call this the "helicopter parent." On the other hand, it can mean their parents were "checked out" or too busy to securely bond with their child.

Shock or trauma can occur if the mother or father shows that they cannot be trusted to provide either consistent enough bonding and attachment support or a structure that the child needs for exploring its environment safely. These children may even prefer strangers as early as three months and stiffen against their parents' efforts to hold and comfort them. This behavior can cause anxiety in the parents. A mother or father may wonder, for example, "Why doesn't my child like me anymore?" Depending on their self-esteem, they may perceive the child's attempts to separate early as a threat to their identity as a "good mother or good father. "

In either case, the movement from bonding into separation is a delicate process, requiring that both parents not only have good information and skills, but also have healed their own developmental shocks or traumas around their bonding and separation experiences. Any hidden, unhealed shocks or traumas that the parents still have will show up during this transition period of their child.

The Four Sub-Phases of the Counter-dependent Stage of Development. Children's inner struggle between oneness and separateness creates the framework for the journey towards individual Selfhood. In Table 4.2 below, I summarize the essential developmental processes of the four sub-phases of the counter-dependent stage of development and suggest some ways to support this completion process. In addition, I present a narrative description of each of these sub-phases in the section that follows it.

Table 4-2
The Essential Developmental Processes of Each of the Four-Sub-phases of the Counter-development Stage of Individual Development[4]

Counter-dependency Sub-phase	Essential Developmental Processes	Suggested Experiences for Completing the Sub-phase
Early Exploration Stage (6 to 9 months) *First Steps*	• Becoming aware there is a world beyond the oneness of mother and father • Differentiating between familiar and strange faces • Introducing short periods of separation between mother and infant • Learning to sit alone • Learning to physically move away from caregivers, first through creeping and then through crawling experiences • Learning to self-regulate emotions when distressed	• Exposure to non-familiar faces both in the home environment and through excursions outside the home • Comfort and reassurance during episodes of anxiety or discomfort due to disruption in the parent-child attunement in strange environments • Make sure that the father or a second bonded parent figure is heavily involved in the child's life during this stage • Sensitive and aware parents who are able to pace the child's exposure to strange faces, experiences and environments • Parents looking into the child's eyes and talking directly about any changes in the parent-child relationship, such as the introduction to professional childcare, care by family members or by new people coming to live in or visit the home

Counter-dependency Sub-phase	Essential Developmental Processes	Suggested Experiences for Completing the Sub-phase
Early Exploration Stage (6 to 9 months) *First Steps* *(cont.)*		• Parents offer timely help to heal any narcissistic wounds or developmental traumas in both themselves and the child that disturb resonance • Parents introduce transitional objects such as stuffed animals, blankets or soft dolls for the child to carry with them or to sleep with (avoid using pacifiers for this purpose)
Full Exploration Stage (10 to 15 months) *The Love Affair With the World*	• Mastering the evolutionary shift from creeping and crawling to standing upright • Mastering the challenge of walking unassisted • Mastering the art of falling and returning to standing upright • Learning to say "no" • Learning that mother's or father's absence is not personal or permanent	• Parents give permission and support to safely explore the home environment Parents give the child twice as many "yes's" as "no's" while he/she is exploring his/her world • Parents arrange environment to provide safety • Parents give clear limits and rules for exploring • Parents help child internally regulate his or her emotions, especially shame, when limits are given • Parents help child differentiate between his or her own needs and the needs of others • Father or second bonded parent figure regularly takes child on excursions away from mother, first inside the home and then gradually outside the home • Parents model for the child how to meet needs effectively

Counter-dependency Sub-phase	Essential Developmental Processes	Suggested Experiences for Completing the Sub-phase
Full Exploration Stage (10 to 15 months) *The Love Affair With the World* (cont.)		• Adults help the child to quickly reestablish the resonance with his/her mother or father when it is disrupted • Parents use non-shaming responses to the child in setting limits & giving consequences• Caregivers authentically mirror the child's essence rather than performance, compliance, or mirroring parents' narcissistic needs
Early Separation Stage (16 to 24 months) *The Splitting Stage*	• Coping with emotional outbursts and tantrums caused by the inner conflict between the desire to explore and the fear of separation • Learning that mother or father are their own persons with separate needs • Learning that mother's or father's love is unconditional but that she/he has limits on her/his energetic resources • Learning to cope with the "mother of separation" and recognizing that she is a different mother than the "mother of bonding"	• Caregivers offer empathy & compassion as the child learns to regulate his or her conflicting emotions, thoughts and behaviors related to inner conflicts related to separation and bonding • Avoiding the use of punishment and shame as tools for diminishing the ego • Caregivers stay emotionally separate during emotional outbursts and tantrums, allowing the child to express these difficult feelings without judgment or shaming • Caregivers support the child who is becoming a separate individual by giving them choices (food preferences, dressing options, which comfy objects to sleep with, their own glass for drinking)

Counter-dependency Sub-phase	Essential Developmental Processes	Suggested Experiences for Completing the Sub-phase
Early Separation Stage (16 to 24 months) *The Splitting Stage* *(cont.)*	• Developing an internal mother or father representation to cope with their physical absence• Mastering the "splitting" stage in which the child sees the parents as all good or all bad	• Parents give positive support for the child's efforts to develop an autonomous Self • Supporting the child as he/she copes with mother's limits regarding safety, disobedience and rule-breaking • Keeping photos of mother in childcare setting or carrying something with mother's photo on it • Being able to hear mother's voice over a telephone • Being able to watch a short video of mother talking to the child • Father or second bonded caregiver must focus on supporting the child's feelings when mother is not available and not agree with the child's perception that mother is "bad" • Parents support any regressive behaviors that might appear, such as the need for more cuddling or wanting to sleep in their bed for a short time • As the separation process is a reciprocal and mutual dance and the mother or father are also separating from the child, they must be sensitive to their own cues about when to set limits on regressive behaviors.

Counter-dependency Sub-phase	Essential Developmental Processes	Suggested Experiences for Completing the Sub-phase
Early Separation Stage (16 to 24 months) *The Splitting Stage* *(cont.)*		• Parents must act in unison to hold the child's psyche during the splitting stage by working out their own conflicts away from the child • Parents must recognize their own tendencies to split when the child is splitting by supporting each other or even getting therapy • During this stage, parents must reinforce limits in a consistent way that often looks very black and white • Parents must recognize their own narcissistic needs for perfect mirroring from their child and keep them separate from their parenting • Utilizing the "Guidelines for Completing the Individuation process" included in this chapter
Complete Separation Stage (25 to 36 months) *Object Constancy*	• Achieve "object constancy" during stressful periods of separation from the parents, particularly the mother • Mastering both/and thinking • Developing solid cause-and-effect thinking • Move towards cooperative and self-sufficient behaviors • Learn to accept limits without oppositional behaviors	• Providing clear limits regarding the environment and the child's behavior and boundary violations • Reinforcing limits without physical punishment or emotional punishment involving shaming, belittling, humiliating and name-calling • Allowing the child to have his/her feelings about it's loss of the inflated ego and loss of perceived adult powers while parents remain empathic and maintain emotional equilibrium

Counter-dependency Sub-phase	Essential Developmental Processes	Suggested Experiences for Completing the Sub-phase
Complete Separation Stage (25 to 36 months) *Object Constancy* *(cont.)*	• Heal any developmental traumas from previous stages of development	• Father and other caregivers take an increasingly larger role in interacting with the child and taking them out into the world. • Parents do not permit the child to dominate them because they lack experience in setting limits and giving consequences • Parents and other caregivers need to assure child about his/her own capacity for self-care, emotional regulation and personal sufficiency • Parents and other caregivers support child during periods of regression when they demonstrate "baby" behavior by providing "baby" comfort. This support and comfort must be provided with an open heart and without criticism or judgment. • Parents help the child heal any signs of unhealed developmental trauma from earlier stages of development.

THE ESSENTIAL DEVELOPMENTAL PROCESSES FOR THE FOUR SUB-PHASES OF THE COUNTER-DEPENDENT STAGE

Mahler and Stephen Johnson,[5] another developmental psychologist, found that the internal conflict between oneness and separateness gets resolved when children are able to successfully complete the essential developmental processes in four distinct sub-phases of the counter-dependent stage described in the table above. As you look more carefully at each of these sub-phases, you may recognize essential developmental processes that were not completed and are still keeping you stuck as an adult.

For example, you may see that your lack of patience as an adult stems from the frustration you first experienced in this early stage of development. If you can locate specific developmental traumas related to what you perceive you got or didn't get in each of the four sub-phases of the process, then you can begin to heal them in present time.

The following information on the four sub-phases of the counter-dependent stage of development describes the essential developmental processes in each. There is an accompanying set of developmental needs that must be met for each essential developmental process.

As you read the following descriptions, ask yourself: "Knowing what I do about my parents, what do I think my experiences were with them during these sub-phases?" This will help you connect the dots to any issues you have in your adult life that involved developmental traumas during the separation stage of development.

The Early Exploration Phase (6 months to 9 months). I am going to describe the developmental processes that occurred during each of the sub-stages as you might have experienced them. I want you to be able, if you can, to identify with how you might have handled these early experiences at that time in your life. Therefore, I will use the personal pronoun "you" to describe these experiences. Pay close attention to your reactions as you read about them.

During the Early Exploration Phase, you became aware that there is a world outside of the oneness between you and your mother and father or other caregivers. At first, you looked at this world from the edge of your mother's lap or over your father's shoulder while being held or burped. You were curious about many things that you saw.

You saw your mother or father smile and you smiled back. Imitation helped you learn new responses of watching and doing. In addition, you first began to notice strangers and may have reacted to them at first with some fear.

However, if the relationships with your mother and father were strong, supportive, and nurturing, you eventually grew more curious than scared of strangers. If the relationship was weak or you were not yet ready to separate, then the fear may be stronger and you clung to your parents when strangers approached in order to feel safe.

In the Early Exploration Phase you had no way of holding on to an image of your mother or father when either one was out of physical sight ("out of sight, out of mind"). You may have coped with this fear of loss, as best you could, by trying to keep your mother or father always in your view.

Eventually, you were able to imagine that your parents were with you even if they were not. You could only sustain this for short periods at first, but gradually you learned to tolerate longer periods of being physically separated from your parents.

If your "mother of oneness" was available, nurturing, warm, and secure, you could hold on to memories of these experiences even when she was not present. Your mother also may have assisted you in developing these qualities by being trustworthy and reliable. For example, when she had to leave, she would let you know in advance that you were going to be cared for by a sitter or by your father.

She knew the quickest way to destroy your newfound trust was to sneak away when you were not looking. In addition, she knew any prolonged absence of several days while you were very young could leave you feeling abandoned. She did not want to add that trauma to your life so she was careful not to stay away for too long.

One of my client's suffered from severe anorexia particularly when someone close to her left her. She had to be hospitalized and fed intravenously during these episodes in order to save her life. What we found out was that when she was about 2 years old her parents took her to visit her grandmother. While her grandmother took her to the kitchen and fed her milk and cookies, her parents sneaked out the front door for a two-week vacation.

The Servant Leader's Role in Handling the Vicissitudes of the Separation Process. During the Early Exploration Phase, you moved away and back many times during a day to confirm that the bond with your mother or father was still intact. You may also have gotten touched, given a loving smile, a brief snuggle, a bottle by your father or an opportunity to nurse on your mother's lap.

Each time, however, you were lured back to exploring the world because your inner drive to explore the world around you grew stronger by the day. Operating as a servant leader, your father knew that his role was to play with you, hold you, and help you move away from your mother. Soon you learned that your father wasn't just a part of your mother, but a separate person. You saw these differences and similarities between your father and your mother. She let you know in many ways that she trusted your father, which also helped you trust him.

If your mother tried to keep you from your father, then you likely picked this up and began to fear your father. You also needed other relatives and friends to bond with you. Again, you relied on their judgment and learned to trust people that your mother or father trusted.

One of the essential developmental processes of this phase involved developing a specific smile of recognition for your mother, father or other caregivers. Games of peek-a-boo are common ways to interact with your child during this stage. It was also a good time for you to learn to discriminate between your parents and strangers.

If the bonding and attachment with your mother and father was strong, you showed more curiosity and wonderment toward strangers and aspects of your environment. If it was less strong, you might have pulled back from strangers out of fear and uncertainty, especially when you were around eight to nine months of age.

The Full Exploration Phase (10 months to 15 months). During this phase of counter-dependency, you began to crawl and walk and ventured out even further. Learning to walk was a celebration of your ability to master your world. This skill would lead you to the natural development of a "love affair with the world." Separation and exploration became almost a full-time occupation for you, coupled with occasional trips back to your mother's lap or your father's knee for needed comfort and reassurance. Teething or too many "dont's" may have slowed you down, but your elation over new discoveries could easily distract you from any pain.

The innate drive for separateness and wholeness was in high gear by the end of this phase and you probably had some transitional objects such as a teddy bear, a doll, or a blanket that represented your mother or father when they were not available. You may have carried these comfort objects everywhere you went.

Eventually, you abandoned these objects when you were able to develop an inner sense of your mother or father that you could use to soothe or comfort yourself when you needed it. This is called emotional reregulation and is essential that you develop this skill if you wish to complete this stage of development successfully.

The Servant Leader's Role in Supporting the Child's "Love Affair with the World." During this period, you loved the thrill of being mobile.

In this expansive period, you found you could explore a large area in your home and discover all kinds of new things each day. Your excitement often reached a state of euphoria, causing you to temporarily forget about wanting to be close or even eating, unless something scary happened.

Because your mother or father seemed so big and so powerful, you saw them as omnipotent. Because you were not separate from them, you often felt omnipotent—able to do grandiose things and entitled you to have everything that crossed your path. Life seemed limitless to you.

One of the essential developmental processes for this phase involved learning that there are limits to your mother's or father's presence, energy, patience, time, and resources. Because you needed to learn about their limitations gradually, they gave them to you incrementally. When either of them had to leave you with another bonded caregiver, the other stayed away only as long as he or she knew you could comfortably tolerate it.

At first, this was just for a matter of minutes. As you grew older, they expanded this to hours. They made sure that you had a reliable person to care for you while they were gone who could support your feelings if you were unhappy about their absence.

They also helped you learn how to take care of your own needs and to be self-sufficient while they were gone. They provided you with transitional objects, such as soft animals for comfort, so that you could comfort yourself in their absence. They knew that this would help you to develop a "nurturing parent" inside yourself.

Other essential developmental processes for this phase involved learning that mother's or father's absence wasn't personal and that they were separate persons with their own needs and interests. Parents or other caregivers helped you express your feelings of frustration when you weren't able to have things go your way all the time.

You also needed a constant adult presence that could monitor your exploration and make sure you were safe. They helped you when you struggled with two contradictory fears: the fear of too much separation (abandonment) and the fear of too much oneness (engulfment).

The Early Separation Phase (16 months to 24 months). Near the beginning of this phase, you began to realize that you are a person are totally separate from your mother and father. When you first understood this, you may have felt scared and returned to your mother or father to be cuddled.

It may have looked to others as though if you were regressing back to an earlier phase of development, but if you received the comfort you desired, it was usually short-lived. Again, your innate drive to become separate took over and you returned to exploring and mastering your world.

Your mother and father kept encouraging your efforts to separate during this phase, while providing you with support and nurturing when you needed it. You were likely to feel angry and frustrated when you were unable to master certain tasks or when your parents placed too many restrictions on you. Your parents accepted this anger and frustration and responded empathetically to you.

A warm hug and some assurance that you were still loved even when you were angry or frustrated was all that you really needed. Humiliation, isolation, shame or punishment only set up further cycles of tension that you needed to discharge. Your parents' repeated reassurances helped you develop a sense of your Self, separate from them. You began to be able to hold both the feelings of being loved and accepted by them and the ability to stay connected to your inner feelings.

Your Parent's Role in Avoiding "Splitting." Another important part of this phase is the phenomenon called "splitting." There were times when you mastered a task or returned to your mother or father and found a receptive warm reunion. When this happened, you experienced your mother or father as "good" and everything looked and felt good for you during these times.

However, there were other times when you were unable to master a task or when you needed a warm hug, and you found your mother busy cooking dinner or your father working on his computer or talking on the telephone.

If they were not available for any reason to meet your needs, you experienced them as "bad," and this feeling was generalized to everything. Mother or father became either "good mother" or "good father" when they were available or "bad mother" or "bad father" when they were not available. In addition, since you were not separate from them, you saw yourself as "bad" or "good" as well at those times. The healthy resolution to this inner conflict occurred gradually as you learned two important things.

First, you realized that your mother and father had a mix of good and bad qualities and still you could trust them. You began to see them as good persons in spite of not always being readily available to be with you. You eventually learned that if you waited a bit, they would respond to your needs.

Second, you also saw yourself as having good and bad qualities that were separate from your mother and father. You learned that this mixture of good and bad qualities in yourself was also okay. You realized that you were both okay. This is the resolution of this inner conflict.

In addition, because you were becoming separate, you also had to come to terms with your own humanness. Here is where you learned the limits of your natural narcissistic urges toward omnipotence, grandiosity, entitlement, and euphoria.

If you didn't complete these processes successfully, it is likely that you became stuck at this phase of your development, creating a reality split of polarities of good/bad, all/nothing or always/never. You also may not have successfully tempered your narcissistic urges toward grandiosity, entitlement, euphoria, and omnipotence.

As an adult, you may express these leftover narcissistic urges through behaviors involving manipulation, pride, arrogance, self-centeredness, and addictions to activities and substances that help you maintain your euphoria. If all else fails, you may experience rage attacks when you were asked to accept a limitation in yourself or others.

This is the most critical point in completing your psychological birth. During this time-period, you made a decision either to become separate emotionally from your mother or father or to remain co-dependent with them.

If you chose to return to the safety of oneness, you developed more co-dependent behaviors and decided in order to feel safe and get your needs met, you would remain emotionally dependent on others. However, if you had repeated experiences of emotional, physical or sexual abuse, neglect, or repeated developmental shocks or traumas you likely decided that oneness and closeness was unsafe and too scary. Out of a need to protect you, you might have prematurely chosen to separate emotionally from your mother or father and developed a False Self.

This False Self, for example, helped you to wall off your feelings of vulnerability and fears. You try to ignore your need for closeness by creating defensive behaviors that pushed people away and/or showed people how much you didn't need them. This False Self helped you to look capable and act strong.

You also developed ego defenses so that you would never let anyone see your vulnerability and wounds again and risk getting hurt feelings. If this happened during this phase, you may end up using similar adult versions of two-year-old like temper tantrum behaviors to cope with adult situations where you are faced with limits or when you feel vulnerable.

The Servant Leader's Role in Helping Achieve Object Constancy. Parents and other bonded caregivers play a critical role in helping you move through the splitting sub-stage of development toward object constancy. Object constancy is your ability to maintain a sense of equanimity, even when your narcissistic urges were challenged.

Your parents' most difficult task was to avoid participating in your perceptual splits. Behaviorally, any split manifests as the two-against-one game in which you ally with one parent against the other via some kind of secret, or taking sides in some conflict. Here, you test the strength of the bond between your parents or caregivers, as well as the adults' psychological maturity.

Adults who have not completed their own psychological birth will inadvertently display splitting behaviors of their own in the midst of a conflict with you and get into needless power struggles. The saying is, "never get into a power struggle with a skunk or a two-year-old."

When this happens, the adults often find it difficult to validate their child's reality and reflect their feelings, making their separation process even more difficult. A father with unresolved abandonment issues, for example, may reveal his split by criticizing his wife and making her bad in front of his child when she appears to pay more attention to the child's needs than she does to his needs.

Most men without servant leader skills often feel trapped in the middle of a "no-win" struggle between their partner and their two-year old child and don't know how to handle the situation. It is no surprise, therefore, that the most common time for fathers to leave a marriage or file for divorce is when the first child is about two years old. This is where the need for a father with servant leader skills is most critical.

The Complete Separation Phase (25 and 36 months). If you had loving parents who supported your need for emotional separation between 25 and 36 months, you were developing an initial sense of separateness and identity by the age of three. The ability to hold yourself as an object of worth, separate from other people is called "object constancy."

As a three-year-old, you had only enough object constancy to feel safe in the world as a separate person if you had built up enough good-mother, good-father and good-self experiences. The struggle to maintain object constancy continues during the rest of your life in your encounters with new problems and crises that threaten your sense of Self.

During this stage, you constantly have to balance your yearnings to return to paradise and the bliss of oneness with your intense longings to be a separate, autonomous individual. The resolution of this issue between ages two and three involves completion of a complex set of essential developmental processes.

For example, when you went to your father and complained about your unavailable mother, he needed to know how to respond to your feelings effectively. If he used your complaining as an opportunity to vent his own feelings about having an unavailable wife, you may have learned to devalue women and overvalue men.

Fathers often feel abandoned when their wives become so consumed by taking care of their children's needs and end up not paying enough attention to their needs. However, if your father takes the side of your mother and criticizes you for complaining about her, you learn that there is no emotional support available from your father to help you become separate from your mother.

You may have felt betrayed and defeated if any of these things happened repeatedly. What your father with servant leader skills needed to do was listen to and support your feelings without agreeing or disagreeing with your definition of your mother's "badness." ("I see you are really upset that Mommy's gone and until she comes back I am here to play with you.")

This empathic response does not blame anyone and acknowledges your feelings. This can be difficult for men to use if they never learned how to make empathic responses.

Some fathers get scared and feel helpless when they find themselves in the middle of the intense separation struggle between your mother and you. They find reasons to work longer hours or have an affair or even leave the relationship altogether.

It is almost impossible for you to complete your psychological birth between ages two and three unless you have the emotional support of a father with servant leader skills. If you do not complete this essential developmental milestone at age 2-3, you will remain emotionally dependent on others for the rest of your life and not be able direct your own life effectively. You likely will use the Drama Triangle to try to manipulate others to get your needs met.

Jung believed that for most people the completion of this milestone was the major developmental task of mid-life, because he realized that almost none of his patients had completed their individuation process earlier in life. My belief is that all men who are fathers can learn these servant leader skills and help their children complete this vital process by age three.

The Servant Leader's Role in the Completion of the Essential Developmental Processes in the Counter-dependent Stage. In order to support the completion of the essential developmental processes during the counter-dependent stage, the basic responsibilities of both parents are to:

- Identify and heal any remaining developmental traumas from your own separation stage of development.
- Avoid being personally triggered by your child's good-bad.splits in perception.
- Give your child twice as many "yes" as "no" responses while they are exploring their world.
- Childproof your home to allow safe exploration thus reducing the number of limits that need to be set.
- Set appropriate and safe limits without the use of shame or physical punishment.
- Show respect and compassion for the feelings of your child.
- Take your child's needs seriously.
- Meet your child's needs in appropriate and timely ways.
- Use "time in" rather than "time out" to discipline your child.

Use of 'Time in' Versus 'Time Out' in Limit Setting. I would like to call particular attention to the use of "time out" as the most common way of disciplining young children at this stage of development. While it is a big improvement over corporal punishment, I personally think it is a big cause of developmental trauma during the counter-dependent stage of development.

So I want to say very clearly: Time outs mostly are designed to serve the emotional needs of adult caregivers rather than the needs of the child. They provide you with time to re-regulate your own emotions after an emotional conflict with your toddler.

Time-out, however, can become a way that you can justify separating from your child so you can calm yourself down. You may frame it as a time-out for your child to think about and correct their behavior and to re-regulate themselves emotionally. However, the exact opposite is actually true.

While time-outs are helpful for you, they are absolutely one of the worst things you can do to your toddler. Why? Because time-outs violate the most basic principles of adult-child relationships and the research of Allen Schore and others that I have cited earlier in this book.

In Chapter Three, for example, we presented Schore's research about how the output from the mother's (or father's) right brain hemisphere regulates the child's right brain mechanisms. This creates emotionally synchronized, psycho-biologically attuned face-to-face, right brain-to-right brain interactions.

Schore is very clear in his position that the attuned parent-child dyad is the mechanism that controls children's ability to regulate their biological, psychological and emotional states. The closer in proximity the child is to you, the easier it is for children to re-regulate themselves during or after an emotional meltdown.

Isolating you from your parents when you are emotionally dysregulated causes a developmental trauma in the process and helps hardwire it even more into your nervous system. When you correctly understood the cause of your toddlers' emotional outbursts, you recognize that "meltdowns" are an extreme case of emotional dysregulation in your child.

The cause of an emotional outburst is usually an inner conflict between wanting to be separate and exploring and while wanting the love and approval of your parents. Toddlers need help in understanding their feelings of frustration and anger at having natural limits set on their exploration and their desire to be independent.

What happened to you when you got a "time-out" is that you are now more physically separated and disconnected from your parents. This actually increases your emotional dysregulation rather than decreases it. Many adults, unfortunately, make the situation worse for a two to three-year-old child by saying; "I don't want to be close to you when you are behaving this way. Go to your room until you can get yourself quieted down."

This message often comes with a look of scorn, which you may have internalized as, "There is something wrong with me. I feel ashamed of myself and I don't know how to stop my feelings. I need help." This dynamic creates even more inner conflict and gives rise to toxic shame where you believe that "There actually is something wrong with me because I don't know how to get myself to feel better."

If this happens repeatedly, it is reinforced over time. This is the foundation of shame-based behavior in adults. What you really needed is a "time-in" where you could sit on or by your parent and be talked to in a calm, soothing way. This not only helps you re-regulate your feelings, it prevents you from developing feelings of shame. ("There is something wrong with me.")

When this support is available, children realize there is nothing wrong with having these feelings and they can calm down. You are much more empathetic when you can understand correctly that the emotional outburst is a symptom of your child needing help to re-regulate his/her emotions.

Rather than feeling angry and frustrated at your child, you can intervene empathetically in ways that truly help your child. This normalizes the negative feelings and communicates an acceptance of your child's struggle to become independent and learn how to regulate his/her own feelings.

The developmental traumas that are caused by "time outs" and the resulting prolonged shame are very difficult for toddlers to endure emotionally. They have long-term damaging consequences. Children not only fail to learn how to discharge or regulate their feelings of shame in a healthy way, they learn to blame themselves or others as a way of coping. They also learn to project the energy of their shameful emotions out of their body onto others in order to relieve their inner stress.

If you are a conscious parent or caregiver, you need to work on yourself to heal your own developmental traumas. If you do that, you are more able to help children successfully complete their psychological birth and the essential developmental processes of the counter-dependent stage of development between ages two and three. With your support, your children are able to maintain object constancy, go on "internal power" and demonstrate "I'm okay, you're okay" thinking.

Below are some examples of time-in techniques that you can utilized with your children. They are organized by age, so that you might know which one is appropriate to use at each age.

Table 4-3
Time-In Techniques for Children
LAP TIME-IN: AGES 1–3 [6]

Works best for:	Children who are hitting, biting, throwing toys or who are too upset to follow directions.
Adapted from:	Kathleen Gray, child development specialist at the University of California-Davis

How to do it:	1. Ask the child to stop the problem behavior. If this does not work, then gently control the child by placing your hand on their shoulder or thigh. 2. If this does not work, then pick up the child and walk away from the scene. Sit down in a quiet place and hold the toddler on your lap. Say, "You seem upset. Let me help you quiet yourself." 3. Become an ally to the child. Talk about what just happened, indicating that you understand the circumstances surrounding the child's behavior.
How to do it: *(cont.)*	4. Describe your limits regarding the problem behavior and stress the standard you will maintain on it. ("Children are not allowed to hit each other here. If you hit, I will stop you and you will sit on my lap until you can stop hitting." 5. Even very young children understand the tone of your words and the meaning behind them.
Dos and don't's:	1. Make eye contact with the child, if this is culturally appropriate. 2. Speak firmly, calmly, respectfully and kindly to establish your authority. 3. When physically engaging a child, avoid grabbing, jerking and using other forms of physical disrespect. 4. If the child refuses to sit on your lap for a short time, indicate via a firm touch and a firm voice that "You may not get up yet because you are still upset and not ready to play with other children. You need to sit on my lap until you can quiet yourself." 5. This affirms the goal (self-quieting) and that the child is not being punished. 6. The more that you use gentle but firm touch, the more that the child will comprehend your message and attune with you.

SIT IN A CHAIR TIME-IN: AGES 2 1/2–6

Works best for:	Children who need help building internal structure.
Adapted from:	Donna Corwin, Beverly Hills, CA author and mother.

How to do it:	1. Pull a chair close to you and have the child sit in it so that she is looking at a blank wall. 2. Apply a hand lotion containing lavender oil to the child's hands. This physical contact plus the lavender in the lotion will help to calm her. 3. While applying the lotion, tell her that you want to help her become more calm and to help her learn the rules. Ask her if she knows what rule she has broken.
How to do it: *(cont.)*	3. Once she understands the broken rule, she must sit quietly in the chair for a specified number of minutes. Use one minute per year of age. During this time, she is encouraged to calm her self and to think about why she broke the rule so that she will remember it in the future. 4. Set a timer for the specified amount of time. 5. During the time that she is sitting close to you, quiet yourself, touch her and surround her with "quiet energy." 6. When the timer rings, ask the child if she is quiet yet. If not, set the timer again. Once she is quiet, ask her to repeat the rule and what she will do differently in the future.
Dos and don't's:	1. Use the same chair and same place in the room each time. 2. Using the timer indicates your seriousness about the need to quiet and about the behavior rule. 3. If she gets up, reseat her firmly, gently and respectfully. 4. Be calm and firm and avoid showing anger by raising your voice. 5. Do not talk about her misbehavior with others if your child is within earshot. This is considered shaming and public humiliation.

The Role the Servant Leader in the Development of Healthy Narcissism[7]. Children need to be seen as real and authentic persons, to be understood, to be able to express their feelings and needs, to be taken seriously, and to have their feelings and needs respected by you. It often takes mothers and fathers who have servant leader skills to do that effectively. These are normal healthy narcissistic needs.

If these needs are met adequately during the codependent stage, for example, your child probably will develop healthy self-esteem. One of the initial ways that children can get their narcissistic needs met during the bonding process is through their mother's or father's mirroring of their essence while they gazed up at their parent's face. This is how infants learn who they really are.

Children who are mirrored appropriately by you during the codependent stage develop healthy narcissism and eventually move on. It is as though the child experiences enough unconditional love, enough nurturing, enough mirroring, enough protection and limits and enough consequences to feel loved.

If you were able to develop a strong sense of Self as a child, you can become a true humanitarian and are able to serve others or to be in an intimate relationship without losing your boundaries. This is essential for the successful completion of the separation process.[8]

If your mother or father mirrored back their desire for you to be a certain way or expected you to meet their unmet narcissistic needs or to fulfill their incomplete dreams, this may have twisted or distorted your self-image. You may have stayed fused with them in order to be loved and cared for. You may have ended up trying to meet their needs more than getting them to help you meet your needs.

Parents must be able to meet their own needs with other adults rather than through their children. Otherwise, it creates "parentized" children who operate as a surrogate spouse and activates something known as a "reversal" process in which children strive to meet the needs of their parents rather than the other way around. This is the most common characteristic of a disorganized attachment style.

Reversal dynamics anchored in the counter-dependent stage of development make you vulnerable to subsequent reversal dynamics inside larger systems such as the workplace, schools, churches, and governments. This keeps you trapped in recreating co-dependent of counter-dependent relationships.

Alice Miller[9] lists the ways that your children develop healthy narcissism. As you read this list, ask yourself, "Can I imagine my parents doing these things for me when I was two to three years old?"

- React calmly and reassuringly to any of my aggressive impulses.
- Support my attempts to become separate and autonomous instead of being threatened by them.
- Allow me to experience and express my natural feelings and urges such as rage, fear, jealousy or defiance.

- Allow me to develop and follow my natural curiosities safely during each developmental stage, rather than over-protecting me or requiring me to be a people-pleaser.
- Be available both physically and emotionally when I became emotionally dysregulated.
- Permit me to express my conflicting or ambivalent emotions and treat those feelings seriously and with respect.
- See me as separate from themselves, as someone with my own needs, feelings, wishes, preferences, dreams, and accomplishments.

With this kind of support, your children can develop healthy narcissism and grow up without being narcissistically wounded and developmentally traumatized during the separation process. The only truly unselfish, genuine people in the world are those who were able to get these healthy narcissistic needs met appropriately at this stage of their development.

Unfortunately, very few people get this kind of support, so it is likely that you still have some "narcissistic wounds" as an adult. You then build defenses around them to protect yourself against any further wounding. These narcissistic wounds are caused by developmental traumas that have to be healed in order to achieve healthy narcissism.

Alice Miller describes people who did get their narcissistic needs met in childhood this way: "Children who are respected learn respect. Children who are cared for learn to care for those weaker than themselves. Children who are loved for what they are cannot learn intolerance. In an environment such as this they will develop their own ideals, which can be nothing other than humane, since they grew out of the experience of love."[10]

The Servant Leader's Role in Resolving Conflicts. Navigating the conflicts that naturally occur during the counter-dependent stage of development requires very specific fathering skills. These are designed to prevent the development of splitting in the child during the counter-dependent stage.

- As a father, you have to be very aware of tendencies to be drawn into in a "two against one" dynamic. Here are some suggestions on how to navigate this delicate process:
- When your partner is not available to the child, you or another bonded caregiver needs to be available to physically and verbally support the child's feelings of anger, grief, fear, and sadness: "I can see that you are upset because your mommy left."

- You need to assure the child that their absent or unavailable parent will return: "I'm here to take care of you while your mommy is gone tonight."
- Avoid making anyone bad during conflicts and focus on supporting the child's feelings: "You seem angry because your daddy left. You don't like mommy when she leaves. It is okay to feel upset when mommy leaves."
- Both parents or caregivers must create clear communication patterns between themselves and between themselves and their child to prevent two-against-one or triangulation dynamics: "I can see that you are angry at mommy because she asked you to put your toys away. Perhaps you want to go to her and tell her how you feel. Would you like me to go with you to talk to her?"

The key to the Functional Family Triangle is a strong bond between all three members—mother-father, mother-child and father-child. If there is a weak or missing bond in any of these relational links, then the child is conditioned to experience the two-against-one dynamics common in most dysfunctional families.

The Servant Leader's Role in Initiating the Completion of the Psychological Birth Process. The successful resolution of the conflicting drives between the desire for oneness and the desire for separateness occurs between the ages of two to three. This happens when your children's normal, healthy, narcissistic needs are acknowledged and met by caring, self-assured, aware, and psychologically whole parents and adult caregivers like you.

If you did not have a father or other bonded caregiver who could be empathic or compassionate during this process, you likely failed to complete the individuation process at age 2-3. Instead, you had to develop a False Self to make you look strong and independent ("fake it till you make it").

You hoped this False Self would be more acceptable than your True Self would. Your True Self was unobtainable without the support of a father who could be empathic and compassionate or a bonded caregiver with servant leader skills, in addition to your mother. As an adult, you retain aspects of your False Self until you finish this essential developmental process. Failure to complete your individuation process can interfere with intimacy in your adult relationships.

People with developmental traumas from the bonding process generally develop a deflated False Self. Inside they feel weak and helpless. If you suffered from developmental traumas related to the separation process, you had to develop an inflated False Self in order to cope with your feelings. If you had very early developmental shocks or traumas during the co-dependent stage, you may be more prone to depression. If you suffered from developmental traumas during the separation process, you are more likely to be grandiose and adrenalized into hyperactivity.

This helps you avoid feeling depressed, but you become more manic instead. To complete your psychological birth as an adult, it is necessary for you to master your internal struggle between two seemingly opposite forces: the natural drive toward oneness and closeness and the equally powerful drive to be an emotionally separate, self-determining individual. If you have not completed your psychological birth, your need for the intimacy of oneness can also bring up intense fears of being engulfed or consumed.

This experience can feel like a "psychological death" and dismemberment of your False Self. The counterforce of separation can produce intense fears of existential alienation, aloneness and abandonment even by God.

Navigating these intense experiences as an adult requires that you have spiritual courage. Carl Jung once said that such experiences are an integral part of the process he called "individuation." Jung saw it as both a psychological and spiritual process that he said generally isn't completed by most people until during or after mid-life.

He said people must move beyond the conventional wisdom in order to discover "gnosis," or the knowledge of the heart that renders human beings free.[11] This involves using your servant leader skills of empathy, compassion, intuition, emotional intimacy and the ability to give and receive unconditional love.

Jung also realized that humans can't fulfill their potential if they become too attached to the trappings of the external world. He said people needed to be" in the world, but not of the world" in order to feel free. He urged people to find their spiritual truths inside themselves and not in established religions.

Jung saw this spiritual rebirth as a prerequisite to the completion of the individuation process by adults. He said you also have to individuate from society in order to feel free. You will have to question all your beliefs that you learned from your family, your schooling, your church and the sub-culture where you grew up. Likely most of them proved to be false or damaging to you.

In either case, understanding what happened in your childhood, healing your developmental traumas and developing new relationship skills will help you complete your psychological birth. Clients often ask, "How will I know if I have completed it?"

What I tell them is that they will have a keen sense of who they really are and handle life's challenges and conflicts with a minimum of stress while feeling good about themselves and good about others. You will be able to maintain your object constancy in the midst of most of your life challenges.

You will be able to be both close and intimate and be separate and alone when you want. Only the adult who has worked on himself or herself, both psychologically and spiritually, can expect to complete this essential developmental process successfully.

So what about single-parent families? No research has been done about how bonded caregivers such as a babysitter or grandparents can fill the missing parent's role. However, if a male child's primary parent is a woman and the father is either absent or very emotionally unavailable, he will have more difficulty in separating from her. This area certainly needs much more research and study.

At this point in our evolution, most of us have not had enough sustained experiences of deep emotional attunement and biological synchrony to heal our unhealed developmental shock or trauma. Healing these early developmental shocks or traumas is essential for servant leaders to do in order to be able to utilize their inner resources effectively.

Guidelines for the Servant Leader in Helping Children Complete the Psychological Birth Process.[12] As I wrote earlier, the psychological birth and individuation process requires the support of two bonded caregivers for the child to become emotionally and psychologically separate. Ideally, both of them need to have servant leader skills, but it is essential that the father or another bonded caregiver separate from the mother have these skills. Here are some guidelines that you can use to help children (large and small) complete the individuation process:

1. **When one bonded caregiver is not available to meet the child's needs and the child complains or gets upset, the available caregiver should do the following:**

- Support the child's feelings. ("I can see that you are upset because your mommy left.")

- Refuse to participate in the child's judgment about the "badness" of the unavailable parent, but instead offer empathy and compassion to the child. ("It's hard for you when your mommy leaves you alone. You'd like her to stay here with you.")
- Reassure the child that his or her needs will be met. ("I'm here to take care of you while your mommy is away.")
- Inform the child that the missing caregiver will return. ("Your mommy will be back at four o'clock and she will be glad to see you.")
- Inform the returning caregiver about the child's reaction to the separation. ("Kevin was upset today when you had to leave. He wished that you would stay with him you when you left.")

2. The returning caregiver should do the following:

- Ask the child if this is true. ("Were you upset today that I had to leave? Did you want me to stay with when I left to visit my friends?")
- Support the child's feelings and offer closeness. ("It sounds like you were sad and mad today. Is that true? What do you need from me right now?")
- Express his own feelings about separation to the child.) ("I miss being with you too. I feel sad when I have to leave you.")
- Give the child reasons for the absence.) ("Mommy has friends that she needs to visit occasionally or they will feel sad that they don't get to see her enough.")

3. When the child has a conflict with one caregiver and brings the conflict to the second caregiver, the second caregiver should do the following:

- Support the child's feelings. ("I can see that you are upset with your mother. You look angry. Are you angry?")
- Do not agree or disagree with the judgment the child has about the first caregiver's" badness" but instead offer empathy to the child. ("You are angry because your mother made you clean up your toys. You don't like to pick up your toys just because she told you to.")
- Support the child in dealing directly with the first caregiver to resolve the conflict. ("Are you willing to talk to her and tell her how you feel?")
- Help the child talk to first caregiver. ("Do you need my help when you go to talk to your mother?")
- Let the child know that it is not okay to triangulate and have family secrets. ("If you are not willing to tell her how you feel, I will tell her that you are upset about your conflict with her.")

- Let the child know that you will not resolve his or her conflict with the other parent or caregiver but that you are available to support both the child and his/her mother or caregiver whey they are ready to resolve it. ("I do not want to get in the middle of this conflict between you and your mother. I will not go to your mother and speak for you. I will only let her know that I am aware you are angry at her and support both of you.")
- Inform the child that if he or she resolves the conflict without you that you would like to know the outcome. ("When you and your mother talk about your feelings about having to pick up your toys, please let me know what happens.")

At first, you may feel awkward and unfamiliar using these kinds of responses. This is normal when you are learning a new skill. The truth is, we are all in a learning curve developing new skills we need to help children to successfully complete the individuation process. Very few people have ever experienced this kind of communication in their lives. When you do use your servant leader skills in this kind of situation you will see how effective it is in helping your children feel more accepted and understood.

What "Not" to Do. Below is a summary of the guidelines on what not to do in the above situations:

- Do not contribute to making anyone bad. ("She is never here when you need her.")
- Do not take sides. ("You are right. She doesn't care about you. She doesn't care about anyone.")
- Do not ignore or discount feelings. ("Don't cry. Here, have a cookie.")
- Do not discount the importance of the child's situation. ("Can't you see I'm busy. Go play.")
- Do not create secrets. ("I won't tell her you are angry at her, if you don't.")
- Do not rescue. ("I'll talk to your mother and tell her that you shouldn't have to pick up your toys.")
- Do not play "two against one." ("Let's go talk to your mother. We'll tell her that you shouldn't have to pick up your toys.")

Using both sets of the above guidelines is critical for facilitating the completion of the individuation process during the counter-dependent stage of development. If you find yourself using the incorrect responses, you can always go back and change them. You can always ask for an apology and start over.

It is never too late to seize an opportunity to complete this process during a recycled separation experience later in life. Since most of us still have unresolved inner conflicts about wanting to be separate, the communication guidelines above are also useful for resolving conflicts in your adult relationships where these same dynamics are present.

These protocols also help support a functional family triangle. Through repeated successful trials, using the best servant leader skills that you can display, your child eventually learns that neither mother nor father are all-bad and eventually adopts "I'm okay--you're okay," both/and thinking. Your child becomes free to use his/her emotions and inner knowledge to direct his/her life. He or she is also emotionally prepared to handle frustration and to move forward to independence, the next stage of development.

When functional family dynamics are not present in the parent-child structure, a dysfunctional family triangle known as the "drama triangle" develops instead. The dynamics of the drama triangle are the result of developmental traumas originally from the counter-dependent stage of development. I discuss the Drama Triangle more in Chapter Eight. In addition, our book, Breaking Free of the Drama Triangle and Victim Consciousness, is available from Amazon.

WHAT "NORMAL" EVENTS CAUSE DEVELOPMENTAL TRAUMAS IN THE COUNTER-DEPENDENT STAGE AND CAN CAUSE PROBLEMS FOR POTENTIAL SERVANT LEADERS.

- Too many "nos" or restrictions during the exploratory process.
- Limits are set in angry, rigid or abusive ways.
- Use of physical punishment, shaming or name-calling to set limits
- No limit-setting present at all.
- An emotionally or physically absent father.
- Separations of two weeks or more, without any contact with the child.
- Sibling rivalry promoted or supported by parents.
- Not enough "kid proofing" of the environment
- Physical injuries that lead to a belief that the world is not safe.
- Parental expectations are too high causing performance anxiety.
- Little support for the child to become a separate person.
- Holding on and keeping your child dependent to meet your needs.

WHAT ARE THE LONG-TERM EFFECTS OF DEVELOPMENTAL TRAUMAS IN THE COUNTER-DEPENDENT STAGE ON POTENTIAL SERVANT LEADERS

- A belief that the world is a scary place. Paranoid actions.
- OCD behaviors.
- Social disengagement/dissociation.
- Low self-esteem.
- Frequent experiences of severe emotional dysregulation.
- Difficulty in reregulating yourself, without assistance.
- A stressful disorganized lifestyle.
- Becoming overly involved in the lives of your children or spouse.
- Not feeling lovable, leading to compulsive "doing."
- Difficulties with intimacy.
- Erect walls to keep people from getting too close.
- Defensive behaviors. Inability to apologize for mistakes.
- Developing Personality Disorders such as Anti-Social, Avoidant, Obsessive-Compulsive, Schizoid and Narcissistic.

NOTES

1   Weinhold, J. & Weinhold, B. (2011). *Healing developmental trauma: A systems approach to counseling individuals, couples and families.* Denver, CO: Love Publishing CO. pp 122.

2   Mahler, M. (1968). *On human symbiosis and the vicissitudes of individuation.* New York: International University Press.

3   Mahler, M. (1968). *Ibid.*

4   *Healing developmental trauma.* (2011). pp. 125-127.

5   Johnson, S. (1987). *Humanizing the narcissistic style.* New York: W. W. Norton & Company

6   Weinhold, B. (2014). *The male mother.* Colorado Springs, CO: CICRCL Press, pp. 119-123.

7   Weinhold, B. (1014). pp. 124-126.

8   Weinhold, J. & Weinhold, B. (2008). *The flight from intimacy.* Novato, CA: New World Library.

9   Miller, A. (1981). *Prisoners of childhood.* New York: Basic Books, Inc.

10 Miller, A. (1984). *For your own good.* New York: Farrar, Straus & Giroux, p. 97.

11 Hoeller, S. (1989). *The Gnostic Jung and the seven sermons to the dead.* Wheaton, IL: Quest Books.

12 Weinhold, B. (2014) *The male mother.* Colorado Springs, CO: CICRCL Press/ CreateSpace.

CHAPTER 5

THE ROLE OF THE SERVANT LEADER IN HELPING OTHERS DEVELOP INDEPENDENCE

"The deepest change begins with men raising children as much as women do and women being equal actors in the world outside the home. There are many ways of supporting that, from something as simple as paid sick leave and flexible work hours to attributing an economic value to all caregiving and making that amount tax deductible."

— *Gloria Steinem*

THE ROLE OF THE SERVANT LEADER IN RAISING CHILDREN

As in the last stage, in the next stage of development, the Independent Stage, the role of the servant leader father is also highly crucial. Fathers are the one who usually initiates your child to the external world. The more time you as a father can spend with your child during this stage of development the better.

Many fathers are either too busy or too wounded themselves to play with their children. Play is the work of children who are in the Independent Stage of development. This occurs between 3 and 6 years of age.

If you are a father, you need to play with your children. This is how you can teach your 3-6 year-old how to master their everyday tasks such as brushing his/her teeth, bathing properly, "going potty," or getting something off the counter or out of the refrigerator.

Your children will want to learn how to make their own breakfast or how to use your tools and eventually how to tie their shoes or dress themselves. With safe instruction from you, they will learn to feel confident about their ability to understand how and why things work the way they do, but also begin to master some everyday tasks with adult supervision.

They learn most at this age by imitation. That is, they watch you do things and then they try to imitate what they saw. It is trial and error learning. They may have to try something repeatedly until they get the "ah ha" that tells them how and why something works. Eventually they learn how to do it for themselves the first time. The most commonly used word of a child in this stage is "why." They want to know why everything works the way it does.

You need to engage your children as they try to figure out how to master their everyday tasks. If you are a father, you must tune into what your child of this age feels inside. The way you respond to your son or daughter is extremely important. If you or their mother for that matter, respond to the excitement of a child who just mastered an everyday task by saying, "You did a great job" you have missed the boat.

The skill for you to use in this kind of situation is to reflect back the feeling of excitement you see being expressed by your child. Using your servant leader skill of empathy, you can say the following: "Wow, you must be feeling very happy inside that you were able to do that." Or "You must feel excited to be able to button your shirt. Yesterday, you were having trouble doing that and now you can do it. Congratulations."

If you respond by telling your child how you "feel" that they accomplished this task, rather than focus on how they feel also you have missed an opportunity. The opportunity you missed is to strengthen your child's connections to his/her own inner feelings.

Even by saying something like, "good job," you are missing an opportunity to strengthen your child's inner feelings. That kind of response is more of an evaluation of what you saw the child doing. If you continue to respond in that way, your child will look likely outside him or herself for validation that they did "a good job." This will begin to substitute for them learning how to connect with their inner feelings.

This causes children to build a "self" based on what you or others say or do rather than on how they feel inside about what they have said or done. Parents and teachers are guilty of using this method of praise to reward their children and students.

You and other adults do a great disservice to children or students if they respond to a child's or student's accomplishments in this way. It truly robs them of the inner experience and causes children to grow up feeling that they need validation and approval from others.

This means they become "other-directed" in their orientation to life and they lose track of the "inner wisdom" that they could use to direct their lives. Your intervention using your servant leader skills is vital in helping your children develop their inner wisdom.

This is what is needed in the next stage of development to help strengthen the completion of the individuation process. Without your constant support, your child can lose the connection they had previously in their inner resources.

Below is Table 5-1 that shows the essential development processes that need to be completed during this stage of development.

Table 5-1
The Essential Developmental Processes for the Independent Stage[1]

Independent *(three to six years)* ***Mastery of Self*** ***& Environment***	• Master basic self-care • Master the process of becoming a functionally autonomous individual separate from parents • Develop object constancy • Develop trust in your core values and beliefs •Achieve secure bonding experiences with nature • Learn effective social engagement skills • Develop secure internal working model of self/other •Achieve secure bonding with peers	• Parents rearrange home environment to support mastery of self-care for the child (eating, dressing and toilet training) • Parents support the child in developing effective internal limits and consequences • Parents teach the child appropriate ways to defer gratification of his/her wants and needs • Parents support the child in learning effective emotional self-regulation & control • Immediate & extended family members offer the child nurturing, supportive and consistent contact • Parents support the child in learning to trust his/her inner sense of wisdom and guidance

Independent *(three to six years)* *Mastery of Self & Environment* *(cont.)*		• Parents provide child with experiences for safe exploration of nature • Parents support the child in developing sensory relationships with nature • Parents provide the child with reciprocal social interactions with other children • Parents teach the child cross-relational thinking including empathy & respect for others • Parents support the child in developing cause/effect problem-solving skills • Adults model partnership solutions to conflicts

If you use your parenting skills in your interactions with your children, you are modeling how to respond to the world around them. By being actively involved in helping the child complete the essential developmental processes of this stage of development, you are helping your child to build a self. Even if the completion of the individuation process at the end of the previous stage of development was successful, your child still needs you to use your servant leader skills to help him/her continue to use what he/she learned in the previous stage.

In a previous chapter, we introduced the concept of "Time In." We discussed the reasons why this was far superior to "time out" as a discipline strategy. In this stage, there are additional opportunities to use "time in" to help your children handle times when they are emotionally dysregulated. Below are some suggested ways to use your skills in "time in" situations with a 3-6 year-old child.

Table 5-2
NO TIME LIMIT TIME-IN: AGES 2–4[2]

Works best for:	Children who demonstrate some degree of self-discipline and emotional self-regulation. This teaches children self-control rather than needing adults to serve as "policemen."
Adapted from:	Charlotte Petersen, child psychologist in Eugene, Oregon.
How to do it:	1. Create a place where children can sit in a neutral environment that is either on or by you. There should be no toys or other things to play with. 2. When a child behaves in an unacceptable way (throwing toys around in anger), clearly state what you want him to do. ("I want you to pick up all these toys now.") and give one warning: ("If you choose not to pick them up, it will tell me that you need to sit by me in the time-in seat.") 3. Once the child is seated in the time-in seat, say "You need to sit here by me until you are quiet and ready to..." 4. Surround the child with "quiet energy" and attune with their energy. 5. Allow the child to know when they are ready to get up. Observe their behavior after this to make sure that they are re-regulated. If not, kindly repeat this process until they are ready.
Dos and dont's:	1. With this form of time-in, never say to the child, "Okay, you can get up now." 2. Allow the child a period of time to sit quietly. 3. If the child leaves the seat, simply ask "Are you quiet and ready to...?" 4. If the child says "no," then say, "Oops. You aren't allowed to get up until you are quiet and ready to...You can get up whenever you are ready to.."

CREATIVE PLAY COOLING OFF TIME-IN: AGES 3–6

Works best for:	For children and adult caregivers who need time to cool off following rowdy, disruptive behavior.
Adapted from:	Evonne Weinhaus, family counselor in St. Louis and mother of three.

How to do it:	1. When a child misbehaves, say, "I can see that you are out of control. Please come and sit by me so that I can help you can get quiet." 2. Let her decide how long she needs to become quiet, or
How to do it: *(cont.)*	3. If the adult is the one who is out of control, say "I am getting out of control and I need a time-in. I am going to sit quietly with myself until I can get quiet. I don't want to say something that I don't mean and hurt some- one. I will talk to you again after I get myself quiet." This kind of modeling is perhaps the most important tool for teaching emotional self-regulation.
Dos and dont's:	1. When the time-in is over, avoid a big dramatic scene involving joyful embraces and hugs. This can be perceived as a "payoff" or reward for misbehaving and getting attention. 2. This normalizes the process of emotional self-regu- lation.

HOW TO DISCIPLINE YOUR CHILDREN USING SERVANT LEADER SKILLS[3]

Limit setting and disciplining your child is one of the most important functions where you can use your servant leader skills. If you do not set ef- fective limits or are inconsistent with your limit setting that sends a message to your child that you do not care very much about them and their welfare.

Parents who are seemingly loving and do not do a good job of setting limits for their children, are often seen by their children as too busy or too distracted to care very deeply. Children need limits in order to feel safe and when the limits are not consistent or clear, children will naturally act out to test them more. Below are ten suggestions on how to discipline your child using your servant leader skills. Read over these suggestions and see if any of them reflect areas where your limit-setting skills are weak.

1. **Take a deep breath and get centered before saying or doing anything.** Never discipline when you are feeling upset or off center, if you can help it. When you are centered, you will be able to think more clearly and the decisions you make will make more sense to everybody involved.

2. **Engage your brain before opening your mouth.** Think about what you want to say and what would be the kindest way to say it. There are many ways to express your thoughts and feelings, but often the first thing that

you think of is not necessarily the best thing. If you do happen to utter some unkind words before you engage your brain, you can always go back and apologize to your child and make amends. This creates an important model.

3. **Be specific and ask directly for what you want from your child.** Avoid complaining or using "always" or "never" to justify your request. Anger is usually a signal that there is something that you want or need that you currently don't have. Use your anger at your child to first think about what it is that you want or need from him or her and then ask him/her for it, without whining, blaming or shaming.

   The other important aspect of any conflict you are having with your child is to determine how the child's behavior tangibly effects you. Leaving dishes in the sink where you have to work around them may have more tangible effects on you than your teenager having a dirty room.

4. **Ask your child if he or she knows what rule was broken.** If consequences were set before the rule was broken, also ask your child to tell you what the consequences were for breaking that rule. It is best when the child can tell you what the rule was and what consequences were agreed on ahead of time in case the rule got broken. In this kind of situation, your role is merely to help carry out a consequence that was previously agreed to by you and your child.

   Consequences should be agreed upon ahead of time and the criterion for an effective consequence is that it should help your child to remember and abide by the rule. If there are repeated violations of the rule, this is an indication that the consequence is not strong enough to help your child remember the rule.

5. **Let your child tell his or her side of the story.** Your job is to listen and using your best listening skills to reflect back to what you heard and understood. Confirm with your child that you heard them say without judging or shaming them.

   This step is crucial if you are going to keep the lines of communication open and find a win-win solution. You need to stay open to how your child views the situation and this often provides you with an opportunity to better understand how your child thinks through problems and conflicts and problem solves them.

6. **Ask your child what he or she would suggest to fix the problem.** Consider this suggested solution and agree or make a counter proposal un-

less your child's suggested solution meets your needs. This negotiation stage is very important to set the stage for a possible win-win solution. By giving your child, some say in finding a solution to the problem that he or she may have created, you are teaching your child how to assume responsibility for his her actions.

7. **Ask your child what he or she will do the next time when faced with this rule.** This question asks your child to think through the situation and project that thinking into the future. When children can think about what they would do the next time they are faced with this rule or situation, they are more likely to remember what they need to do to stay on track.

8. **Ask your child what he or she thinks should happen if the rule is broken again.** This is where you can set consequences ahead of time to cover a future problem like this one. If you child can come up with his or her own consequences that they believe will help them remember the rule the next time, then they are likely to remember and not break the rule.

9. **Reassure your child that you believe their behavior caused a problem, not them as a person.** It is sometimes hard for your child to understand that it is their behavior that is in question here, not their worth as a person. A reassuring comment from you may help remind your child of this fact. Letting them know that they are still lovable even though they did something that you reacted to with anger, is very reassuring.

10. **Give your child a hug or ask for a hug.** When you have completed your discussion and have found a win-win resolution to the problem, it is important to let your child know that you still love them. This makes it possible to prevent any undo relationship fallout as a result of the problem. It is possible to provide limits with love. In fact, limit-setting is one of the most important tasks that parents have to perform and when it is done consistently with love your child will be more willing to cooperate with you and not have to test your limits.

One of the parents of young children who responded to a survey I did wrote about what he learned that didn't work in setting limits with his toddler. He wrote, "I have found out it does not work to force a 1.5 to 3 year child to do something more quickly or something he/she really doesn't like to do or doesn't understand. All you can get is crying and trauma.

I remember, one episode, when my older son was nearly 2 years and 4 month. He was scattering his toys around the room and when I asked him to stop, he continued and acted like he didn't hear me. Therefore, I began to shout at him, but his reaction was opposite to what I expected and finally out of frustration, I slapped him.

He cried and I don't think he understood what I wanted, so it caused a trauma for him. I regretted what I had done and realized I was trying to control his behavior and was frustrated that what I tried was not working."

If you were faced with this kind of opposition to your limits, what would you do? How would you get this child to pay attention to what you wanted them to do without hitting them? If you make a mistake like this, you can apologize to your children.

UTILIZING YOUR CHILDREN'S PLAY TO TEACH INDEPENDENCE SKILLS[4]

Play is a powerful component of any child's life. In play, they learn how to use their imagination to solve problems, to explore their world, to learn to cooperate with others and how to interpret new events in their life. They also learn to work through their feelings through their play by experimenting with new roles and acting out their feelings.

Use your parenting skills to provide guidance to your children by choosing toys to play with that have lots of possibilities. Blocks, dolls and art supplies can provide endless opportunities for creative play. Toy guns, toy tanks and toy artillery weapons are not appropriate toys for raising kind kids. Also, remember to buy toys that are age-appropriate. A set of walkie-talkies is not appropriate for a two-year old, but a set of blocks is.

Using your servant leader skills, you will need to provide many opportunities for your child to have unstructured and creative play. You can enhance unstructured play by providing many props such as dress up clothes, sand, water, art supplies, etc.

Make sure that you allow enough uninterrupted time for play. Avoid intruding on their play when it is intense. Give your child choices in their play. Let your child choose what toys he or she wants to play with and encourage your child to initiate play when he or she wants to.

Play is a way to begin to teach children cooperation. Encourage cooperation and sharing without placing undue pressure or expectations on very young children. Finally, help your child refrain from aggressive play with others by offering acceptable alternatives such as pounding a pillow or supplying play dough or building something at a workbench. Another easy way to get more "bang for your buck" is get them to burst the bubbles in the bubble wrap.

WHAT ARE THE "NORMAL" EVENTS THAT CAN CAUSE DEVELOPMENTAL TRAUMAS IN THIS STAGE FOR POTENTIAL SERVANT LEADERS?[5]

- The unhealed developmental traumas from the previous two stages. What isn't healed is "dragged along" as excess baggage making it harder to complete the essential developmental processes of the next stage.
- No comfort or support to help children cope with the frustration involved in mastery of everyday tasks.
- A lack of patience with and criticism of the child's efforts at mastery.
- Contaminated or lack of "safety parent" messages leading to injuries.
- Too high parental expectations leading to low self-esteem.
- Over-protectiveness; unwillingness to allow the child to take the risks involved in the master process.
- A parent who is an overly solicitous caregiver. They try to organize the life of their child in order to cope with their own disorganized attachment disorder.

WHAT ARE THE LONG-TERM EFFECTS OF DEVELOPMENTAL TRAUMAS IN THIS STAGE ON POTENTIAL SERVANT LEADERS?[6]

- An unwillingness to try new things. Compulsively sticking with what they know how to do.
- Having to rely on others to do things, they do not know how to do or are unwilling to learn to do.
- A lack of patience with self and others.
- Self-blame.
- Judgments of others who try and fail to help them.
- Develop faulty beliefs such as "the world is a scary place."
- Usually not comfortable in unpredictable situations.
- Withdraw from or avoid social situations.
- Have low self-esteem.
- Suffer from depression or anxiety.
- Performance anxiety in many situations.

- Hypervigilance when out in public.

NOTES

1   Weinhold, B. (2006). *Raising kind kids. Swannanoa, NC: CICRCL Press.*

2   *Ibid, p. 122-124.*

3   *Ibid.*

4   *Ibid.*

5   Weinhold, B. (2015). *Freaked out 101: How hidden developmental traumas can disrupt your life. (An online course available at http://weinholds.elearnux.com/ courses/freaked-out-introduction/ Colorado Springs, CO: CICRCL Press.*

6   *Ibid. Freaked Out 101. Class # 2.*

CHAPTER 6

THE ROLE OF THE SERVANT LEADER IN HELPING OTHERS LEARN TO COOPERATE AND RESOLVE CONFLICTS

"We can either emphasize those aspects of our traditions, religious or secular, that speak of hatred, exclusion, and suspicion or work with those that stress the interdependence and equality of all human beings. The choice is yours."

— *Karen Armstrong,*
Twelve Steps to a Compassionate Life

HOW DO SERVANT LEADERS TEACH INTERDEPENDENCE?

Servant leadership begins with parenting your children. Parents with servant leader skills need to teach their children how to get along with others. Mostly you will be teaching them these skills by allowing them to observe how you do it. They will need to see how you negotiate to get your needs met, particularly when there is a conflict of needs with someone else. You also need to teach them how to cooperate with others. They will learn to do this as well by observing how you cooperate with them and with others with whom you interact.

Table 6.1 below describes the essential developmental processes that need to be completed during the Interdependent Stage of Development. This occurs roughly between the ages of 7 and 18, although it can extend in the late twenties for some children due to other factors that prevent completion of this stage. The main skills that you need to teach your children are to learn to cooperative with others, how to negotiate to meet their needs in healthy, straightforward ways and how to resolve conflicts in a win-win way.

What I have found is that if the essential developmental processes are met in each of the previous stages of development, this stage is a lot easier on parents and on their kids. If any essential developmental processes were not completed during the previous three stages of development, they will show up again during this stage and make it more difficult to complete this stage.

Table 6-1
The Essential Developmental Process of the
Interdependent Stage of Development[1]

| Interdependent (six to 18 years) Cooperation & Negotiation Skills | • Learn how to cooperate with others
• Learn how to negotiate with others to get needs met
• Learn to accept responsibility for personal behaviors and life experiences
• Experience secure bonding with peers & other adults
• Develop a social conscience
• Achieve secure bonding experiences with the main culture
• Develop secure bonding experiences with the planet
• Live out of an authentic adult self
• Achieve secure bonding with their own children
• Understand the influence of incomplete developmental processes on their life and the how to heal their developmental shocks or traumas successfully | • Parents model effective cooperative social engagement skills in couple, family & peer relationships
• Teach the child negotiation skills to get his/her needs met in healthy ways
• Parents seek solutions to the child's conflicts that honor the needs of all parties involved
• Parents teach the child the importance of keeping his/her relationship agreements
• Provide adult models that can teach the child empathy and compassion for others
• Provide adults who can teach the child intuitive language and thinking skills
• Provide the child with nurturing, supportive and consistent contact from immediate & extended family members
• Teach the child how to build sustainable relationships with other adults and suitable ways to find a find primary love partner |

Interdependent *(six to 18 years)* **Cooperation &** **Negotiation Skills** *(cont.)*		• Provide adult input on the values of the child's cultural group & teach the child how to overcome any limits imposed by family & culture • Adults encourage the child to develop an internalized safety parent by allowing him/her to engage in safe risk-taking behaviors • Teach the child how to find personal meaning and a personal mission within the context of the "global family" • Teach the child how to heal his/her developmental shocks or traumas

The Pattern of Recycling Unfinished Business. You can actually predict when any incomplete developmental processes will show up again. After counseling hundreds of parents of teenagers, it became clear that there is a pattern to when unfinished essential developmental processes will show up again to get completed during transition times during teen years.

Generally speaking, the following unfinished issues will show up at times of transition. The first being when the child enters fist grade in school. This can bring up fears of abandonment in some children stemming from a lack of secure bonding/attachment in the codependent stage. Some children get very clingy at this time and don't want to leave the security and comfort of home.

You might also see your child getting sick so they don't have to go to school. Other children will act out and get defiant, telling they are not going to school and you can't make them. These kinds of responses are confusing to parents and often they don't know what to do.

My best advice is to hug or hold your child until they feel safe and then ask them open-ended questions like, "Will you tell me what is going on inside of you?" "What are you feeling?" With some children, you may ask them to draw you a picture of them going to school and then ask them to tell you what is going on in the picture.

Another time is when your child enters Middle School. Again, this is a transition from the familiar to the unfamiliar. Often anything left unfinished in the early bonding process will surface at this time. Any traumas that occurred early on will surface. If their mother or father had a prolonged illness that caused some separation, this may surface at this time

If there are some incomplete developmental processes from the counter-dependent stage, from 9 months to three years, they will surface about age twelve to fourteen. I have had too many mothers in my office screaming, "either she goes (meaning her daughter) or I do." I have had fathers say similar things. It is the terrible twos all over again. You see oppositional behavior that seems to come out of nowhere.

If you can be aware of where these sudden outbursts of regressive behaviors are stemming from there is a chance to help your child finish what was not finished at an earlier age. Again, treat them in age-appropriate ways, but realize that they are actually regressing back to some point where some earlier developmental process was interrupted and left incomplete in some way.

If you have a whiny or clingy 12-13 year-old, think of what a six-month-old might still need and provide it. As a result, you might see miraculous recoveries. When a teenage child starts acting out, it is likely that he/she needs more structure or limits to help them reregulate their emotions and behaviors.

Remember what is effective with toddlers and try some age-appropriate interventions and see what happens. You may have to try several approaches until you hit on the one that works and you will see an almost instant shift out of the behavior.

The next time there is a transition, it is usually when your child graduates or leaves high school and goes either to work or on to college. This is another transition where effective servant leader parenting behaviors can save the day.

I remember when my daughter left for college, she was very clingy and needed a lot more support than I thought she should need. I drove her to her school and helped her set up her dorm room and buy the supplies that she needed.

I was surprised by the amount of fearfulness and uncertainty coming from a kid who was very successful and confident during her high school years. I was grateful that I was able to support her and as a result, we shared a moment of wonderful closeness when I hugged her as I was leaving her dorm room.

Eight Ways A Servant Leader Can Support Children Who Are 6-18 Years Old[2]. These are some suggested ways that you can use your servant leader skills during The Interdependent stage of development. The challenge is to be able to model for your kids what you want them to grow up to become.

That can be difficult at times, especially if you didn't get much male mothering from your father. You may have to do some serious work on yourself, if you are going to meet the challenges that this stage of development presents. Here are some ideas.

1. **Saying something kind and encouraging to your child every day.** By saying something kind and encouraging to your children daily, you are empowering them and telling them that you appreciate them. These small daily kind and encouraging acts are ways to model kind behaviors. Children who are told they are loved learn to love others and feel good about themselves. A simple saying "I love you" is invaluable.

2. **Create a warm, friendly home atmosphere where kindness abounds.** Home is where a child needs to feel safe. Some ways of creating that safe haven are with simple acts such as: leaving kind notes on the refrigerator, placing your children's drawings certificates of achievement on the wall or, greeting your children with a hug when you or your children return from school or work.

3. **Be willing to listen to your child and treat him or her with respect.** Let your child know that his or her needs and feelings are important to you. Listening to and treating your child with respect are not only kind acts, but are forms of unconditional love. Though you may not agree with your child, at least let your child have his/her say in the matter. Your child will then feel that you respect them enough to listen to his/her thoughts and feelings without judgment.

   When you listen, you are also saying that you value his/her thoughts, needs, and feelings. This is how you can tell them they are important to you. Remember, if you treat your children with respect, you'll deserve to get respect in return.

4. **If your child fails in some endeavor, listen to his or her feelings and then remind him or her of the many ways that he or she has been suc-**

cessful. Failure is tough to take especially when you're a child. Help your child with his or her feelings regarding the failure by listening to them and supporting him or her. You need to help your child work through and express those feelings.

After you have done that, you can then help your child by pointing out the many successes in his/her life. By doing this, you are saying that they are still loved by you even when they fail and that they are still important and valued as a person. I once told my son who was rebellious at the time, "There is nothing you can do or say that will make me stop loving you."

5. **Treat each of your children as individuals; each with unique talents and strengths.** Remind each of them often of the talents and strengths that you believe each one has. Respecting children and valuing their differences, shows each of them that they are special and that you love them. If your children feel this love, then they don't have to compete or act out to get your love and attention.

6. **When you discipline your children, do not shame them.** Help your children understand that you dislike the specific behavior they did and that you do not dislike them as a person. Separating the behavior from the person is very important when disciplining hour child.

If you tell your children, they are bad rather than their behavior, in some way you are attacking them as a person. This may negatively affect their self-esteem and cause shame. Their behavior is what you dislike and not them, thus, it must be expressed in this manner in order to avoid putting judgments and shameful feelings on your children.

A good way to do this is by simply stating what behavior you disliked. For example, for a child who hit another child and made that child cry, you can say that hitting people is unacceptable and this behavior will be punished. This is more effective than just saying that the child is "bad" for hitting another child.

7. **If you make a mistake in parenting them, admit it and apologize to them.** This provides an effective model of the responsible behavior that you want them to learn. Again, you are modeling to your children that everyone makes mistakes, even parents. By owning up to that mistake, you are taking responsibility for your action or mistake. This type of modeling will teach your children what you want them to learn. They

too will learn that we all make mistakes and they can do something positive about their mistakes by offering a simple apology.

8. **Every child needs attention and recognition.** Make sure your children get more positive attention and recognition than negative. Be a cheerleader for them. Attention is very important to children, thus, children will try to get attention any way possible. If you pay attention to the positive things they do and say, you will see positive behaviors from them.

A good rule of thumb is to remember that whatever behavior you pay attention to or recognize, you will see more often. A good way to do this is by praising your children for the positive things they do. You can say things like: "I really like the way you helped you sister with that problem." As a result, you will see your child doing this more often. After emphasizing that, you need to help your child focus on his/her inner feelings and wisdom in making choices. You can say, "How did you feel when you were helping your little sister?" It is still okay to praise them when they deserve it. You can say it with something like, "You must feel very good about that, and so do I."

NORMAL EVENTS THAT CAN CAUSE DEVELOPMENTAL TRAUMAS IN THIS STAGE THAT CAN CAUSE PROBLEMS FOR POTENTIAL SERVANT LEADERS[3]

- The burden of carrying unhealed developmental traumas from the previous three stages.
- Parents 'rescue" their children to prevent them from learning natural consequences of their behaviors.
- Child is not expected or encouraged to accept responsibility for their actions or their feelings.
- Poor or no limit setting by parents.
- Sibling rivalry promoted by parents.
- Bullying by peers at school or in the neighborhood.
- A lack of peer friendships in the neighborhood or at school.
- Accident-prone behavior leading to repeated injuries.

THE LONG-TERM EFFECTS OF DEVELOPMENTAL TRAUMA IN THIS STAGE ON POTENTIAL SERVANT LEADERS[4]

- Compulsive avoidance of conflict due to a lack of skills.
- Victim behavior: blaming all problems on others.
- Victim behavior.

- Cutting on themselves.
- Addictions to substances or activities.
- Bulimia or anorexia.
- Taking wild or unnecessary risks.
- Poor decision-making skills.
- Poor relationships with siblings.
- Bullying or dominating others.
- Rigid behavior and an unwillingness to compromise.
- Lack of empathy toward others.
- Isolated with poor social skills.
- A tendency to be accident-prone that causes injuries.

NOTES

1 Weinhold, B. (2014). *The male mother: The missing skill set for fathers. Colorado Springs, CO: CICRCL Press.* pp. 162-163.

2 Weinhold, B. *Raising kind kids. Colorado Springs, CO: CICRCL Press.*

3 *The male mother. Pp. 168-171.*

4 Weinhold, B. (2015). *Freaked out 101: How hidden developmental traumas can disrupt your life. Colorado Springs, CO: CICRCL Press. (Online course and link: http://weinholds.elearnux.com/courses/freaked-out-introduction/*

CHAPTER 7

THE BRAIN DEVELOPMENT OF THE SERVANT LEADER

"The intuitive mind is a sacred gift and the rational mind is a faithful servant. We have created a society that honors the servant and has forgotten the gift. We will not solve the problems of the world from the same level of thinking we were at when we created them. More than anything else, this new century demands new thinking: We must change our materially based analyses of the world around us to include broader, more multidimensional perspectivest."

— *Albert Einstein*

RESEARCH ON THE ROLE OF THE PRE-FRONTAL CORTEX

I found a lot of scientific support for my clinical findings from new research on the function of the brain's prefrontal cortex.[1] What does that have to do with servant leadership?

Well this research clearly shows that the brain of someone with servant leadership skills is more highly developed than the brain of people that do not have these skills. They particularly found that the prefrontal cortex of people who had what I call servant leader skills is more highly developed than others who do not have these skills.

Before talking about why the prefrontal cortex of those with servant leader skills are different, I want to share with you what the researchers also found out about people with unhealed developmental traumas. They have different brains as well. When reenacting unhealed childhood trauma, people become emotionally dysregulated and respond from memories hard-wired into their limbic brain or lower brain. They cannot access information from their thinking brain: the cerebral cortex.

While they are aware of being in present time, their brain is simultaneously accessing information from a previous time and using a more primitive part of the brain where these memories are stored. This information floods their central nervous system and causes them to become emotionally dysregulated, scared and confused.

The long-term effects of these early, unhealed experiences can cause people to be biologically disconnected from their prefrontal cortex. When this happens repeatedly over many years, it prevents them from developing synapse connections between the limbic brain and the pre-frontal cortex. This makes it even more difficult for them to respond to others with empathy and compassion.

The pre-frontal cortex also stores relational information about love and nurturing. It is also where our imagination resides. In order to reconnect to the pre-frontal cortex, a person with unhealed developmental traumas must consciously intercept the signal from the hard-wired limbic memory.

Then they have to replace it with new signals that connect to the pre-frontal cortex. This is where trauma reduction tools such as EMDR, EFT and our own TET can be utilized to interrupt the signal and create a new signal[2]. Chapter Ten shows you how to do this.

The Prefrontal Cortex and Its Role in Servant Leaders. The prefrontal cortex (PFC) is located in the very front of the brain, just behind the forehead. In charge of abstract thinking and thought analysis, it is also responsible for regulating our behavior. This includes mediating conflicting thoughts, making choices between right and wrong, and predicting the probable outcomes of actions or events.

This brain area also governs social control, such as suppressing emotional or sexual urges. Since the prefrontal cortex is the brain center responsible for taking in data through the body's senses and deciding on actions, it is most strongly implicated in human qualities like consciousness, general intelligence, and personality.

The Functions of The PFC. This vital region of the brain regulates thought in terms of both short-term and long-term decision making. It allows humans to plan ahead and create strategies, and also to adjust actions or reactions in changing situations.

Additionally, the PFC helps to focus thoughts, which enables people to pay attention, learn, and concentrate on goals. This area is also the part of the brain that allows humans to consider several different yet related lines of thinking when learning or evaluating complex concepts or tasks. The pre-frontal cortex also houses active, working memory.

Since the PFC controls intense emotions and impulses, it is sometimes referred to as the seat of good judgment. As such, a properly functioning pre-frontal cortex inhibits inappropriate behaviors —including delaying gratification of needs, for things like food or sex— while encouraging wise, acceptable choices. In part, this occurs because it works to allow humans to balance immediate reward with long-term goals.

The Evolution of the Prefrontal Cortex. The prefrontal cortex has re-markably expanded in size throughout human evolution, culminating in modern Homo sapiens. This suggests a strong selection pressure in favor of its continued growth and development. The size of the PFC relative to the rest of the brain has also increased over that time; while the brain itself has only increased in size about threefold in the past five million years, the size of the PFC has increased six fold.

Medical studies have shown that the PFC is the last section of the brain to mature. In other words, while all other brain regions are fully developed early in life, its development is not complete until around age 25. Magnetic resonance imaging (MRI) research has revealed that the prefrontal cortex changes a great deal during adolescence, as the brain's myelin matures and connects all regions of the brain together.

This late growth and development is likely the reason that some other-wise intelligent and sensible teens engage in high-risk or excessive behaviors even though they understand the potential dangers. This probably is why men don't live as long as women because young men take unnecessary risks that end up taking their lives.

The Pre-Frontal Cortex of the Servant Leader. When you are using your servant leader skills as a parent in interacting with your children, you are building connections to the pre-frontal cortex that help support the fol-lowing important psychobiological functions:[3]

1. **Body regulation.** Helps you regulate your body to handle any sudden or unexpected experiences. You can remain calm in the middle of chaos
2. **Attuned communication.** When connected to the PFC you can connect with another person's mind as well as your own mind. You can attune

to another person without words only by looking into their eyes. This is what Schore believes is essential for secure bonding with your children.

3. **Emotional balance.** It helps us re-regulate our emotions quickly when we get triggered by the memory of an unhealed trauma.

4. **Response flexibility.** It allows us to think before we act and then respond after we have more completely assessed the situation.

5. **Empathy.** It enables us to know what someone else is feeling and be able to connect with them at a feeling level.

6. **Insight.** The PFC helps us begin to make sense of our thoughts and feelings by connecting past and present behaviors to predict any potential future behavior at any given moment. It is essential for self-reflection and self-correction.

7. **Fear modulation.** Has the capacity to help us calm down when the "fear factory" in our limbic brain goes into over-production.

8. **Intuition.** It is where we process signals from various parts of our brain and enables us to intuitively decide the best course of action. It also helps awaken our imagination.

9. **Morality.** It is where we construct our sense of morality and can apply that to our beliefs about ourselves, other people and the world around us.

Access to an integrated pre-frontal cortex enables us to live a flexible, adaptive, coherent, energized and stable life with a fully realized Self. If the pre-frontal cortex is disintegrated or disconnected, it cannot transmit information to help override the more primitive impulses from the lower brain containing memories of unhealed developmental trauma. Interestingly, people who are diagnosed as Narcissists or Psychopaths lack the ability to perform these pre-frontal cortex functions.

The Biology of The Servant Leader[4]. A recent study showed that men who were actively involved in the care of their children had lower testosterone levels.[5] Those fathers who were directly involved in nurturing activities with their infants and toddlers had significantly lower testosterone levels.

The researchers were clear about the nurturing finding. They wrote, "Caregiving fathers had lower [testosterone] than fathers who did not invest in child care." Furthermore, they reported that the more hours the fathers spent with their children, the lower their testosterone levels.

"We found that [testosterone] … was lowest among fathers reporting more hours spent in childcare." The researchers were not surprised to find the hormone-nurturing link. Earlier research has shown that testosterone drops in other male mammals that are involved in caring for their children. Their question was: would this be true for humans?

They found their nurturing fathers in the Philippines, in Cedu City, where, the report stated, "it is common for fathers to be involved in day-to-day care of their children." This leads one to wonder what would happen if this research were conducted in the United States.

Perhaps men in this country are not yet as evolutionarily advanced as these men are in their ability to nurture their children. The researchers agree that evolution is involved. "Our findings suggest that human males have evolved neuroendocrine architecture ... supporting a role of men as ... caregivers."

All of this is not surprising, really. If testosterone is the hormone that contributes to aggression in men, then it makes sense that nature would reduce that hormone when men are caring regularly for children. Earlier, I discussed the role of Vasopressin that keeps the testosterone levels low in fathers who are engaged in childcare for their newborn baby. This hormone helps to keep the father contented to be a nurturing caregiver.

Fatherhood as a biological achievement, is accomplished in partnership with a mother, but the presence of a male nurturing parent is something else entirely. This is a man who spends attentive, loving, extended time with his child emotionally, seeing the world through their eyes, teaching them, and feeling, at times, the delight that his selfless nurturing can give. In short, this is a father with male mother skills.

The benefits for an increase in male nurturing might be more than personal. Many people have wondered for at least a century if politics would change if men become more involved in childcare. Jane Addams, the Nobel Peace prize winner and women's suffrage advocate, wrote as early as 1913, that she thought if the government were under women's control instead of men's, its chief purpose would not be to fight or prepare for war, but the nurturing of children and the protection of the weak and sick.

This is not because women are inherently nurturing, but because historically women "had always exercised these functions." This is now changing and we are beginning to realize that men with servant leader skills can be just as nurturing to his children as women can.

THE ROLE OF SERVANT LEADER SKILLS IN
CONSCIOUS CONCEPTION & PARENTING

Bruce Lipton and his colleagues in the field of pre- and perinatal psychology are active proponents of this new paradigm. Pre- and perinatal psychologists believe that the energetic structure of an individual's template actually begins prior to conception. Regardless of the exact point, it begins very early—much earlier than once believed.

The first stage of our model of individual development, codependency, begins with conception and goes through the age of 6–8 months. During this period, the essential developmental task involves creating a secure bond between the child and both parents.

In Lipton's book, The Biology of Belief[6] his chapter on "Conscious Parenting: Parents as Genetic Engineers," describes how parents act as "genetic engineers" during the months prior to conception. In the final stages of egg and sperm maturation, a process of genomic imprinting adjusts the activity of specific groups of genes that will shape the character of the child yet to be conceived.[7] A father who has servant leader skills can help facilitate this process.

Lipton's interpretation of the research in this area is that, during the process of genomic imprinting, the events in the lives of parents prior to conception have a profound influence on the mind and body of their yet-to-be conceived child. He agrees with Thomas Verny in that "it makes a difference whether we are conceived in love, haste or hate, and whether a mother wants to be pregnant."[8]

An impressive body of research on prenatal development documents the impact of parental attitudes at the time of conception on the subsequent development of the fetus. Studies show that unborn children are energetically attuned to their mother's and the father's every action, thought, and feeling. From the moment of conception, the experience in the womb shapes the child's brain and lays the groundwork for the personality, emotional temperament, and higher thought.

Mothers and fathers, Lipton says, are in the conception and pregnancy business together, even though it is the mother who carries the child. According to Lipton, what the father does profoundly affects the mother, which in turn affects the developing child.[9] The essence of conscious parenting is that both parents have important responsibilities for fostering healthy, intelligent, productive, and joy-filled children.

Some parents report having spiritual or transpersonal encounters with their babies before they have been conceived. They may have vivid dreams, visions, and telepathic encounters that come weeks, months, or even years in advance of physical conception. Some parents even report communing with the soul of the incoming child and negotiating the appropriate time for conception.[10]

NOTES

1   J. Weinhold & B. Weinhold. "The Impact of Developmental Trauma on Human Evolution," Journal of Pre and Perinatal Psychology and Health. 25:1, Fall 2010, pp. 17–31.

2   Weinhold & Weinhold (2011). Healing developmental trauma. P.23.

3   C. Thompson. (2010). Anatomy of the soul. Carol Stream: IL, Tyndale House. p. 163.

4   Knight, L. (2011). The biology of nurturing fathers. http://www.womensmediacenter.com/feature/entry/the-biology-of-nurturing-fathers

5   Gettler, L., McDade, T., Ferain, A., & Kuzawa, C. (2011) "Longitudinal evidence that fatherhood decreases testosterone in human males." CrossMark. http://www.pnas.org/content/early/2011/09/02/1105403108

6   Lipton, B. (2005). The biology of belief. Santa Rosa, CA: Mountain of Love/Elite Books.

7   Surani, 2000; Reik & Walter, (2001), cited in Lipton, (2005), p 172.

8   Verny & Weintraub, (2002), cited in Lipton, B. (2005), p. 172.

9   Lipton, B. (2005), p. 173.

10   Chamberlain, D. (2003). Early and very early parenting: Very early parenting starts before conception. https://birthpsychology.com/free-article/very-early-parenting-starts-conception

CHAPTER 8

PERSONAL/PSYCHOLOGICAL BARRIERS TO OVERCOME TO BECOME A SERVANT LEADER

"He who controls others may be powerful, but he who has mastered himself is mightier still."

—*Lao-Tsu*

PERSONAL/PSYCHOLOGICAL BARRIERS

I contend that the most challenging barriers for a servant leader to overcome are personal/psychological. In the previous four chapters, I have outlined what the childhood development of a potential servant leader needs to be. This underscores the importance of servant leaders having a good psychological foundation. Mostly, servant leaders have to be able to rely on their inner resources to assist them in making the decisions they need to make to effectively serve others, without depleting themselves. This can only happen if the servant leader is psychologically secure.

Most important is that servant leaders need to be able to rely on their own inner resources when they need them, like their intuition, empathy toward themselves and others, exhibiting true compassion and unconditional love for self and others. In Chapter Eleven, I discuss how to overcome any of these personal/psychological barriers, including how to heal any developmental traumas from childhood that might interfere with you becoming a true servant leader.

The two most important skills that you need to overcome any personal/psychological barriers are self-reflection and self-correction. If you have good self-reflection skills you can connect the dots and see how what happened or didn't happen to you as a child relates to the issues you are coping with as an adult. Self-correction skills help you change those things that might be obstacles and turn them into assets.

UNHEALED DEVELOPMENTAL TRAUMAS

Our Developmental Systems Theory is a blueprint to help track human evolution. The Developmental Trauma Track of human development shows how developmental traumas interfere with the completion of important essential developmental processes in each of six human systems and how they impede further evolution in each system.

We look at the evolution of six main human systems: the individual, the couple, the family, social organizations, nation-states and the history of the human race. Our research and the research of others clearly indicates that undiscovered and unhealed developmental traumas can have long-term effects on the functioning level of each of these human systems, starting with any individual who wishes to become a servant leader.

One of the effects of early childhood developmental traumas is the creation of a weak or insecure attachment in the first year of life. Often this is because your mother and/or father were too stressed to pay sufficient attention to your needs. This means that you could not count on them to be there for you when you needed them.

As a result, you stopped trusting them to be there for you and you found other ways to get your needs met. The kinds of insecure attachment styles are avoidant, anxiety/ambivalent and disorganized. As I mentioned earlier, one of the main the characteristics of the disorganized attachment style is to compulsively try to take care of the needs of others. This becomes a way of avoiding taking care of your own needs. This can create a pseudo-servant leader.

If you have a disorganized attachment style, you may be drawn to do and say things that will be self-serving rather even though it looks like you are serving others. The good news is that you can change your attachment style by using your self-reflection and self-correction skills.

The research of Mary Main and Eric Hesse, who created the Adult Attachment Interview, shows that adults can change their attachment styles. One of the main ways they suggest from their research is for you to reexamine your life's story and make sure it is cohesive and coherent. If you can effectively connect the dots and understand how your attachment style affects you adult behavior, you can "earn" a secure attachment style and avoid the pitfalls of an insecure attachment style.

One of the long-term effects of an insecure attachment style is that people use greed and power to try to cover up or compensate for their unhealed developmental traumas. If they don't have the tools or understandings to effectively heal their developmental traumas, people will do almost anything to try to make themselves feel better when they suffer from the long-term effects of hidden developmental traumas. Mostly they turn to a myriad of addictions to self-medicate and avoid healing their traumas. These people will not become genuine servant leaders.

THE LONG TERM EFFECTS OF ADVERSE CHILDHOOD EXPERIENCES[1]

In 1995, the Centers for Disease Control and Kaiser Permanente conducted a study to determine the long-term effects of Adverse Childhood Experiences on adult physical and mental health. They asked 17,000 adults 10 questions about their adverse childhood experiences (ACEs). They found that the number of ACEs predicted the mental and physical health problems of these adults with surprising accuracy. Here are some of the results:

- Individuals who had faced 4 or more categories of ACEs were twice as likely to be diagnosed with cancer as individuals who hadn't experienced childhood adversity.
- For each ACE Score a woman had, her risk of being hospitalized with an autoimmune disease rose by 20 percent.
- Someone with an ACE Score of 4 was 460 percent more likely to suffer from depression than someone with an ACE Score of 0.
- An ACE Score greater than or equal to 6 shortened an individual's lifespan by almost 20 years.

Here is the set of questions that participants were asked to answer. Take this self-quiz and see if you have hidden traumas related to these ACEs. If you do have hidden traumas, you will need to heal these in order to be effective as a servant leader. Chapter Eleven provides you with strategies to heal any hidden childhood traumas.

ACE'S QUESTIONNAIRE[2]

Prior to your 18th birthday:

- Did a parent or other adult in the household often or very often... Swear at you, insult you, put you down, or humiliate you? or Act in a way that made you afraid that you might be physically hurt?
No___ If Yes, enter 1 __

- Did a parent or other adult in the household often or very often… Push, grab, slap, or throw something at you? or Ever hit you so hard that you had marks or were injured?
  No___ If Yes, enter 1 __
- Did an adult or person at least 5 years older than you ever… Touch or fondle you or have you touch their body in a sexual way? or Attempt or actually have oral, anal, or vaginal intercourse with you?
  No___ If Yes, enter 1 __
- Did you often or very often feel that … No one in your family loved you or thought you were important or special? or Your family didn't look out for each other, feel close to each other, or support each other?
  No___ If Yes, enter 1 __
- Did you often or very often feel that … You didn't have enough to eat, had to wear dirty clothes, and had no one to protect you? or Your parents were too drunk or high to take care of you or take you to the doctor if you needed it?
  No___ If Yes, enter 1 __
- Were your parents ever separated or divorced?
  No___ If Yes, enter 1 __
- Was your mother or stepmother: Often or very often pushed, grabbed, slapped, or had something thrown at her? or Sometimes, often, or very often kicked, bitten, hit with a fist, or hit with something hard? or Ever repeatedly hit over at least a few minutes or threatened with a gun or knife?
  No___ If Yes, enter 1 __
- Did you live with anyone who was a problem drinker or alcoholic, or who used street drugs?
  No___ If Yes, enter 1 __
- Was a household member depressed or mentally ill, or did a household member attempt suicide?
  No___ If Yes, enter 1 __
- Did a household member go to prison?
  No___ If Yes, enter 1 __
  Now add up your "Yes" answers: ___ This is your ACE Score.

BREAKING FREE OF THE MATRIX

The Matrix movies are a metaphor and framework for understanding how much of our world is illusion and its people are living in a prison. A servant leader has to be able to see through these illusions, so he/she can effectively lead others out of this prison.

The defining moment in The Matrix films is when Morpheus offers Neo a choice between taking the red pill and the blue pill. Morpheus tells Neo that taking the red pill promises "the truth, nothing more."

Here is what Morpheus says to Neo: "The Matrix is a system, Neo. That system is our enemy. But when you're inside, you look around, what do you see? Businessmen, teachers, lawyers, carpenters. The very minds of the people we are trying to save. But until we do, these people are still a part of that system and that makes them our enemy. You have to understand, most of these people are not ready to be unplugged. And many of them are so inured, so hopelessly dependent on the system, that they will fight to protect it."

Neo decides to take the red pill and suddenly he awakens to a reality that is utterly different from anything he was aware of. What Neo thought was reality turned out to be a collective illusion fabricated by a Matrix mainframe computer and fed to a sleeping humanity, cocooned in grotesque embryonic pods.

Rather than a computer creating our illusionary Matrix, a small group of very wealthy, powerful, international, corporate leaders use the corporate media to help them weave a false reality. This conglomerate of con artists control and manipulate the mass consciousness in ways that seem very similar to the Matrix films. Throughout history, this group and other groups of self-serving leaders chose political and religious leaders to help them sell us this fabricated reality that embodies their lies. This elitist group also uses their fabricated reality to benefit their families, organizations and corporations.

Like Neo, I was unaware of the reality matrix when I began my own search for truth. I had vague and uneasy hunches that what I was observing was not what it seemed to be. So I began an exhaustive seven-year period of research to determine what was true about what I perceived and what was not.

MY PERSONAL JOURNEYS FOR TRUTH

As a criterion for knowing when I found the truth, I looked for cross-validation of the same information from at least three independent sources. I was cautious in my research, and looked for sources that didn't cross-validate each other's research. This step was very important, because I discovered that much of the matrix was created by people disseminating disinformation that was subsequently cited by others in order to make it appear valid.

The main task of the would-be servant leader is to question everything he/she has been taught to believe as the truth. If you do this kind of personal search for the truth, you will be able to be freed from any disinformation and lies that you were taught about the way the world works.

Out of my research, I identified six levels of "knowing" about my individual and collective matrix where I searched for "the truth, nothing more." I organized our research into six areas: My developmental history, the history of my country, the history of my religion, the history of the Earth, the history of the human race and finally the history of your human soul as it has traveled through many lifetimes.

Then my wife and I wrote a six-part series of Breaking Free of the Matrix books.[3] I encourage you to do similar research and perhaps look at what we found in our research. While we documented our sources and research done between 2000 and 2007, some of them may now be outdated, and some of the links to our online sources may now be inactive.

So I encourage you to read these books with an open mind, take everything that we share with a grain of salt, and then do your own investigative research. Question everything! Here is a short description of the six areas we researched:

The Truth About Your Developmental History. You need to learn the truth about your pre-natal development and your birth experiences in creating your personal matrix. The next step is understanding how your family-of-origin participated, knowingly or not, in programming you with Matrix patterns. Family-of-origin patterns are hardwired into you by the age of three and create what is known as the internal working model of reality.

Unless you recognize how these early programs were created and how they have shaped your development, you will continue to be controlled by them in your adult life, and ultimately pass them on unexamined to the next generation. In our other books and e-books, (my wife and I co-authored other books) you'll find many tools and resources to help you recover the truth about your developmental history.

The Truth About Your Religious History. Recovering your religious history is an extension of the programming you got from your family of origin. It is the next larger influence outside of your family of origin. Any distortion in what you were taught prevents you from breaking free of the

Matrix, so you need to identify exactly what values and beliefs from your religion and culture keep you trapped in the matrix.

The Truth About Your National History. Creating a false and misleading history of one's country is an excellent way to preserve the Matrix. Those who wrote American history books and then taught this distorted history to trusting students intentionally excluded parts of that history that provide people with inspiration and hope of liberation. While American history books point to our ideals of freedom and justice, in reality people discover that there are serious restrictions limiting the achievement of these ideals.

They become disillusioned or cynical and hopeless to ever change the conditions that block them from finding more freedom and equal justice. As a result, they are easily manipulated and controlled.

The Truth about the Earth's History. This is our home, yet we have been influenced by myths about the Earth's creation and evolution that are not true. In order to break free from the Matrix, it is important to understand know this very amazing truth about Earth's history and evolution. This one proved to be the most revealing area of research. I realized that much of the history of the Earth that I had learned in school and elsewhere was distorted and full of untrue myths.

The Truth about the History of the Human Race. While there is a considerable amount of accurate information available about the history of the human race, most of it is not available to the average person. Life on Earth is much older than most people think or were told. Much of this pre-history about ancient civilizations can be found in the traditions of indigenous people.

The Truth about the History of Your Soul. Recovering the journey of your soul through many lifetimes requires some deep soul-searching work. The Matrix, through our family, religion, culture and nation encourages us to believe that this is our only lifetime. To go beyond this programming requires the leap of faith that recognizes the soul is not is limited to one lifetime and one body.

Other Personal/Psychological Obstacles. Self-serving leaders utilize numerous methods of misinformation and lies all designed to keep the masses under their control. Below, I describe the various ways that these leaders attempt to scare, confuse and manipulate the masses in order to control them.

PSYCHOPATHS AND PREDATORS AS
PSEUDO-SERVANT LEADERS

People who suffered severe early developmental traumas often become psychopaths or people who never developed a conscience. They may have suffered from long breaks in their bonding during the first year of life or they may have suffered from severe abuse and/or neglect. If their bonding and attachment was very weak, they developed dysfunctional ways to try to overcome this problem.

Their understanding of right and wrong is twisted and they try to get their needs met by manipulating others. They are usually very smart and because they don't have a conscience, they are very good at lying through their teeth.

A good psychopath can stand in front of you and tell you "the world is flat" and you will be tempted to believe them, even though you know otherwise. A good servant leader must be able to detect these manipulators and not fall for their deceit. They are cleaver manipulators and servant leaders need to know how to stay steady in the face of their manipulations.

A study conducted by Daniel Bartels, Columbia Business School, Marketing, and David Pizarro, Cornell University, Psychology found that people who endorse actions consistent with an ethic of utilitarianism—the view that what is the morally right thing to do is whatever produces the best overall consequences—tend to possess psychopathic and Machiavellian personality traits.

In short, a servant leader has to be able to identify the morality of a utilitarian philosopher who is a manipulative con artist that cares little about the feelings and welfare of anyone but himself/herself.[4] Below are some suggested ways to identify psychopaths and how to respond to them in such a way that you aren't victimized by them.

Characteristics of Psychopaths and How To Spot Them[5]. Evidence of a lack of conscience or moral judgment. Present them with opportunities to show you if they have a conscience or not.

- **Lack a depth of empathy toward the misfortune of others.** Watch how they react to the misfortune of others.
- **Lack the full range of human emotions.** You might ask them how they are feeling when something happens requiring feelings.
- **Learn to fake emotions.** Watch for a lack of matching non-verbal signals that give away their mimicry.

- **Enjoy playing practical jokes or tricking others in ways that may be harmful.** Notice if people you know seem to get great enjoyment out of tricking others.
- **Playing mind games with people to try to prove they are smarter than others.** Notice how you feel in their presence. Do you feel drained of energy when you are around certain people?
- **Exhibit great charm, magnetism and charisma.** People like them and often trust them because of these qualities. Pay attention to your tendency to idealize others. If they seem too good to be real, they probably are.
- **Act as if they are the great expert on whatever topic you discuss.** They have a great need to be one-up. Do you feel one-down around these people?
- **Are good at out-smarting others.** They are good at finding and exploiting the weaknesses of others. Do you feel used in any way by any people you know?
- **Say and do grandiose things.** They also appear extremely self-confident. Do these people frighten you by their ideas and actions?
- **Are pathological liars.** They are at complete ease and act cool even when they know they are lying through their teeth. Notice if people you suspect are exceptionally "smooth talkers."
- **Do not assume any responsibility for their actions.** It is always someone else's fault if they are caught. Notice if people you know refuse to accept any responsibility for their actions. This is an important warning signal.
- **Lack shame, guilt or remorse for any of their statements or actions.** Ask yourself if you would feel any remorse, shame or guilt if you did what they did. If you would and they don't be careful.
- **Utilize twisted moral reasoning to justify their actions.** Watch for the twists in their thinking, usually justifying their actions.
- **Are addicted to power and greed.** They never get enough of either to satisfy them. Notice if people seem to have upper limits on these qualities. If they do not seem to, be very careful.
- **Engage in high-risk behaviors and often crave novel stimulation.** If the behavior of these people seems over-the-top much of the time, limit your contact with them.

OTHER TYPES OF PSEUDO-SERVANT LEADERS

Other types of Pseudo-Servant Leaders are also prevalent. The research of Mary Ainsworth and Mary Main showed that infants achieve either a secure attachment or an insecure attachment with their parents in their first year of life. The most common insecure attachment is the disorganized attachment. Research shows that infants who achieve a disorganized attachment by age six have become "solicitous care givers" or "little generals." They organize their life around taking care of others.

Many of these people become members of the helping professions and can look like they are taking good care of those they serve. Unfortunately, they usually cannot organize their own life, so taking care of others is often limited by the chaos that exists in their own life. Be wary of these people, because they often become victims of their own disorganized attachment style and may drag you down with them. You can spot them by their use of the "Rescue" position in the Drama Triangle. Below is an explanation of the Drama Triangle and its counterpart, the Need/Obligate System.

THE DRAMA TRIANGLE[6]

One of the most common ways that people with a disorganized attachment style try to get their needs met is by using the Drama Triangle to try to get their needs met. The Drama Triangle consists of three rotating roles: Rescuer, Persecutor and Victim. The objective of the game is to get your needs met by manipulating others instead of asking directly. The Persecutor is the "bad guy" role in the Drama Triangle. For this reason, most people avoid it unless they have a need to vent "justified" negative feelings such as anger or rage.

In these instances, they must identify some excuse to feel justified or right so they can express their negative feelings. Once they have a good reason for making someone bad, they can dump their repressed feelings. This is one of the Persecutor payoffs. Righteous indignation, the most common form of Persecutor behavior, is putting others down by using guilt and shame.

According to Berne, there are first-degree games that just involve making someone uncomfortable. Second-degree games involve threatening someone's safety. Third-degree games can be life threatening. While the Drama Triangle can also be played at any of these three degrees, they typically begin at the first degree and then escalate to second or third degree. Below is a brief description of the three roles plus the psychological games they can play using that role and the payoff they want by using a particular psychological game:

The Persecutor Role/Games. "NIGYSOB" "It's All Your Fault" & "See What You Made Me Do."

- Set unnecessarily restrictive rules & limits.
- Blames others for whatever happens.
- Criticizes all actions of others.
- Keeps the Victim oppressed.
- Expresses justified and righteous anger.
- Uses guilt and shame to put the other person down.
- Provokes conflict and drama.
- Takes a rigid, authoritative stance.
- Acts and sounds like a critical Parent.
- Comes from an I'm okay/good, you're not okay/bad position.

The Payoff. A Persecutor gets to be "right" and therefore is justified in releasing pent-up emotions. The Persecutor role allows a player to remain in control and dominate others. When someone rejects the heavy-handed behavior and expresses justified anger in return, this catapults them into the Victim and victim consciousness.

The Rescuer is the "good guy" role in the Drama Triangle. It provides people with a look-good opportunity to get their ego needs met. Rescuing allows people to look important and competent and to feel superior. Rescuer acts are often accompanied with woeful messages of self-sacrifice and martyrdom that also obligate the Victim in some way, if they buy into the guilt.

The Rescuer's attempts to help someone usually fail in some critical way, which then permits the Victim to get angry. This is also where people can quickly switch roles—from Persecute the Rescuer. The Rescuer then switches into the Victim role, saying indignantly, "I was only trying to help you!"

We discovered that most Rescuers are usually acting out their own unmet need to be rescued. They unconsciously project this need from unresolved childhood trauma, and then use it to justify rescuing of others. Here's a summary of the Rescuer role.

The Rescuer Role/Games. "I Am Only Trying To Help You" & "Look How Hard I've Tried."

- Feels obligated to rescue & often really doesn't want to.
- Does things for others that they don't ask for and could do for themselves.

- Feels guilty if they don't help others.
- Acts and sounds like an "authoritative" Parent, keeping the Victim dependent and helpless with their Rescuing.
- Supports the Victim's perception of being weak and a failure.
- Expects to fail in his or her own attempt to Rescue the Victim.
- Often a pleasing, marshmallow person who avoids conflict and drama.
- Comes from an I'm okay/good, you're bad/not okay position.

Payoff. Get to look okay, strong, capable and be one-up. Ultimate Payoff: Become a Victim when their Rescuer attempts to help others don't work.

The Victim role is key in the Drama Triangle because the whole game revolves around getting to be the victim. It is the one role where you can get your needs met without having to ask directly. Those in the Victim position also have to take responsibility for their behavior or feelings. They blame whatever isn't working in their lives on someone or something else.

There are two types of Victims: the Pathetic Victim and the Angry Victim. The Pathetic Victim plays one-down games, holds pity-parties, uses woeful, poor me facial expressions and body language, and one-down verbal language.

The Angry Victim pretends to be powerful, using guilt and shame to get others to feel sorry for them. The underlying motive of the Angry Victim is revenge. Both types want someone to blame for the feelings they have and for their troubles. Always operating in the background, of course, is their desire to attract a Rescuer who can take care of them. Here's a summary of the Victim role.

The Victim Role/Games. "Poor Me," & "Ain't It Awful."

- Acts victimized, oppressed, helpless, hopeless, powerless and ashamed in order to manipulate others.
- Looks for a Rescuer to help perpetuate his or her negative self-beliefs and to try to get needs met without asking directly.
- Uses the Victim role to avoid making decisions, solving problems and taking responsibility for his/her actions.
- Uses conflict situations to play victim.
- Refuses to learn how to avoid or create conflict situations.
- Has a slouched dejected body posture.
- Operates from a "I'm not okay/bad, you're okay/good" position.

Payoff. You can get what you want and need without asking.

Martyrs are a special class of Victims. Sometimes described as "emotional vampires," they act out toxic theatrical vignettes that escalate into hysteria and "high drama."

Martyrs use their Victim status to invoke extreme pity, and to prove that there is nothing that will improve their situation. Rather than blaming other people for their troubles, they blame them on God or some other omnipotent force that no one could win against. Martyrs are the most eloquent and committed kinds of victims.

The drama part of the Triangle comes from the fact that game-players rotate roles. They typically start out in the Rescuer role, but end up as the Victim. This rapid role switching confuses people. It disrupts their attempts to think logically and to express their authentic emotions. In dysfunctional families, this plays out as the Talk fast, Don't Listen game.

Drama Triangle players must become adept at switching roles if they are to insure confusion in their social interactions. They use the Three Rules of Chaos so that they can switch roles quickly and defend, deny and protect themselves.

- Make a game out of everything,
- Deny everything, and
- Blame others for everything and put them on the defensive.

The faster that roles change on the Triangle, the more the drama increases. As people's brains short out, they become more frustrated and angry. At some point the emotional intensity peaks. Then players can express rage, scream and lose control of their emotions, and maybe even get violent.

WHAT KEEPS THE GAME GOING?

Competition for the Victim role keeps the game going. Let me repeat this. It is competition for the Victim role that keeps the Drama Triangle game going.

Each player secretly strategizes in order to get to the Victim role. The Victim role is the prize! Here you can get others to help you meet your needs without having to ask them directly, and you can blame others for your problems.

The Persecutor initially feels righteous in his/her anger at the Victim, but then may feel guilty after attacking someone who's weak and helpless. The Victim can then push the Persecutor's "guilty" button and blame him/her for a lack of compassion or appreciation about the Victim's challenging problems. Then the Angry Victim can turn the Persecutor's anger back on them. This act of revenge flips the Persecutor into the Victim role.

The Rescuer may also secretly envy all the attention the Victim is getting without having to be accountable. The Rescuer's unconscious envy and associated ego wounds are often related to their own need to be taken care of and get attention. This unconscious yearning for being cared for often provokes the Rescuer into doing or saying something that causes the Victim to collapse and become worse.

This may motivate the Angry Victim to switch to the Persecutor role, where they express their anger at the Rescuer for failing to help the way they said they would. The Rescuer then collapses and gets to be the new Victim (this is where the Rescuer secretly had hoped to eventually end up). The Rescuer exclaims, "But, I was only trying to help you."

If you are feeling confused after reading about players' rapid role switching, their unconscious agendas and the associated chaos... welcome home! This is exactly how it feels when you are on the triangle and being catapulted from one role to another.

THE NEED/OBLIGATE SYSTEM

The Need-Obligate System, which is at the core of co-dependency, is a variation of the Drama Triangle. It's woven into the "good old boy" and "good old girl" networks found in organizations and corporations. Here is how it works:

- Someone does something for you without first asking you.
- Then they expect you to be grateful for what they've done for you, and
- You return their favor without them having to ask for it.

The implicit agreement (never spoken) is that "I did this favor for you, now you are obligated to return it." This means you've been Rescued and are expected to Rescue someone. In this game, you must figure out what this other person needs and give it without he or she ever having to ask for it. That's why it's called the Need-Obligate System.

If you don't repay the other person's favor in just the right way, you run the risk of being persecuted. Your failure permits them to get justifiably angry about your lack of thoughtfulness. If you accept the person's Rescue and don't repay their favor, the Rescuer feels cheated and becomes a Victim. This game is so prevalent in organizations that it permeates all their day-to-day operations. It's also the source of most organizational conflicts, gossip and rumors.

The Purpose of the Need/Obligate System. The purpose of the Need/Obligate System clearly is manipulation and control. It is designed to make you take care of other people without them having to ask for it. This is also the defining quality of all co-dependent interactions. It is the primary reason that people get stuck playing on the Drama Triangle.

The Need/Obligate system is also a way of controlling large groups of people at one time. Like families, large groups can use persecution, rescue and victim dynamics in ways that turn people into "examples"—humiliating, shaming and dehumanizing them ways that make those witnessing this "punishment" more compliant and less assertive. This is also known as "vicarious traumatization," a very effective form of mind control.

How Lobbyists Use the Need/Obligate System to Manipulate the Lawmakers. All Washington lobbyists and politicians use the Need-Obligate system all the time. A lobbyist approaches a member of Congress, for example, and donates a sum of money to his campaign fund without the Congressman ever asking directly for it. Then the Congressman is obligated to vote a certain way on legislation that related to the lobbyist's interests.

Nothing is ever transacted directly or written down. The members of Congress know that if they do not vote the way this lobbyist wishes, that will be the end of the campaign contributions from that source.

Once the Supreme Court's Citizen's United decision legitimized corporations as people, it allowed corporations to secretly give large sums of money to support candidates for reelection. Super-PACs are able to receive money without disclosing its source, which makes the need-obligate system a real game. The Citizen's United decision permits secret Need/Obligate system transactions in both the national and state legislatures.

We believe that the best way to protect yourself from the Need-Obligate and other dysfunctional, codependent Drama Triangle structures is know thyself very well. The better you understand yourself, the better your bullsh*t detector will work. It will help you to avoid manipulation and entanglements.

TWISTED BELIEFS AS A PERSONAL/ PSYCHOLOGICAL OBSTACLE

Throughout history, we see that many people died defending their beliefs. In my opinion, this defense has been and continues to be the greatest cause of violent conflicts in the world. These conflicts have been mostly over differences between the long-standing religious and spiritual beliefs of different groups of people.

In reading how these disputes start and end-up, I could not help but wonder why smart people did not find better ways to handle their differences in beliefs. These struggles end up with these smart people doing self-defeating things where nobody wins and many lives are lost or ruined.

What I have observed is that even the smartest people I know still do self-defeating things. I have wondered, "Why do they do that and how can they stop 'shooting themselves in the foot?'" For starters, I think these so-called smart people might look deeper into their own beliefs to find why they believe what they do.

Then they could reflect on whether or not what they believe actually makes sense in the real world. Without a willingness to examine our beliefs and possibly change them, unfortunately, we will continue to see these smart people often say and do stupid, self-defeating things.

In addition, we see that some of these smart people and groups end up preying on others using twisted logic to try to manipulate and control them. What causes people to develop predatory twisted beliefs? I wonder, "What causes these people to think the best way to get along with others is by trying to manipulate and control the actions of others?"

Most research suggests that people form their core beliefs by age ten or earlier, but my research indicates that the first three years are when most of us formed our beliefs. From my research, it appears that early childhood experiences and especially traumas during this early stage of development have a large and often unseen effect on creating twists in our beliefs. It also seems to depend on whether or not you have traumas in the co-dependent stage (from pre-natal time to about age nine months) or in the counter-dependent stage (from about ten months to three years of age). The traumas during the co-dependent stage tend to twist personal beliefs about:

- Trusting others,
- What you have to do to get your basic bonding needs met, and
- What you have to do to survive.
  Traumas during the counter-dependent stage tend to twist beliefs about:
- How close is "safe" for you in your relationships,
- How you can get the support you need from others, and fears about how much others might hurt you.

The above list of twisted beliefs and many others like them lead to self-defeating actions. Unfortunately, if our lives are not working, our usual strategy is to take what we are doing and try harder. Almost no one thinks of looking at his or her beliefs for the reason why things are not working. As a result, people seem to do the same self-defeating things over and over again. Have you done seemingly self-defeating things over and over again? What about any of the following:

- Repeatedly picking a relationship or marriage partner that ends up with you getting abused and then going back to the same person or similar people over and over again for the same abuse.
- Voting for the same political candidates repeatedly whose stated agenda is clearly counter to protecting and advancing your needs.
- Living far beyond your means, believing there will never be a time you will have to pay for anything.
- Never letting others really get to know you and putting up barriers to intimacy in your relationships to keep you from getting hurt.
- Repeating the same mistakes over and over in your life without knowing why or how to change your actions.
- Acting like you are smarter than everybody else and trying to manipulate and trick them into giving you things that you want or need.
- Acting weak and helpless in order to get others to take care of you in some way.
- Staying with the same dead-end job that you hate.
- Picking friends who continually take advantage of you in many ways.

My research shows that the long-term effects of early childhood traumas can inhibit the development of the neural pathways to the pre-frontal cortex where our moral, religious and spiritual values and beliefs are formed. All early childhood traumas are recorded in the more primitive part of the brain called the "limbic brain," particularly in the amygdala, which is part of the limbic brain. This is also responsible for the twists in the thinking processes of the adult population in general and is responsible for a lack of empathy and compassion toward others as seen in predators who are diagnosed as psychopaths, sociopaths and narcissists. These people do not connect with their pre-frontal cortex. Suffice it to say, part of the healing from the effects of early traumas requires the following:
- Examining your core beliefs,

- Understanding how you formed them, and
- Looking for twists and distortions in what you think and believe.

This means of you want to be a servant leader you have to learn the skills of self-reflection and self-correction. Finally, you need to learn how you formed your own beliefs, particularly religious and spiritual beliefs, independently without twists or distortions. Later in Chapter Eleven of this book, I provide specific tools and techniques to help you learn how to spot any twists in your beliefs and how to change them.

Premature Hardening of the Categories. A recent book by David McRaney You "Are Not So Smart" helps explain why this happens.[7] McRaney describes two psychological defenses that contribute to the persistent twists in the beliefs of people who likely are being influenced by early trauma. He does not seem to understand what causes these defenses so he can only describe their effects.

One of the common defenses designed to cover any hidden and unhealed traumas is what he calls the "confirmation bias." This is the tendency for people to favor information that confirms their preconceptions regardless of whether or not the information is true. They literally fear learning any some new information that might force them to change their beliefs.

As a result, people gather evidence and recall information from their memory selectively and interpret it in a biased way. Research on this tendency showed that these biases appear more often for emotional issues and for long established or core beliefs. This supports my assumption that the lingering effects of early trauma twist their beliefs. People usually try to defend what they believe in order to avoid feeling any unwanted feelings connected with their earlier unhealed traumas, even if they have to make things up to do so.

The other defense that people utilize to protect themselves from feeling their unwanted feelings is called the "backfire effect." McRaney says that when someone tries to correct the facts that these people are using, tries to point out any misconceptions or errors in their thinking, it backfires and only serves to strengthen their beliefs.

Over time, the backfire effect helps these people become more rigidly attached to information that allows them to confirm their beliefs and attitudes as true and proper. They usually try to avoid any situations (hypervigilance) where they might encounter information that would challenge their beliefs. They see people who have different beliefs from theirs as being "misinformed" or "brain-washed." Then any information they do give out to others has a twist in it that they do not even see.

The confirmation bias and backfire effect seem to cause people to resort to repeat "sound bites" that they have heard others say. They generally do not examine any possible twists in their beliefs connected with these ideas. In some cases, these people are cut off from any feelings of empathy or compassion toward others. While these psychological defenses have been around since we had to fend off the saber-toothed tigers, what makes their effect more dangerous today is the presence of the Internet and social media.

McRaney predicts, "As social media and advertising progresses, confirmation bias and the backfire effect will become more and more difficult to overcome. You will have more opportunity to pick and choose the kind or information that gets into your head along with the kinds of outlets you trust to give you that information."[7] This means that people will be better able to screen out all information that does not conform to their beliefs and only receive the information that supports them. What a formula for creating what I call "premature hardening of the categories."

Have you noticed that when you get lots of positive comments about your behavior from co-workers or people you are close to you do not pay much attention to them, but one critical remark will send you into a tailspin? People who are dealing with the effects of early childhood trauma have to constantly guard against something triggering a memory of their earlier trauma. They are constantly on the lookout for a possible negative remark that might bring up their unwanted feelings. This is called hypervigilance and is a classic sign of Post Traumatic Stress Disorder (PTSD).

People who suffered from early trauma have a harder time warding off their unwanted fears. So as the media's ability to bring the bad news from everywhere in the world instantly into our living room increases, these messages become harder to block out. This causes people to feel more fearful and unsafe and this makes it harder to keep their unwanted feelings at bay. In addition, these people will continue to feel unsafe as many of the mainstream institutions that operate on twisted beliefs that they trust begin to break down.

For example, the financial world almost totally collapsed in 2008 because of a twisted belief that the banks and other financial institutions were too big to fail. There also was a twisted collective belief (maybe a "Big Lie") that these institutions would police themselves and did not need any government regulations to limit their excesses. These twisted beliefs contributed enormously to the creation of the worst worldwide economic crisis since the Great Depression.

Our whole global capitalistic economic system is based on the twisted belief that economic growth is essential to our economic survival. However, at some level we must recognize that continuous economic growth is not good for our environmental survival. In order to avoid changing this twisted belief about continuous economic growth, we defend this belief with the backfire effect by attacking those who believe in global climate change.

STAGES OF CONSCIOUSNESS AS BARRIERS FOR SERVANT LEADERS

Robert Kegan researched the stages of consciousness in individuals and groups as well as the stages of culture, and how these two interface. He developed a meta-theory that helps explain why smart people do self-defeating things. Kegan divides consciousness into five distinct stages, each with requiring increasingly more complex beliefs necessary to handle the demands of modern life.

He looked at the mental demands of three models of culture present in our country today: Traditionalism, Modernism and Post-Modernism. His work is summarized in his book, In Over Our Heads, with the subtitle, The Mental Demands of Modern Life).[8] He contends that most of us are in a state of overwhelm most of the time because our consciousness and our beliefs have not sufficiently evolved to where we can cognitively handle all that is being thrown at us by "modern life."

His stages are developmental in that each builds on what was learned in the previous stage, however, he found that people can be all over the map in their lives. They can be in very different stages of consciousness based on what they believe related to various areas of their lives. For example, they might operate at Stage Four at work, but operate at Stage One or Two at church, largely because they have either not examined or changed their religious beliefs.

Early childhood traumas can cause people to develop twisted beliefs and can contribute to this fluctuation of stages of consciousness in various areas of our life. Because of the effects of hidden and unhealed traumas, certain situations cause people to regress and operate using more beliefs that are primitive. For example, in very intimate relationships, they can be triggered by a memory of an earlier trauma and be flooded with feelings that inhibit any critical thinking.

They may turn to beliefs about protecting themselves from great danger and act accordingly without much thought of the effects on others around them. This is where a seemingly mild-mannered person can suddenly be triggered into becoming a violent person who is acting on a belief that he or she is in great danger.

Over the past twenty-five years, I have seen many people transform themselves and their relationships by learning effective ways to resolve their conflicts. For many people, however, their early negative experiences with conflict causes them to avoid conflict at all costs. This means their avoidance of conflict may cause them to miss important opportunities for personal transformation.

Another group of people simply lack the skills they need to resolve conflicts in ways that would raise their consciousness. The skills taught in our book, Conflict Resolution: The Partnership Way,[9] make it possible for people to effectively utilize their conflicts, particularly those that are long-standing or intractable, as tools for transforming themselves and their relationships.

One of the first skills I recommend that people develop is the ability to identify their current stage of consciousness. We discovered that one of the best ways to do this is around the beliefs people have about their conflicts. Harvard psychologist and educator, Robert Kegan, devised a taxonomy of stages of consciousness that he describes in his book. The SOC Inventory below is a good way to begin to locate where you are in his taxonomy regarding your beliefs about conflict.

The SOC Inventory. The SOC Inventory is a tool based on Kegan's theory that I developed and validated to assist people in their effort to identify what stage of consciousness they live in most of the time. As I said above, no one lives in just one stage all the time and depending on the issue involved can slide back and forth among various stages. Fill out the SOC Inventory below and score it to better understand your stage of consciousness.

THE SOC INVENTORY[10]

Directions: Place the number that represents your best response in the blank before the number of each statement.

Use the following scale to determine your answers:

1= Almost Never, 2= Sometimes, 3= Often, 4= Almost Always)

_____ 1.   Conflicts just seem to happen to me and I have no idea why.

_____ 2. In a conflict situation, someone has to win and someone has to lose.

_____ 3. In a conflict situation, I feel victimized by the actions of others.

_____ 4. I can see the underlying patterns in my recurring conflicts.

_____ 5. I have the skills to help others successfully resolve their conflicts.

_____ 6. If I have a conflict, I turn it over to God or my higher power.

_____ 7. In a conflict situation, I tend to see myself as right and the other person as wrong.

_____ 8. In a conflict situation, I try to "shoot down" the arguments of the other person.

_____ 9. As the result of resolving my conflicts, I am able to better understand myself and why I got into a conflict with this person.

_____10. I have altered some of my values and beliefs as the result of my conflicts.

_____11. I wish that the people who bug me would just go away.

_____12. In a conflict situation, I end up not getting what I want and the other person does.

_____13. I lack confidence in my ability to resolve my conflicts successfully.

_____14. I can see the causes of my current conflicts stemming from similar unresolved conflicts I had as a child.

_____15. I have the ability to locate and resolve any unresolved conflicts from my past.

_____16. In a conflict situation, I am afraid that I'll lose myself if I consider the other person's position or needs.

_____17. I believe that the past is the past, you have to put it behind you and go on.

_____18. I depend on the instruction of my teachers because they have more knowledge and experience than I do.

_____19. I am able to see how the patterns of unresolved conflicts from my past are controlling my life.

_____20. I am able to change the major underlying dysfunctional patterns of behavior that have controlled my life.

Scoring: To get a score for each of the five stages of consciousness, add the numbers for the four items keyed to each stage (See below);
Stage One (Add items 1, 6, 11, and 16) = _____
Stage Two (Add items 2, 7, 12, and 17) = _____
Stage Three (Add items 3, 8, 13, and 18) = _____

Stage Four (Add items 4, 9, 14, and 19) = ____
Stage Five (Add items 5, 10, 15, and 20 = ____

Interpretation. After receiving information about what each stage represents, you can use the following interpretation of your scores: The stages of consciousness where you had your highest scores are the ones that you are most likely to use in a conflict situation. The higher the stage of consciousness where you have your highest scores, the better chance you have of keeping any twisted beliefs from interfering with your ability to resolve your conflicts.

In each of the five stages of consciousness, a score of 10-16 = a high score, 5-9 = a medium score, and 1-4 = a low score. Now that you have taken the Self-Inventory, look below at what Kegan says about each of the stages he identified.

Stage One. Magical Beliefs[11]. Individuals in this stage of consciousness lack good cause-and-effect thinking and often attribute events in their lives to magical sources or causes. They often act impulsively and engage in fantasy projections. In conflict situations, they typically blame their conflicts or problems on some unforeseen coincidence or on the other person without any awareness of how they might have participated in causing the conflict. They have very low self-awareness or self-reflection skills and almost no self-correction skills. The world around these people is a scary place and they are always on guard waiting some something bad to happen to them.

Stage Two. Concrete Beliefs Individuals in this stage of consciousness base their reality on what is visible and concrete. They are unable to grasp the meaning of abstract concepts such as "human rights" or "fairness." Everything must be quantified in concrete, visible ways for them to grasp its meaning or significance. During conflicts, they often focus on the most visible and obvious aspects of the conflict and ignore the rest. These people display very limited self-awareness and almost no self-correction skills. Their self-reflection is centers on trying to figure out what's wrong with others that causes these people to create conflicts for them. They typically feel defeated by the actions of others.

Stage Three. Cross-Relational Beliefs. Individuals in this stage of consciousness are able to think abstractly. While they are able to see the relationships between categories of information, they tend to see the world as acting upon them.

175

They typically think, act and feel like a victim. In conflict situations they usually feel victimized by others or the situation and believe the conflict is caused by the other person or circumstances. They also tend to victimize others for the same reason and experience conflicts as either win-lose or lose-lose. The self-reflection that occurs at this stage is focused on how they are being victimized or how to victimize others first. People at this level still do self-defeating things.

Stage Four. Systemic Beliefs. Individuals in this stage of consciousness can think holistically and systemically. They are able to perceive the underlying patterns of thoughts, feelings and behaviors that recycle and control their lives. In conflict situations, they are able to correlate a current conflict with similar ones from the past. They can understand how and why a current conflict might be caused by an unresolved conflict from their past, but they usually can't figure out what to do to change this pattern or conflict. People at this level of consciousness are very self-aware, but still are not able to do much self-correction. Most of the time these people do not do stupid things.

Stage Five. Trans-Systemic Beliefs. Individuals in this stage of consciousness can not only see the relationships between their current conflicts and their past unresolved conflicts, but they are able to figure out how to change these life-restricting patterns. They are able to see why they have been unable to resolve past conflicts, how these unresolved conflicts are currently affecting their lives and how to resolve these intractable conflicts at their source. They can truly utilize conflict situations as opportunities to change their lives and their relationships. The people at this level of consciousness are able to self-reflect and self-correct, so they are mostly free from twisted beliefs.

A Summary of Kegan's Research Findings. Based on his and other research findings, Robert Kegan concluded that up to 70% of the adult population of the United States operates most of the time at Stage Three or below. He calls these people "Traditionalists." This group likely suffers from the long-term effects of unrecognized and unhealed developmental traumas and operates out of a false self. People in stage four he identifies as "Moderns" and those at stage five he calls "Post-Moderns." According to his research, up to 30% of adults are entering or at Stage Four and less than 1% are entering or at Stage Five.[12] These people have the consciousness needed to heal their traumas and create a fully functioning self.

Kegan claims that because of their lower stage of consciousness, many people are clearly "in over their heads" in their attempts to understand and cope with the complexity of modern life. He says this group of people with lower consciousness is not able to meet the mental challenges of modern life. I have found that these people often have twisted beliefs that help them cope with their overwhelm but keep them from evolving. Generally, they do not have enough of a self to figure out how to meet these mental challenges.

FAMILY OF ORIGIN BARRIERS

You need to question everything you were taught in your family of origin. Most of what we came to believe as the truth about our family of origin was highly distorted and often untrue. Below is a description of the 12 most common family patterns that often are transmitted unconsciously from one generation to another.

The 12 Most Common Family Patterns[13]. Below is a description of the twelve most common intergenerational family patterns that may still be operating subconsciously as you parent your children as a servant leader. Locating and changing these patterns is extremely important if you want to be a servant leader in parenting your children. What I have found is that if you don't identify and change these intergenerational family patterns, you will unconsciously pass them on to your children.

Below is a brief description of the three General Family Patterns. Following that, I include a description of each of the Specific Family Patterns that fall under each General Family Pattern.

General Family Pattern #1: The Reappearance of Unresolved Parental Traits. What you know about how to form close adult relationships you learned in your relationships with your parents and siblings or from other adults such as teachers, relatives, and friends.

All your attitudes, values, beliefs, feelings and perceptions that occur in your current relationships are anchored in what you learned by the age of ten. The traits of your parents that were the most difficult for you to cope with as a child will show up again in your adult relationships.

Your interactions with your parents left you with many un answered questions. You will continue to seek answers to these questions in your current adult relationships. As a result of these gaps in your understanding, you likely will unconsciously recreate adult relationships with people who have some of the same difficult behaviors, attitudes, needs and feelings you experienced as a child in your interactions with your parents. If you had a rageful father, you will draw rageful bosses, friends and spouses to you as an adult.

The main reason this happens is that the natural learning style of humans is to repeat something that left you confused or hurt so you can better understand it and learn to do something different as a result. It is common to selectively perceive and even provoke reappearance these traits of your current partners, co-workers and bosses. For example, if you had a father who had a bad temper and you never learned how to cope with his temper as a child, you may draw to you a spouse, boss, co-workers or friends who have a bad temper "just like my dad."

General Family Pattern #2: Instant Replay of Co-dependent & Counter-dependent Family Patterns. If your relationship with one of your parents was full of conflict or confusion and contained little emotional acceptance, you may recreate in your current relationships the same kind of relationship dynamics that you had with that parent. For example, if you were expected to take care of your parents' feelings or needs by being obedient, thoughtful and subservient to their wishes instead of taking care of your own wants and needs, you will find yourself doing the same kinds of co-dependent caretaking in your adult relationships.

Most children are never given the tools they need to become emotionally and psychologically separate from their parents, so their most familiar adult relationship pattern is a co-dependent one. When children leave their parents, it is often from a position of counter-dependency ("I'll show you I don't need you anymore. I can make it on my own."). If you left your parents out of some counter-dependent acting out behaviors, you will likely recreate this kind of action when you form your adult relationships.

As a result, you will fall back on the more familiar co-dependent patterns and alternate them with counter-dependent ones. This "co-counter" dance in relationships is one of the primary barriers to intimacy and why you will have trouble sustaining your adult relationships. When the going gets tough in our adult relationships, you will likely leave the relationship the same way you did with your parents.

General Family Pattern #3: Living Out Your Parents' Relationship. If your parents' relationship was conflictual and confusing to you, you will try to understand their relationship by recreating the dynamics of your parent's relationship in your own adult relationship. You will find yourself fighting the same way that they did and even fighting over the same issues the way that they did. It often is money, child-rearing methods or religion. In addition, you will find yourself still trying to "fix" your parents' relationship as a way of finally winning their love and gaining their acceptance of you.

SPECIFIC FAMILY PATTERNS

Under each of the three general family patterns there are three specific family patterns that relate to the general one. They are each described briefly below

Specific Family Pattern #1a: Parental Disapproval. Under the first general pattern, the personality traits of your parents that you were unable to cope with as a child, will show up in your current relationships. You will find that the same things that your parents disapproved of in you when you were a child and are some of the same things that you are "sensitive" about and where you can be easily hurt by with others. You will find yourself disapproving of your children the same way they did of you.

Your old wounds will cause you to be "triggered" into a body memory of the times when someone disapproved of something you did or said. These represent traumas that have not been healed. If not healed, it will seem to you that you are actually drawing this kind of person to you. In truth, that is exactly what is happening. It is your attempt to finally heal the wound connected to these traumas by drawing someone to you who is like your parents in some way.

Labels like "selfish" or "unappreciative" will cut deeper if these were ways you were disapproved of as a child. You will use them to disapprove of yourself. In addition, you will disapprove of the same things in others and your children that your parents disapproved of in you. In short, you may hold prejudices, beliefs and values similar to your parents, although you may not even be aware of it.

Specific Family Pattern #1b: Getting Even. You may find yourself using these same disapproval methods to get even with those you perceive as weaker than you. This is another attempt to try to heal your wounds by finding others where you feel safe to act out your hurt or angry feelings. Bullies are people who are trying to get even.

However, the only way these wounds can heal is by feeling the feelings and expressing them in more appropriate ways. Acting them out tends to keep you from your true feelings. You may "blow up" at someone in order to avoid feeling the hurt or sadness that you are experiencing.

Specific Family Pattern #1c: Self-Condemnation. The other way you act out this first general pattern is by "beating yourself up" by using the same disapproval methods and expressions your parents used on you as a child. Sometimes you may hear yourself criticizing your mistakes, saying almost verbatim what your parents said to you as a child.

This kind of self-hatred is very destructive to your self-esteem. Have you ever done something embarrassing and then heard yourself calling yourself names such as "stupid" or "you jerk" or some other degrading term that you remember your parents said to you as a child?

Specific Family Pattern #2a: Acting Weak and Helpless. Under the second general pattern, you tend to recreate in you current relationships the same kinds of conflictual relationships you had with you parents when you were a child. You may find yourself acting weak and helpless toward your spouse or boss the same way you did toward your mother when you were a child to get her to pay attention to you.

You may let others take responsibility for your life either because you don' t feel able to do it for yourself or because it is easier to blame them if something goes wrong. Many people are stuck in infant behaviors and spend the rest of their lives trying to get other people to take care of them. Most alcoholics have this pattern.

Specific Family Pattern #2b: Life Is a Struggle. Because of the struggles you had with your parents while growing up, you may find comfort and familiarity in the struggles you are experiencing in your adult lifestyle and relationships. Therefore, when there is an absence of struggle or conflict, you may get anxious and uncomfortable and attempt to create struggle or conflict.

It is possible to become addicted to the steady flow of adrenal stress hormones from the drama of struggle and conflict, making it difficult to tolerate peace and harmony in your life for very long. Adrenaline is a very addictive substance and it is hard to overcome this addiction.

Specific Family Pattern #2c: Sexual Repression. This specific issue concerns repressed sexual feelings, which can also effect your adult sexuality. Because you are a sexual being, and because in most families sex is never openly discussed, normal sexual feelings between parents and children are never verbally acknowledged.

Instead, many parents and other adults either overtly or covertly act out their repressed sexual feelings on their children or push them away both physically and emotionally when the child begins to develop sexually.

If this happened to you, you may have learned to repress your sexual feelings or were victimized by your parents' sexual acting out or their rejection. In these cases, your adult sexual relationships can be profoundly affected.

Repressed sexual feelings are the most common causes of impotence and frigidity in both men and women and can severely limit your freedom to express your sexual feelings appropriately in your adult relationships. Promiscuous sexual behavior and teenage pregnancies often result from perceived parental rejection.

Specific Family Pattern #3a: The Parentized Child. The third specific family pattern involves growing up too fast and taking on adult responsibilities while still a child. This is very common if one of the parents is absent from daily household activities or if a parent is incapacitated by mental and/ or physical illness or from drug or alcohol abuse.

Another cause of this pattern is underlying compatibility problems between your parents that leave both of them with unmet emotional needs. In this case, fathers may "parentize" their daughters and mothers may parentize their sons by discussing issues and problems that should be addressed only by the adults, such as finances, job problems, and extended family conflicts. This is also called "triangulation."

Most damaging, however, is parents who discuss their marital and sexual problems with their children. These kinds of behaviors, which are considered emotional incest, can be very damaging to children's emotional development.

Unresolved loyalty and legacy issues with your family of origin can confuse matters even more for you. You may feel you owe your parents great debts that you can only repay by being loyal to them and conforming to their wishes. Becoming an extension of your parents' unresolved lives is another form or "parentizing."

Here you serve as an object that your parents can manipulate to satisfy their unmet needs. You must break this particular pattern before you can build sustainable adult relationships.

Specific Family Pattern #3b: The Fear of Success. If you were taught to take care of your parents wants and needs first and deny your own wants and needs, you may find yourself feeling afraid of being more financially, socially, educationally and psychologically successful than your parents. You may limit yourself and your adult relationships in these ways so as not to "make your parents feel bad or appear unsuccessful."

Specific Family Pattern #3c: The Fear of the Unfamiliar. Under the influence of this pattern, you may limit your adult relationships just because you are afraid of the unknown. Breaking your family patterns means venturing out onto unfamiliar waters well beyond those traveled by your parents. Your success in dealing with the unknown will depend partially upon how your parents supported your attempts to explore new and unknown territory as a toddler.

Most parents encourage and support their children's ventures into new and better relationships. They recognize the limitations that they had to overcome and will want their children to have an easier and happier life.

In your innocence, you may expect this kind of love and support from your parents. Instead, you were greatly disappointed and confused when they held on, criticized, controlled and discouraged your efforts to live freer and happier lives, often asking you to live out their fear of the unknown.

As you become aware of these intergenerational patterns, you can see how your parents are (or were) as also scared children with unhealed developmental traumas and hurts. You can have compassion for their struggle as wounded adults and parents rather than holding on to your resentment and anger over their lack of effective support.

When you are able to see your parents as they really are and stop idealizing them, then are able to see yourself and others the way you and they really are. This more realistic perspective will set you free to grow up and take charge of healing your wounds, finally establishing the loving, effective adult relationships that you have always wanted.

NOTES

1   Felitti VJ, Anda RF, et. al. (1998). "Relationship of childhood abuse and household dysfunction to many of the leading causes of death in adults: The Adverse Childhood Experiences (ACE) Study," 14:245–258. Detailed article on the ACE Study: http://acestoohigh.com/2012/10/03/the-adverse-childhood-experiences-study-the-largest-most-important-public-health-study-you-never-heard-of-began-in-an-obesity-clinic/

2   Starechecki, L. (March 2, 2015). Take The ACE Quiz - And Learn What It Does or Doesn't Mean. http://www.npr.org/sections/health-shots/2015/03/02/387007941/take-the-ace-quiz-and-learn-what-it-does-and-doesnt-mean

3   Weinhold, J. & Weinhold, B. (2008). Breaking free of the matrix (Six books). Swannanoa, NC: CICRCL Press. www.weinholds.org

4   Sona, R. (September 30, 2011). "Social Personality Traits Predict Utilitarian Responses To Moral Dilemmas." sr2763@columbia.edu Columbia Business School.

5   Weinhold, B. (2013). The twisted beliefs of human predators. Asheville, NC: CICRCL Press/CreateSpace.

6   Weinhold, B. & Weinhold, J. (2015). How to break free of the drama triangle and victim consciousness. Colorado Springs, CO:CICRCL Press/CreateSpace.

7   McRaney, D. ((2012). Your are not so smart; Why you have too many friends on Facebook and 46 other ways you are deluding yourself. New York, NY: Avery Publishing Co.

8   McRaney, D. p. 7.

9   Weinhold, B & Weinhold, J. (2009). Conflict resolution: The partnership way. Denver, CO: Love Publishing Company.

10   Kegan, R. (1994). In over our heads. Cambridge, MA: Harvard University Press.

11   Kegan, (1994), p. 314.

12   Kegan, pp. 191-197.

13   Weinhold, B. (2015). Breaking free: How to identify and change your addictive family patterns. Colorado Springs, CO: CICRCL Press/CreateSpace.t

CHAPTER 9

SOCIAL, ECONOMIC AND POLITICAL BARRIERS TO OVERCOME TO BECOME A SERVANT LEADER

"It is no measure of health to be well adjusted to a profoundly sick society."

— *J. Krishnamurti*

THE FAILURE TO QUESTION

One of the most important traits of a servant leader is his/her willingness to ask questions about the social, economic and political barriers to his/her values and beliefs. One of the greatest failings of the 20th century was the failure of the people to ask tough questions of elected officials. We need servant leaders who will ask the tough questions and encourage others to do the same. Unfortunately, self-serving leaders have shied away from asking the tough questions and instead tried to protect their turf.

There is no such thing as being "neutral" and not holding others accountable for their actions. That too is a political position and one that is an obstacle to human progress. Primarily, servant leaders must question their own values and beliefs and understand where they came from. Actually asking the questions, "why" or "why not," about everything is the key to any human progress.

Servant leaders have to be fierce seekers of the truth. They have to value seeking the truth as being more important than their loyalties to their culture, religion, race, or any ideology they hold; in short their inherited identity. Without questioning everything, they will never make any progress at all. Unfortunately, too many people are afraid to "rock the boat," are obedient and do what they are told, without questioning it. Unfortunately, they then become cynical about change. Well-informed cynicism is actually just another form of conformity. I am going to start this chapter with a discussion of self-serving psychopaths and human predators.

I show how they try to imitate servant leaders in order to manipulate others into believing they are serving the needs of others. It is important for servant leaders to be able to ask the right questions to expose these imposters and not be taken in by their deceptions. I have fallen prey to some of these people because often what they were offering seemed too good to be true. What I have learned, sometimes the hard way, is that if it seems too good to be true, it probably is. Caveat Emptor ("Let the buyer beware").

Psychopaths and Human Predators Become Self-Serving Leaders. People who suffered severe early developmental traumas often become psychopaths or people who never developed a conscience. They may have experienced long breaks in their bonding/attachment during the first year of life or they may have had traumas due to severe abuse or neglect. If their bonding and attachment was very weak for whatever reason, they developed dysfunctional ways to try to overcome this problem. Their understanding of right and wrong got twisted and they try to get their needs met by manipulating and cheating others. They become human predators and are totally self-serving.

Human Predators and Other Life-Takers. Human Predators come as wolves in sheep's clothing and wreak havoc in your relationships. They show up on Wall Street and on Main Street. Finally, they roam the legislative corridors of our nation's and our state's capitol. They have a well-practiced smile on their face and will steal you blind, if you let them. They are life-takers. The life-takers are thankfully a very small minority of human beings, perhaps less than ten percent, but their influence is powerful and widespread.

They are the con artists, manipulators, psychopaths, sociopaths, and narcissists of our world who prey on other human beings to satisfy their need for power, greed and control. They are self-serving leaders of one kind or another. They are the war makers of the world and those who profit from war making. They are the greedy Wall Street bankers and many of the so-called wealth makers.

Since they are a small minority, they have to use certain life-taking weapons to manipulate the majority of life-givers into assisting them in order for them to reach their goals of excessive wealth accumulation, power and control. Primarily, they use three methods to achieve their goals. They attempt to intimidate and instill fear in the life-givers, they tell lies, sometimes big lies, and they operate covertly so they can manipulate information and resources to remain in control.

WHAT HAPPENS WHEN SELF-SERVING LEADERS ARE IN CHARGE?

Below, I describe what has happened to this country because self-serving leaders have been in charge of more and more of our lives. A self-serving leader is a cleaver manipulator who often does not even have a conscience. Unless you have been living in a cave somewhere with no contact with the outside world, you likely have heard of most of the examples I list below, but there may be a few surprises in the list.

What you may not know is how these self-serving leaders operate to increase their personal gain at the expense of all others. I believe we have more self-serving leaders in this country than in any other country in the world. In these examples below, I show the ways the unsuspecting public is being preyed upon by self-serving leaders:

1. **Predatory Lending.** During the financial meltdown in 2008, it was the practice of major banks and mortgage companies to prey on unsuspected poor risk and minority borrowers. There were enough predatory lenders to fill a stadium. To date, none of these predators have ever been prosecuted or sent to prison.

2. **Predatory Capitalism.** These are the self-serving corporate leaders who are lobbying for an unregulated free market so they can make more profits at the expense of the general public. Instead of championing democracy, this form of unregulated predatory capitalism is used to undermine democracy. The owners of this wealth control the levers of investment and get to make all the decisions about what is produced, where, how and for whom.

3. **Predatory Cronies: The Bernie Madoff Story.** The capture of Bernie Madoff, who made off (isn't this a great last name for his chosen profession) with millions of dollars of money from investors who trusted him with their hard earned savings, is an interesting case. Even the New York Mets baseball owners and many famous people invested millions of dollars with him. His Ponzi scheme was unlike many others because of its size and that he was unusually successful in hoodwinking his best friends and cronies. He was the former Chairman of the NASDAQ and Chairman of a prominent Wall Street firm. He used his position to swin-

dle over $64 billion from his over 4,800 clients, which ranks as the biggest fraud case in history.[1]

4. **Predatory Religious Leaders.** This is not a new happening in Christianity and even the Apostle Paul condemned the early Christian Church for its practice of pederasty involving priests and young boys. However, not all the abuse was directed against boys. Priests frequently abused little girls as well. Pedophilia in the Roman Catholic Church has been a problem since early times, during its early history, the Church tried draconian methods to stop child abuse. For example, one church official in the Middle Ages recommended keeping offenders on a diet of bread and water for between three and twelve years. If strictly enforced, this diet would probably lead to the death of the offender by malnutrition.[2] Unfortunately, more recently, the Roman Catholic Church has become far more tolerant of these abuses. Priests who sexually abused children were simply moved on to other parishes where all too frequently they're offended. Pope Benedict XVI personally issued a document telling Bishops to cover up allegations of abuse. He knew this document would cause problems. He instructed church leaders to keep the sensitive document in a safe at all times. Victims were sometimes pressured into silence when possible with the threat of excommunication to keep them in line while other victims were bribed into silence.[3]

5. **Predatory Coaches: Getting Up For the Game.** The recent sex scandals involving a predatory coach at Penn State University, represents only the tip of the iceberg. Actually, after this scandal broke, many other sexual predator cases surfaced at other colleges and universities.

Again, what is most disturbing about these scandals is the way they were covered up and that put more young men and women at risk as a result. Had the first alleged Jerry Sandusky incident involving a young boy in the locker room shower been reported, many more young men could have been protected from his predation. He continued to prey on boys through his foundation whose stated purpose is to help troubled young men. He also preyed on high school students.

Wayne Drehs in a recent online article on ESPN Outside The Lines writes the following: "Anyone who spends a few minutes online can find a high school or middle school coach in their state who has been charged with some form of sexual abuse. One blog that tracked such arrests from May 2007 to May 2011 tallied 625 coaches who had been charged with everything from propositioning a student for sex to child molestation to statutory rape.[4]

6. **Human Traffickers.** Another area where sexual predators have been exploiting minors is in human trafficking. It is actually one of the fastest growing predatory activities in the world. The National Center for Missing & Exploited Children (NCMEC)[5] estimates that at least 100,000 American children are the victims of commercial sexual trafficking and prostitution each year. While it is often seen as just sexual exploitation, human trafficking also includes forced child labor that includes millions of children worldwide.[6]

7. **Identity Thieves.** One of the most invasive kinds of predation is identity theft. There are criminals who specialize in this form of predation and it is on the increase. Identity theft is a form of stealing someone's identity by pretending to be someone else, typically in order to access that person's resources or obtain credit card information and other benefits in that person's name. The victims of identity theft can suffer adverse consequences if the theft results in them having to pay for what the thief spent.

Identity theft occurs when a predator uses your identifying information, like your name, Social Security number, or credit card number, without your permission, to commit fraud or other crimes. The term identity theft was coined in 1964, however it is not literally possible to steal somebody's identity, so less ambiguous terms are often used like identity fraud or impersonation.[7]

Perhaps one of the best identity thieves of all time was Frank Abagnale, who impersonated as an airline pilot, a teaching assistant, a medical doctor and an attorney. He was finally captured and eventually went to work for the FBI to help them catch other psychopaths like him.[8]

8. **Predatory Foreign Policies: War Is the Answer; Now What Was the Question?** When the only tool in your toolbox is a hammer, everything serving predatory foreign policy. The lack of effective skills in negotiation and peaceful conflict resolution has led the U.S. to even adopt preemptive war policies. Since the 9/11 attack, this automatic urge to use war as our only tool in the foreign policy toolbox has gotten even stronger. By creating the Department of Homeland Security, we have created an internal monster to help us fight the "War on Terror" at home while we fight this invisible enemy around the world.

9. **Predatory Politics: The Best Self-Serving Candidates That Money Can Buy.** It isn't two big a leap to move from self-serving financial operators to self-serving politicians. Politics has always seemed like a dirty business with back room deals and wealthy contributors demanding ambassadorships and other positions in the government for plunking down millions of dollars to support a candidate.

There has been ample evidence that the politicians themselves also enjoy many perks as the result of lobbyists and wealthy backers giving them tickets to sporting events, funding lavish golf vacations and other incentives to buy their votes on certain legislation. While some rules seem to limit this activity, there are still enormous and stupid loopholes they can use. For example, it is illegal for a lobbyist to buy lunch for a politician, but if the lunch involves a fund-raiser, it is perfectly legal.

Not bound by term limits and the fact that over 80% of incumbents get re-elected, the climate is ripe for predators to use their elected office to line their own pockets and only pay lip service to the needs of their constituents. Most elected officials at the federal level are millionaires and greatly increase their wealth during their term of office.

10. **Predatory Environmental Policies: The Attack of the Climate Change Deniers.** Talk about people who are in denial, the climate change deniers are in a special category. The Republican Presidential candidates all label it the "global warming hoax." The mainstream media has almost stopped reporting anything about climate change to help with the denial.

However, the mainstream press still prints stories about scientists who claim it is a hoax, when later it is shown to be inaccurate reporting by someone who holds a twisted belief about global climate change. Yet, there is overwhelming scientific evidence to prove the existence of global climate change. Almost all legitimate climate scientists have published the facts based on their research that show that the rapid climate change is mostly due to carbon emissions from the use of fossil fuels.

11. **Universities As Self-Serving Corporate Factories: Learning To Earn.** Economic and other self-serving practices have all but taken over our public university system. We all carry fond memories of the university as a citadel of democratic learning. Unfortunately, a university eager to define itself largely in economic terms, is rapidly replacing this image. For example, university presidents largely ignore public values and shy away from addressing major social issues and problems.[9] Instead, they

now display their corporate affiliations like a badge of honor, sitting on corporate boards and pulling in huge salaries. A survey conducted by The Chronicle of Higher Education reported that, "…19 out of 40 presidents from the top 40 research universities sat on at least one company board."[10]

12. **Predatory Farming and Food Distribution: Let Them Eat Cake.** One of the most frightening coups by the predatory self-serving capitalists involves our agriculture industry. Farming and food distribution giants like Monsanto and Archer, Daniels, Midland now control everything from seeds to weeds. Monsanto now forces farmers to buy their "terminator" seeds that self-destruct every year, meaning that you cannot collect your own seeds.

These seeds have been genetically engineered to contain Round Up, (Glyphosate) the weed killer that Monsanto makes. This also can cause other seeds to become sterile as well. As a result, each year farmers will have to only buy Monsanto's GMO seeds.

Monsanto has been the leader in introducing genetically modified seeds that have unknown and possibly devastating effects on human body, with the FDA's tact approval. Monsanto has successfully prevented our government from regulating the use of glyphosate-treated seeds despite considerable scientific evidence that it is having serious health effects.

Various studies have linked glyphosate to the following diseases: ADHA, Alzheimer's, Birth Defects, Autism, Brain Cancer, Breast Cancer, Prostate and Lung Cancer, Celiac Disease, Gluten Intolerance, Kidney Disease, Colitis, Depression, Diabetes, Heart Disease Hypothyroidism, Lou Gehrig's Disease, Multiple Sclerosis, Non-Hodgkin Lymphoma, Parkinson's Disease, Obesity, Reproductive Problems and Respiratory illnesses.[11] This substance in our food and water is killing us.

There is currently a huge political fight in the European Union over whether or not to ban Round Up and similar products. Forty-eight Members of Parliament of the EU from 13 different countries volunteered to take a urine test to see how much glyphosate was present. The results showed that on average, the MEPs had 1.7 micrograms/liter of glyphosate in their urine, or 17 times higher than the European drinking water norm (0.1 microgram/litre).

This means that everyone they tested was way above the limit for residues of pesticides in their drinking water.9 GM corn, soybeans, canola, and sugar beets have made their way into approximately 80 percent of current U.S. processed grocery store items. Up to 90 percent of U.S. grown crops use genetically engineered seeds. In addition, ice cream, cheese, and myriad of other dairy products are made from milk, containing genetically engineered bovine growth hormone or rBGH, known to cause cancers. Recent studies show that glyphosate has even contaminated organic crops. Experts are not sure how this is happening, so further research is being done to determine the cause.[12]

13. **Predatory Violence & Abuse: Bullies & Bystanders.** The largest group of human predators in this country are bullies who believe in "might is right." Fed by a media that promotes the use of violence to resolve all conflicts, bullies act out their rage, often to cover up their deep fears of inadequacy. Every classroom in the country has bullies who are often encouraged by a school climate that promotes a version of getting your way at all costs. I can walk into any school in the country and within five minutes I can tell you what behaviors are most rewarded.

From research I conducted, all schools tend to over-focus on catching someone doing something wrong. This "gotcha" climate interferes with student learning and gives bullies free reign. Actually, what I found in my research was that some of the worst bullies in the school were teachers who sadistically put-down and bullied their students. Generally, students had no one to protect them from this kind of predatory behavior and were forced to submit to cruel and unusually punishments.

14. **The Secret Government and False-Flag Events.** As the result of Edward Snowden's leaks of secret government files, the public has gotten a glimpse of the covert, secret activities of the self-serving leaders of our Secret Government. Besides constantly spying on its own constituents, there is emerging evidence of the use of "false-flag" events to instill widespread fear in the populace.

This enables the self-serving predators to manipulate the life-giving public into supporting their life-taking efforts. The Iraq war is a clear example of how the widespread fears caused by the 911 attacks was used to invade Iraq, even though none of the 911 terrorists came from Iraq.

Throughout history, there have been examples of "false flag" events that were designed to raise widespread fears in order to gain the support of life-givers in carrying out life-taking ventures. For example, Hitler staged to Reichstag Fire in 1933 in order to gain public support for his

Third Reich. There is strong evidence that the 911 attacks were staged or promoted by forces within our government in order to gain support for the Iraq war.

There is good evidence that Pearl Harbor was another false-flag event that was created to give the U. S. a reason to enter World War II. Roosevelt had been given prior warning of the attack and did nothing to prevent it. The same strategy likely was utilized in the World Trade Center attacks in 2011.

The Revival of Social Darwinism. Robert Kegan's research showed that nearly seventy percent of adults are likely to be influenced by twisted beliefs that involve being either a victim or victimizing others. They lack a fully individuated Self and operate primarily out of a False Self.

For example, these people are more likely to accept twisted beliefs portraying them as victims of the government or "corporate" interests. They might accept a twisted belief that, "The government stands in the way of me succeeding financially." They might also have less empathy and compassion for those they perceive as competing with them for limited resources.

This group is more likely to believe that, "It is every man for himself in this dog-eat-dog world." The Predator Society propagandists aim their lies and manipulative tricks at the people who see themselves as victims or as victimizers. They are masters at creating "us versus them" mind games.

They know they can influence people who operate mostly from this kind of thinking more easily than those who have a secure individuated Self. People at this higher stage of consciousness are more likely to see through the deceit and manipulation. Those lacking a fully individuated Self have difficulty getting beyond their own twisted beliefs and are more vulnerable to being obedient to authority.

Social psychologist, Stanley Milgram, conducted experiments on obedience. He set up an experiment where adult "teachers" were instructed to administer shocks to adult "students" (who were part of the experiment and not harmed by the shocks). Every time the student made a mistake, the teacher was instructed to administer an increasingly higher level of electrical shock to the student. The student was instructed to scream in pain at each shock.

Even though participants expressed discomfort at administering the shock, they were told to obey the instructions of the experiment and continue to administer the shock. It turned out that 2/3 of the participants obeyed the instructions of the experimenter and administered the highest level, near fatal, shock to the students. Their obedience to the authority figure, who told them to continue, overrode their discomfort at seriously hurting the student. This study was replicated numerous times with similar results.[13]

Social Darwinism Was Born During the Gilded Age. There is a set of twisted beliefs that was part of America since the so-called Gilded Age from about 1870 to 1910.

The robber barons such as financier Jay Gould, railroad magnate Cornelius Vanderbilt and oil tycoon John D. Rockefeller used twisted beliefs to justify their control over much of American industry. During that time the gap between the rich and the poor had grown into a deep chasm, with urban slums everywhere. Children were forced to work long hours in sweat shops, women could not vote, and blacks were subject to Jim Crow laws.

Sacks of money were literally deposited on the desks of eager legislators by lobbyists representing the rich. Does some of this sound familiar? Well it should, because today the predators are increasing their use of this victim/victimizer propaganda to again mask their greed.

About 1870, Yale social science professor, William Graham Sumner, took Charles Darwin's theory about the survival of the fittest and twisted it into an economic and social theory to support predation. Graham called it "Social Darwinism," which stated that life was a natural competitive struggle in which only the fittest will survive.[14] According to Graham, this "natural order of things" contains victims and predators. Graham believed that societies evolved and became stronger because of this struggle between victims and victimizers. He also believed that government should do little to help those in need because that would interfere with natural selection. Sumner warned against giving handouts to people who he termed as "negligent, shiftless, ineffective, silly and imprudent."

More than a century ago, Sumner also said the following: "They (millionaires) may fairly be regarded as the naturally selected agents of society." He added that although they live in luxury, "... the bargain is worth it."[15]

Theory X and Social Darwinism in Businesses and Corporations. Social predators utilize their twisted belief system in many places in today's modern world. Perhaps it is most visible in business management theory and practice. Douglas McGregor, in his classic management book, The Human Side of the Enterprise,[16] proposed two theories of how to manage people: Theory X and Theory Y.

The assumptions and beliefs that are part of Theory X are the modern version of Social Darwinism that the Illuminati utilize in their business management. This is the prevalent theory practiced in the corporate management of people today.

The twisted beliefs of Theory X about what workers are like and what motivates them are as follows: Workers are basically lazy and will avoid work, if allowed to do so. Workers do not want to be held responsible for anything they do or say. Workers would much rather follow a strong leader than lead themselves.

According to Theory X, workers are self-centered and do not care about organizational or societal goals. Their only focus is "what's in it for me." Workers are gullible, somewhat stupid and are easily manipulated and controlled. If these workers are not controlled and closely supervised, they will drain off the profits of your business.

They will work for money and you have to use what you pay them to keep them dependent on the job. Don't give them any benefits, if you can avoid it. By utilizing these twisted beliefs, those in corporate management generally use coercion, implicit threats, close supervision and tight controls to get people to perform at work. Unions have served as a counter balance to these oppressive practices, but they have gradually been undermined by an emphasis on "corporate interests" and the bottom line. In Chapter Twelve, I discuss Theory Y and how it is changing the way some companies are doing business.

The Revival of the Southern White Plantation Culture. When a Southern white conservative talks about "losing his liberty," he is talking about the loss of this absolute domination over the people and property under his control. Even worse, he is referring to his loss of status and the resulting risk of being held accountable for laws that he was once exempt from. This is what liberty means to him. In this view, freedom is a zero-sum game. Anything that gives more freedom and rights to lower-status people is seen by him as putting serious limits on his freedom to do as he pleases. This twisted belief is the foundation of the Tea Party movement. This is mainly why they see any compromise as giving up their liberty or rights.

Knowing this, we can understand the traditional Southern antipathy to education, progress, public investment, unionization, equal opportunity, and civil rights. When Southerners quote Patrick Henry's, "Give me liberty or give me death," what they're really demanding is the unquestioned, unrestrained right to turn their fellow citizens into supplicants and subjects. As long as America runs according to the rules of Southern politics, economics and culture, we're no longer free citizens exercising our rights to life, liberty and the pursuit of happiness as we've always understood them. Instead, we're being treated like serfs on the Master's plantation, and increasingly, we're being granted our liberties only at the Master's pleasure.[17]

ECONOMIC BARRIERS

Perhaps the biggest barrier for the servant leader to overcome is the secret, privately owned central banking monetary system that operates outside the law in the U. S. Since 1913, the currency of the United States has been owned and operated by a private corporation of international bankers known to all of us as the "Federal Reserve System." This private corporation prints "Federal Reserve Notes" and then loans them to the U. S. Treasury at an interest rate totally determined by them. The Fed has never been audited, so no one knows how much money they actually control.

If these banks were to fail, as some did in 2008-9 due to reckless financial greed, the taxpayers would have to bail them out because their failure would send us into a deep depression like in the 1930's. In addition, most of the so-called "national debt" is basically owed to the Federal Reserve. They make lots of money by "loaning" the currency they print to the U. S. government and collecting interest on those loans.

When Democratic Party Candidate Bernie Sanders is talking about breaking up the banks, he is not calling for the elimination of this corrupt system. His proposals are for new laws that would force them to decentralize more, so they are no longer "too big to fail." This is not a game-changer.

This system of Central Banks also operates in almost all other countries by the Global Elite. As discussed earlier, the Global Elite consists of a small group of super-rich families that also set up shell companies outside their country's border to avoid paying any taxes on their wealth. Estimates are that over $50 trillion dollars is being held in offshore, non-taxed accounts. If recovered, the taxes on this amount of money would be enough to end poverty in the world.

This practice is what privately owned central banks have been doing for centuries. Among other things, they have funded all major wars. Wars are very profitable and they fit the self-serving agenda of the "banksters," no mater what the cost in human lives happens to be. They usually fund both sides of the conflict so whomever wins, they can collect from them.

Most workers have very little control over their employment. They are selling their best hours in their life to "the man." As a result, most employees do not enjoy the freedoms that our democracy promises them. This results in a gigantic collective Stockholm Syndrome. Every employee has to act as if they enjoy being held captive. If they want to survive in the workplace, they are forced to be obedient workers and do as they are told. As a result, we are all caught in a monetary system that enslaves us.

We have had to sell our talents to employers. When people are having trouble paying their bills, they tend to see it as a personal problem of their own making. They don't understand the systemic problems of a manipulated economy and money system. The whole system is corrupt and is designed to keep people enslaved.

The Evils of Toxic Capitalism. Capitalism is accepted as a normal way of life in this country. No one questions the toxic effects that capitalism has on all of us. Ownership of wealth obviously confers power to whoever controls the money. It gives wealthy individuals an upper hand in the "voluntary" exchanges they make with others. Lacking the means otherwise to support themselves, most workers must hire out their ability to do work in exchange for wages. They might do quite well, if they are educated and talented, lucky or white, but even so, they ultimately produce more value than for what they are paid - that is, after all, the reason they were hired.

Wealth ownership, thus, gives an upper hand to employers in any so-called voluntary exchanges with working people. The extra value that workers create flows steadily into the hands of wealth holders and the workers do not have a say over what it is used for. This upper hand in these so-called voluntary exchanges provides an ongoing and increasing source of wealth accumulation that is self-reinforcing. Money begets money. That is after all what capital is: money advanced for the purpose of making more money.

Excluding people from having a say over what happens to the wealth that they help create is the first and the most fundamental way that any capitalist system undermines democracy. Employees are fundamentally disenfranchised in the places where they work. Wealth owners control the levers of investment and, thus, the "needs" of capital always trump the "needs" of workers when it comes to making decisions about what gets produced, how and for whom.

In addition, capitalism is based on competition, which means for everybody who "wins" there is somebody who loses. In addition, it is not a level playing field, and some have as better chance of winning than others.

Beyond this, wealth managers use the wealth we create to enforce a virtual dictatorship by using it to control the political sphere. One percent of the wealthiest capitalists control the lives of the other 99 percent. Finally, the most obvious manifestation of this dictatorship by wealth is the unlimited corporate financing under Citizen's United of our elected representatives.

Therefore, it is a fact of American life that capitalism is equated with democracy, while at the same time, it acts as democracy's most toxic force. Let's look at some of the outcomes of capitalism.

- Over twenty percent of the world's population is undernourished with over nine million people (five million are children) dying each year from malnutrition. More than eleven million children die each year from preventable diseases like malaria and diarrhea.
- Half of the world's population lives on less than $2 a day.
- Over a billion people have no access to safe, fresh drinking water.
- More than 2.4 billion people don't have access to the toilets we all take for granted.
- Three million people die every year from water related diseases that could be prevented.
- There are still 27 million slaves in the world.

Taken together, this is an astonishing set of indictments against toxic capitalism. We should ask, "if capitalism cannot solve any of these problems then what good is it anyway?" All these outcomes can be traced back to a capitalistic system that is controlled by self-serving leaders. We can do better then this and servant leaders can use other methods that are available to help solve all of these problems. I discuss some of these in Chapter Twelve.

The Effects of Income Inequality in the U.S. When it involves income inequality, Americans fare even worse than most countries. The U.S. has one of the highest levels of income inequality among its peers and is among the worst in offering equal opportunities for advancement. This roots of this problem stem from the prevailing belief of Social Darwinism, that the rich are the fittest to survive and therefore deserve the most wealth. This has become one of the major issues in the 2016 Presidential campaign with candidates from both sides of the isle offering their prescriptions for solving the growing income and wealth gap.

The post-World War II era was prosperous for both the American economy and its workers. However, since then wages have stagnated, with the median income falling to where it was 40 years ago. During the same time, CEO pay has risen to 300 times the average worker's income, up from 30 times where it was 40 years ago. Minimum wage jobs are increasingly being held by the family's primary breadwinner, instead of being held by a teen looking for part-time work.

Economic Inequality: Worse Than You Think. In a candid conversation with Frank Rich last fall, Chris Rock said, "Oh, people don't even know. If poor people knew how rich people are, there would be riots in the streets." Probably Chris Rock is right. People in this country have no idea how unequal our society has become. Studies show that Americans estimated that the CEO to worker pay ration is 30-1 while the actual ration is 354 to 1. Fifty years ago is was 20 to 1.

George Carlin once joked that, "the reason they call it the American Dream is because you have to be asleep to believe it." How can we wake up?[18] The servant leader needs to understand this issue and work diligently to help overcome these economic barriers.

POLITICAL BARRIERS

I have discussed some of the political barriers earlier, so I will briefly summarize what these barriers represent. In the U. S., the political system is totally broken. It has come under the total control of the wealthiest 1 percent, mostly bankers. In essence, we have created a fascist system where the two parties are only the two wings of the corporate bird. The left wing and the right wing.

The corporate media has helped sell this form of government as "democracy." Many of us believe we are "free," and that we have choice and free will. These are illusions we were presented to make us believe that we still have basic human rights. We are told we have human rights, a bill of rights, liberties, democracy, majority rule, freedom, and so on. In order to get elected, candidates for office have to sign on with corporate donors, who then dictate what laws get passed and what do not.

Unfortunately, the opposite of what we were told is true. What we were told is "free will" is just a cleverly disguised set of options all of which lead to predetermined outcomes that benefit those with the wealth and control. Actually, we do not even have choices. We are allowed to make selections from what the self-serving capitalist leaders have determined are going to serve their best interests. This is a system of economic and political slavery. Goethe once wrote, "none are more enslaved than those who believe they are free." In Chapter Twelve, I address this issue and propose strategies the servant leader can use to overcome these obstacles.

Predatory Politics. Not usually bound by term limits and the fact that over 80% of incumbents get re-elected, the climate is ripe for predators to use elected office to line their own pockets and pay lip service to the needs of their constituents.

Most elected officials at the federal level are millionaires and greatly increase their wealth during their term of office. With the predatory media blowing their horn, politicians can market such lies as "Government regulators are job killers," or "Voter IDs are needed to protect us from widespread voter fraud." They have learned how to spin their messages to play to the irrational fears and unhealed traumas that voters carry with them into the voting booth. This may help explain why so many voters seem to vote for candidates whose stated agenda is almost the opposite of what the voters' needs are.

Psychologist Jonathan Haidt in his article, "What Makes People Vote Republican?" writes that "...conservatism is a partially heritable personality trait that predisposes some people to be cognitively inflexible, fond of hierarchy, and inordinately afraid of uncertainty, change, and death. People vote Republican because Republicans offer "moral clarity"—a simple vision of good and evil that activates deep seated fears in much of the electorate."[19]

He cautions liberals to remember that a large block of the voting public still places high moral importance in rallying around the flag, believing in the sanctity of our founding fathers (even though most of them were slave owning elitists), and the power of our military in order to feel like a patriotic American. While this may seem too simplistic for some liberals, it is what many voters turn to when faced with a barrage of lies that trigger their deep-seated fears and unhealed traumas.

Twisted Beliefs. In my book, Twisted Beliefs: Why Smart People Suffer From Premature Hardening of The Categories,[20] I quote David McRaney who identified two factors that effect how voters respond to information. One he calls the "backfire effect," where people get more rigid in their beliefs when they are confronted with information that counteracts their beliefs in some way. The other is the "confirmation bias," where people filter out or ignore information that runs counter to their beliefs.

In either case, this means that giving people information designed to get them to change their vote does not work and actually backfires. I found that most people do not examine their beliefs very much and often rely on the opinions of others. They are prey to the lies of those who wish to trick them not because they are stupid or lazy, but because they are confused as to what to believe.

NOTES

1   http://en.wikipedia.org/wiki/Madoff_investment_scandal
     Accessed May 20, 2012.

2   Ruden, S. (2010). Paul among the people. New York: NY, Image Books.

3   Perry, A. (January 12, 2011). Roman Catholicism's Long History of Child Abuse.
     http://www.suite101.com/content/roman-catholicisms-long-history-of-child-
     abuse-a331760
     Accessed May 21, 2012.

4   Ibid.

5   National Center for Missing and Exploited Children
     http://www.missingkids.com/missingkids/servlet/NewsEventServlet
     Accessed Jan, 20, 2016.

6   Drehs, W. (Dec. 16, 2011). Not My Coach. Not My Town.
     http://espn.go.com/espn/otl/story/_/id/7349583/protecting-young-athletes-sexual-
     predators-espn-magazine
     Accessed May 21, 2012.

7   Identity Theft. http://en.wikipedia.org/wiki/Identity_theft
     Accessed May 25, 2012.

8   Frank Abagnale. http://en.wikipedia.org/wiki/Frank_Abagnale
     Retrieved May 25, 2012.

9   Newfield, C. (2008). Unmaking the public university, (Cambridge: Harvard
     University Press.

10   Ibid.

11   Results of Glyphosate Urine Test: "It's Not Good News. Glyphosate in Water and Food.
     Lorraine Chow May 12, 2016, Global Research
     http://www.globalresearch.ca/results-of-glyphosate-urine-test-its-not-good-
     news-glyphosate-in-water-and-food/5525529?utm_campaign=magnet&utm_
     source=article_page&utm_medium=related_articles
     Accessed June 1, 2016.

12   Brian Shilhavy ALERT: Certified Organic Food Grown in U.S. Found Contaminated
     with Glyphosate Herbicide.
     http://humansarefree.com/2016/06/alert-certified-organic-food-grown-in.html?utm_
     source=feedburner&utm_medium=email&utm_campaign=Feed%3A+humansarefre

e%2FaQPD+%28Humans+Are+Free%29
Accessed on June 5, 2016.

13 *https://en.wikipedia.org/wiki/Milgram_experiment*
    Accessed June 2, 2016.

14 *https://en.wikipedia.org/wiki/William_Graham_Sumner*
    Accessed June 2, 2016.

15 *Bok, D. (2002). The cost of talent. New York: Simon & Schuster, p. 246.*

16 *McGregor, D. (2006). The Human side of the enterprise. New York: McGraw-Hill.*

17 *Robinson, S. (2012). "Southern Values Revived." Salon Magazine. Accessed 4/9/2016.*

18 *Fritz, N. (March 31, 2015). "Economic Inequality: It's Far Worse Than You Think." Scientific American. Accessed April 13, 2016*

19 *Haidt, J. (Sept. 8, 2008). "What Makes People Vote Republican?" Edge.*

20 *Weinhold, B. (2013). Twisted Beliefs: Why Smart People Suffer From Premature Hardening of The Categories. Asheville, NC: CICRCL Press.*

CHAPTER 10

CULTURAL, RELIGIOUS AND EDUCATIONAL BARRIERS TO BECOMING A SERVANT LEADER

"Men express themselves in harmony with their land. And superiority, as far as culture is concerned, lies in this harmony and nothing else. There are no higher or lower cultures. There are cultures that are more or less true."

— *Albert Camus*

CULTURAL BARRIERS

Every person is born into a social and cultural setting—family, community, social class, language, and religion—and eventually develops many social connections. The characteristics of a child's social setting affects how he or she learns to think and behave, by means of instruction, rewards and punishment, and example. This setting includes home, schools, your neighborhood, and perhaps the local religious and law enforcement agencies.

Then there are also the child's mostly informal interactions with friends, other peers, relatives, and the entertainment and news media. How individuals will respond to all these influences, or even which influence will be the most potent, tends not to be predictable. There is, however, some substantial similarity in how individuals respond to the same pattern of influences—that is, to being raised in the same culture.

Furthermore, culturally induced behavior patterns, such as speech patterns, body language, and forms of humor, become so deeply imbedded in the human mind that they often operate without the individuals themselves being fully aware of them.

Every culture includes a somewhat different web of patterns and meanings: ways of earning a living, systems of trade and government, social roles, religions, traditions in clothing and foods and arts, expectations for behavior, attitudes toward other cultures, and beliefs and values about all of these activities. Within a large society, there may be many groups, with distinctly different subcultures associated with a region, ethnic origin, or social class.

If a single culture is dominant in a large region, its values may be considered correct and may be promoted—not only by families and religious groups but also by schools and governments. Some subcultures may arise among special social categories (such as business executives and criminals), some of which may cross national boundaries (such as musicians and scientists).

Fair or unfair, desirable or undesirable, social distinctions are a salient part of almost every culture. The form of the distinctions varies with place and time, sometimes including rigid castes, sometimes tribal or clan hierarchies, and sometimes a more flexible social class. Class distinctions are made chiefly on the basis of wealth, education, and occupation, but they are also likely to be associated with other sub-cultural differences, such as dress, dialect, and attitudes toward school, gender roles and work. These economic, political, and cultural distinctions are recognized by almost all members of a society—and resented by some of them.

The class into which you were born affects what language, diet, tastes, and interests you will have as children, and therefore influences how you will perceive the social world. Moreover, class affects what pressures and opportunities you will experience and therefore affects what paths your lives are likely to take—including schooling, occupation, marriage, and standard of living. Still, many people live lives very different from the norm of their class.

What is considered to be acceptable human behavior varies from culture to culture and from time period to time period. Every social group has generally accepted ranges of behavior for its members, with perhaps some specific standards for subgroups, such as adults and children, females and males, artists and athletes.

Unusual behaviors may be considered either merely amusing, or distasteful, or punishably criminal. Some normal behavior in one culture may be considered unacceptable in another. For example, aggressively competitive behavior is considered rude in highly cooperative cultures.

Conversely, in some subcultures of a highly competitive society, such as that of the United States, a lack of interest in competition may be regarded as being out of step or lazy. Although the world has a wide diversity of cultural traditions, there are some kinds of behavior (such as incest, violence against kin, theft, and rape) that are considered unacceptable in almost all of them.

UNDERSTANDING THE IMPACT OF YOUR CULTURAL ROOTS

The culture you were born into and the culture your parents and grand-parents were born into determine most of the values and beliefs you learned. It is necessary for a servant leader to understand how these intergenerational cultural values and beliefs can influence their behavior. It becomes a barrier, if you do not understand the origin of your values and beliefs and how the culture you were raised in has influenced your perception of yourself, other people or the world around you.

This set of perceptions is called your "internal working model of reality." It forms during infancy and toddlerhood through early childhood experiences while interacting with your family and community culture. It is generally well formed by age ten and likely remains the same unless you engage in extensive self-reflection and self-correction activities designed to question your own values and beliefs. If the subculture you grew up in was not very homogenized, you likely had few encounters with people from different cultures. Your internal working model of reality determines much of your behavior.

It also can be difficult to question your values and beliefs, because you were probably taught to accept without question what you are told to value or believe. Some cultures do value questioning one's values and beliefs, like some Jewish cultures, but most do not.

For example, if you were born in this country, research shows it may be difficult to understand someone else's point of view because you were taught the value of individualism. In contrast, if you were born in China, you would have no trouble understanding another person's perspective, because that behavior is valued in a collectivistic culture.

When you encountered people from different cultures, you may have broadened you perceptions of "what is right and what is wrong" about these people. Either you learned to fear these differences or you realized the differences were not a threat to you and your values and beliefs.

Cross-cultural psychologist, James Prescott, decided to study the factors that cause a culture to be considered a violent culture or a peaceful culture. He decided to study 49 different tribal cultures. He found that one behavior predicted with 80 percent accuracy whether that culture would be violent or non-violent. That one behavior was mother/infant bonding as demonstrated by continuous baby carrying on the body of the mother or a close relative acting as a mother throughout the day for the first year of life.

The peaceful or violent nature of the remaining ten cultures could be predicted from whether or not youth sexual expression was supported or punished. In violent cultures, it was punished and in peaceful cultures it was supported. In short, these two culturally supported behaviors predicted with 100 percent accuracy the peaceful or violent nature of these 49 tribal cultures distributed throughout the world.[1]

Each culture has its own unique set of values and beliefs that it deems important. Some of these values and beliefs are very functional and others have become recognized as dysfunctional, but often persist anyway. This is called "cultural relativity." It means a particular behavior might work for most people in one culture, even though it might not work in the culture you were born into. In the best of all worlds, we could determine which values and beliefs from each culture are the most functional for all people and then create a culture that offers a blending of all these cultural gems.

THE MYTH OF THE AMERICAN DREAM

In this country, one of the prevailing values and beliefs is social and economic mobility. For example, people say things like, "Every person born in this country can become President." It is part of what is referred to as "The American Dream." All the candidates in this year's Presidential elections are hawking their version of the American Dream. How real is that cultural belief?

While this cultural belief may have been true at one time, it now is nothing more than a myth. First, let's look at social mobility compared to other countries. The notion that anyone in America who is willing and able to "pull themselves up by their bootstraps" can achieve significant upward social mobility is still deeply embedded in U.S. society. Conventional wisdom holds that class barriers in the United States are the lowest among the world's advanced economies. Motivating this belief is the notion that there is a tradeoff between market regulation and mobility; advanced European economies are characterized by higher taxes, greater regulation, more union coverage, universal health care, a more comprehensive social contract, etc. Because some see these policies and institutions as impediments to mobility, social and economic mobility is believed to be greater in the United States.

While faith in the American Dream is deep, strong evidence suggests that the United States lacks policies that ensure the opportunities that the dream envisions. According to the data, there is considerably more mobility in most other developed economies.

The report, The State of Working America, 12th Edition,[2] measures the relationship between earnings of fathers and sons in member countries of the Organization for Economic Co-operation and Development (OECD) with similar incomes to the United States and for which data are available. A score of zero would mean there is no relationship, and thus complete intergenerational mobility, with poor children just as likely as rich children to end up as rich adults. The higher the score, the greater the influence of the socio/economic class of his/her birth family on later life position.

The relationship between father-son earnings is higher in the United States than in most peer OECD countries, meaning mobility in this country is among the lowest of major industrialized economies. The relatively low correlations between father-son earnings in Scandinavian countries provide a stark contradiction to the conventional wisdom. They found that people living in the United States have less chance of moving up than people living in Finland, Norway, and Denmark. This means if you are born into a poor family, the chances are greater in this country you will likely stay there when compared to other industrialized nations.[3]

EPIGENETICS

So, what is epigenetics? It is the study of genes and how they are able to express themselves in a variety of ways without actually changing their basic genetic code. It draws language and concepts from the quantum sciences, such as energy, resonance, synchrony and attunement. The field of epigenetics is exploding with new research findings, stirring the age-old debate about nature vs. nurture and whether genes are "set" and create our destiny, or are "fluid" and changeable.

Genetic code can be thought of as "potential." It's a library of possibilities, a "software bank" from which we can download what we need to survive or thrive. Think of newborn infants as computers. They come with an operating system (OS) called "human nature," along with a host of "human nurture" software programs that are available for activation.[4]

The "nurture" experiences in an infant's environment energetically identify which software programs to activate—multiple languages, music, engineering, martial arts, mechanics, childrearing, affection, surviving violence or abuse, sports, art, deprivation, abundance, or adversity. The infant gets a steady stream of "nurture" energy and information from the environment indicating which genetic "nature" software programs are needed for surviving or for thriving. The genes cooperate by downloading or expressing the appropriate software. This invisible process happens through an exchange of energy and information between the child's cells and what is being received from the cultural and family-of-origin environment.[5]

Language and concepts from epigenetics describe and explain how babies develop because of the epigenetic exchanges of information and energy between their Mind/Body/Spirit's and what is happening around them in their environments. Ultimately, epigenetics is about relationships. This invisible interplay is happening all of the time and at an unconscious level. It is largely unconscious, and it can be made conscious.

Let's begin by looking at the role epigenetics plays as a causative factor in trauma, abuse and neglect. Nurturing experiences have a primary influence on how genes express themselves. Nurture is everything that happens in the environment—attachment, parenting, and family-of-origin experiences, including ancestral influences. Nurturing experiences influence our health and our children's health, our ability to learn and remember, and our responses to stress. Nurture is the fabric of the lives led by our parents and grandparents, from their diet to their education, and the care they received as children. It also includes the traumas they suffered and perhaps many other experiences that left their legacy written inside our DNA as "instructions for interpretation."[6]

Epigenetics explains "why Jews whose great-grandparents were in concentration camps, Chinese whose grandparents lived through the ravages of the Cultural Revolution, young immigrants from Africa whose parents survived brutal civil wars and genocidal massacres, and adults who grew up with alcoholic or abusive parents are alike in some ways. They all carry with them more than just their memories. Our experiences and those of our forebears are never gone, even if they have been forgotten. They become a part of us, a molecular residue on our genetic scaffolding. The DNA remains the same, but many psychological and behavioural tendencies are inherited."[7]

An epigenetic experiment unintentionally took place in the Netherlands during World War II. The "hunger winter" was a very cold period from November 1944 to the late spring of 1945 during which a German blockade forced the Dutch to survive on less than a third of their regular caloric intake. For decades afterwards, Dutch and British scientists studied the children who had been exposed to this famine in-utero. These children grew smaller than the Dutch average and their children were also smaller. They also turned out to be more susceptible to diseases of metabolism including diabetes, obesity and cardiovascular disease.[8]

Like the Dutch, the Scots experienced several generations of starvation after the mid 1700's. The lack of sufficient food killed off those with a fast-burning metabolism, while those with slow metabolisms survived. This caused generations of Scots to be prone to obesity. This starvation culture legacy is also common in African Americans and Native Americans, both of which experienced many generations of starvation and a lingering legacy to be over-weight.

It is very clear, now from a scientific perspective, that childhood neglect, physical abuse, and sexual abuse (broadly termed, child maltreatment) have profound and long-term effects on a child's development. This is exactly what the Adverse Childhood Experiences Study revealed. It's also now possible to extrapolate the long-term epigenetic impact of childhood maltreatment on future generations.

The long-term effects of chronic early maltreatment within a caregiving relationship (also known as Developmental Trauma Disorder) on a child shows up in higher rates of psychiatric disorders, increased rates of substance abuse, and a variety of severe relationship difficulties. Child maltreatment is an intergenerational problem. Most frequently, the perpetrators of abuse and neglect are profoundly damaged people who have been abused and neglected themselves.

Abused and neglected children exhibit a variety of behaviours that can lead to any number of diagnoses. However, the effect of early abuse and neglect on the child can be seen in several critical areas of development. These areas include emotional regulation, behavioural regulation, attachment, neurobiology, response flexibility, a coherent integrated sense of self across time, the ability to engage in emotional attunement with significant others (empathy and emotional connectedness). In addition, it affects self-concept, cognitive abilities and learning, and conscience development.[9]

During the first year of life, nature and nurture interactively create a child's Internal Working Model of Reality and attachment style. Both will remain relatively stable into adulthood unless there are significant changes in the child's environment, such as the parents getting therapy and changing the quality of the care-giving input, or the child getting therapy.

Epigenetics is also major factor in healing trauma, neglect and abuse. Working from an epigenetic, resonant field model, what we know is that a person's Mind/Body/Spirit is always interacting with the environment, exchanging information and energy. The protective and defensive structures constructed during the bonding and separation stages in the first three years of life are hard-wired in the brain.

That's not to say that they can be changed, because they can be deconstructed and reconstructed in both therapy and learning experiences. The deconstructing/reconstructing process does, however, require using intervention tools based on epigenetic theory and language to help make the invisible processes of healing and learning become conceptually "visible."

There are two reasons why servant leaders need a basic understanding of the role of epigenetics in human development. The first is from a causative perspective. Epigenetics helps those with histories containing traumatic, neglectful or abusive experiences make sense of what happened to them in their childhood, particularly recognizing what is "right" about their developmental traumas. The second reason is from a healing perspective. Epigenetics helps teachers and therapists use their contractual relationship to support their students and clients in deconstructing and reconstructing Self-parts caused by adverse childhood experiences.

RELIGIOUS BARRIERS

Most of the monotheistic religions are patriarchal in structure. In the Christian religion, the Old Testament of the Bible is a history of patriarchy. The Protestant version of Christianity has softened their patriarchal stances, with many denominations allowing women to become ordained clergy. On the other hand, the Catholic Church has maintained its patriarchal structure with male only clergy. Nuns are allowed to have some power, but are denied full clerical status in the church.[10]

The Belief in Original Sin. If you are interested in being a servant leader and you grew up in a Christian family, you may need to examine more fully some of the beliefs that you were asked to accept. It is hard to define "Christianity" because there are so many variations. What I settled on for my definition was those forms of "Christianity" that believe in original sin. This turns out to be almost all Christian denominations, except for a few.

The exceptions are the Orthodox Church; the so-called Restoration Movement Churches, such as the Church of Christ and the Disciples of Christ; and the Church of Latter Day Saints. This means that about 136 million current Christian church members in this country belong to churches where they believe in the doctrine of original sin.

In many ways it is hard to criticize Christianity because so many people have embraced it as an important part of their lives. I am suggesting that while there are many good things to celebrate about Christianity there maybe some bad things that I believe people should understand. I believe that once people understand both the possible positive and negative effects of some of their Christian beliefs, they can decide what to do with this information that could improve their lives. The best and worst I can say about Modern Christianity is that it promises more than it delivers and it likely has been used to advance the agendas of human predators.

The early Gnostics living in Alexandria, Egypt in 100-200 AD were critical of the emerging Christian doctrines because they saw them as not being able to deliver what they promised and they feared that Christianity was in danger of falling under the influence of the self-serving Illuminati branch of the Mystery teachings. Some members of their Gnostic Mystery Schools, called the Illuminati, misused their initiated knowledge to manipulate the masses into believing that the Christian Church could free the masses from what they called "sinful behavior" and save them from going to hell because of their sins.

Most Gnostics, however, saw through this promise of salvation as a trick to manipulate the masses as self-serving and finally broke their silence and began to speak out against the emerging Christian church. Gnostic teachers, such as Hypathia in Alexandria, were able to easily refute the logic in the Christian arguments, which was done in public oral debates and in their prolific writings. The Gnostics offered spiritual guidance to those who were interested, but did not proselytize or try to convert anybody to their way of thinking.

They had over a thousand years to refine their ideas and were very articulate in defending them. They saw through the Salvationist doctrines that arose in Palestine after about 150 AD as a twisted belief system that trapped the human species in religious codependency with a victim, persecutor, rescuer dynamic. Gnostics believed that this doctrine did not lead to salvation, but instead to servitude of the masses to a false God. They saw the footprints of the self-serving Illuminati all over the doctrine of salvation and decided to speak out against it.[11]

I want to examine the twisted belief of original sin that played a vital role in setting up the salvation scenario. Without an acceptance of the twisted belief in original sin, the rest of the salvation dynamic could not be utilized: No sin, no salvation.

The Origins of Original Sin. Not all Christians accept the doctrine of "original sin." Actually, Augustine of Hippo is said to have invented the concept in the 5th century A.D. After that, it was mostly dormant for almost six centuries until it was re-introduced by Anselm in the 11th century AD, and eventually found its way into medieval church philosophy. From there, it became an accepted belief of the Roman Catholic Church dogma, and was eventually adopted by the Protestants.[12] Neither the Gnostics nor the Pagans believed in original sin or sin itself.

They called what others would call a "sin" merely "ignorance" or a mistake. They believed that people 1) learn by making mistakes 2), need to learn from their mistakes by being able to self-reflect and self-correct and 3), if they failed to learn from their mistakes they were seen as evil, but not sinners. Gnostics also saw that people who were capable of deepening their self-awareness could nip evil in the bud. I would call this becoming aware of and reclaiming your "shadow" parts. It is a vital part of learning to be a servant leader.

Original sin is completely unknown in Judaism and among the indigenous Christian churches of Greece, the Balkans, Africa, Eastern Europe, Russia, and the Muslim faith in the Middle East, Iraq, Iran, and India. According to Islam, every one is born clean. That is why according to a Muslim belief every child will go to heaven no matter whether he/she was born to the worst family on earth or the most religious. The Prophet Mohammad even said that, "He who makes a pilgrimage to Mecca with sincerity will return like the day he was born" - that meant clean of any sin.[13]

In another account, Muslims do not even believe in sin by derivation. They do not believe that Sin is transferable and therefore it should be limited to only the person who committed it. Therefore, in their teachings, a child does not inherit the sins of the father or mother. In Islam, the Quran says in the 2nd chapter (surat al Baqara), that after Adam and Eve sinned, God taught them how to repent, they did, and he forgave them. That's where the issue of the "original sin" ends for Muslims.[14]

The whole concept of original sin seems to be based on a misinterpretation of Romans 5: 12, which teaches us that sin came into the world when

Adam disobeyed God. Eve got the blame for getting him to listen to her instead of obeying God. The result of that sin was his spiritual death or separation from God. The verse goes on to state that everyone since then has also sinned. However, it does not say that we inherited our sin from Adam.

That's an assumption that gradually found its way into the text. In John 3:7 Jesus said, "Flesh gives birth to flesh, but the Spirit gives birth to spirit." In other words - when we are born, we are not spiritual. Without a spiritual connection to God, we follow the impulses of our bodies. We do what feels good. There is nothing inherently sinful about our emotions or our bodily pleasures.

Unfortunately, sin became defined as doing what pleases us without regard to what others have decided is God's will. Since we begin at birth to do what comes naturally - fulfilling our physical and emotional needs - we learn to commit ourselves to our own pleasure. As we grow and begin to become aware that there is something called "right and wrong," we see that others have needs and rights as well. That is when we become aware that we have been seeking self-fulfillment instead of any higher purpose. James 2:14-15 states "each one is tempted when, by his own desire, he is dragged away and enticed. Then, after desire has conceived, it gives birth to sin; and sin, when it is full-grown, gives birth to death."[15]

The other source, said to prove this doctrine, comes from Psalm 51:5 - "Behold, I was shapened in iniquity, and in sin did my mother conceive me." This is all about David's conception and relates to his mother being defined as a sinner, but it does not say that therefore he was born a sinner. That interpretation was added much later.7 Why has this twisted belief persisted for so long? Likely it has persisted because it has become a powerful tool of Christianity to control the masses and win converts to their religion.[16]

Believers are promised redemption from their original sin and salvation if they follow the doctrine of the church, contribute money to the church and continue to look to the church to "rescue" them from their natural sinful ways. If you follow the very lofty standards set up by the Church, your soul will be saved and you will be granted everlasting life. Otherwise, you will burn in hell for eternity. What a choice!

This twisted belief makes you dependent on the approval or disapproval of your behavior by the authority of the church leaders and teaches you to rely on what others tell you is true. As a result, you are programmed to be other-directed rather than self-directed.

In addition, by having to compare yourself to God or Jesus, (What would Jesus do?) you always will fall short and are found wanting or sinful. As a result, someone else now is in charge of determining your self-worth and you are dependent on the hoops they ask you to jump through in order to be saved (from eternal damnation in hell) and be granted everlasting life.

This is a trap that very few people escape from and leads to a lifelong codependency with the church or their religion. This is antithetical to what the servant leader needs to believe. The servant leader strives to free people and not enslave them.

The Twisted Beliefs of the Savior Complex. It is very difficult to criticize established Christian beliefs, because they have been around for so long and so many people seem to believe them. My hope in offering a critique of these core beliefs of Christianity is that it will raise your awareness and, if you are a Christian, cause you to re-examine some of your core beliefs.

I mean no harm to Christians who hold these beliefs. If you claim to be a Christian, I hope you will take another look at these core beliefs of Christianity. If this critique stirs some further study, I hope you will look even deeper into the source of these beliefs. I also hope this analysis helps you see possible negative effects of these beliefs and presents an alternative set of beliefs for you to consider.

I sincerely believe this will support greater awareness of which Christian beliefs advance human potential and which beliefs hold it back. I believe that once you reflect on the positive vs. negative effects of your beliefs; you might consider changing some of them. What are the beliefs that I think Christians need to examine and possibly change? The early Christians built their religion around a set of beliefs that I am calling the "savior complex." It has evolved over the centuries and is still at the core of Christian beliefs. In order to adopt the "savior complex" you have to believe most of the following things:

- There is a heaven and a hell.
- If you do not confess your sins and are not saved you will burn in hell for eternity.
- You have to worship a God who lives in heaven, which is somewhere up in the sky.
- You have to have faith in and believe in the existence of an "unknowable off-planet God."
- Jesus, the Son of God, died on the cross to redeem humans of their sins.

- If you are saved, you will not die and live forever in a place called heaven.
- In order to be saved, you first have to accept the fact that you were born a sinner (original sin) and you will always be a sinner, even if your sins are forgiven.
- You need to be told what is a sin and what is not by the "experts" on these matters because otherwise you wouldn't be able to figure it out for yourself.
- You have to be part of a church and employ the clergy of that church to decide whether or not you have done what you need to do to be saved.
- Because of your sinful nature, you need the church and its clergy to help you keep from sinning and/or to forgive you when you do.
- Otherwise, if you follow your natural urges, you will continue to commit sins and therefore are constantly at risk of eternal damnation.
- In order to determine whether or not you are measuring up, you have to compare yourself to Jesus and be able to accomplish what he reportedly was able to do.
- Otherwise, you are falling short of what a good Christian should be and are instead are a lowly sinner.
- If you believe this set of beliefs, it will determine how well your life works.

What the Gnostics saw in the "savior complex" was a program that led people away from trusting themselves and instead trusting religious authorities to determine their goodness or badness as persons. If I applied this set of dynamics to a psychological context, I would have to say this is a great formula for how to create a False Self to please others. As a result, you do not have to create your own fully individuated Self and can instead rely solely on what pleases the church. Such a Deal!

The church does the job for you and you fall into a trap of believing that they know what is good for you better than you do. This is a formula for victimhood, learned helplessness and codependency. When you give away the power to create your "Self" to others, it is hard to get it back again. The Gnostics spoke out against this belief system because they saw that it led people down a blind alley and did not advance their consciousness. They also were critical of the "savior complex" because they saw how the Illuminati were using this complex to keep people trapped in dependency and victimhood.

The Beliefs of the Gnostics[17]. The set of beliefs that Gnostics held were designed to lead people to develop their ability to think for themselves and advance their consciousness. These beliefs include:

- There is no heaven or hell. Heaven or its equivalent exists here on earth. Hell is a made up concept to scare people.
- The deity to worship is Sophia who is part of everything you see here on earth. There is no off-planet God that you need to worship.
- Faith and belief in an "unknowable off-planet God" is replaced with knowing God from within your own heart and experiencing God all around you on earth.
- Jesus was a wise master, but he did not die on the cross to save us from our sins.
- The resurrection is a story made up by Christians to support the savior complex.
- Salvation comes from freeing yourself from living out of a False Self (other directed) and creating a fully individuated Self (inner directed) to guide your life.
- In this definition, salvation means developing your divine potential and living a moral/ethical life.
- There is no such thing as sin, only mistakes that, with consciousness, can be corrected.
- Evil is a failure to correct the mistakes you are aware of.
- You need to discover the wisdom of your heart to guide your life and you do not need someone else to tell you how to live your life.
- You do not have to be part of a church to be a good person.
- You can discover the true goodness of your heart by coming to know yourself at deeper levels and healing any wounds to your heart that prevent you from knowing and loving yourself.
- You can find that simply by living a conscious life.
- You create your own ethical system and do not need someone else such as the church telling you about what Jesus would do to set the moral/ethical standards for you to live up to.
- Following your natural urges will help you find your true Self. By following your natural urges and by using self-reflection and self-correction you can learn what works and what doesn't work in your life.

As you can see these are two very different sets of beliefs. When Christianity was forming in Egypt and the Middle East around 100 A. D. the Gnostics remained silent at first. They finally decided to speak out when they realized that the savior complex created a trap, a prison where people would not be able to create a fully individuated Self. In addition, they saw that the early Christian beliefs were being used by the Illuminati to control the minds of people and promote their patriarchal agenda.

When the early Christians realized that the Gnostics could rather easily refute their core beliefs, they set out to systematically eliminate them as a threat. Currently, an overwhelming percentage of Republican citizens profess a belief in the end-times (76 percent in 2006). This suggests that any governmental attempts to curb greenhouse emissions will encounter stiff resistance even if every Democrat in the country voted to curb them. They state, "an end-times believer would rationally perceive such efforts to be ultimately futile, and hence ill-advised."[18]

In addition, people who hold this belief see the increasingly more severe weather due to climate change as a fulfillment of the end-times prophecy and conformation of their belief. It appears that changing this twisted belief is virtually impossible.

These people believe that the Bible predicts the future and that we are all living in our last days. This twisted belief is rooted in the Bible's oldest prophetic passages, especially those in Daniel and Ezekiel in the Old Testament and the Book of Revelation in the New Testament. In addition, in a 2006 survey by the Pew Research Center's Forum on Religion & Public Life and the Pew Research Center for the People & the Press, fully 79% of Christians in the U.S. say they believe that Christ will return to Earth. This belief is tied to the belief in end-times in that the Second Coming is supposed to happen immediately after the Armageddon.[19]

The Belief in End Times is Worldwide. A new poll conducted by Reuters found that 1 in 7 people worldwide people also hold a belief that we are living in the end times on Earth. Researchers at Ipsos Global Public Affairs polled 16,262 individuals from more than 20 countries to gather the data. The U. S. and Turkey had the highest percent of end-time believers at 22 percent. France had the lowest.[20]

Twisted Beliefs and Religious Persecution. The twisted beliefs of the Catholic Church and later the Protestant Churches in this country led to the killing of hundreds of thousands of women. The church condemned them to die as witches and heretics. The war against witches by the Catholic Church reached its peek between 1580 and 1660, and officially ended on June 17, 1782 after the Witch Trials, when the last execution took place in Switzerland. The decline and end of witch-hunts and the end to the war against witches in Europe was a very gradual and multifaceted process. It was caused by gradual changes in political, social, philosophical/intellectual, and institutional beliefs arising in late seventeenth century Europe.

As Europe started to step from the 17th century into the 18th century, many societies began to gain stability again, and this helped people realize the craziness that had been going on. The hysteria raged mainly in France, Germany, and Switzerland, but also extended throughout western Europe, into pockets of northern and eastern Europe, and eventually to the American colonies in New England. It is sad to think that all these so called witches were guilty of was their pagan earth-wisdom beliefs that threatened the authority of the Church. Many were victims of vindictive neighbors and others were victims of mass hysteria.

To this day the Church has not admitted that innocent people had been punished on suspicion of witchcraft and yet there is no doubt that sensible people would never permit such a terrible thing to happen. An estimated two hundred thousand suspected witches were accused and about one hundred thousand were executed in Europe even before the Salem Witch Trials. The way the European people thought and believed about such things as witches had a great impact on what happened in Massachusetts.

The European views had a lasting impression on the Puritans, since none of this would have ever happened if they had not been the ancestors of the Europeans themselves. They actually held many of the same twisted religious beliefs that those they fled from had held. We now know that what we likely saw in these witch hunts were unwanted fears related to undiscovered and unhealed developmental trauma that were projected and acted out against others.

Spiritual Bypasses as A Barrier to Understanding Yourself. Another religious barrier to avoid or overcome if you want to be a servant leader is the tendency to use a "spiritual bypass" as a way to avoid working on yourself. Some people who claim to be very religious or spiritual, often use their spiritual beliefs to avoid doing their psychological work. They try to "rise above" the trials and tribulations of everyday life and pretend that they have evolved to a higher level of consciousness.

In truth, these people are often afraid to face their own demons and therefore deny their existence. They focus on "Love and Light" and hope they can hide from their psychological problems. What happens when people do that is that they drive their psychological problems further from their awareness and their problems go deeper into their body and can cause degenerative diseases.

EDUCATIONAL BARRIERS

The servant leader must begin by understanding the true purpose of education as it is currently structured. The purpose of our current educational system is to prepare people to fit in society. What is expected under this structure is that people have to take orders, be obedient and endure boredom. A substantive quality education should teach the curious developing mind to be critical and discriminating, willing to ask questions, challenging the status quo of preconceived suppositions and accepted dogma. Servant leaders need to be willing to do this and help restore this quality to our nation's schools.

The Dumbing Down of K-12 Education. The deliberate "dumbing down" of Our K-12 schools stared around the turn of the 20th century. It was a time of progressive reforms and the members of the Global Elite were frightened that kids would read in their textbooks about the "robber barons" and the greedy industrialists who savagely repressed workers, maintained sweat shops and mistreated minorities. Therefore, Andrew Carnegie, through the Carnegie Foundation offered all the leading writers of U. S. history books grants to rewrite U. S. history books.

They all submitted their revisions to the Foundation Staff who then chose the version that made the robber barons look like the good guys and those striking workers like the bad guys who demanded more than they were worth. They also omitted all references to the labor strikes where they hired thugs to beat up and kill workers. They also removed all references to the Native Americans and how they were exploited by the government and corporations. Finally, they omitted most of what we now call Black History.[21]

The Rockefeller Foundation, not to be outshined, created a General Education Board, as part of the Foundation. Here is what the Chairman of the Board, Frederick Gates, wrote in 1912 about "The Country School of Tomorrow:"[22] "In our dreams...people yield themselves with perfect docility to our molding hands. The present educational conventions [intellectual and character education] fade from our minds, and unhampered by tradition we work our own good will upon a grateful and responsive folk. We shall not try to make these people or any of their children into philosophers or men of learning or men of science.

We have not to raise up from among them authors, educators, poets or men of letters. We shall not search for embryo great artists, painters, musicians, nor lawyers, doctors, preachers, politicians, statesmen, of whom we have ample supply. The task we set before ourselves is very simple...we will organize children...and teach them to do in a perfect way the things their fathers and mothers are doing in an imperfect way."

Some have called our modern K-12 educational structure "factory schooling." The school day is structured much the same way a factory is structured with a rigid schedule. Bells ring to separate tasks, students have to sit in rows of desks and obey the rules that they did not make and then if they are compliant they get rewarded with a short lunch break where they get to eat food that has low nutritional value. All this is an attempt to make our schools look like the factories these students would eventually work in.

For most of the 20th century, The Global Elite and its member organizations and think tanks have been involved in a grand experiment. They have been engaged in social engineering with America's youth to homogenize a lowest common denominator product of sub par mediocrity, creating generations of young Americans who can neither read nor write, nor think for themselves in any critical manner.

According to a study last year by the US Department of Education, 19% of US high school graduates cannot read, 21% of adults read below 5th grade level and that these alarming rates have not changed in the last ten years.

The main purpose of educating the masses used to be to prepare people to think critically and be able to make wise decisions essential to living in a democracy. The current educational system is no longer about even learning the basic A-B-C's, but simply cranking out a subclass of work force laborers, who will obey the rules and not cause any trouble.

Schools also age-grade both boys and girls, when everybody knows girls develop at a faster rate for the first 16 years. Boys eventually catch up developmentally. Who knows the effects on males of always playing catch up to females? They also use a punitive approach to learning where all mistakes are highlighted and only the top students in the class get any rewards.

Traditionally, our schools were considered a local matter. Locally elected School Boards made sure the schools were meeting the educational needs of the local children. Gradually, the federal government sent money to the states to funnel to the local school districts. The states took the federal money because that meant they did not have to use as much of their budget to fund the schools in their state.

Then came the federal mandate, No Child Left Behind, a program designed to gain federal control of our nation schools. It was a transparent corporatized privatization takeover. Behind the double speak deceit of No Child Left Behind, Washington began blackmailing school districts across America with the threat of cutting off federal funds should their test scores fail to make the cut. This has forced schools to "teach for the tests."

Now Washington could unlawfully dictate mandates to the 1600 US school districts to make them comply with in order to avoid a cutoff of any federal dollars. Thus, local school districts throughout this nation came under a subversive assault from the long arm of our authoritarian totalitarian government. Should a school district accept even $1 from the federal government, it automatically had to relinquish control to the feds, thus providing no choice to the locals.

The federal government busily ramroded its agenda pushing standardized tests and test performance as the packaged panacea in the form of Common Core standards and privatized charter schools under the guise of tax paid public education. Of course, school privatization in many districts around this Christian nation also means Creationism was now going to be being taught instead of evolution. Naturally, this systemic dumbing down of our educational system also permeates a parallel process in the dumbing down of textbooks sold to the schools. The omission of truth and inclusion of false disinformation and propaganda in school textbooks are just another form of indoctrinated mind control.

As states reduced their educational budgets, teachers were burdened with more overcrowding in their classrooms, with 30 or more students as is extremely common today. This became a deliberate a setup for failure to provide an enriching learning environment.

Predictably this leads to the above scenario of a dumbed down ADHD-drug pushing classroom culture. Yet, this is typically what happens to children and young people who are generally sharper in intellect and creativity, but are inadequately engaged, stimulated and challenged in the classroom.

The one size fits all cookie cutter educational system stifles learning, cognitive and intellectual development and creativity. It rewards those who acquiesce and simply do what they are told as good little boys and girls on their way to being good little employees and citizens. They are now easily manipulated, controlled and subdued. They become the lifeless, walking dead who merely go through the daily motions on autopilot, too beaten down, numb and/or fearful.

The Dumbing Down of Higher Education. Around 1973 David Rockefeller founded a conservative think tank called the Trilateral Commission. The membership of the Trilateral Commission is composed of about 400 distinguished leaders in business, media, academia, public service (excluding current national Cabinet Ministers), labor unions, and other non-governmental organizations from the three regions. The regional chairmen, deputy chairmen, and directors constitute the leadership of the Trilateral Commission, along with an Executive Committee including about 40 other members.[23]

Since 1973, the Trilateral Commission has met regularly in plenary sessions to discuss policy position papers developed by its members. Policies are debated in order to achieve consensuses. Respective members return to their own countries to implement policies consistent with those consensuses.

The original stated purpose of "New International Economic Order." Its current statement has morphed into fostering a "closer cooperation among these core democratic industrialized areas of the world with shared leadership responsibilities in the wider international system."

Since the Carter administration, Trilateralists have held these very influential positions: Six of the last eight World Bank Presidents; all the Presidents and Vice-Presidents of the United States (except for Obama and Biden); over half of all US Secretaries of State; and three quarters of the Secretaries of Defense. In 1973,

One of their first tasks was to examine the role of education in our democracy. They wrote a position paper titled, "The Crisis of Democracy."[24] The conclusion of this report was that the population of the U. S. is overeducated. As a result of what they were taught in school children expected to have a life of their own and to be in control of how their life works. They decided to deliberately "dumb-down" our higher education system in every way they could.

They reduced federal and state spending on public higher education. Ronald Reagan helped their cause by eliminating free public higher education in California. Their goal was to lower the job expectations of those who received a college degree.

Within two years they had most of the top federal cabinet officials, including President Carter, in their membership. The first move was to make sure that the history that was taught in our nations schools contained nothing about the roots of social or economic inequality or the workings of capitalism. They did not want anybody to ask hard questions. Our history also omitted what was needed to understand how power works in this country and thus those in power protected themselves from public scrutiny.

Four years prior to the Trilateral Commission report, in 1971, the infamous and secret 'Powell Memo' was issued. It was written by a corporate lawyer and tobacco company board member, Lewis F. Powell, Jr. (whom President Nixon nominated to the Supreme Court two months later). It was addressed to the Chairman of the Education Committee of the U.S. Chamber of Commerce, representing American business interests.

Powell lamented the conclusions of reports indicating that colleges were graduating students who "despise the American political and economic system," and thus, who would be inclined to move into power and create change, or outright challenge the system head on. This marked a form of "intellectual warfare" being waged against the system. Powell, who then quoted economist Milton Friedman of the University of Chicago (and the 'father' of neoliberalism), who stated: "It [is] crystal clear that the foundations of our free society are under wide-ranging and powerful attack—not by Communists or any other conspiracy but by misguided individuals parroting one another and unwittingly serving ends they would never intentionally promote."[25]

Powell elaborated, "there is reason to believe that the campus [university/education] is the single most dynamic source," as "social science faculties usually include members who are unsympathetic to the enterprise system." These academics, explained Powell, "need not be in the majority," as they "are often personally attractive and magnetic; they are stimulating teachers, and their controversy attracts student following; they are prolific writers and lecturers; they author many of the textbooks, and they exert enormous influence—far out of proportion to their numbers—on their colleagues and in the academic world." Such a situation he saw as, naturally, horrific and deplorable! Imagine that, having magnetic, stimulating and prolific teachers.

His twisted beliefs looked at this with horror and despair for what this would bring the world. He urged the Chamber to create "a staff of speakers of the highest competency" which "might include the scholars," and establish a 'Speaker's Bureau' which would "include the ablest and most effective advocates form the top echelons of American business."

This staff of scholars, which Powell emphasized, should be referred to as "independent scholars," should then engage in a continuing program of evaluating "social science textbooks, especially in economics, political science and sociology." The objective of this would "be oriented toward restoring the balance essential to genuine academic freedom." This meant, of course, implanting ideological indoctrination and propaganda from the business world. Powell described this move as the "assurance of fair and factual treatment of our system of government and our enterprise system, its accomplishments, its basic relationship to individual rights and freedoms, and comparisons with the systems of socialism, fascism and communism."[26]

Powell lamented that the "civil rights movement insisted on re-writing many of the textbooks in our universities and schools," and "labor unions likewise insisted that textbooks be fair to the viewpoints of organized labor." Thus, Powell contended, in the business world should re-write textbooks and education to be fair to business, He concluded that, this process "should be regarded as an aid to genuine academic freedom and not as an intrusion upon it."[27]

He said that the "only alternatives to free enterprise" are to be presented as "varying degrees of bureaucratic regulation of individual freedom–ranging from that under moderate socialism to the iron heel of the leftist or rightist dictatorship."[28] In 1973, a mere two years after the memo was written, the Heritage Foundation was founded as an "aggressive and openly ideological expert organization," which became highly influential in the Reagan administration.

These right-wing think tanks helped bring in the era of neo-liberalism, bringing together "scholars" who support the so-called "free market" system (itself, a mythical fallacy), and who deride and oppose all forms of social welfare and social support. The think tanks produced the research and work, which supported the dominance of the banks and corporations over society, and the members of the think tanks had their voices heard through the media, in government, and in the universities.

They facilitated the ideological shift in power and policy circles toward neo-liberalism. The era of neoliberal globalization marked a rapid decline of the liberal welfare states that had emerged in the previous several decades, and as such, directly affected education.

Reports from the World Bank and the Organization for Economic Co-operation and Development (OECD) in the 1990s transformed these ideas into a "policy template." This was to establish "a new coalition between education and industry," in which "education if reconfigured as a massively undervalued form of knowledge capital that will determine the future of work, the organization of knowledge institutions and the shape of society in the years to come."

In the revised neoliberal model of education, "economic productivity was seen to come not from government investment in education, but from transforming education into a product that could be bought and sold like anything else–and in a globalised market, Western education can be sold as a valuable commodity in developing countries." Thus, within the university itself, the meaning of 'productivity' was shifted away from a generalized social and economic good towards a notional dollar value for particular government-designated products and practices.

The new 'management' strategy for universities entailed decreased state funding while simultaneously increasing "heavy (and costly) demands on accounting for how that funding was used," and thus, "trust in professional values and practices was no longer the basis of the relationship" between universities and government. It was argued that governments were no longer able to afford the costs of university education, and that the efficiency" of the university system–defined as "doing more with less"–was to require a change in the leadership and management system internal to the university structure to "a form of managerialism modeled on that of the private sector."

The solution for the self-serving elites was simple: less democracy, more authority. In the educational realm, this meant more elite control over universities, less freedom and activism for intellectuals and students.

Universities and the educational system more broadly was to become increasingly privatized, corporatized, and globalized. The age of activism was at an end, and universities were to be mere assembly plants for economically productive units, which support the system, not challenge it.

One of the key methods for ensuring this took place was through debt, which acts as a disciplinary mechanism in which students are shackled with the burden of debt bondage, and thus, their education itself must be geared toward a specific career and income expectation. Knowledge is sought for personal and economic benefit more than for the sake of knowledge itself.

One of the consequences of this economic slavery is that many young people have to move in with their parents. This used to be a rare occurrence, but now it is quite the norm. Over 32 percent of millennials (18-34) now live with their parents because they cannot find a job that covers their expenses, like repayment of student loans. This is up form about 20 percent in 1956. It is actually higher for young men than young women. Over 35 percent of young men lived with their parents in 2014 and about 28 percent of young women.[29]

Graduating with extensive debt then implies a need to immediately enter the job market, if not already having entered the job market part time while studying. Debt thus disciplines the student toward a different purpose in their education: toward a job and financial benefits rather than toward knowledge and understanding. Activism then, is more of an impediment to, rather than a supporter of knowledge and education.[30]

This process has left us with an almost illiterate population that is compliant and unquestioning. Some students, who didn't get the message, protested and were severely punished or expelled to show others what happens to you when you don't go along with the system.

This condition now makes it possible for demigods to run for public office and never present any ideas that would bring about progressive change in this country. Donald Trump took advantage of this situation and seized the GOP nomination.

THE THREAT OF AI

This part of our technology advancement is rather shocking. It doesn't seem possible to have advanced so quickly in the field of cybernetics. The rapid advancement of this filed now poses a threat that was unknown ten years ago.

This was science fiction as some of your might remember in watching the Terminator movies. Starting in 1984 with release of the original Terminator film we were introduced to cyber world technology. In case you haven't watched this movies, here is a short summary of them. In the year 2029, Skynet, a global computerized defense network that controls machines called Terminators, is losing the war against the humans.

Just before the resistance is victorious, Skynet sends a cyborg Terminator, a Cyberdyne Systems T-800 series model 101, back in time to the year 1984 to kill Sarah Connor, the mother of John Connor who is the future leader of the human resistance. Sergeant Kyle Reese volunteers to go back in time to protect Sarah. Reese ultimately stops the Terminator. Sarah becomes pregnant with John, Reese's child. The Terminator's endoskeleton arm is left behind in a hydraulic press.

Ten years later, a manufacturing corporation called Cyberdyne Systems uses the endoskeleton arm to make advances in technology. Skynet sends a new liquid metal Terminator, the T-1000, back through time to kill the 10-year-old John Connor. The resistance sends the T-800 back to protect him. Sarah Connor, now in a mental health facility in California, teams up with her son and the T-800 to break into Cyberdyne. Together with Miles Bennett Dyson the creator of Skynet, they blow up Cyberdyne Systems. Dyson dies in the explosion. The T-800 destroys the T-1000 and himself. They believe they have stopped Judgment Day.

In 2003, CRS (Cyber Research Systems) has taken over the work of Cyberdyne Systems. Sarah Connor is dead, without a purpose in life; John Connor becomes a drug-addicted drifter living off the grid. Judgment Day is inevitable, it has only been delayed. Because John Connor can't be found, a new weaponized Terminator called the T-X is sent back to terminate future officers of the resistance. In the future John Connor is dead, killed by a T-800 infiltrator.

Kate, John's wife, sends the T-800 back in time to protect her and John before Judgment Day. In order to shutdown a malicious computer virus that is attacking military networks, Skynet is given system wide control over the military. Skynet becomes self-aware and launches an attack on mankind initiating Judgment Day. The T-800 is destroyed while defeating the T-X. John and Kate survive the attack inside an old military fallout shelter called Crystal Peak.

In 2003, a murderer on death row named Marcus Wright donates his body for research to Cyberdyne Systems. He mysteriously wakes up in the year 2018 to find an ongoing war between machines and humans.

Wright teams up with a teenage Kyle Reese, who will become John Connor's father in the future. The resistance uncovers a way to cut off a signal that Skynet uses to communicate with the machines. John Connor volunteers to test it.

When Reese is captured and taken back to Skynet, Wright, who is really a Cyborg with a human heart, must team up with a reluctant Connor to save Reese. At Skynet, Marcus Wright learns he was programmed to infiltrate the resistance and lead Connor back to Skynet so he can be killed by the T-800. Together Wright and Connor defeat the T-800 and blow up Skynet. Connor is injured during the battle. Wright volunteers his human heart to save Connor and symbolically receives salvation for his past crimes.[31]

We are no longer talking about science fiction. By 2020 experts predict we will enter the Cyborg Age. This means that computer scientists working with Artificial Intelligence will be able build a super human robot that will exceed human intelligence. In the computer sciences this point is known as "Singularity."

At that moment machines will no longer need human control to operate (and potentially can control us). They plan to offer a "chip" or series of chips that will be surgically imbedded under our skin that will produce a "super human" or a machine that will take over our brain and nervous system and allow us to be connected to super intelligence, super strength, and be able to heal all our diseases granting us eternal life.

Doesn't this sound wonderful? So why is it a threat? Well, the devil is in the details as they say. What humans will have to give up is their free will, their soul and their ability to have feelings, the good ones as well as bad ones. Many people, who do not want to do their inner work and are feeling unhappy with their life, will jump at this opportunity to live a better and longer life.

The real threat is that these machines can decide that organic humans are like a virus on the Earth and decide to get rid of them. Awareness of this diabolical possibility may help shape the way we utilize this technology. It will be up to servant leaders to help those with less consciousness understand the consequences if they choose this method to raise their consciousness.[32]

NOTES

1   Prescott, J. (Nov. 1975). Body pleasure and the origins of violence. Bulletin of the Atomic Scientists. pp 10-20. http://www.violence.de/prescott/bulletin/article.html

2   Mishel, L., et. Al. (November 2012). The state of working America, Twelfth Edition. Ithaca, NY: Cornell University press.

3   Gould, E. (October 10, 2012). U.S. lags behind peer countries in mobility. Economic Policy Institute. http://www.epi.org

4   Weinhold, B. (2014). The twisted beliefs of human predators. Swannanoa, NC: CICRCL Press

5   Lipton, B. (2005). The biology of belief. Santa Rosa, CA: Mountain of Love/Elite Books.

6   Peckham, H. (July 17, 2013). Epigenetics: the dogma-defying discovery that genes learn from experience. International Journal of Neuropsychotherapy, 1, 9-20.

7   Becker-Weidman, A. (2014). Attachment-Focused Psychotherapy & Epigenetics: What your grandparents passed on. www.center4familydevelop.com/Epigenetics.pdf

8   Starvation effects handed down for generations, Science News, July 31, 2015 https://www.sciencedaily.com/releases/2015/07/150731105240.htm

9   Becker-Weidman, A. (Sept. 22, 2015). Child Abuse and Neglect: Effects on child development, brain development, psychopathology, and interpersonal relationships. http://www.center4familydevelop.com/CHILD%20ABUSE%20AND%20NEGLECT-effects.pdf

10 Tarico, V. (June 11.2012). 8 Ugly Sins of the Catholic Church. Alternet.

11 Weinhold, B. (2014). The twisted beliefs of human predators. Asheville, NC: CICRCL Press.

12 Ibid.

13 Lash, J. (2006). Not in his image. White River Junction, VT: Chelsea Green Pubs.

14 Ibid.

15 Wikipedia. Original Sin. http://en.wikipedia.org/wiki/Original_sin

16 Wikipedia. Original sin.

17 Lash, J. Not In His Image. p. 18.

18 Ibid. p 239.

19 Ibid. p. 238.

20 One in Seven (14%) "Global Citizens Believe End of the World is Coming in Their Lifetime." (May 1, 2012). Ipsos Change Changers. http://www.ipsos-na.com/news-polls/press release.aspx?id=561021

21 Weinhold, B. Twisted beliefs of human predators. p. 53.

22 Hagopian, J. (Aug. 14. 2014). The Dumbing Down of America–By Design. Global Research. http://www.globalresearch.ca/the-dumbing-down-of-america-by-design/5395928

23 Gates, F. (1024). The country school of tomorrow. New York: General Education Board.

24 Marshall, A. Class War and the College Crisis: The "Crisis of Democracy" and the Attack on Education. https://andrewgavinmarshall.com/2012/04/02/class-war-and-the-college-crisis-the-crisis-of-democracy-and-the-attack-on-education/

25 Ibid.

26 Giroux, H. (Oct. 01, 2009). The Powell Memo and the Teaching Machines of Right-Wing Extremists. Truthout/Perspective http://www.truth-out.org/archive/item/86304-the-powell-memo-and-the-teaching-machines-of-rightwing-extremists

27 Ibid.

28 Ibid.

29   Bahrampour, T. (May 25, 2016) For millennials, living with mom and dad is the norm. The Gazette. p.1.

30   Marshall, A. (April 2, 2012). Class War and the College Crisis: The "Crisis of Democracy" and the Attack on Education. https://andrewgavinmarshall.com/2012/04/02/class-wa-and-the-college-crisis-the-crisis-of-democracy-and-the-attack-on-education/

31   John, V. (December 5, 2014). Terminator movies Explained in Four Paragraphs. Movienewz. http://www.movienewz.com/terminator-movie-explained-in-four-paragraphs/

32   Henry, W. (2015). The skingularity is near. williamhenry.net

CHAPTER 11

STRATEGIES FOR OVERCOMING ANY PERSONAL/PSYCHOLOGICAL BARRIERS TO SERVANT LEADERSHIP

"In order to have sustainable community you have to make sure the people are sustainable. This means healing trauma."

— *Jarmbi Githabul, Narakwal/Gitabul Custodian*

STRATEGIES FOR OVERCOMING YOUR PERSONAL/PSYCHOLOGICAL BARRIERS

HEALING YOUR DEVELOPMENTAL TRAUMAS

Our research over the past 26 years has helped me better understand why even smart people have twisted beliefs and suffer from premature hardening of the categories. They are suffering from hidden and unhealed developmental traumas that started in the first three years of their lives. In order to become a servant leader, you will need to identify and heal these hidden developmental traumas.

Once you learn how to "connect the dots," you will begin to understand the sources of your current conflicts and relationship problems. Once your begin to understand the power of hidden and unhealed developmental shocks, traumas or stresses to cause relationship conflicts, you will have a better idea of what you need to do to heal the effects of these early traumas on your relationships. If you are interested in identifying and healing these traumas, I suggest that you to do some or all of the following:

1. Read one of our books to help you identify the unseen and unhealed developmental shocks, traumas or stresses that are still influencing your life. The two books I recommend are Healing Developmental Trauma: A Systemic Approach to Counseling Individuals, Couples and Families[1]

and Developmental Trauma: The Game Changer in the Mental Health Profession.[2] These books are available on our website and at Amazon.

In addition, read the four new e-books in the Twisted Beliefs Series available on Amazon. There are many self-inventories in these books to help you identify what events in your life have contributed to developing twisted beliefs and how they might be affecting your life.[3]

2. Learn to utilize some kind of trauma reduction techniques that eventually change the neural pathways in your brain and body. These create sensory distortions because of an early childhood shock, trauma or stressor. You will need to create new neural pathways to replace the ones created because of these early shocks, traumas or stresses. In our book, Healing Developmental Trauma, we describe several techniques that have proved successful to heal these traumas. The four books in the Twisted Beliefs Book Series also include tools to help you change these beliefs.

3. Use the tools that we offer you to clear your mind-body of the memories connected with the early shocks, traumas or stresses. All the books we mentioned above describe many ways that have proven successful in clearing these early memories.

4. Change some of your mistaken thoughts and beliefs connected to your early experiences of developmental shock, trauma, and stress. Again, our books describe tools to help you do this.

5. Learn how to re-regulate your dysregulated emotional responses that are connected to the long-term effects of unhealed early developmental shocks, traumas or stresses. This is a skill that you can utilize in your relationships. Again, we have described many tools in our books to help you learn how to do this.

6. Heal any inner splits you may have in your thoughts and feelings. The experience of early developmental shock, trauma or stress can cause you to dissociate and experience an inner split between or among the various inner parts of yourself. We have developed a number of effective tools to help you reconnect your internal splits that are described in our books.

7. Change your twisted beliefs or distorted perceptions. The last and perhaps the most important step is to change any of your distorted perceptions of your self-other relationship dynamics caused by early developmental shock, trauma or stress. The early shocks, trauma or stresses

occur in relationships with the most important people in your life. It is only natural that when your adult relationships get close enough, these distorted beliefs will show up. We have created tools that committed couples can use to heal these distortions. Our books describe how a couple might use these tools to help each other heal the effects of early shock, trauma or stress and help each other change your twisted beliefs.

WHAT IS A BELIEF?

A belief is a choice or a decision to accept a statement, truth, or fact without direct personal experience or observation, based upon the testimony or work of another person or a source that you trust. Common sources of beliefs are gossip, secondhand information, and parental stories. Beliefs also can come from cultural myths or from religious texts such as the Koran, Bible, or Torah. Beliefs usually create a philosophical foundation that people can use for moral guidance and direction in their lives. Most beliefs are formed very early in life (usually before the age of ten.) I suggest that you examine all the beliefs you may have formed early in life and see if they actually are still true in your life. Usually, to change your behavior, you also have to change your beliefs.[4]

IDENTIFYING YOUR TWISTED BELIEFS

Below is a list of common twisted beliefs that people hold about themselves, other people and the world around them that cause them to suffer from premature hardening of the categories. Servant leaders have to examine their beliefs and change any beliefs that are twisted in some way.

1. **"Deep down, I believe I am unlovable."** (Try listing your good qualities and your bad ones and see which list is longer).
2. **"It is risky to ask others directly to help meet my needs because I believe they might reject me.** Instead, I have to manipulate them into giving me what I need without ever having to ask them directly."
3. **"I believe I am permanently flawed in some important way: I am not pretty enough, smart enough, rich enough to succeed, etc."**
4. **"I believe it is best to avoid conflicts at all costs because they are dangerous."**
5. **"I believe that other people are much smarter than I am, therefore I should listen to what they tell me to do."**
6. **"I believe that once I became an adult, I left behind all the bad things that happened to me as a child and they longer affect my life."**

7. "I believe that other people are lazy and motivated mostly by fear."

8. "I believe I have to beat others to the punch in order to get ahead in the world."

8. "I believe I have to beat others to the punch in order to get ahead in the world."

9. "I believe the world is a scary place and I must always be on guard to prevent something bad from happening to me."

10. "I don't believe I have to be bound by the rules or laws of society like everybody else. This is because I am smarter than they are so I won't get caught if I break the rules or laws."

This set of twisted beliefs supports what many have called, "vulture capitalism." Malcolm X said this about capitalism, "Capitalism used to be like an eagle, but now it's more like a vulture." Albert Einstein cited the crippling of individuals as the worst evil of capitalism. He said, "Our whole educational system suffers from this evil. An exaggerated competitive attitude is inculcated in the student, who is trained to worship acquisitive success as a preparation."[5]

Many of us who want to be servant leaders have been tricked or manipulated into supporting the lies we have been told, and find ourselves in the unpardonable position of unwittingly giving support to vulture capitalism. If you find yourself in this kind of dilemma, there are many things you can do about this problem. The first step is to recognize who these self-serving leaders are and how to avoid supporting their nefarious agenda. This book will help you identify where you might be supporting self-serving leaders of the world and what to do about it.

This book is designed to help you learn ways you can withdraw your support for these self-serving belief systems and how to create alternative servant leadership belief systems. Before you can withdraw your support from these self-serving belief systems, you need to be able to look inward and ask yourself some of the following questions:

1. What beliefs do I have that have caused me to give my support to these self-serving systems?

2. How can I educate myself so I know when I am being lied to and manipulated into supporting self-serving behaviors?

3. How can I improve my life by changing some of my beliefs and get free from supporting self-serving systems?

4. How can I learn not to give my support to self-serving systems?

5. How can I contribute my servant leader gifts and talents to help create a world where the self-serving leaders no longer are in control?

FIVE QUESTIONS YOU NEED TO ASK TO CHALLENGE ANY BELIEF

1. What is the evidence for this belief? Looking objectively at all of my life experience, what is the evidence that makes this true?
2. Does this belief invariably or always hold true for me?
3. Does this belief look at the whole picture? Does it take into account both positive and negative ramifications?
4. Does this belief promote my well-being and/or peace of mind?
5. Did I choose this belief on my own or did it develop out of my experience of growing up in my family?

A STRATEGY FOR BREAKING FREE OF THE MATRIX

In Chapter Eight, I briefly discussed the need to break free of six levels of the Matrix. Learning how to break free of this illusionary reality can be a daunting task. We have attempted to develop strategies and tools that make this shift of consciousness possible. Below is a simple, but profoundly important strategy for breaking free of the Matrix. I invite you to use this exercise to challenge your assumptions and beliefs, as well as change the behaviors that stem from these assumptions and beliefs.

Have You Ever Surrendered Unconditionally? I believe that this is a necessary step in breaking free of the Matrix. What does it mean to "surrender unconditionally?" First, you need to understand what "surrender" means. It is not what you think it is.

There are two forms of "surrender" and you will need to master both forms in order to be able to truly surrender unconditionally and break free of the Matrix. First, there is a feminine form of surrender. This means "the willingness to receive without resistance." This involves taking in what others say and do that may be very unpleasant to receive. It also means truly receiving and understanding what is being said or done, without "screening out" the parts you don't want to hear or see.

Most people have developed ways to screen out whatever they don't want to hear or see before it really reaches them and thus have resistance to accepting what is happening. This can involve thinking of what you are going to say or do to counter what is being said or done before you have actually taken it in and experienced it inside yourself. You may be thinking of what you can say to make what the other person wrong in some way. You may tighten your stomach muscles or even shorten your breath to avoid in the moment taking in what is happening. Another form of is resistance trying to fix the other person. This often involves "rescuing" them instead of just listening to them.

Receiving without resistance will take practice, so be gentle with yourself as you learn how to do this. It took me about 5 years to truly learn how to do this consistently. I hope that it will not take you that long.

A second form of surrender is the masculine form, which is "taking charge without guilt or shame." Here it involves taking action on your own behalf to get your needs met without sabotaging yourself with built-in excuses that are designed to protect your ego if you fail in your efforts. You might say to yourself or others, "I could have done that but...." I would have been successful if so and so hadn't interfered." "I just don't deserve to get my needs met" or "Things always seem stacked against me." In short there is always some excuse or "but" in your thinking that prevents you from fully taking charge of your life. You need to get that "but" out of your way if you are going to adopt the masculine form of surrender.

WHAT ARE THE ELEMENTS OF A DECLARATION OF UNCONDITIONAL SURRENDER?

There are four main elements in a declaration of unconditional surrender. They are experienced as an internal process, so you will have to go deep inside to fully experience each of these elements. This process was taken from an ancient Hawaiian healing process called, ho'oponopono.[6] I suggest that you meditate on each of these elements and look for the deepest meanings of each of them for you. In Chapter Fifteen, I describe even more about this process, including the history of how it was created, how it has been utilized and the potential for its uses in the future.

The First Element: "I am sorry." To gain access the first element say to yourself, "I am sorry." This means confessing your role in helping to create the Matrix and believing in the most basic tenet of the Matrix, which is, "We are all separate." The truth is that you belong to one human race and "we are all one."

This truth was hidden from you while you were participating in the Matrix, but must now be experienced at your deepest awareness, if you ever hope to break free of the Matrix. You will need to feel the deep grief and re-

236

morse that goes with accepting this truth. What does it mean to you to finally embrace this truth and accept your true place in the human race?

To fully experience the true meaning of this element, you will have to utilize the feminine form of surrender and allow yourself to fully receive this truth without any resistance. This means letting the truth sink in and then utilizing the masculine form of surrender.

This means taking charge of changing all your beliefs and behaviors that were based on the lies that you were taught about those "other people" who were portrayed as being different from you. You need to do that without feeling guilty or shameful. To fully embrace this truth you have to develop deep empathy for yourself and for others.

The Second Element: "Please forgive me." In order to break free of the matrix you have to forgive yourself for not knowing any better. You may think of yourself as an evolved, conscious being but when you see your areas of blindness or ignorance, you have to forgive yourself. By doing this you will free yourself from the guilt and shame that keeps you trapped in the Matrix.

Forgiveness actually means to "give back" or "for-give." What you have to give back is all the misinformation that you took in as the truth to whomever it was who gave it to you. You may want to turn this into a writing exercise where you make a list of everything that you learned that you now see was not true.

You can associate this information with certain people like a teacher who taught you a version of American History that you now know is false. I suggest you not blame these people because remember they like you were also trapped in the Matrix. Give them back the misinformation and send it through them to the sources of the misinformation from the unknown people whoever they might be.

The second part of forgiveness involves giving back to yourself the truth about who you really are and fully accepting yourself as a divine member of the human race. You have to let go of any limiting beliefs about yourself that you mistakenly took on as defining who you are. This actually may have been a projection of something someone gave you that they didn't want to look at. By forgiving yourself for believing these untruths, you can take charge of fully actualizing your true self without guilt or shame.

The Third Element: "Thank you." Now you can begin to express your appreciations to others and to yourself for breaking free of the illusions of the

Matrix. You need to thank yourself for being willing to forgive yourself and others and let go of the burdens that kept you trapped in the Matrix.

You may want to write out a list of affirmations you wish to use to remind yourself of how you have surrendered unconditionally, like: "I am grateful that I have let go of all the burdens and mistaken beliefs that have trapped me in the Matrix." or "I completely let go of the illusion that I am separate from others and fully accept my common connection to all other human beings."

As for others, your task is to thank them for being willing to let go of any illusions of separateness they may have held and for accepting your apology. Finally, thank them for having compassion for our common struggle to break free of the Matrix.

The Fourth Element: "I love you." The final task in the process of unconditional surrender is to love yourself unconditionally. This means being willing to let go of your negative self talk and totally accepting and loving all your flaws and shortcomings. This can be an enormous task, because a big part of living in the Matrix has been accepting the notion that there is something wrong with you and or you are flawed in some essential way.

When you live in the Matrix, you are supposed to feel guilty for having needs and shameful if you try to get them met. This is what traps you in the Matrix and keeps you from trying to break free. Breaking free in itself is an attempt to get your needs met and is considered a shameful act and is forbidden. You will need to pay close attention to your thoughts and let go of any negative thoughts designed to condemn yourself for having needs or shame you for trying to get them met.

This process will require that you give careful attention to not only your conscious negative thoughts, feelings and beliefs, but also those in your sub-conscious. Under the conscious mind lurks the vast reservoir of unconscious negative thoughts, feelings and beliefs connected with what you were taught about who you are and your role in the Matrix. The best way to break through this illusion is to begin to surrender unconditionally to all the good things about yourself again without guilt or shame or without resistance.

Make a list of all the good things you see in yourself and then ask a loved one to add to your list. Be willing to take in and fully receive all these good qualities about yourself without any resistance. Notice if you have a tendency to qualify or in some way resist taking in all these good things.

Next, you will have to do the same for others. Instead of focusing on any perceived shortcomings, you will need to acknowledge all the good you can identify in others, especially those that you are prone to judge in some negative way. This can get difficult in the cases of those who engage in life-taking behavior.

You may need to first take a look at your own life-taking behaviors, even though they are not as extreme as those you are prone to judge. As part of the Matrix, we all were taught life-taking behaviors and we need to go through the four elements to uncover and free ourselves of our own life-taking behaviors. Once you have done that, it may become easier to forgive and love those who still engage in life-taking behavior.

SUMMARY

This journey through the process of unconditional surrender can be quite painful if you are truly honest with yourself. If done well, it should bring up sadness, grief and remorse as we fully realize what we have missed by being trapped in the Matrix. It also should help you lift a huge burden from your shoulders that you and everybody who is trapped in the Matrix is expected to carry. Removing this burden should bring joy as well as sadness and excitement as well as fear.

Once outside the Matrix you are in uncharted waters and you will have to take charge of your life without guilt or shame and assume full responsibility for all your actions. No longer can you blame anything that is happening to you on someone else or your "bad luck" or any other circumstance. This can be difficult at first, but when you learn how to chart and navigate these open waters, you will be able to fully enjoy your life without the invisible anchor chains that have held you back all these years.

TOOLS FOR SHIFTING YOUR CONSCIOUSNESS

If you want to be a servant leader, you will need to shift your consciousness. I have found that it is possible to utilize your present relationship conflicts as tools for shifting your individual and collective consciousness. I recommend that you consider the following principles:

1. All unresolved conflicts you presently have are reminders that your conflict resolution strategies are incomplete. If you can accept this limitation, you can create an opportunity to test the effectiveness of your strategies and make them more effective and complete, not a reason to attack others for their ineffectiveness. Through open dialogue or self-reflection, it is often possible to discover how to improve your conflict resolution strategies.

2. Those with whom you have conflicts are not going away. You have unconsciously drawn them into your life to help you transform some aspect of yourself and possibly to help you identify and heal your developmental shocks, traumas and stresses. Welcome them as your teachers not as your enemies. The key here is to be able to look for the gift they are bringing you.

3. Value and utilize your relationships with those you have conflicts with to help you become more whole and integrated by helping you recognize and recover aspects of yourself that you have disowned. Only in genuine, trusting relationships can you hope to recover that which you have disowned.

4. Accept the plurality of the world and accept the fact that every form of life has a reason for being on this planet and has a purpose. Acceptance of differences and a willingness to engage those who differ from you in some way is an important strategy for breaking down the tendency of "premature hardening of the categories" between different peoples, races and cultures.

5. Recognize your intractable conflicts as doorways to change and transformation. They are an indication that you have undiscovered and unhealed developmental shocks, traumas or stresses. They contain keys to things that are blocking your healing and evolution. Only with a receptive heart and mind can you hope to find the keys in unblock your evolution.

LEARN HOW TO RESOLVE CONFLICTS

As the above strategies suggest, one of the most important skills you need as a servant leader is how to resolve conflicts in effective ways. Most people try to avoid their interpersonal conflicts like the plague. Avoiding your conflicts takes an enormous amount of energy that could be utilized in endeavors that are more productive.

Conflicts cause an Adrenal Stress Response in your body and either you freeze, flee or fight when you become aware of the conflict. None of these responses actually resolves the conflict. These are ways to avoid resolving the conflict. A servant leader has to be able to resolve his/her conflicts effectively or risk not being able to serve those who are counting on him/her.

The Partnership Way of Conflict Resolution[7]. Below is a protocol to follow to help you resolve any conflicts of wants and needs with others. To be an effective servant leader, you will need to be able to negotiate and resolve your conflicts with others in as win-win way.

In our book, Conflict Resolution: The Partnership Way, my wife and I describe how to resolve conflicts of wants and needs, values and beliefs and intractable conflict. The last category of conflicts relates to unresolved conflicts connected to developmental traumas from your past.

How to Prepare Yourself for a Conflict Resolution Session. There are some practical considerations to keep in mind to prepare for the conflict resolution session. Here are some of them:

1. Pick a time when neither of you is rushed. Tell the other person that you have a conflict with something he/she said or did and you would like to resolve it with him/her. Ask this person if he/she would be willing to take some time resolve it in a way that meets his/her needs and meets your needs as well.

2. Since your child or the other person doesn't have the same information or skills that you have or does not realize that something he/she has said or done that has caused a conflict for you, you will have to take the lead. You are the one who has the conflict and the tangible consequences of the unresolved conflict.

3. Think about what you are feeling and what unmet needs are causing this conflict. Identify how this unresolved conflict is affecting you in real and tangible ways. For example, if the conflict is that your child refuses to pick up his toys after playing in the living room, the tangible consequence for you is that, if he doesn't, you will have to pick them up or risk stepping on them.

4. Follow the step-by-step process described below to help you resolve your conflict of wants and needs.

THE PARTNERSHIP WAY TO RESOLVE CONFLICTS OF WANTS AND NEEDS

Directions. Below is a step-by-step process to follow that outlines how to effectively resolve conflicts involving wants and needs. If you have a current unresolved conflict of wants and needs with others, you can use these steps to help guide you to resolve this conflict.

Step 1. Describe objectively your perception of the problem or behavior that is preventing you from meeting your needs. Begin with "I" statements.

Avoid using harsh or judgmental language, "you" statements, threatening body language or a strident voice. For example, you might begin with a calm statement that just deals with the facts: "I noticed that you didn't pick up your toys when you were done playing with them."

Step 2. Share the way you feel because of the other person's behavior and what needs it prevents you from meeting. Keep your focus internally, specifically on your inner experience of the conflict to help you stay centered so that you do not escalate or lose your objectivity. Continuing with the above example, you might say, "I felt upset when I saw your toys on the living room floor and I my need is to be able to walk into the living room without stepping on them and possibly breaking them."

Step 3. It is important to think about and express the tangible effects that the conflict has on you and meeting your needs. It could also have a tangible effect on the kind of relationship you want or need with your children. Speak authentically in such a way that helps your child realize that his/her behavior has had some real or tangible effects on you and on your relationship as well as what feelings you have about them and the conflict.

Here you have to let the other person know how what they said or did tangibly affected you. You might say, "If I have to pick up your toys I am going to feel resentful toward you and feeling this way it will make it harder for me to enjoy being with you tonight the way I usually do."

Step 4. State directly what it is you want or need from the other person. Formulate this request ahead of time in your mind so that you can speak directly and clearly. Emphasize how much you value and care for the other person by saying, "What I need you to do is keep your agreement to pick up your toys after you are done playing with them. If you are willing to do that I will be able to feel better about spending time with you tonight."

Step 5. You need to ask the person directly for what you want or need from them. Asking directly gives the other person a choice. When people have choice, they are more likely to act cooperatively and are more willing to negotiate with you if your initial suggestion does not meet their needs. It is important to ask directly, "are you willing to do that?"

Step 6. At this point, if the other person gives you a defensive explanation for their behavior or refuses to agree with your request, use the skill of reflective listening and repeat back what you hear them say by identifying their feelings. This will help them feel heard and understood before you go onto the next step.

Your child might say something like, "I was going to pick them up, but Mom called me to come to the kitchen for my snack." Avoid being bogged down here by allowing him/her to defend him/herself, blaming him/her, complaining about him/her or escalating by bringing in other unrelated issues.

Stick with "I" statements and focus on your feelings of compassion and caring for the other person as you reflect back what you think they are feeling. You can say to them, "When I got upset about you not picking up your toys, you looked like you were feeling a little hurt and maybe you thought I was being unfair. Is that true?"

Once you have reflected back their statement and gotten their response to your reflection, you may want to return to your original question: "Are you willing to do what I asked?" If they say "no" at that point then move on to the next step.

Step 7. Negotiate any remaining differences between what you need and what the other person seems to need. In this step, be prepared to enter into a negotiation process, if necessary, to get your needs met by proposing a series of additional options or solutions that might meet your needs.

If the other person indicates that they don't believe they can get their needs met by agreeing to your request, ask them, "What are you willing to do to resolve this conflict?" or "What do you want from me in order to resolve this conflict." Then negotiate various options with him/her until you reach a satisfactory resolution that meets your needs and meets his/her needs.

Step 8. If you are unable to negotiate the differences, you need to look for other reasons for the conflict. In this case, you may have to agree to disagree in the moment and invite the other person to join you in exploring the conflict further.

You might say, "I see that we just don't agree on this issue and I accept our disagreement." Then ask, "Would you be willing to discuss this further to see if there are other reasons for this conflict that we have not discovered?" In these cases, probably what you will discover is that the conflict is about something else other than what either of you realized.

If you have created enough safety for your child by the respectful way you approached the conflict, he or she likely will agree to explore what else is involved that is causing the conflict. Once you discover the "hidden" causes then you can start over with this process and see if you can reach a partnership resolution to the conflict.

When you can resolve your conflicts with your children in a manner that respects their needs, they will learn how to do this with their friends and siblings. If you show respect for their needs, then you are on solid ground in asking them to respect your needs as well. This is an important servant leader skill so you can teach negotiation and conflict resolution skills to your children during the Interdependent stage of development (ages 6-18).

THE PARTNERSHIP WAY OF RESOLVING CONFLICTS OF VALUES AND BELIEFS

This skill is extremely important for a servant leader to develop. In our partnership model of conflict resolution, the tools that we use for resolving conflicts of values and beliefs are far different from those you use to resolve conflicts of wants and needs.

These kinds of conflicts tend to be more emotional than conflicts of wants and needs, and tend to be anchored in traumatic experiences, which means that they offer more opportunities for discovery and transformation. Finding a cooperative approach for resolving conflicts of values and beliefs seemed like an impossible task when we were creating our model of conflict resolution.

Values and beliefs also have a collective or universal aspect. They are formed during early childhood through experiences in our family of origin, neighborhood, school, church community, culture, and nation. They help us define our niche in the larger world. They often serve as a means of creating an identity related to membership in particular groups, such as male/female, adults/children, Caucasians/people of color, North Americans/Europeans, old/young, and rich/poor.

Values and beliefs can also be used to create separation, conflict, and even wars about whose beliefs are "right" and whose beliefs are "wrong." In addition, we may regard our values and beliefs as right or "true" because we are most familiar with them. Then we regard as wrong or "false" those values or beliefs with which we are not as familiar.

Because of the universal nature of our values and beliefs, it is difficult to both identify and change them. Changing values and beliefs also raises the risk of feeling outside or excluded from social and professional peers. The formative experiences that led to the development of values and beliefs actually may be less difficult to uncover.

Changing values and beliefs often brings up sadness or guilt. We feel sad that we are leaving something we held as dear to us behind, and guilty because we are telling those who gave us these values and beliefs, and still hold them that we prefer other values or beliefs. There is also that people will reject us if we hold different values or beliefs. We may even be afraid to share our values with because we now have values and beliefs that are different from theirs.

Conflicts involving values and beliefs are some of the most difficult to resolve and require a very different approach from resolving conflicts of wants and needs. Resolving conflicts of values and beliefs requires a shift in perception and the ability to understand another person's experience without attempting to change that person's values or beliefs.

We found that this shift in perception and capacity for understanding emerges most quickly when the people in the conflict feel safe enough to identify the foundational or early developmental experiences that helped form their values and beliefs. When these two criteria are met, the power struggles over who is "right" and who is "wrong" usually disappear.

WHAT ARE SOME TYPICAL CONFLICTS OF VALUES AND BELIEFS?

Common value conflicts between parents and teenagers often involve differences about the cleanliness of the teenager's room, how teens dress, how they wear their hair, or whether or not they can get a tattoo or a body piercing. This kind of conflict can escalate into a family power struggle. When we've helped families resolve these kind of conflicts, it has become clear that the teenager's dirty room, dress, hairstyle, tattoo, or earring frequently had little or no tangible effect on the parents, other than they would prefer that their son or daughter would do as the parents wished.

The parents' values around cleanliness, dress, hairstyles, or preferences about their bodies' appearances simply are different from those of their teenage children. When asked why their children have to behave according to their parents' preferences, the parents often say, "Do it because I said so." It usually isn't productive to create a major power struggle over these kinds of differences in preferences.

The important questions that parents must ask themselves in such a situation is, "How important is it that I impose my value on my children?" and "What cost will it have on our relationship?" On the other hand, if your child tells you he or she has been selling illegal drugs to friends, this situation is likely to involve more than just a heated clash of values. This has a tangible effect on the parent who is still legally responsible for the actions of that child.

Both values and beliefs are formed very early in life, usually before the age of 10 or 12. Value formation, particularly if it is imposed in a forceful manner, can create intense emotional experiences or traumatic events that leave a powerful imprint on a child's psyche.

As a result, values and beliefs often have an irrational quality that makes it difficult to change them through cognitive and rational discussions. Neither values nor beliefs can be truly changed without examining the experiences and circumstances that helped shape or form them.

WHY IS THERE A NEED FOR PEACEFUL DIALOGUE?

On a global as well as personal level, people are learning to use power without resorting to triangulation, aggression, and violence. The principles and practices set forth in the U.S. Constitution support this shift and promote the use of dialogue and the rule of law for resolving conflicts. While far from perfect, our American democratic tradition gives us hope for a better world. This better world may not be without conflict, but we as individuals can utilize peaceful dialogue that reduces the need for war and violence to resolve conflicts.

In 1985, John Murray wrote, "A republic is made up of people locked in civil argument. In addition, the point of the argument is neither to win nor to end the diversity of opinion and power. Peace means keeping the argument going, ad infinitum."[8] In this context, peace becomes as Sam Keen put it, "fierce men, women and nations struggling together to define their boundaries and enhance self-respect with love and politics as a playing field. I see rivals facing each other not as incarnations of evil, but as worthy opponents."[9]

Albert Camus, possibly one of the most unsentimental thinkers of the 20th century, wrote, "It would be completely Utopian to wish that men should no longer kill each other. Skeptical though we are, realism forces us to this Utopian alternative. When our Utopia has become part of history men will find themselves unable to conceive of reality without it. For history is simply man's desperate attempt to give body to his most clairvoyant dreams. [10]

Arnold Mindell wrote, "If you cannot dream it, it cannot happen. If you dare to dream it, it is already happening."[11] According to his theory, if you can imagine a better, more peaceful world, then it already exists in some form and makes it easier to actualize.

Why Is Dialogue Is the Key? For a more peaceful world, however, we need more than a common vision of peace. We need skills that help us achieve our common goals and realize our dreams. One of the most important skills for a peaceful world is the ability to dialogue.

We believe that dialogue is the key not only to peace, but to scientific achievements and all other cooperative efforts. Werner Heisenberg, one of the greatest minds of the 20th century, argued, "Science is rooted in conversations. The cooperation of different people may culminate in scientific results of the utmost importance."[12] Heisenberg recalled that his dialogues with Wolfgang Pauli, Albert Einstein, and Niels Bohr led directly to the theories that literally reshaped our understanding of the physical world.

Dialogue is actually a very old practice. It was revered by the ancient Greeks and used by many early societies, such as the American Indians. Physicist David Bohm developed the contemporary theory now used in the practice of dialogue. He believed that the purpose of science is not the accumulation of knowledge but rather the creation of mental maps that guide and shape our perception and action. These mental maps, Bohm said, are best created by groups who have learned the skill of dialogue.

What is the Difference Between Dialogue and Debate? Dialogue and debate are very different forms of interaction. The purpose of a debate is to convince other people or groups that one's views, beliefs, or values are correct. Although you might accept part of another person's perspective during a debate in order to strengthen your own position, the basic goal is to be "right," or win the debate. This often leads people to exaggerate the truth and disregard certain facts. Debate is necessary when a group is trying to reach some agreement on a course of action to be taken. Other times it can stifle creative input for solving a problem.

The goal of dialogue is different. Dialogue does not seek agreement but rather to discover new courses of action. The word dialogue comes from the Greek word dialogos, which is defined as "meaning." Senge wrote that Bohm saw the purpose of dialogue as helping a group of people access a larger pool of common meaning that could not be accessed individually.

In a dialogue, people participate in the discovery of this pool of common meaning. At the same time, they become more aware of the assumptions that shape their actions and the events from their pasts that have shaped those assumptions. Table 8-1 is a summary of the main differences between dialogue and debate. As you read this list, think about how the skill of dialogue can be used to help resolve conflicts of values and beliefs.

Table 8.1 Comparison of Dialogue and Debate[13]

Dialogue	Debate
Dialogue is collaborative: two or more sides work together toward common understanding.	Debate is oppositional: two sides oppose each other and attempt to prove each other wrong.
Finding common ground is the goal.	Winning is the goal.
One listens to the other side(s) in order to understand, find meaning, and find agreement.	One listens to the other side in order to find flaws and to counter its arguments.
Dialogue enlarges and possibly changes a participant's point of view.	Debate affirms a participant's point of view.
Dialogue reveals assumptions for reevaluation.	Debate defends assumptions as truth.
Dialogue causes introspection on one's own position.	Debate causes critique of the other person's position.
Dialogue calls for temporally suspending one's beliefs.	Debate calls for investing wholeheartedly in one's beliefs.
In dialogue one searches for basic agreements.	In debate one emphasizes differences.
Dialogue involves a real concern for the other person and seeks to not alienate or offend.	Debate involves a countering of the other position without focusing on feelings or relationships and often belittles or deprecates the other person.

What Is Necessary for Dialogue to Be Effective? For dialogue to be effective, it is necessary to meet three basic conditions:

1. All participants must be willing to suspend their assumptions, reveal them to others, and open them to examination.
2. All participants must be willing to regard one another as equals or as colleagues.

3. In a group there has to be a facilitator who keeps the dialogue process moving, or the group needs to use a written protocol for everyone to follow.[14]

According to Bohm, once an individual "digs in his or her heels" and decides "this is the way it is," the flow of dialogue stops. In a dialogue, different assumptions can be presented as a means for discovering a new idea or enhancing the understanding of other people's assumptions. Because of the dire need for dialogue to help resolve conflicts at all levels, the Dalai Lama[15] proposed that the 21st century be named the century of dialogue.

Dialogue utilizes the skills of reflective listening and inquiry, which are important components of the Partnership Way. You will have an opportunity to practice these skills by completing the worksheet and exercise at the end of this chapter.

Learn Empathy Skills and the Seven Skills of Dialogue. Learning how to respond empathically to others is an important skill that servant leaders need to utilize in many settings. The servant leader skill of empathy involves learning how to "dialogue" with someone either verbally or non-verbally. There are seven skills of dialogue that include empathy skills. These skills are also necessary to resolve conflicts of values and beliefs. See the protocol below on how to use dialogue skills to resolve conflicts of values and beliefs.

In order to tune into what other people are thinking or feeling you need to learn these seven skills of dialogue. The seven skills of dialogue involve deep listening, respecting others, inquiry, self-reflection, suspending assumptions and judgments, balancing advocacy and inquiry, and reflecting content and feelings. Each of these skills is briefly explained below.

1. **Deep Listening Skills.** In its most simple form, deep listening derives from a conscious choice to listen. It involves quieting the voice in your head so that you can hear the whole story of the person to whom you are listening. As you listen to understand their whole story, you literally stay quiet and just listen. Instead of readying yourself for your turn to speak, your focus needs to be on listening and understanding the speaker. Non-verbally you can do the same thing a listen by observing what the other person is doing and what look they have on their face.

2. **Skills in Showing Respect for the Needs, Values and Beliefs of Others.** Voltaire, a French author, humanist, rationalist and satirist is reported to have said, "I disapprove of what you say, but I will defend to the death

your right to say it." This perspective lies at the heart of respecting the needs, values and beliefs of others. Clearly, this is particularly difficult if you interact with people whose needs, values and beliefs are different from yours.

Practicing this skill therefore becomes imperative if you are to develop the true capacity to dialogue. While respecting the needs, values and beliefs of others does not mean that you have to agree with them, it does mean that you are willing to respect their right to express them.

It is a perspective that is valid because it contributes, maybe even only in a small way, to your understanding of a more 'complete' picture of who the other person is and why they are expressing what they are. Often you learn something new about yourself when you dialogue with others who have different needs, values and beliefs.

3. **Inquiry Skills.** This is the capacity to ask genuine open-ended questions. As such, open-ended questions enhance our understanding of different perspectives, and allow the deeply held mental models that lie behind many perspectives to come to the surface.

    An example of an open-ended question would be, "Expand on what you just said, I want to understand it better?" If you ask closed-ended questions that require just a "yes' or "no" answer, you will not get very far in developing an understanding of what the other person is thinking or feeling. For example, if you ask, "Were you happy with what happened?"

4. **Self-Reflection Skills.** Many of us are quite talented at using this skill, at least in part. Self-reflection is the capacity to say what you think and to be able to explain why you think that way. Unfortunately, many people struggle to share their opinions. All opinions are important for the development of a true understanding of any situation. If you do not share your opinion, then a part of the picture may be missing. This is why voicing your opinion is so important in the context of dialogue.

5. **Skills in Suspending Your Assumptions & Judgments.** This allows you and your child the opportunity to explain why you are doing what you are doing. Firs, you have to be willing to share your assumptions and judgments to let the other person know why you believe what you do. Then it is necessary to set aside or suspend your assumptions & judgments in order to hear and understand what the other person is really saying or doing.

Much like you hang your clothes on a line for them to dry, suspending your assumptions and judgments means that you 'hang out' of reveal your reasons for your views. This allows people who are interacting to see them, question them. This even assists you in developing a deeper understanding of your own perspectives.

To suspend your assumptions & judgments illustrates a willingness to discover more about what you and the other person are thinking and feeling. Should you discover that your views are not useful through the act of having suspended them, you have the opportunity to adopt a new understanding of yourself. This experience is often described as self-correction.

6. **Skills in Balancing Self-Reflection with Inquiry.** This skill is as simple and as complex as balancing the act of sharing your views and why you have them. Your also need to be able to ask genuine questions to better understand another person's views. To practice this skill involves utilizing all the other skills listed above: deep listening, respecting others, asking open-ended questions, inquiry, voicing your views openly and suspending your assumptions & judgments.

Even if the other person with whom you are conversing is not consciously trying to dialogue with you, practicing this skill significantly enhances the quality of your conversations. People will notice when you use this skill because the quality of your conversations will be enhanced by your contributions to them.

7. **Skills in Reflection of Content and Feelings.** The capacity to reflect back what you heard from the other person and checking with them to see if you correctly understood what they said greatly enhances your capacity to engage in dialogue. This needs to be done before you state your own views on the topic.

Then you need make sure you heard exactly what they meant to say before saying what you have to say. With some people, when you feed back to them what you heard them say, it may actually help them become more concise in explaining their point of view.

People ask me, "How old do my children have to be before I can use these skills with them?" The answer is as soon as they have language to express their needs, feelings and beliefs directly to you. That can begin as early as one year of age in a more limited way. It is never too early to try to engage with your children in this way.

251

The Partnership Way to Resolve Conflicts of Values and Beliefs. The Seven-Step Method for Resolving Conflicts of Values and Beliefs contained in the Partnership Way is described in more detail below. Remember that conflicts of values and beliefs are often masked as conflicts of wants and needs. If you tried to resolve a conflict of wants and needs and were not satisfied that the conflict was totally resolved, the next step is to complete the Worksheet below: "The Seven-Step Method for Resolving Conflicts of Values and Beliefs."

Some important differences exist between the processes and the intentions of the methods for resolving these two kinds of conflict. The intention in resolving conflicts of wants and needs is to reach a mutually agreeable resolution. The intention in resolving conflicts of values and beliefs is much broader. It includes discovering more about the other person and developing and communicating respect, compassion, and acceptance (not agreement) for the other person's values and beliefs. The intention also involves identifying the source of each other's values and beliefs, and noting any shifts in those values and beliefs that come as a result of the dialogue process.

Through dialogue, the people involved have the opportunity to get beyond any labels or stereotypes and get to know each other in important ways. It is important for people who are dialoguing to understand that their values or beliefs are not necessarily complete, nor are the other person's values or beliefs. The purpose of the dialogue is for each person to end up with a more complete understanding of his or her own values or beliefs and a more complete understanding of each other's values or beliefs.

The following steps summarize the key points for resolving a conflict of values and beliefs using the Partnership Way. Remember to express compassion, respect, and understanding of the other person's values and beliefs. This helps create a safe context for both of you to explore the sources of your values and beliefs.

Step 1. Take Turns Listening to Each Other's Views of the Conflict, Using Reflective Listening. Be sure to identify the feelings as well as the content of each other's values or beliefs. Follow the rule that you cannot state your opinion or position until you have first restated what the other person has said and reached agreement that you understand the other person's view. For example, you might say, "You seem to be saying that you think I am trying to control you, and you also seem a little angry and scared. Do I understand accurately what you are saying and feeling?"

In discussions or debates about a value-laden subject, the people involved often focus more on what they are going to say next to the other person rather than listening carefully to what the person is saying. Adding this step prevents them from not listening carefully to what the other person is saying. It is important to listen carefully to identify any unstated feelings and include them in your reflection. Agree that neither of you can state your opinion or position until you have first restated what the other person has said and reached agreement that you understand what the other person said.

Kind, reflective listening helps to create an atmosphere of trust and respect. Most people are not used to being listened to so carefully, and they usually feel honored that the other person cares enough to actually listen to them. This step helps set the tone for the conflict resolution process and makes it possible for true dialogue to occur.

It also sets the stage for the next step, which requires that the participants look at how they may have formed the values or beliefs around which the conflict is centered. Without some trust, created through the mutual respect displayed in the first step, this next step can be difficult.

Step 2. Take Turns Finding the Sources of Our Value or Belief Conflict.
Again, it is important for each person to listen to and restate the feelings and content the other person expresses before going on. Asking questions such as, "What experiences have you had earlier in your life in which you have felt people were trying to control you?" can lead to much new awareness and exciting discoveries. The goal is for people to get underneath the surface of the conflict and explore the personal experiences that may have influenced the formation of their values or beliefs. When people examine the sources of their values and beliefs, they often uncover traumatic or unusual experiences that helped to form them. Once the source of a particular value or belief is located, it is possible to change that value or belief.

For example, a client told us about an incident that occurred when she was 10 years old, and she saw her mother fall down a flight of stairs in a drunken stupor. She remembered deciding at that time to never again allow herself to get close to anyone. This woman formed the belief that

253

it was too frightening to risk losing someone you were close to and that the only safe choice was to avoid getting close to anyone.

Many lonely years passed before she remembered this incident and was able to change her belief. The key to changing a value or belief is to first remember how and why you formed it and to then express the feelings connected to the causal events. This step is an excellent exercise in developing kindness and compassion toward yourself regarding the way you formed your values and beliefs.

Step 3. Take Turns Finding the Sources of Our Feelings Related to the Conflict. The focus here is on the feelings attached to the values or beliefs expressed. Each person states his or her feelings and reflects back what the other person said. Asking questions like, "What other times in your life have you felt this way?" can get the dialogue started. When a person has intense feelings about a value or belief, it is almost certain that these feelings relate back to some developmental trauma or unresolved conflict from the past.

It is usually impossible for the person to change the value or belief until that person can identify the source of the attached feelings. If, for example, you get very angry when you feel someone is treating you unfairly or when you see someone else being treated unfairly, your anger may be related to times when as a child you felt you were treated unfairly.

Once you remember the incidents you experienced, you can decide what is unresolved about them. Perhaps as a child you never got to express your feelings directly to those who treated you unfairly. By having your partner role-play a parent who treated you unfairly, you can release those repressed feelings. Finding the source of your feelings and coming to terms with the earlier incident will help you reframe the way you look at this conflict and may cause a shift in awareness that causes you to change your value or belief.

Step 4. Determine Any Shifts in Our Awareness. This step enables both people to reflect on whether their values have changed because of what they have uncovered regarding the sources of their values or beliefs. Asking a question like, "Based on what you have discovered about the sources of your values or beliefs and your feelings, do you have any new perceptions of your value or belief?" is a good way to start the dialogue. The participants should take turns restating any new perceptions expressed by the other person.

Indeed, each of the prior steps can lead to new awareness, and it is important to check how this awareness may have affected the conflict or perceptions of values and beliefs. Although people at this stage of the process are not usually ready to change their value or belief completely, they may have softened their position and often feel more compassionate toward each other's views. It is useful to spend some time exploring these shifts in perception before moving on to the next step.

Step 5. Explore Remaining Areas of Agreement and Disagreement. If the dialogue has been successful, it may now be possible to explore areas of mutual agreement and disagreement. For example, in a scenario centered around the issue of control, one partner might say, "I think we now can agree that what we identified as control was really a desire for more directness in our relationship. Because of our past history of having had people try to control us, we are prone to be indirect with each other. Do you agree that this could be a problem for us?"

Armed with the knowledge of the sources of their values or beliefs, the partners can work to sort out the various parts of the conflict that were uncovered in the dialogue process:

- The partners may find that they are now closer to agreement on many aspects of the conflict than they first realized.
- They may uncover any core disagreements that remain. They may have to agree to disagree on these.
- They will likely have a better understanding of why such disagreements exist.

When you can see that the other person has formed his or her value or belief out of unique or traumatic experiences, then it is easier to accept that partner and the value or belief he or she holds, even if it differs from your values and beliefs.

It is unlikely that the partners in a conflict of values or beliefs will reach complete agreement, even when important shifts in perception have occurred as a result of their dialogue. However, from the dialogue, they may have acquired enough mutual understanding and compassion to feel closer to each other.

When areas of disagreement remain, it is useful for the partners to identify kind and compassionate ways to handle these disagreements in their relationship. One may say, for example, "I think if either of us is feeling controlled by the other in any way, that person should raise the issue and we can talk about it again."

Step 6. Make Plans to Handle Any Areas of Disagreement. If the partners have successfully completed the previous steps, they will probably be able to agree to disagree, if that is still necessary. The process will inevitably create more intimacy, understanding, compassion, and trust between the two people or groups. It is likely that the areas of disagreement that still exist no longer pose a major conflict in their relationship. Even though they did not agree completely, they did reach a more complete understanding of the areas of disagreement. Such understanding leads to more compassion, as well as tolerance and acceptance for different values and beliefs, and allows partners to develop a mutually acceptable plan for handling these differences.

Learning to understand, accept, and welcome differences of values and beliefs in others can be an unexpectedly positive experience. Many people learn to fear differences and avoid people whose values or beliefs are different from their own.

By engaging in the dialogue process described here, you can learn to better understand and accept such differences and may even, in the process, revise some of your own values and beliefs. If a conflict brings up strong feelings and reactions in you that the dialogue does not resolve, you may want to find the source of those strong feelings and reactions. They may be related to undiscovered and unhealed developmental traumas.

Step 7. Make Plans to Handle Any Strong Feelings or Reactions. If you still have strong feelings or reactions at this stage of the conflict resolution, this usually is a good indicator that the conflict relates to some unhealed developmental trauma or unresolved conflict from the past that is being activated by the current conflict. Any leftover elements of the conflict that have not been adequately explored so far should be addressed at this time.

WHAT IS INDIVIDUATION?

The most important step in overcoming any psychological barriers is to create a fully individuated Self. This process is much the same as Breaking Free of the Matrix that we discussed earlier.

Carl Jung called the process of reaching psychological maturity as "individuation." The basic psychological principles of individuation came directly from early Gnostic teachings in Egypt. The goal is to emancipate yourself from the one-sided pursuit of people-pleasing and attempts to be accepted by everybody.

This could mean rejecting the external laws and commandments of the Christian Church and instead developing your own set of moral-ethical standards with which to live your life. People need to learn to make conscious moral choices of their own design, winning individual victories and suffering their personal defeats according to the just constellations of their inner life. This means taking full responsibility for all your thoughts, feelings and behaviors. There is no place for victims in this picture.

According to Jacobi, a Jungian scholar,[16] there are four general guidelines to follow in pursuit of individuation:

1. We must become conscious of the shadow parts of ourselves. The shadow, according to Jung, contains those things about ourselves that we have repressed or tried to ignore. It becomes important to be able to acknowledge and accept our shadow parts in order to become a whole and complete person.

2. The need to discover our "anima" and "animus" or the feminine and masculine parts of ourselves. This means we are aware of those parts of ourselves that society might label our feminine parts such as our feelings or our ability to nurture ourselves and others. We have to integrate that feminine part of us with our masculine parts that can think through things logically and can take positive action in the world. We all have both parts inside of us and individuation requires that we are conscious of both parts and can integrate them in productive ways.

3. We need to become aware of our archetypal spirit. This archetype is often represented in myths and fairy tales as the wise old man or the earth mother. Again the task is to unite the seeming opposites in our personality. This part of the process often requires that we liberate ourselves from the constraints imposed on us by twisted beliefs of either our mother or our father or our culture.

4. We need to become conscious of a separate "Self." Jung called this final step "self-realization." This requires that we develop our ability to self-reflect and to self-correct. It also means making a conscious shift from other-directedness to inner-directedness. It makes it possible for us to be of the world but not in the world.

Jung's concept of individuation is not much different from Maslow's concept of self-actualization. According to Jung, the individuation of humankind involves uniting the two sides of our personality. The one side reaches into the heavens where the divine mother of the eternal mind (Mater Coelestis) waits to receive us.

The other side it is rooted in the subterranean power of the phallic Eros (Phallos), the earthly father, whose strength and energy furnishes the force that enables us to be liberated. The final union of heaven and earth begets the androgynous Anthropos, or the divine Sophia of the Gnostics. Jung called it, "the paradigm of the transformed and individuated ego of every individual and of all humanity."[17]

NOTES

1   Weinhold, J. & Weinhold, B. (2011). Healing developmental trauma. Denver, CO: Love Publishing Co.

2   Weinhold, B. & Weinhold, J. Developmental trauma: The game changer in the mental health profession. Colorado Springs, CO: CICRCL Press.

3   Weinhold, B. (2013). Twisted beliefs. Asheville, NC: CICRCL Press. (This is a series of four books listed on Amazon. All were published by CICRCL Press.

4   Katz, N. & Lawyer, J. (1985). Communication and conflict resolution skills. New York: Kendall/Hunt.

5   http://www.quoteland.com/author/Malcolm-X-Quotes/1509/

6   https://en.wikipedia.org/wiki/Ho'oponopono

7   Weinhold, B. (2009). Conflict resolution: The partnership way. Denver, CO: Love Publishing Company.

8   Peck, S. (1998). A different drum. New York: Simon & Schuster.

9   Murray, J. C. (1985). We hold these truths: Catholic reflections on the American proposition. Kansas City, MO: Sheed and Ward, p. 96.

10   Camus, A. (1980). Neither victims nor executioners. New York: Continuum Publishing Co., p. 51.

11   Mindell, A. (1983). Dreambody. Santa Monica, CA: Lao Tsu Press.

12   Senge, P. (1990). The fifth discipline. New York: Doubleday, pp.238–239.

13   Ibid, pp. 238-239.

14   Adapted from a paper prepared by Shelley Berman, which was based on discussions of A Guide to Training Study Circle Leaders by the Dialogue Group of the Boston Chapter of Educators for Social Responsibility (ESR), 1993, Pomfret, CT: Topsfield Foundation, Study Circles Resource Center. Adapted with permission.

15   Bohm, D. (1987). Science, order and creativity. New York: Bantam.

16   Jacobi, J. (1999). Compex/archetype/symbol in the psychological of c. G. Jung. London: Routledge.

17   Hoeller, S. (2002) Gnosticism: New light on the ancient tradition of inner knowing. Wheaton: IL, Quest Books.

CHAPTER 12

STRATEGIES TO OVERCOME THE SOCIAL, ECONOMIC AND POLITICAL BARRIERS TO SERVANT LEADERSHIP

"The greatest terror a child can have is that he is not loved, and rejection is the hell he fears. I think everyone in the world to a large or small extent has felt rejection. And with rejection comes anger, and with anger some kind of crime in revenge for the rejection, and with the crime guilt—and there is the story of mankind."

—James D Prescott, Ph.D.

STRATEGIES TO OVERCOME THE SOCIAL BARRIERS TO BECOMING A SERVANT LEADER

Eliminate the Drama Triangle and Need/Obligate System. Dynamics or the Need/Obligate System. This is extremely important in your social transactions with others. If you don't break free of the Drama Triangle and the Need/Obligate System, you will have trouble sustaining your true servant leader role.

How To Exit the Drama Triangle[1]. Stephen Karpman, the founder of the Drama Triangle, says that the exit point in the Drama Triangle is usually through the Persecutor role. Once you decide to get off the triangle, you will be perceived as the bad guy or gal. The other game players will feel angry, hurt and rejected because you are leaving them and the pseudo-intimacy you've had together. Therefore, you must learn how to accept them making you bad and not make them bad in return. This is critical, if you are to break free of the power of the Drama Triangle.

Encountering the Coke Machine Syndrome[2]. What will happen as soon as you attempt to exit the Drama Triangle is that you will encounter the Coke Machine Syndrome. This metaphoric game is how people keep you trapped in the Drama Triangle. It is similar to putting your money in a coke machine and pushing a certain button with the expectation that you'll get the soda of your choice. If you push the button and nothing happens, you will likely push it again, only harder. If that doesn't get you what you want, you might try pushing another button, after realizing you are not going to get your favorite soda.

If these options don't work, you might try pushing a third or fourth button. Finally, if you are really thirsty, you might push all the buttons. If none of those actions gets you what you want, you might resort to shaking the machine or cursing at it. Eventually you try pushing the coin return. If that doesn't work, you will have to leave and search for another machine.

Those with whom you play on the triangle know exactly what your buttons are. As soon as you declare that you are exiting the game, they will begin pushing your buttons, hoping to get you to re-engage in the game.

If they don't get the response they want from you, they'll keep pushing different buttons and until they finally realize that you are not going to give them what they want, which is to rejoin the game. Then they will make you bad, declare you a traitor or some other terrible name, and finally go looking for another person to join their game. Staying off the Drama Triangle requires that you become non-reactive and unfazed by other people's attempts to draw you back into the game. You must learn how to resist these manipulative attempts to draw you back into the game, particularly when you are being blamed as the "bad guy or gal" for not playing the game anymore. (this is one of the buttons they will push).

One way to side-step the angry and blaming button-pushing messages they direct at you, is by making one of the two following replies. You can say to them, "Thank you, I am aware of that" or "Thank you, I wasn't aware of that." That's all you need to say, and you can repeat it like a broken record, if you need to. Take my word for it, this works!

You can also use communication skills such as reflective listening that acknowledge other people's feelings. Ex: "You are angry at me because I am no longer willing to give you money to support your drinking habit." This helps you sidestep being blamed, feeling guilty or being manipulated back into the Rescuer role.

How to Stop the Blame Game. An excellent blame-and-drama-stopper statement is to ask: "Is there something that you want from me?" This makes people shift their focus from blaming you or complaining about your behavior and asks them to be direct and accountable for their behavior.

It forces them to ask directly for what they want from you and gives you the opportunity to either give them what they are asking for, or you can say no, giving them your reasons for refusing to give them what they are asking for. These straightforward transactions leave no room for discussion, manipulation, enabling or game playing.

Staying off the Drama Triangle also requires that you learn how to use your own emotions effectively and honestly. You must acknowledge and experience your emotions and so that others cannot use them to subvert, govern, and control your behavior. For example, if you carry around unprocessed anger, it's easy to provoke an angry outburst with only a little effort.

Suppressing emotions isn't good for you physically, and a primary cause of panic attacks, anxieties, compulsions, depression, and addictive behaviors. A goal in relationships is finding a balance point between:
- Creating a space where people can express authentic feelings and
- Not using their emotions to manipulate or control others.

Most people need help in identifying and naming their strong feelings because they are usually associated with unmet needs.

Anger, for example, means that there's something you want and need that you are not getting. Sadness means that you have lost something that's important to you and you need comfort. Fear means that you don't feel safe and that you need some form of protection.

When you are feeling hurt, or sad or afraid and can say so. Here's an example of honest communication: "I don't believe you heard me. Would you please listen to what I am saying and repeat it back to me so I know you heard me?" If you do that, people will respond more authentically and honestly.

Once you decide to exit the Drama Triangle and feel strong enough to tolerate being seen as the bad guy or gal, you become a role model for others who also want out of the game. It's important that you not align with those who are leaving the Drama Triangle by making others who chose not to bad. Otherwise, you've just created a new team of players and you will only start a new Drama Triangle.

Being Willing to Ask Directly for What You Want. If your commonly held position on the triangle is the Rescuer role, then you can do the following: The primary way to get off the triangle and stay off is by being willing to ask for what you want directly from others 100 percent of the time.

It is necessary to take responsibility for getting your own needs met. You must also make sure that you do or not do something or give something to another person, unless they have asked you for it directly. This prevents Rescuing and enabling. If you would like to help another person, you can ask them for permission to help them: "You look like you could use a hug. Would you like a hug?"

Focus on asking directly for what you want, stay grounded in your own inner experience and listen to other people's feelings. If you get off-center, take a time-out from the intensity by taking a deep breath and going inside. Remember that what keeps you playing on the Drama Triangle is competition for the Victim role and not asking for what you want. If you remain committed to asking for what you want directly 100 percent of the time, you will be able to resist temptations to return to the Drama Triangle. If you find yourself being sucked into a Drama Triangle at work or in your relationships, excuse yourself and take a time-out immediately.

STRATEGIES FOR OVERCOMING THE ECONOMIC BARRIERS TO SERVANT LEADERSHIP

Once you understand how the crooked money system works, you will have to look for alternatives to that system. It is likely that this system will collapse on its own soon because it is already showing early warning signs of collapse. Banks in Europe are already charging "negative interest," meaning you have to pay them to keep your money. You may have to help yourself and others prepare for this collapse because there is probably going to be a period of chaos and unrest that follows this collapse.

The biggest problem is that the world's economy runs almost entirely on credit. There is only about $250 million in actual dollars in circulation to cover debt that may exceed $60 trillion dollars. In other words, it is a gigantic Ponzi scheme. Banks keep less than 1 percent of actual cash in their vaults to cover the deposits they have collected. If many people went to the bank tomorrow to withdraw the deposited money from their account, the bank would have close its doors. It does not have the money it collected from you.

The banks will close down and the ATMs will stop working. Your credit card will not work as well.

Therefore, you will need some actual cash on hand. I recommend keeping at least a month's worth of dollars to cover your usual expenses. The grocery stores will run out of food in two to three days or even sooner. You should have a pantry full of food (at least two-weeks to a month's worth) to tide you over. Fresh water could also be a problem, if the usual supply is shut down. Store containers of water in your garage, in case your usual supply of water is cut off. If you have a well, this is good, but if the power grid goes down, the well pump will not work.

We had a near financial meltdown in 2009, but the situation has gotten much worse. Despite federal legislation, such as the Dodd-Frank Act, banks are bigger than ever, still buying and selling Credit Default Swaps. These were central to the near collapse in 2009. All the big banks would have failed, if the government and taxpayers hadn't bailed them out.

The amount of debt being held by banks today is also far greater than it was in 2009. This is now too much for the government and the taxpayers to bail out. The Fed itself has now become too big to fail, without causing serious effects. The banks will fail this time and we all will suffer.

Bernie Sanders has campaigned vigorously during the 2016 Presidential Campaign saying he would break up the big banks and regulate their risky transactions. Sanders wrote, "You would determine is that, if a bank is too big to fail, it is too big to exist. Then you have the secretary of treasury and some people who know a lot about this, making that determination. If the determination is that Goldman Sachs or JPMorgan Chase is too big to fail, yes, they will be broken up."

His campaign released a statement on how a Sanders administration would break up the banks, also stating that he and rival Clinton "have very different points of view on how to reform Wall Street and the largest financial institutions in this country."

The statement reads, in part: "Within the first 100 days of his administration, Sen. Sanders will require the secretary of the Treasury Department to establish a 'Too-Big-to Fail' list of commercial banks, shadow banks and insurance companies whose failure would pose a catastrophic risk to the United States economy without a taxpayer bailout."[3] Within a year, the Sanders administration say they will work with the Federal Reserve and financial regulators to break these institutions up using the authority of Section 121 of the Dodd-Frank Act.

Sen. Sanders also says he will also fight to enact a 21st Century Glass-Steagall Act to clearly separate commercial banking, investment banking and insurance services. Secretary Clinton opposes this extremely important measure.

President Franklin Roosevelt signed the Glass-Steagall Act into law precisely to prevent Wall Street speculators from causing another Great Depression. And, it worked for more than five decades until Wall Street watered it down under President Reagan and killed it under President Clinton. That is unacceptable and that is why Sen. Sanders says he will fight to sign the Warren-McCain bill into law that would replace the Glass-Steagall Act. Let's hope this action is not too late to change the current unstable situation.[4]

One problem with Senator Sander's strategy is that it depends on other leaders cooperating and working with him to make this kind of change. Most of those currently in leadership positions are self-serving leaders and will likely oppose or try to undermine his efforts. Most of his ideas will likely fall victim to the efforts of self-serving leaders who will try to block them to protect their special interests. Without removing money from politics none of his ideas will get much traction.

Sanders' rival for the Democratic Party nomination, Hillary Clinton, is less enthusiastic about this idea and others he has proposed. However, pressure is coming from many directions that suggest she may try to get in front of the parade that is forming. Her campaign said she would break up banks that the regulators deem "too large and too risky." Since she has strong financial ties to these financial institutions, one wonders if this is her way of slowing down the push for reform.

Her approach also calls for taxing certain forms of computer trading by banks. She says she favors improved transparency in markets where prices are publically disclosed and harsher penalties for banking executive whose subordinates violate the law. Since 2009, none of the banking executives involved in the 2008 meltdown were prosecuted or jailed.

As long as the Federal Reserve is in charge of our monetary system, very little will change. The Federal Reserve System is the most powerful banking system in the world today and it is lead by self-serving leaders. It is designed to try to stabilize currency rates around the world, since most currencies are dependent on the dollar as the standard currency.

Since wars are the biggest moneymakers for the Fed, they start them and then fund both sides so they will win no matter how the war turns out. Servant leaders will have to call for the removal of the Federal Reserve System, in order for any significant changes to occur. None of the candidates is calling for this kind of drastic reform.

Interestingly, the Central Banks in Europe are mostly publically owned by their government. The Great Depression shook public confidence in privately owned banks in Europe. They were all private until after WWII, when they became public. There is some private influence by the banking cartel to try to keep the banks from failing. It is like the FDIC in this country, that supposedly protects your bank deposits up to $250,000. In Europe, a private firm called Mutual Credit, is supposed to do the same thing.

STRATEGIES FOR OVERCOMING POLITICAL BARRIERS TO SERVANT LEADERSHIP

Public Financing of All Elections. The biggest political obstacle that a servant leader has to overcome is the private financing of all elections. Since Citizen's United was upheld by the Supreme Court, it opened the door for unlimited secret financing of elections by Super PACs. Since these Super PACs are not required to disclose the donors or amounts contributed by them, there is no way to prevent undue influence of rich donors on all elections. Servant leaders have to support public financing of all elections and eliminate all private donations to candidates or issues.

Congress enacted various reforms during the early 1900s, but it was not until 1971 that reformers came up with an alternative to private campaign financing. The Federal Election Campaign Act of 1971 not only required candidates for federal office to disclose their funders and set limits on their spending, but for the first time provided public funding of elections for presidential campaigns, though not for Congressional races.

The idea was to match funds raised by the candidates themselves with public monies–provided that the candidates agreed to spending limits. The public funds came from voluntary contributions by individual taxpayers through a check-off on their income tax returns, designating a small donation to public campaign funding.

For six electoral cycles, from 1976 to 1996, public financing worked well for the campaigns of Presidents Jimmy Carter, Ronald Reagan, George H. W. Bush, and Bill Clinton, and their opponents. Availability of public financing encouraged transparency in campaign funding and sharply reduced the influence of wealthy donors.

Many political observers credit the public funding system with giving voters a wider choice of candidates, including two underdogs who went on to win the Oval Office–Jimmy Carter in 1976 and Ronald Reagan in 1980. So public funding worked well in presidential races for a quarter of a century.[5]

How the Public Funding for Elections Broke Down. However, the presidential public financing system began to fray during the 2000 campaign. Republican George W. Bush became the first nominee of either major party to pass up public matching funds during the primaries and to rely solely on money raised contributed by big donors to his own campaign.

In the general election, however, Bush accepted public funds, as did his Democratic opponent, Al Gore. In 2004, President Bush and his Democratic opponent, Senator John Kerry, both declined public matching funds during their party primaries, but accepted public funding in the general election.

It was Democrat Barack Obama in 2008, who became the first nominee of either major party to break away entirely from using public funds for both the primaries and the general election. His Republican opponent, Senator John McCain of Arizona, followed the Bush-Kerry pattern, using public funds in the general election. However, Obama's decision to opt out was the death knell for the system. Since 2008, no presidential candidates have used the public financing system at all.[6]

Why Public Funding for Elections Broke Down. The system broke down because the old arithmetic of public funding no longer fit reality. The sheer cost of running for president has risen astronomically since 1976, outstripping the amount of available public funding, in part because Congress never established a mechanism to index available public financing to the inflation in campaign costs.

An even more basic problem was the sharp decline in taxpayer participation in funding the system–from 30% in 1980 to 9% in 2008, meaning that less money was in the government coffers to fund campaigns. For the 2012 general election, the tax return check-off generated only about $80 million, a tiny fraction of the $2.3 billion actually spent on the 2012 presidential campaign.

Finally, the rise of independent campaign expenditures by Super PACs, permitted to operate without limits by Supreme Court rulings, created a huge disadvantage for any candidate who agreed to abide by campaign spending limits in order to quality for public funding. In short, public funding became impractical.[7]

Public Funding Closer to Home–States and Cities. Yet, while public funding of presidential campaign was falling by the wayside, public funding has achieved some notable successes at the state and city level since the late 1990s. States as varied as Arizona, Connecticut, Maine and Minnesota and cities such as Los Angeles and New York have developed effective systems of public funding.

Some seek to empower small donors and to reduce the influence of billionaire and corporate donors, by providing matching funds at a high 6-to-1 ratio for small donations up to $175. The idea is to give candidates a strong incentive to go after small donors.

Two other ways of empowering small donors are giving them a tax credit for limited donations (up to $100, for example) or else giving all voters a small publicly funded voucher ($50 or $100), which voters can then donate to candidates of their choice.

An alternative strategy is to adopt Clean Elections reforms aimed at fostering a statewide culture of limited campaign spending and of spurning outside money. Under such a system, states or cities require candidates, whether for governor, mayor, legislature or city council, to qualify for public funding by raising a set number of small donations to prove they are viable candidates. Once candidates qualify and apply for public funding, they must agree to forego any further fundraising on their own. These systems work to keep campaign costs down and eliminate obligations to lobbyists.[8]

The New Push for Public Funding of Elections. The recent explosion of Mega Money in American campaigns–presidential races costing in the billions, individual Senate races topping $100 million–have reignited public concern about the excessive influence of fat-cat Mega Donors.

In Congress, there has been a rebirth of interest in public funding of campaigns to offset the impact of wealthy or corporate interests flush with cash and to give more power to small donors. Several proposed bills incorporate reform strategies already working at the state or city level.

The reform measure with the broadest support is the Government by the People Act, first sponsored by Rep. John Sarbanes, a Maryland Democrat. This bill provides matching funds for donations up to $200 on a 6-to-1 ratio, as well as a $25 refundable tax credit for donations up to $200. It has attracted 155 co-sponsors–154 Democrats plus Republican Congressman

Walter Jones of North Carolina. However, so far, the House Republican majority has blocked it from coming to a vote on the House floor.

Empowering Small Donors, Engaging the Young. Public matching funds for small donors, Congressman Sarbanes argues, are a way to give some leverage back to average voters "Americans want to see Congress putting their priorities first, but the problem is that Big Money gets in the way," he says, pointing to the campaign funding and influence of oil companies, Wall Street banks, and U.S. multinationals.

Like many others in public life, Sarbanes worries about the alienation of young people who are disenchanted with money-dominated politics. To him, public funding is an antidote. "It can be very motivating in terms of getting them involved again in the political process," Says Sarbanes.

In the U.S. Senate, Illinois Democrat Dick Durbin has proposed the Fair Elections Now Act that creates a small donor matching system of public funding for both Senate and House candidates. Durbin's bill, co-sponsored by 17 Democrats, provides a 6-1 match for small contributions up to $200 but no refundable tax credit. "This bill," says Durbin, "will give candidates the opportunity to focus on dealing with our nation's problems, not on chasing after campaign cash."

While Republican leaders in Congress have generally opposed using taxpayer money to fund election campaigns, some Congressional Republicans have recently come out for tax credits for small donors. In what he calls the CIVIC Act -Citizens Involvement in Campaigns, Wisconsin Republican Representative Tom Petri has authored a bill that offers tax credits for donations up to $200.

"Most would agree that the ideal way to finance a campaign is through a broad base of donors," Petri observes. "Unfortunately, most Americans aren't in the position to donate hundreds or thousands of dollars—but they want to get involved. We should be encouraging political participation."[9]

This will require all of the skills of the servant leader to change. Without this change, it is very difficult for a true servant leader to be elected. The special interest groups can spend an almost unlimited amount of money to defeat any candidate who tries to change the system of private financing of elections.

Bernie Sanders in a press release in August 2015 said he would introduce legislation that would call for public funding of elections. He said in the press release, "We're going to introduce legislation which will allow people to run for office without having to beg money from the wealthy and the powerful."[10]

STRATEGIES FOR OVERCOMING THE CORPORATE/ORGANIZATIONAL BARRIERS TO SERVANT LEADERSHIP

Interest in the meaning and practice of servant leadership continues to grow. Hundreds of books, articles, and papers on the subject have now been published.

Many of the companies named to Fortune Magazine's annual listing of "The 100 Best Companies to Work For" espouse servant leadership and have integrated it into their corporate cultures The following seventeen organizations from Fortune's 100 Best Companies to Work For are also considered companies that are practicing servant leadership:

- SAS (#1 on the list of Best Companies to Work For)
- Wegmans Food Market (3)
- Zappos.com (6)
- Nugget Market (8)
- Recreational Equipment (REI) (9)
- Container Store (21)
- Whole Foods Market (24)
- QuikTrip (34)
- Balfour Beatty Construction (40)
- TD Industries (45)
- Aflac (57)
- Marriott International (71)
- Nordstrom (74)
- Men's Wearhouse (87)
- CH2M Hill (90)
- Darden Restaurants (97)
- Starbucks (98)

As more and more organizations and people have sought to put servant leadership into practice, the work of The Spears Center for Servant-Leadership continues to expand in order to help meet that need. Servant leadership characteristics often seem to occur naturally within many individuals; and, like many natural tendencies, they can be enhanced through learning and practice. Servant leadership offers great hope for the future in creating better, more caring, institutions.[11]

Theory Y Organizations. Theory X and 'Theory Y are theories of human motivation and management. They were created and developed by Douglas McGregor at the MIT Sloan School of Management in the 1960's. These theories describe two contrasting sets of beliefs about what motivates workers. Theory X stresses a belief in the importance of strict supervision, external rewards, and penalties: in contrast, Theory Y highlights the role of job satisfaction and encourages workers to approach tasks without direct supervision. Servant leaders generally hold Theory Y beliefs about people.

Theory Y is almost the complete opposite to that of Theory X. Theory Y managers have the following beliefs about people in the work force:

1. They are internally motivated,
2. They enjoy their labor in the company, and
3. They work to better themselves and the organization without a direct "reward" in return.

Theory Y employees should be considered as one of the most valuable assets to a company, and can truly drive the internal workings of the corporation. In addition, Theory Y states that these particular employees thrive on challenges that they may face, and relish on bettering their personal performance. Workers additionally tend to take full responsibility for their work and do not require the need of constant supervision in order to create a quality and higher standard product.

Because of the drastic change compared to the "Theory X" way of directing, "Theory Y" managers gravitate towards relating to the worker on a more personal and relatable level, as opposed to a more conductive and teaching based relationship. As a result, Theory Y followers may have a better relationship with their bosses, as well as potentially helping to create a healthier atmosphere in the work place.

In comparison to "Theory X", "Theory Y" adds more of a democratic and free feeling to the work environment allowing employees to design, construct, and publish their works in a timely manner in co-ordinance with their work load and projects. A study was done to analyze different management styles of deans and department chairs professors at a Turkish University. This study found that the highly supervised Theory X management style affected the research performance of the academics negatively. In general, the study suggests that the professional setting and research-based work that professors perform are best managed with Theory Y styles.

While "Theory Y" may seem optimal, it does have some drawbacks. While there is a more personal and individualistic feel, this leaves room for error in terms of consistency and uniformity. The workplace lacks rigid rules and practices, and this can result in an inconsistent product, which could potentially be detrimental to the quality control standards and strict guidelines of any given company.

Based on a theoretical analysis, empirical research, and case studies, there is sufficient evidence to suggest that Theory Y forms of servant leadership may indeed qualify as the best leadership style for all situations for the following reasons:

- Being freed from egotistic concerns, such as insecurity and self-advancement, Servant leaders are able to devote their full attention to developing workers and building the organization.
- Servant leaders have a positive view of workers as individuals who are capable of developing their full potentials and becoming leaders, if they are given a supportive and caring work environment.
- Being concerned with individual needs and sensitive to individual differences in personality, servant leaders are able to bring out the best in the workers.
- Being situational leaders, servant leaders recognize situations in which absence of their power actually facilitates self-management and productivity.
- Being good stewards, servant leaders will do whatever necessary and appropriate to maximize leadership effectiveness in all kinds of situations.
- Being worker-centered and growth-oriented, servant leaders can turn ordinary workers into future leaders by developing their strengths.
- The servant leader serves as an antidote to corruption and abuse in power positions.
- Servant leadership can help reduce burnout and build an emotionally healthy organization.
- The servant leader focuses on cultivating the intrinsic motivation through inspiring workers to believe in their own growth and embrace the vision and purpose of the organization.
- Servant leadership seems most suitable for the next generation of workers, who are very cynical of authority and demand authenticity from their bosses.

- Servant Leadership seems most suitable for knowledge workers, who value independence and creativity.
- Servant leadership recognizes that leadership is a group process, which should not be centralized in one or two individuals. Therefore, servant leadership is based on team building.
- Servant leadership is deeply rooted in humane, spiritual and ethical values.
- Servant leadership represents the most effective and comprehensive approach to human resources management and development.

Research on What Makes A Great Servant Leader. Servanthood by itself does not make you a great leader. One needs to blend a servant's heart with good leadership skills. After an extensive review of the literature on what makes a great leader, Wong identified twelve defining characteristics of exceptional leaders:[12]

1. **Great capacity for productive work—They seem to possess boundless energy and thrive under stress.** They are able to work indefatigably for years on end in order to accomplish an important project. Their stamina and tenacity give them a decided advantage. They manage to work with great enthusiasm even when they cannot get into a state of "flow". Their consistent productivity is based on their deeply ingrained habits of commitment and discipline.

2. **Great vision for the right direction—They can see things clearer and farther than others.** They have insight into just what is needed and the foresight to see what will succeed in the long run. They can feel the pulse of the world, which they inhabit and anticipate the world which is not yet born. Time and time again, they prove that they have the right answer, even when conventional wisdom and tradition dictate otherwise. Their vision is neither a grand illusion, nor abstract ideal. Rather, it is a living document that inspires, unites and energizes others.

3. **Great intellect and knowledge— They are intelligent, knowledgeable and competent not only in their specialty, but also in the general area of humanities, social sciences and business administration.** They have a good grasp of complex issues and the ability to get to the crux of the matter. They have the genius of holding two opposing views and the wisdom to navigate crosscurrents.

4. **Great people skills—They work well with all kinds of people from different cultures, because they have a deep understanding of human**

nature and basic human needs that transcend cultures. They see both the bright and dark side of people, without losing faith in the human potential for positive change. They don't judge others based on their beliefs, values or other cultural characteristics, because they respect the basic human dignity of all people. Understanding and flexibility characterize their leadership style. They know how to resolve conflicts effectively and foster harmony. They know that different folks need different strokes, and they apply different management skills to handle different situations.

5. **Great team-builders—They do not surround themselves with people who are subservient and loyal only to them, but select competent and creative people who are faithful to the same vision and mission.** They welcome diverse opinions and value people who are smarter than they are in various areas of expertise. They know how to put together and manage an A-team to insure organizational success.

6. **Great motivators—They create a supportive and meaningful work environment and make people feel that they matter to the organization.** They generate intrinsic motivation by involving people in the excitement of doing something significant and purposeful. They capitalize on people's strengths and know how to unleash these inner energies. They see the potential in every person and want to bring out the best in them. They empower workers to develop their potential to become great workers and leaders. They set challenging but realistic goals. By setting an example of excellence in everything they do, they make it the standard for all aspects of their operations.

7. **Great heart—Their heart is big enough to embrace the entire organization and the whole world.** They are neither partisan nor petty. They reach out to those who do not agree with them. They do not mind being proven wrong or outshone by others; their main concern is for the common good. They don't hold grudges; they are always ready to forgive and apologize. Their capacity for compassion is equivalent to their understanding.

8. **Great communicators—They can articulate a vision and tell compelling stories to rally people around a common goal.** They know how to inform as well as inspire. Above all, they are good listeners. They understand people's needs and feelings by talking to them on a personal level. Their ability to resonate with others is based not so much on com-

munication skills as on their deeply felt sense of connectedness with the organization and humanity.

9. **Great optimists—They stay optimistic even when circumstances are bleak.** Their optimism stems from personal faith more than anything else. They have faith that good will prevail over evil and persistence will eventually lead to success. They know how to inspire hope through difficult times, while battling their own inner doubts. Their proven capacity to endure and overcome inspires others to be optimistic about the unknown.

10. **Great courage—They have the courage to confront their worst fears and risk everything in order to remain true to their own convictions and other people's trust.** Courage is not the absence of fear, but the ability to persist and act effectively in the presence of fear. They know how to live with the continued tension between despair and hope, doubts and confidence, and fear and courage. They grow stronger as a result of this constant opposition.

11. **Great self-knowledge—They know who they are and what they stand for.** They know that their strengths also contain the seeds of their destruction (e.g., over-confidence). They also accept their own weaknesses and limitations as the essential conditions of being human. They are willing to accept negative feedback in order to improve themselves. They would not let their ego get in the way of doing what is good for the organization. Feeling comfortable in their own skin reduces their defensiveness. Their humility comes from their emotional maturity and self-knowledge.

12. **Great character—Above all, they possess integrity and authenticity.** They have the moral courage to stand up for their beliefs and do what is right, no matter how much it will cost them. To them, integrity is more important than success. Their leadership is principle-centered and purpose-driven, regardless of the pressure to make expedient. They are transparent and genuine; they say what they mean and they walk their talk. They accept responsibility for their choices and do not blame others for their own mistakes. They do not steal credit from others. One of their greatest assets is their "reputational capital". Others can always rely on their trustworthiness, because they serve as symbols of moral fortitude.

It is self-evident that the best practices of servant leadership listed above all contribute the development of an effective leadership, especially in matters related to the heart and character of the leader. In fact, servant leaders are more likely to be characterized by personal humility and a fierce dedication to a larger cause. Servant leaders with these qualities are able to give and receive unconditional love in their interactions with those they serve.

NOTES

1   Weinhold, B & Weinhold, J. (2013). How to break tree of the drama triangle and victim consciousness. Colorado Springs, CO: CICRCL/ClearSpace/Kindle e-book)

2   Ibid.

3   http://www.commondreams.org/news/2016/04/06/fact-sanders-has-very-clear-plan-how-break-too-big-fail-banks
    Accessed on June 1, 2016.

4   Ibid.

5   Blair, E. (May 4, 2011). 5 Alternatives to the Federal Reserve. Activist Post. http://www.activistpost.com/2011/05/5-alternatives-to-federal-reserve.html

6   Ibid.

7   Ibid.

8   Ibid.

9   Issue Brief: Empower Small Donors, Public Campaign Funding http://reclaimtheamericandream.org/brief-public/ Accessed May 9, 2016.

10 https://berniesanders.com/press-release/sanders-proposes-public-funding-of-campaigns/ Accessed May 9, 2016.

11 Spears, L. (2010). The Journal of Virtues & Leadership, Vol. 1 Is. 1, 25-30. School of Global Leadership & Entrepreneurship: Regent University.

12 Wong, P. T. P. (2007). What makes a great leader? Retrieved on July 16 from http://www.meaning.ca/archives/presidents_columns/pres_col_jun_2007_great-leader.htm

CHAPTER 13

STRATEGIES FOR OVERCOMING RELIGIOUS, CULTURAL AND EDUCATIONAL BARRIERS TO SERVANT LEADERSHIP

*"True leadership must be for the benefit of
the followers, not to enrich the leader."*

—*John C. Maxwell*

STRATEGIES FOR OVERCOMING CULTURAL BARRIERS TO SERVANT LEADERSHIP

The chart below outlines the developmental tasks/process of communities and cultures. In the third column of this chart are suggested ways to help complete any developmental process that is complete in any way. These are some of the ways that communities and cultures have healed their developmental traumas and helped communities and cultures to evolve.

Table 13-1
The Developmental Stages of a Community and Culture[1]

Stage of Development	The developmental tasks of a culture	Methods for completing these tasks
Co-dependent	• Build trust • Create a group identity • Provide for the basic needs of all group members • Build esprit 'de corps	• Provide meaning through community or cultural identity • Identify common values and beliefs • Utilize group song, dance and ritual to unify and inspire

Stage of Development	The developmental tasks of a culture	Methods for completing these tasks
Counter-dependent	• Identify unique characteristics of the group • Resolve conflicts of needs between group members	• Encourage creativity regarding the expression of values and beliefs • Offer conflict resolution training to all members
Independent	• Create a set of values and beliefs for the culture • Provide opportunities for sub-groups to form within the larger group • Celebrate the unique characteristics of the cultural group and its sub-groups	• Create forums to encourage the interfacing and interweaving of diverse expressions of values and beliefs • Acknowledge and honor the presence of cultural sub-groups • Teach divergent and convergent thinking • Encourage direct communication between members of cultural sub-groups
Interdependent	• Build consensus between sub-group members	• Identify common goals and visions through collective processes • Utilize sub-group interactions for learning experiences • Create humanitarian organizations to serve the needs of members

STRATEGIES FOR OVERCOMING CULTURAL BARRIERS TO SERVANT LEADERSHIP

THE GREAT TURNING

By looking at the big picture of where we are in our evolution as a community or culture, we can see that these developmental systems are in transition. Some old elements are breaking down and new elements are emerging to replace them. The term "The Great Turning" seems to fit this current situation. Below I describe this concept and how it can provide a framework to understand change. Once you as a servant leader understand how this is happening, you can design strategies that support this change.

The Term "The Great Turning" was first used by Craig Schindler and Gary Lapid to describe the framing idea underlying the work of Project Victory, which they founded in 1985. Their work focused on reducing the risks of nuclear war and conflict transformation. They report that they trained 10,000 leaders in conflict transformation and led a national dialogue on dismantling nuclear weapons. More recently, they sponsored what they describe as "the largest dialogue on race relations ever conducted in the U.S." They used the term "The Great Turning" in their talks, dialogues, and articles.

In 1989, Schindler and Lapid published The Great Turning: Personal Peace - Global Victory,[2] with a marketing endorsement from Joanna Macy. Macy then expanded and deepened the concept and introduced the term and its underlying framework to hundreds of thousands of people through her writing, lectures, and workshops.

David Korten has been the latest and most powerful spokesperson for the Great Turning. Below David summarizes the key elements of how he sees this evolutionary movement. It seems to me an understanding of the key elements listed below should be part of the mission of any servant leader.

The Key Elements of the Great Turning[3]. The version of The Great Turning by Korten provides a powerful framework for the servant leader who wishes to understand our current cultural shifts. It provides a deep historical context for defining the collective choices we must now make as a species. Here are the key elements:

1. We humans face a choice between two contrasting models for organizing our affairs: the dominator model of Empire and the partnership model of the Earth Community.

2. After 5,000 years of organizing human affairs by the dominator model, the Era of Empire finally has reached the limits of the exploitation that people and Earth can peacefully sustain.

3. A mounting perfect economic storm born of a convergence of peak oil, climate change, and a falling U.S. dollar is poised to bring a dramatic restructuring of every aspect of modern life.

4. While technology plays an important role, there is no technological fix for the human crisis. The underlying problem is a consequence of social dysfunction and the only solutions are cultural and institutional

5. We now face a choice between a last man standing imperial competition for what remains of Earth's natural bounty and a cooperative sharing of Earth's resources to create a world that works for all.

6. Empire's power depends on its ability to control the stories by which humans define themselves and their possibilities. Whoever controls the prosperity, security, and the stories that define the mainstream culture, controls the society.

7. The key to changing the human course is by replacing the prevailing Empire prosperity, security, and the stories that define the dominator hierarchy as the natural and essential human order. Replacing that senerario with the Earth Community prosperity, security, and the stories that celebrate the human capacity to live in cooperative balance with one another and Earth.

8. Security and social order depend on strong, caring communities based on mutual responsibility and accountability.

9. Healthy children, families, communities, and natural systems are the true measure of prosperity.

10. To end poverty, heal the environment, rebuild community, and secure the human future it is necessary to turn from growth to the reallocation of resources as the defining economic priority. Eliminate harmful uses (military, advertising, sprawl, and financial speculation), increase beneficial uses (environmental regeneration, food and energy self-reliance, health, education, and productive investment), and give priority to the needs of those the old economy excludes and represses (the desperate, hungry, and indentured). The transition to a New Economy is foundational to navigating the Great Turning.

11. The Great Turning includes the manifestation of an integral spiritual intelligence seeking to know itself through an on-going creative enfoldment process in search of unrealized possibilities.

12. We humans are a choice making, choice-creating species that can choose to create societies that nurture our higher order capacities for compassion, sharing, and commitment to the well-being of all.

13. Meaning is found in discovering our place of service to the whole.[4]

STRATEGIES FOR OVERCOMING RELIGIOUS BARRIERS TO SERVANT LEADERSHIP

There is still a strong push among the evangelical Christians to make this a Christian nation. This would mean, among other things, the extension of the patriarchal model of leadership.

The servant leader has to be able to understand why the current systems of religion are breaking down and how to intervene to create breakthroughs.

Clearly, religions have to adapt to the changing times and examine the beliefs that no longer fit the times and actually impede the evolution of our culture. Your choice of religions is yours, but I would hope you would choose wisely. For it to be an actual choice, there have to be two relatively equal alternatives from which to choose. So, what is the viable alternative to church membership in a Christian or other church? For example, you can choose to be more spiritual than religious.

Religion can be defined as "belief in God or gods to be worshipped, usually expressed in conduct and ritual" or "any specific system of belief, worship, etc., often involving a code of ethics." Spirituality can be defined as "the quality or fact of being spiritual, non-physical" or "predominantly spiritual character as shown in thought, life, etc.; spiritual tendency or tone." To put it briefly, religion is a set of beliefs and rituals that claim to get a person in a right relationship with God, and spirituality is a focus on spiritual things and the spiritual world instead of physical/earthly things.

What religion and spirituality have in common is that they both can utilize false methods for having a relationship with God. Religion tends to substitute the heartless observance of rituals for a genuine relationship with God. Spirituality tends to substitute connection with the spirit world for a genuine relationship with God. Both can be, and often are, false paths to God.

At the same time, religion can be valuable in the sense that it points to the fact that there is a God and that we are somehow accountable to Him. The only true value of religion is its ability to point out that we have sinned and are in need of a Savior. Spirituality can be valuable in that it points out that the physical world is not all there is.

Human beings are not only material, but also possess a soul-spirit. There is a spiritual world around us of which we should be aware. The true value of spirituality is that it points to the fact that there is something and someone beyond this physical world to which we need to connect.[5]

STRATEGIES FOR OVERCOMING THE EDUCATIONAL BARRIERS TO SERVANT LEADERSHIP

What Is the Purpose of Education? As educators prepare young people for their futures in a world that is rapidly changing, it is important to ask: what is the goal? Is it to create adults who can compete in a global economy? Is it to create lifelong learners? Is it to create emotionally healthy adults who can engage in meaningful relationships?

"There are many different points of view on this topic," says Jonathan Cohen, co-founder and president of the National School Climate Center. He says, "I think that my view, and most people's view, is that the purpose of education is to support children in developing the skills, the knowledge, and the dispositions that will allow them to be responsible, contributing members of their community—their democratically-informed community. People need to be a good friend, to be a good mate, to be able to work, and to contribute to the well-being of the community."[6]

Not only should children have civic knowledge—how the electoral college works, the history of political parties, and so on—but they also need to master civic skills, which include respecting others, working collaboratively, acting in a way that is fair and just, and being an active participant in the life of the community.

He adds, "There is a paradox in our pre K–12 schools and within teacher education. Parents and teachers want schooling to support children's ability to become lifelong learners who are able to love, work, and act as responsible members of the community. Yet, we have not substantially integrated these values into our schools or into the training we give teachers,"

The consensus is that there's no need to scrap what has served us well in the past. However, educational policy makers seem to agree that the most significant skill young people can develop in the 21st century is the same skill that served them well in prior centuries: a mind equipped to think critically, the most important work skill of them all.

In addition to teaching students to think critically, students need to be exposed to global ideas. For instance, a Gallup poll reveals that only about one in four Americans can speak a foreign language. Yet, 19 percent of Americans believe it is essential to speak a second language and another 50 percent believe it is a valuable skill.

By contrast, more than 50 percent of Europeans speak a second language, and many of those know a third language as well. The lack of knowledge and understanding of other countries and their cultures could become an increasing liability as the tentacles of the world's economy reach out in various ways. Simple communication and the adaptability to individual cultural rules become more important in the development of this worldwide connection.

Another issue is class size. Researchers have found that gains in achievement generally occur when class size is reduced to less than 20 students.

Here is a summary of the gains students make when the class size is reduced to less than 20 students.

- Gains associated with small classes are stronger for the early grades.
- Gains are stronger for students who come from groups that are traditionally disadvantaged in education — minorities and immigrants.
- Gains from class size reduction in the early grades continue for students in the upper grades. Students are less likely to be retained, more likely to stay in school and more likely to earn better grades.

Academic gains are not the only benefit of lowering class size. A recent study published in the American Journal of Public Health revealed that reducing class sizes in elementary schools may be more cost-effective than most public health and medical interventions. This is because students in smaller classes are more likely to graduate from high school, and high school graduates earn more and also enjoy significantly better health than high school dropouts.

Making Our Schools Safe for Children. James Coleman chaired a massive research study in 1966 (The Coleman Report) to measure the quality of American K-12 education.[7] Using data from over 600,000 students and teachers across the country, the researchers found that academic achievement was less related to the quality of a student's school, and more related to the social composition of the school, the school's climate, the student's sense of control of his environment and future, the verbal skills of teachers, and the student's family background.

It was the largest and most important study on K-12 education in the 20th century. It helped transform educational theory, reshape national education policies, and influenced public and scholarly opinion regarding the role of schooling in determining equality and productivity in the United States.

As a work of sociology, the Coleman Report was full of subtleties and caveats, but the mass media and makers of policy focused on one prediction: that black children who attended integrated schools would have higher test scores if a majority of their classmates were white. This helped spur school desecration.

However, he personally regarded one finding of this study to be its most important one. The researchers found that achievement was determined by how "safe" the school is perceived. He stated that the most important reform was to first make sure students feel safe at school. This finding led me to look at what was making schools unsafe for children and what I thought schools needed to do to improve school safety. I zeroed in on the school climate.

The Kind and Safe Schools Initiative[8]. The program that I designed to make sure a school is safe is the "Kind and Safe Schools Initiative." Over 700 U. S. schools have utilized parts of this initiative. The main goal is to change the school climate from negative to positive by systematically recognizing pro-social behaviors.

It is based on the psychology 101 notion that what you pay attention to you get more of. If you get a majority of students, staff teachers and administrators paying attention to positive things that happen every day in a school, it works and the negative elements of school climate are reduced significantly.

I decided to create this program after being invited to visit over 100 area schools and speaking to the students and faculty. I would always begin my talk to the students by saying something like this: "I am new to your school. Tell me if it is easier in this school to get noticed or recognized for doing or saying something positive or by doing or saying something negative. Let's see the hands of those who say, 'positive' (I would usually get either no hands or just a few hands). Now let's see how many say 'negative.'" (Almost all hands went up. Some kids raised both their hands.) I then began asking these same question to the teachers and I got the same answers.

From this informal survey, I concluded that these schools were part of a "culture of negativity" that was present in families, schools and the workplace. I knew we had to find a way to shift this to focusing on positive behaviors in order to change the climate in schools. Although my sample was not randomly selected, I believe it represented what likely is going on in most schools in this country.

I eventually designed KASSI and made it available in e-book form on my website at a very low price. I believe that this program does change the school climate from being predominately negative to being positive.

Outcomes of KASSI. Schools that implemented the components of KASSI have been able to transform the learning climate in about one to two school years. These are not instant cures, but they have proven to be effective. Here is a list of the outcomes that our research has confirmed:

1. **A more positive school climate.** Our research results show that students who are recognized for positive acts are less likely to put-down or bully others.

2. **Fewer referrals to the office for fighting.** Our research showed that discipline referrals to the office immediately dropped by over 30% after KASSI was introduced. Long-term results over the whole school year showed about a 26% drop. Suspensions & expulsions were also markedly reduced.

3. **Fewer incidents of bullying.** Teachers reported a significant reduction in bullying behaviors after KASSI was introduced. When students saw others getting recognized for positive behaviors, they began to seek this recognition.

4. **Fewer student-to-student put-downs.** Our research shows that student-to-student put-downs dropped significantly when the KASSI was introduced. In some schools, they dropped as much as 94% in the three weeks after the Campaign was introduced into their school.

5. **Kids will resolve conflicts peacefully on their own.** Again, research shows that when the students are taught conflict resolution skills, they resolve their own conflicts without any adult intervention.

6. **School achievement will increase.** In schools where KASSI was well integrated into the daily schedule, student achievement test scores increased. When the school climate was kinder and safer, students felt less anxious and were better able to learn.

7. **School attendance will increase.** Studies have shown that students stay home as much as once a month because of the fear of bullying or harassment. When the school climate improved, students were not afraid to come to school.

8. **Increased participation in school activities.** KASSI encouraged students to participate in school activities and created service-learning opportunities in which students could participate in kindness activities inside and outside the school.

9. **Higher self-esteem of students and faculty.** When kindergarten kids were asked if they like themselves, 95% said "yes." When high school seniors were asked the same question, only 5% replied "yes." When the school climate was improved through KASSI, students and faculty reported more positive self-esteem.

10. **Increased empathy, sensitivity, and friendship skills.** Many of the KASSI classroom activities taught students to be aware of the impact of their behavior. They began to better understand the negative impact of their bullying behavior & put-downs on others.

11. **Increased resistance to peer pressures.** Students were given support for setting limits and speaking up for themselves. This was a key outcome of KASSI.

My book coauthored, with Janae Weinhold, Conflict Resolution: The Partnership Way, contains several chapters that describe more fully the impact that these community-based and school-based programs have had. This program represents an openhearted intervention that a servant leader could use to transform any school or community. It follows the principles of servant leadership. The curriculum for KASSI and instructions on how to implement it in your school is available for purchase at www.weinholds.org.

Revitalizing Higher Education. One of the greatest challenges to higher education is the loss of federal and state funding. As part of the plan to dumb down higher education, most states have cut back on funding on higher education. In addition, online learning has competed with some college and university curricula. These are some of the challenges that the servant leader has to face. There is also a push to better understand the learning styles of their students. Here are five bold predictions about how to overcome the challenges that will define the future of education:

1. **Academic Curricula Will Become More Multidisciplinary.** Current models—reliant upon departmental space where curriculum is developed and fostered independent of the university at large—must change. Today's students demand cross-disciplinary learning and thinking, particularly in science, engineering, and technology. This cross-disciplinary learning demand is manifesting itself in buildings that seek to be academies of tomorrow and entrepreneurial hubs focused on bringing business and creative minds together. Colleges and universities need to think about how these space changes serve as curriculum drivers.

    Examples of this can be found in our project at the University of Utah where they are developing a transformative entrepreneurial building where students can create, live and "launch" companies all in the same space. Elsewhere, the University at Buffalo partnered with Kaleida Health to create a one-of-a-kind facility that brings their academic research center into the same building as a global vascular institute. Incubator spaces within this building extend beyond the notion of "fusion" and empower students to utilize design thinking as a means to create solutions, solve problems and make jobs not take jobs.

2. **Educational Leaders Will Need to Balance Online Learning With Traditional Learning.** Amidst the ongoing discussion relative to online education over the past few years, it is important to remember higher education institutions don't need to choose between online learning and traditional learning; they need to find the right balance. Recent research shows a fifth of Chief Academic Officers (CAOs) don't feel online education is strongly represented in their institutions' long-term strategies, even though they believe it should be. At the same time, new statistics also reveal that while distance education has been growing at a faster rate than traditional higher education ever since 2003, that rate of growth is beginning to slow.

   The truth is that none of the educational delivery models is intrinsically better than the other. Universities need to strategically balance both platforms and think about how they support the never-ending, 24/7 nature of today's learning that extends beyond the classroom.

   Institutions that begin to best leverage an appropriate balance can make better use of time in the classroom and also define tailored approaches to how the professor, student and material work together across the platforms. The University at Buffalo entered into an innovative partnership with Kaleida Health, resulting in a building that stacks their clinical translational research center above Kaleida's Global Vascular Institute.

3. **Student Recruitment and Retention Will Be More Important Than Ever.** To best recruit and retain students, universities need to evaluate how they can offer a student life experience that prepares students to be healthy and dynamic people in the future. That means universities need to embrace sustainability and wellness as key components to campus life. Spellman College recently differentiated itself by diverting all of its athletic funding to create a "Wellness Revolution," focused on best ways to promote the health of its students.

   Scores of other universities are realizing students value their life experience just as much as their academic experience. This is pushing universities to find creative ways to fund new spaces and programming for students. The key here is strategically providing students with resources that give them more opportunity to make the most of their collegiate life experience.

4. **They Need to Invest in Technology.** Today's students aren't just bringing their own technology devices to the classroom, they're also bringing

them to the student center, the gym and the dining hall. This increased use places greater demands on a campus IT infrastructure. Universities seeking to solve today's challenges will need to respond with robust access and bandwidth upgrades. At the same time, institutions need to respond to the "mobility shift" which allows educators and students to be nimble and engaged from anywhere.

Additionally, the education community needs to think about how the emergence of augmented reality devices from Google Glass to Oculus will transform campuses. These devices bring powerful questions related to how they enable students and teachers to maximize the educational experience. Moreover, all of the thinking relative to technology investments needs to also consider security. A cyber security attack at the University of Maryland earlier this year revealed that universities need to balance empowering students with keeping them safe.

5. **Explore New Funding Models.** The historic practice of relying on funding to state institutions based on enrollment is already shifting to performance-based models. These models will redirect educational priorities and investment to help more students succeed, while also redefining an institution's responsibility to its students and its community. While the performance model discussions are more apparent for the state–funded institutions, their impact may extend further as it pertains to incubation, research and corporate support.

Already, these systems are gaining momentum and leaders need to be highly involved with their build-out. There's no magic button to press to ensure educational institutions will have success in the future. However, those seeking to differentiate themselves and are willing to attract the best students and empower them, need to think about these issues and react with strategic plans as soon as possible.[9]

NOTES

1   Weinhold, B. & Weinhold, J. (2009). *Conflict resolution: The partnership way.* Denver, CO: Love Publishing Co.

2   Schindler, C. & Lapid, G. (1989). *The great turning: Personal peace, global victory.* Santa Fe, NM: Bear & Co.

3   Korten, D. (2006). *The great turning: From empire to earth community.* San Francisco, CA: Berrett-Koehler Publishers

4   Living Economics Forum David Korten
    http://www.davidkorten.org/the-great-turning-in-bullet-points
    Accessed 4/28/16

5   *http://www.gotquestions.org/religion-spirituality.html*
    Accessed 5/21/16

6   *Sloan, W. (July 2012). What is the purpose of education?*
    Education Update. Vol. 54, No. 7.

7   *Coleman, J. (1966). The Coleman Report.*
    https://en.wikipedia.org/wiki/James_Samuel_Coleman
    Accessed May, 21, 2016.

8   *Weinhold, B. (2006). The Kind and Safe Schools Initiative.*
    http://weinholds.org/kind-and-safe-schools-kassi/

9   *http://www.fastcoexist.com/3029109/futurist-forum/5-bold-predictions-for-the-*
    future-of-higher-education
    Accessed June 3, 2016.

CHAPTER 14

HOW TO BECOME A SERVANT LEADER

"A new moral principle is emerging which holds that the only authority deserving one's allegiance is that which is freely and knowingly granted by the led to the leader in response to, and in proportion to, the clearly evident servant stature of the leader. Those who choose to follow this principle will not casually accept the authority of existing institutions. Rather, they will freely respond only to Individuals who are chosen as leaders because they are proven and trusted servants. To the extent that this principle prevails in the future, the only truly viable institutions will be those that are predominantly servant-led."

—*Robert K. Greenleaf*

THE JOURNEY TO BECOME A SERVANT LEADER

A person does not wake up one morning and suddenly become a servant leader. It is a journey, mostly an inner one, that gets you to the place where you can begin to take on the role of a servant leader. Below is a summary of the "travel tips" that I have found helpful to remember when you begin the journey to find your inner servant leader.

TRAVEL TIPS FOR THE JOURNEY OF THE SERVANT LEADER

1. **Park your victim consciousness.** It is excess baggage and it will bog you down with needless drama.
2. **Bend your knees and get ready for change.** The only constant is change; be ready to embrace it.
3. **Prepare for unexpected directional shifts.** Keep your knees bent and be ready to shift directions at any given moment.

4. **Keep your life in balance.** Your inner harmony and balance will keep you moving in the right direction.

5. **Learn how to harvest the wisdom contained in your feelings.** Your feelings will show you the way; follow them.

6. **During this journey you will have no ultimate safety, security or guarantees, so don't expect any.** Allow yourself to stay in the moment and stay alert.

7. **Recycle yourself.** Remember what you did yesterday that was successful and use it again today.

8. **The best navigational tools during your journey are your values, beliefs and your intentions.** Stay in touch with your core values, beliefs and intentions and let them be your navigator.

9. **You will need to develop the courage to reach, learn, risk, and leap.** Seize the moment and act with courage. He who hesitates is lost.

10. **Identify your long-term purpose and pair it with short-term goals.** Check how "on purpose" you are with every action you take today.

11. **Do not let your career work define your actions.** Your inner work needs to happen before you undertake any outer work.

12. **Remember: everyone is participating in some way in this journey.** Look for allies and fellow travelers. They are everywhere.

13. **Achieve individuation as a human being.** Becoming fully individuated is your ultimate goal. Don't forget it.

14. **Resolve your conflicts in a partnership way where everybody wins.** Conflict is an opportunity to get closer to your true self and the true self of others.

15. **Keep all your agreements and don't make agreements you don't intend to keep.** Your worth as a person is determined by how well you keep your agreements.

16. **Be truthful without being unkind.** Speak your truth, but don't use it to put others down.

17. **Learn life's lessons.** Life's lessons will keep presenting themselves until you learn them.

18. **Love yourself and others unconditionally.** Unconditional love is your greatest tool for peace and human evolution.

19. **Stay in the NOW.** There is no past or future, only the eternal now. Learn to be here now.

20. **Be 100% responsible for everything you say and do and everything you see outside of yourself.** Being responsible does not mean feeling "guilty." It just means fully exercising your ability to respond in any situation.

WAYS TO DEVELOP INNER KNOWING

In order to become a servant leader, your first step is to get beyond your beliefs about yourself, other people and the outer world. This means developing your spiritual inner knowing skills. It is the place inside of you that knows what is true and what the right action is for you to take in any situation. When you can access this inner knowledge, you no longer have to "believe", you will "know" what is true for you.

Carl Jung called it, "The wisdom of the heart that the mind can never understand." There are literally thousands of tools that you can use to develop your inner knowing. In this chapter, I have chosen some of the most tried and true methods that I have learned. These tools have helped me to develop and refine the quality of my inner knowing.

You may have already been practicing some of these methods. If so, you can skip over them and work with the self-correction exercises keyed to certain practices that you haven't studied or practiced.

Like any set of spiritual practices, the sum of the individual parts does not necessarily equal the whole. The ones I chose are the foundational level practices I have utilized the most over the years, but not necessarily the advanced ones.

I still utilize these practices on a daily basis or when needed. The quest for inner knowing can be a lifetime search for some, as it is for me, while others can develop effective inner knowing quite quickly and easily.

Centering. The skill of centering is basic to many other tools that I utilize. It is also one of the most useful skills I have ever learned and I utilize it almost every day. It is impossible to live your life totally centered all the time, unless you are living in a monastery where you have no distractions. If your life is anything like mine, it will provide you with enough twists and turns that can throw you off center on a daily basis.

Kenneth Cooper, the inventor of Aerobics developed his system by wiring up people measuring their at-rest heart rate and pulse rate. Then he put them under some physical stress, usually, running on a treadmill. After a set number of minutes, he had them stop and he watched how long it would take them to return to their at-rest heart rate and pulse rate.

The shorter the time it took to return to their normal pulse/heart rates the more physically fit they were. The same principle applies to centering. The shorter time it takes you to return to center after you are pulled of center by something, the more psychologically fit you are.

I have been practicing this skill for many years since I learned it from Tom Crum, an Aikido master. The trick is to quickly notice when something pulls you off center and then do what you can to return to center.

For many years I think I was chronically off center in my life and I didn't even notice. So how would I know what it felt like to be on center? First, I had to feel what it is like to feel centered. Then I had to learn to recognize the signals my body was sending me that told me I was off center. When I learned these steps, then I could quickly re-center myself.

I can even use this tool on the tennis court. If I miss a shot I think I should have made, my self-blaming thoughts can pull me off center. If I don't let go of them and return to center, I am likely to miss the next shot as well.

Now, I can quickly notice that I am being pulled off center. It can be my self-critical thoughts about missing a tennis shot or getting angry at someone for cutting me off on the freeway or feeling hurt because someone said or did something that I didn't like.

Then I do a deep connected breath (a long slow connected inhale and exhale) so I feel my body relaxing and returning to center starting at the top of my head and rippling down to the bottom of my feet. After much practice it now takes me only one deep breath to return to feeling centered.

If I am on the tennis court in the middle of a match my thoughts about a missed shot often pull me off center. When that happens, I have learned to take one long, deep breath and return my body/mind to feeling centered. This simple exercise has greatly improved my tennis game.

A Self-Correction Exercise: How Can I Center Myself?[1] Physical centering is the outcome of mentally refocusing your energy. This concept can be demonstrated with a simple activity involving two people.

Person A learning to be centered stands relaxed with his or her feet about shoulder-width apart and knees slightly bent, but not locked. With eyes open, this person is asked to focus his or her thoughts and feelings on something unpleasant that has happened or is anticipated will happen.

Person B stands facing the side of the first person at a 90-degree angle. Person B then applies pressure gently and gradually on the Person A's upper back.

As Person B gradually applies more pressure on Person A's back, this person will begin to feel uncentered and start to fall forward. Person B repeats this process by gently using the left hand to apply gradual pressure to the Person A's upper chest to see if they will begin to fall backward as well.

Notice if there are any differences between the way the Person A responds when pushed off center from the back versus being pushed off center from the front. This can indicate which kind of incident is more likely to cause them to become uncentered: something they are aware of (front) or something unexpected (back).

Next, Person A focuses his or her thoughts on a spot about two inches below the navel near the physical center of gravity of the body. To assist in this focusing, it is useful for Person A to place one hand on this area of the abdomen while Person B again applies pressure on the upper back and then the upper chest of the first person. Again, Person A needs to stay relaxed with knees bent and eyes open.

Both people should see a noticeable difference. Person A should feel very solid and strong without having to exert any extra energy. Person B who is pushing with one hand should find that Person A is no longer a "push over" and has to exert more pressure to push them off center.

After you have completed this with Person A, reverse roles and do the same process again. Taking part in this activity helps people have a physical experience of centering. Once this state of awareness is physically anchored in the body, it is easy to return to by taking a deep breath and focusing on your center of gravity in your abdomen.

Once the skill is learned, it is usually not necessary for a person to place his/her hand on the abdomen. If you return to this state when something happens to pull you off center, you'll find it easier to think clearly and quickly and will be better able to flow with the unfolding elements of the situation.

Prayer. Prayer a reverent petition made to God, a god, or another object of worship is a spiritual tool long extolled for its efficacy in many traditions. Scientific evidence now supports the value of prayer as a form of spiritual healing. Randolph Byrd, a cardiologist and a non-believer in prayer, set out to prove scientifically that prayer had no healing effects.

I was at a professional conference where I first heard Larry Dossey, M.D. speak about a study done by Randolph Byrd on the effects of prayer. Dossey, in his book, Healing Words 2 he cited over 130 studies of the effects of prayer with over half of the studies showing significant effects in favor of prayer.

Byrd used a clinical double-blind study in which he randomly assigned 393 coronary-care patients at a San Francisco Hospital to "prayer" or "non-prayer" groups. Neither the patients nor the doctors or nurses knew which patients were being prayed for and which were not.

Groups of five to seven people located all around the country were given the patient's name and some information about their medical condition and were asked to pray for them every day. The results shocked Byrd. The prayed-for patients compared with the non-prayed for patients had:

- Five times less need for antibiotics,
- Three times fewer cases of pulmonary edema,
- No need for mechanical breathing assistance, and
- Fewer deaths.

The most surprising outcome of the study was that the distance between the prayer groups and the patients being prayed for did not seem to matter. The prayer groups around the corner from the hospital had no more effect than the prayer groups located in New York or Miami.

The study was replicated in 1999 in a double-blind experiment involving 990 consecutive patients who were admitted to a coronary care unit (CCU). Patients were randomized to receive remote, intercessory prayer or not. The first names of patients in the prayer group were given to a team of outside intercessors who prayed for them daily for 4 weeks.

Patients were unaware they were being prayed for, and the intercessors did not know and never met the patients. The medical course from hospital admission to discharge was summarized in a CCU course score derived from blinded, retrospective chart review.

The prayed-for group had about a 10 percent advantage compared to the usual-care group (P = .04). Several other similar studies failed to show significant healing effects of prayer. It appears that it does deserve further study before any clear-cut relationships can be established.

Recently there have been several new studies including a double-blind study by Sicher, Targ, Moore, and Smith,[2] who found positive effects from distant healing in patients with advanced AIDS. This study was conducted at UCSF-California Pacific Medical Center.

Other experiments set out to answer the question: Is there a "best" way to pray? In other words, are there guidelines to suggest how to get the most "bang for the buck" out of your prayers? The Spindrift Foundation designed interesting experiments to attempt to answer this question.[3] Between 1975 and 1993 this group carried out literally hundreds of thousands of replications of their research. They utilized two different types of prayer: directed and non-directed.

A directed prayer was defined as one that was aimed at a specific outcome. Non-directed prayer was defined as prayer that doesn't ask for a specific outcome; only what is in the best interests of the person or plant that is being prayed for. They found that both types of prayer worked better than the control group where no prayer was used. However, the group where non-directed prayer was used did significantly better than the directed prayer group.

Author Greg Braden has examined the way we pray and has identified what he believes to be the best type of prayer. In his book, The Isaiah Effect,[4] Braden lists four types of prayer in common use. They are colloquial prayer, petitionary prayer, ritualistic prayer and meditative prayer. He then adds a fifth type of prayer that he claims to have been discovered in one of the Dead Sea Scrolls called the Isaiah Scrolls.

This form of prayer, Braden explains comes from your heart and is really a feeling that validates that whatever you are praying for has already happened. He contrasts this mode of prayer with the logic-based mode of prayer that is typically used.

Braden asserts that when you pray you need to imagine that your prayer has already been answered. This he says is much more effective than praying for peace in a war zone. The prayer can actually draw the exact opposite energy than you intend and produce more war.

Braden and others, building upon proven non-local effects of prayer, have been conducting various experiments involving a large group of people praying together at the same time all over the world. He speculates that if a number approximating the square root of 1% of the world's population were praying at the same time, (3.14 X the population of the world) it would produce a massive shift in consciousness all over the world.

According to Braden, the relationship between mass prayer and the non-local effect of those prayers is due to a phenomenon known as the "field effect of consciousness." This is an area of prayer research that needs to be explored before any definite conclusions can be drawn.

Beyond this useful information, what else does the research on prayer convey? We can conclude that our apparently 3D world is also non-local in nature. If we can connect our mind to all other moments, places and persons, we can exist in a Reality that is totally multidimensional.

Science can show us that all this is possible, but we may need to feel it and experience it before knowing that this is real. This makes it possible to understand how to connect with the knowledge and the energy that is coming to you from each planet in our solar system, from the magnificent star systems in our universe and our whole galaxy.

Self-Correction Exercise: What Is The Most Effective Way To Pray?[5] If you wish to use a more traditional form of prayer, here are the steps I would recommend you use as you develop your skill to pray effectively.

- Create a peaceful setting for your prayer. Since prayer is a developable skill, it is good to control the externals such as the setting as you develop your ability to pray. Later the externals will not be as important.
- Be specific about what you are praying for. Vague prayers generate vague outcomes. Honor yourself and whom you are praying to with clarity, directness and sincerity. The subject of your prayer should include a request for a specific outcome. It is also important to add disclaimers like, "if this prayer is in my highest good" or "I ask for this or something better that is in my highest good. The same is true if you are praying for someone else.
- Be clear in your intentions. Remember the basic law of prayer: Ask and you will receive. Prayer helps you develop your ability to ask clearly for what you want. Be sure that what you are asking for is what you want in the long run.
- Carefully frame the language of your prayer. Consider writing out our prayer and examining it for clarity, accuracy, intention, consistency, integrity, appropriateness and alignment. As you develop your skills, you probably will not need to write out your prayer.

You may also ask yourself some of the following questions to make sure the language you chose is what you want to say: Is it really what I want? Is it in my highest good? Will it benefit me and all other beings? Do I fully understand the implications of my request and the results I want? To whom are you praying? Do you have to pray to a specific deity for it to be effective? What if you don't believe in God? Most prayer is addressed to the God or deity of your choice, but it doesn't have to be directed at one specific God. The following are some options to consider:

- Direct it to other beings in the spirit realm such as guides, teachers, avatars, angels, and other ascended masters.
- Send prayers to friends or other human beings, sentient beings, ancestors and relatives.
- Communicate with other realms of spirit including the mineral realm, the plant realm, the animal realm and all the spirits connected to these realms.
- Communicate with your own "higher self" to enhance your spiritual self-reliance, compassion, inner strength, personal responsibility and self-trust.
- No matter how you direct your prayer, I recommend adding at the end of the prayer that whatever you are asking for be for the "highest good of all concerned," including yourself.

Meditation. I see prayer as asking for what you want or need and meditation as opening up to receive the information or support you are seeking. It is a less active way of knowing. It requires you to quiet the chatter of your surface mind and listen for the thoughts and feelings that come to you through your deeper mind.

Meditation is an important tool to achieve self-realization and individuation. It helps you get under your daily mental chatter to re-connect with and realize who you really are. If you are over-identifying with the background "noise" in your life it can be very distracting and can keep you from ever noticing the deeper more authentic you that is trying to emerge.

There are many types of mediation. Many are still relatively unknown in the West. An extended listing of all the types of meditation is beyond the scope of this chapter. I will focus on two of the most common forms of meditation used in this country: Transcendental Meditation and Vipassana or Insight Meditation.

Transcendental Meditation. Commonly known as TM, this is a technique brought to this country by the Indian teacher, Mararishi Mahesh Yogi, who credits his teacher and a long line of spiritual masters for preserving this form of meditation for many generations. TM is the most widely practiced form of meditation in this country. It is a relatively simple technique that requires no special postures, diets, clothing, or lifestyle.

The recommended practice is to do it twice a day for about 20 minutes each time. The mechanics of the technique, which must be learned from a teacher, consist of the repetition of mantra or series of words that have been proven to open the mind to deeper thoughts and experiences. You do not have to adopt any particular dogma or beliefs or do anything special except practice it twice a day for twenty minutes each time.

Vipassana Meditation. In 1978, I was taught Vipassana or insight meditation and have been utilizing it on a daily basis ever since that time. Vipassana meditation involves paying attention to your breathing. You either focus your attention on the rise and fall of your abdomen, or the sound or feel of the air entering and leaving your nostrils. You may also imagine an unbroken circle, as I do, with the inhale being the half of the circle and the exhale being the other half.

I begin by picturing a large Ferris wheel with the inhale carrying me to the top of the Ferris wheel and the exhale bringing me down to the ground again. There is no pause at the end of the in-breath or the out-breath, just one continuous circle When you focus your attention on your breathing, your attention will likely wander away as thoughts come into your mind.

You may think, "this is boring" or "I am getting anxious about that job interview tomorrow morning." In this practice of meditation you do not criticize yourself for losing your focus on your breathing, you simply let go of what you were thinking and return your focus to your breathing,

When you get better at holding your attention on your breathing, you at times may reach a point of "no thought." This can be scary at first because it is a very different feeling than what you feel when you are thinking. It is really letting go of all thought, which is a rare occurrence. After all these years of practice, I still can tolerate only a few minutes at a time of "no thoughts."

Improving the quality of your thoughts is another outcome. Deeper insights bubble to the surface and again you are taught to let go of these thoughts as well and return to focusing on your breathing. After a period of meditation, you may want to write down any insights that you received while meditating.

Insight Meditation. Insight meditation, like mindfulness meditation, asks you to explore and focus on one thought or feeling. Before starting an insight meditation session, it's important to have a very calm mind. It might be useful to begin by using mindfulness meditation to quiet the chatter in your mind. Once you feel calm and relaxed, you can shift into doing insight meditation.

You can start by picking a topic to focus on. It could be any topic like "love" or "betrayal" or "truth" or even "death." Once you settle on your topic, you just allow your mind to generate thoughts about that topic. You should not try to control the thoughts that come to you.

For example, if you pick "betrayal," you may think about the times in your life when you felt betrayed in some way. Do not try to control any thoughts that come up after you have picked a topic to focus on. Instead let them pass through without judgment. Don't try to direct them in any way or judge them or try to control them. Just let your thoughts about betrayal go wherever they want to go and see what happens. If you are going to do an insight meditation session with a negative topic such as betrayal, it's important to try and end your session by focusing on something positive you gained from the session.

Try not to leave your meditation session on a negative note. Instead, try to remember what insights you gained about the topic that helped you understand the topic in a new way. You may discover that some thought you initially regarded of as negative turns out to have a positive association for you.

Insight meditation also is extremely useful in clearing you're your mind of meaningless mental chatter. When you are able to quiet your mind, this allows thoughts from your subconscious to bubble up to the surface and give you a new idea or perspective that you had not thought of previously.

I recall doing an insight meditation session on the topic of life after death. In the middle of the session, I suddenly remember understanding exactly what happens to us when we die. It was so clear to me and I was really excited about my insight. However, I decided to let go of these thoughts, fully expecting at the end of the meditation to remember this insight. I was already thinking about sharing this insight with my wife, Janae.

However, when I came out of my meditation session I could not remember anything about what was so absolutely clear for me during the meditation session. I finally, realized that "I got it," but I didn't have permission to share it with anyone else. It was given to me alone and that thought helped me feel at peace with my insight.

Active Imagination. This tool was developed by Carl Jung and is used by many Jungian practitioners.9 It involves dialoguing with several different parts of yourself that live in your own unconscious. This is truly a way to connect with your unconscious much like dreaming except that you are fully awake during the whole experience. Instead of going into a dream to learn more about it, you go into your own imagination and allow images to rise up out of your unconscious.

In this process, you dialogue and interact with your unconscious images. You may be startled to know that your unconscious parts can express themselves from a radically different point of view that those of your conscious mind. They are apt to reveal things you never consciously knew or express startling thoughts or ideas.

Through the use of AI, you learn that the images that appear also symbolize deep split-off parts of yourself. Operating like a figure in a dream, they represent repressed thoughts or feelings or aspects of yourself. The essence of AI is a mindful and active dialogue with your unconscious.

It is active because your ego actually goes into your inner world, walks, talks, confronts, argues, makes friend with or fights with unseen or split-off parts of yourself. It is an internal conversation led by your imagination. This is different from a passive fantasy, which is like daydreaming or simply watching your stream of consciousness flow by you. I have used AI on a number of occasions personally and also I have used it with my clients.

The Three Levels of Active Imagination. There are three levels of alchemy at work while using AI. In the first level, you recognize that you have many parts or sub-personalities. Each has its own needs and wants to participate in your life in some important way.

When you truly realize this, you also begin to see that many of the "intractable or insoluble" conflicts you face in your daily life are actually coming from internal conflicts between different parts of yourself or twisted beliefs. This alchemical process can lead you to a new level of self-integration.

The second level involves making these unconscious elements more conscious in order to reduce the negative effects or undue influence they may have. This could include extending dreams using AI, converting fantasy to imagination, personifying moods or feelings and going on mythical journeys.

The third level is very similar to what people describe as visions. A visionary experience can be a peak experience in which something radical erupts from your depths. An image may seize your imagination with such force that you experience an epiphany with some important unifying truth. The possibilities for uses of this tool are almost endless.

Applied Kinesiology. Applied kinesiology is the scientific term used to describe, "muscle testing." I have been using this tool for over 30 years to determine what nutritional supplements my body needs to stay balanced. This method is based on the premise that if you know how to ask your body for information, it will tell you the truth about anything.

I now use it to verify information about lots of things I see and hear. It is a good way to discriminate between the truth and a lie that you are being told.

David Hawkins in his ground-breaking book, Power vs. Force,12 writes the following about this tool: "Kinesiology is now a well-established science, based on the testing of an all-or-none muscle response stimulus. A positive stimulus provokes a strong muscle response; a negative stimulus results in a demonstrable weakening of the test muscle." There have been numerous studies validating the effectiveness of applied kinesiology led by the work of John Diamond.

Hawkins took this research several steps further "...through the discovery that this kinesiologic response reflects the human Hawkins used to test the effectiveness of applied kinesiology and should be followed if you wish to achieve reliable results.

SOCIAL/POLITICAL ACTIVISM AND SERVANT LEADER

While the 1960's were a time of much social/political activism, many angry activists got caught in the "us vs. them" duality and found that their efforts did not lead to lasting change.

Those who followed the "passive resistance" model of Dr. Martin Luther King, Jr. found that their approach took longer, but did achieve some results in promoting racial equality. Today we are faced with so many diverse problems that we have to invent new "both/and" ways to be effective. Activists need to operate on the principles of servant leadership in these challenging times.

Experts from many fields have concluded that we are in the midst of a great transition or shift in consciousness. In the midst of this great transition, we are seeing old structures breaking down and new, sometimes poorly formed, structures trying to emerge. The latest collapse of the old structures has been our financial structure, including the home mortgage system and the banking system itself. We need to have an inner knowing to be able to see through the crazy twists and turns of these chaotic times.

Our political system is not far behind. In this time of rapid change, it is difficult to know how to act and how to prepare yourself to be a servant leader who helps bring the new structures into form. If you decide to be a servant leader who practices some form of social activism at this time, I believe you need to be well prepared with tools that activists from previous times did not have.

New Social/Political Activism Tools for the Servant Leader. The following are tools you will need in order to be effective agents of change as activists and servant leaders:

- Do most of your personal work,
- Develop inner knowing that allows you to see through the twisted beliefs of others,
- Take back your projections,
- Change any twisted beliefs you had, and
- Heal yourself from the lingering effects of your early trauma.

In addition, you have to enter this fray with an open heart and yet know how to protect your heart from any attacks you might encounter from life-taking predators.

If you don't do these things, you probably will not be successful in your efforts to help bring about fundamental changes in this country. Caution: Do not try to change predators with your servant leadership skills.

Remember, predators do not have a conscience and you are wasting you time and energy trying to change them. They do not want to change, they do not want to "see the light" and suddenly become life-givers. They will only use your attempts to change them as a weapon against you.

There is nothing that they like more than having someone with moral indignation go after them. They now have a target to aim at with their weapons of lies, fear and secrecy. Yes, if you are as well trained servant leader they will not be successful in getting you to serve their life-taking efforts, but you will expend enormous time and energy trying to fend off their attacks.

If you keep your inner weapons sharpened, you will be able to spot them long before they spot you. You will be able to use your weapons to protect yourself from attacks by these predators or at least prevent them from interfering with your essential tasks. You can use your inner weapons to spot them and then do what you need to do to protect yourself from their cons or manipulations.

Remember they are well trained and are able to use their weapons of lies, fear and secrecy much better then you can counter them. You have to be able to see though any attempts they make to invade your life before they can do much if any damage.

Key Questions for the Servant Leader to Address. As a social/political activist who practices servant leadership, you will need to reflect on and find answers to four key questions:

1. Why do lies and twisted beliefs seem to work better for life-takers than straight beliefs and the truth?
2. If the Global Elite is so powerful, as it claims to be, why do they need to use deception, lies and covert manipulations to get what they want?
3. Have you cleared your personal rage and any projections you may still carry?
4. How can you decide what targets to aim at with your servant leadership skills?

The answer to the first question is because no one confronts their lies and by repeating them, they get others to believe them. Servant leaders have to confront all the lies that they see. It seems to me that the only way to combat the strategy of the "Big Lie" is naming the lies every time you see or hear them. You have to make sure that you have the facts to show that what they are saying or writing are lies. You cannot let even one lie go unexposed. Not one of them!

This requires some vigilance and courage to stand up to powerful interests. I believe that if you have done your inner work you will be able to do this with more integrity and strength than you even thought possible.

The second question can also be answered directly. The reason the so-called Global Elite, that claim to be all powerful, use deception, lies and covert manipulations to get what they want **is because they are hiding their unhealed traumas and/or haven't identified or changed their twisted beliefs.**

They are fearful little children who have been trapped as well by running away from their feelings. Instead of doing everything to heal their wounds, they are hiding behind power and control in a desperate attempt to avoid their wounds. They are frauds and deep down they know this and are trying to put their unhealed traumas on others rather than taking responsibility for them and doing their own healing work.

Again, servant leaders will have to call them out and point out how dysfunctional their methods are. They are actually spiritually and psychologically very weak. You have to name the weaknesses that you see and then they may not be able to hurt people with their dirty tricks.

At least, if enough people expose what they are doing and see who they really are, they will not be able to bluff their way out of tight situations. You will have to say to anyone who is listening, "the Emperor has no clothes."

You will need to show, often by example, that it is easy to see through their psychological defenses as liars and as members of the Global Elite preying on others. They refuse to take responsibility for their own lack of healing. Remember there are many more of us than them and our numbers are growing much faster than theirs.

Servant leaders will have to defend against this psychological smoke screen and take back the planet from these impostors. Yes, they are dangerous, only because they are too scared to take responsibility for their own behavior. They have to resort to threats and intimidation to get their way. How much courage does that take?

In answering the third question you will need to make sure your decision to become a servant leader is not based on revenge or personal rage from the hurts you have suffered at the hands of predators or their life-taking agents. You need to make sure that what you are seeing is not a projection of your own unhealed traumas or old hurts and angers. You need to be able to see the life-takers as trapped life-givers and have compassion for their plight.

Empathy is also vitally important in this work. You need to adopt the adage, "For the grace of God, there go I." You might ask, "How will I know if I have cleared my trauma or taken back my projections?" The way you can tell is by the results you achieve. If you are struggling and finding overwhelming resistance, you probably need to do more personal work before continuing to push forward.

One way I tell my clients they can tell they have healed their developmental traumas is if they can ask for what they want from others in such a way that others are delighted to give it to them. People can sense the authenticity of an open-hearted request that does not have some edge to it that makes them suspicious that you are not being genuine.

The answer to the fourth question requires you to ask several more questions:

1. What wakes up at 3 a.m. and disturbs you so much that you cannot go back to sleep?
2. What causes an unmistakable pain in your heart when you think about it?

These experiences will show you where to begin. This is how I decided to start a violence prevention program for communities and schools. I kept waking up with the image of kids in schools who were too afraid to learn and how that would ultimately affect the rest of their lives. I felt the pain in my heart when I visited schools and saw and felt to enormous amount of fear that the students had on their faces.

I also remembered the amount of fear that I experienced when as an eighth grader I was bullied by two ninth grade boys and how that experience impacted my life. These things kept waking me up in the middle of the night and hurting my heart, until I decided to do something about this problem.

Remember, as I indicated above, the three big weapons of life-takers are (1) The Big Lie, (2) spreading fear in the world, and (3) operating in secrecy. All three of these strategies have trapped life-givers with hidden fears, trauma and twisted beliefs that can be changed. You need to do your personal work, develop your inner weapons and then test them out to see if you can reach out with compassion to other life-givers who have fallen prey to life-takers. Below are six inner truths that will help guide your actions.

THE SIX INNER TRUTHS OF THE SERVANT LEADER

In order to become a Servant Leader you will have to understand and live your life out of your own truths. You will not be able to find these truths in the world around you, but they must be found in the world inside of you.

These inner truths are keys on the journey that leads to individuation and self-realization, the essential goals of servant leaders. These are at the core of how you see yourself, if you wish to become a servant leader.

The First Inner Truth. Servant leaders need to focus all their efforts toward the advancement of human consciousness. The way to do that is to attain individuation and self-realization, which is the only way to consciously know God.

The Second Inner Truth. Servant leaders have to pay attention to all their thoughts and feelings as much as their actions. As servant leaders purify their thoughts and feelings, the more pure their actions will be. Their inner knowledge of themselves should be their guide to their actions.

The Third Inner Truth. Servant leaders have to know that who they are is not what they do or how others see them. Who they really are is only discovered as a result of their commitment to self-reflection and self-correction.

The Fourth Inner Truth. Servant leaders have to be resolute in their pursuit of the truth. Nothing should deter them from this pursuit. Their actions will help them determine how well they know themselves. If they encounter failure or resistance as a result of their actions, this only tells them look inward to correct any mistaken thoughts, feelings or beliefs they may be interfering with their actions.

The Fifth Inner Truth. Servant leaders must stay connected to all life. It is all God and if they see "others" as not part of them, they are not connected to God. God dwells in everything and servant leaders need to resist the tendency to see themselves as separate from all life in any way.

The Sixth Inner Truth. Servant leaders need to regard all that they see as in perfect harmony and balance with the universe. If anything seems in conflict with this core knowing, it means the servant leader does not fully understand the perfection of the universe and has to work harder to achieve this core inner knowing. This is just an indication that the servant leader cannot see or understand this perfection.

All conflicts of this sort are because the servant leader does not yet see the truth about what he/she sees and has to continue to do inner work until he/she can recognize that truth. The servant leader will know he/she has found it when he/she sees the perfections that were there all the time.

THE INNER WEAPONS OF THE SERVANT LEADER

After you have begun to live your life according to the Six Inner Truths described above, then you can begin to develop your arsenal of inner weapons in order to operate effectively as a servant leader. These weapons will help you make sound decisions on behalf of your self and in your work with others. Like any tools, they need to stay sharp and this will require your daily attention to them.

Your Inner Spear. Your Inner Spear corresponds with your self-awareness. As a servant leader you must be able to understand what in your personal history has contributed to who you have become today and why you do what you do in various situations.

This skill of self-reflection is vital to your success as a servant leader. It also means that you have the ability to penetrate the false illusions you have created for yourself and have the ability to correct them when you see they do not represent who you really are. Daily meditation and prayer can help you keep this tool sharp and effective.

Your Inner Sword. Your Inner Sword corresponds to your inner discrimination. By utilizing your Inner Sword, you are able to cut through the bullshit and get to the underlying truth about what you are observing. This single-edged sharp instrument represents your sharp, single-minded intellect that you need to have to take decisive action or make quick decisions. The razor-sharpness of your Inner Sword is also used to help you live in harmony and balance with the laws of the universe and with Divine Will.

You must continually sharpen your Inner Sword so that it is ready for use when you are called to take decisive action. As you reflect on what you see on television and read in the newspaper or on the Internet, you need to reflect on what the truth is behind what you are being told.

Your Inner Arrow. Your Inner Arrow corresponds to your inner will power as a servant leader. It refers to your ability to concentrate or develop a one-pointed focus that enables you to hit the center of the center of the target you are aiming at and achieve the goals you want to achieve.

Typically, you will master your Inner Sword and your Inner Arrow before you master your Inner Spear. This means that your will develop your intuition at a later stage than you develop discrimination and will power.

While your intuition is being developed, you should continue to make decisions through deliberation and with good discrimination. However, when your Inner Spear is fully developed it will become the principal weapon you will use as a servant leader.

Your Inner Shield. Your Inner Shield is the love and compassion within your heart. When your love and compassion is very strong, your Inner Shield will deflect all attacks that are directed at you and you can never be defeated. You should carry this Inner Shield everywhere you go to protect yourself from attacks of any kind. If you find yourself in any danger of attack, your foes will not even be able to see you even though you are standing right in front of them.

The Middle Path of the Servant Leader. To become a servant leader, you will need to walk the "Middle Path" between the extremes of behavior, while embracing some of the principles of the balanced philosophy of Taoism. Lao Tsu and other of the great masters throughout history have demonstrated, the best path is the Middle Path that exists between the extremes of the masculine and feminine principles, or Yin and Yang.

Taoism espouses a lifestyle that is the balance of the masculine (fiery, active, intellectual) and feminine (watery, cool, passive, emotional) principles. Too much or too little activity either way can be harmful, just as can too much exposure to either hot or cold, or too much time spent in either light or darkness.

Besides living a balanced outer life, you need to also cultivate an inner balance of masculine and feminine traits. Your goal should be to be prepared for all challenges. You can best do that when you possess an inner balance.

The Self-Discipline of the Servant Leader. To live the life of a servant leader will need to be disciplined in body, mind, emotions and spirit. You will need to keep your physical body fit and healthy, maintain a healthy diet and do regular exercises. Your mind and emotions should be kept in check by striving to focus on generating positive and uplifting thoughts and feelings.

Again, regular meditation is a good tool for assisting you to be completely present in the moment and not succumb to extraneous thoughts. In order to keep your mind steady, you need to adopt meditational practices outlined above. You may also use daily affirmations to help you keep your thoughts focused on your goals.

Open-Heartedness: An Essential Skill of the Servant Leader. As I stated above, if you want to be an effective servant leader you need to have developed your sense of inner knowing. You also will need to open your heart and heal any wounds that you find in there. This will help you see what fundamental problems need to be addressed and how to become part of the solution instead of becoming part of the problem. Having an open heart that has healed helps you connect with other openhearted life-giving people (not just like-minded people) who individually and collectively are actively involved in changing the world.

WHO ARE THE TARGETS OF THE SERVANT LEADERS' WEAPONS?

The target of your inner weapons should be those life-givers who are being manipulated and controlled by the predators for personal gain and are inadvertently engaged in life-taking activities. They have fallen prey to the lies that were told them, the fear that has been cleverly injected into their minds and the secrecy they have been told to use. Because they do have a conscience, they can and will change if you can help them see through the lies, the fears put on them and the secrecy they have adopted.

This is where the servant leader can be the most effective. These people are not your enemies and you need to have compassion not anger in your heart as you engage them with the truth, help them overcome their fears and show them how transparency can set them free.

If the servant leaders are going to be effective in at least neutralizing a well-planned attack by the predators, they need to rely heavily on their inner knowing of the truth and their ability to use the weapons they have at their disposal. Following the principles of Aikido, the servant leader has to fully understand the motivation and strategies of the predators in order to determine the best course of right action.

In the process of engaging those life-givers who have been trapped by human predators it is important to understand why they are trapped and see if there is any way you can help them get free. Remember that your Inner Weapons will stand you well in deciding how to approach those who have drifted away from life-giving activities and inadvertently supporting life-taking activities.

THREE MAIN WEAPONS OF THE LIFE-TAKERS

As I discussed earlier in this book, the three main weapons of the illuminati, Global Elite or con artists, sociopaths or other life-takers are lies, fear and secrecy. They all use the same three basic weapons.

This makes it easier to identify their weapons and how they are using them. By understanding how the weapons that the life-takers have used to trap the life-givers, you will know how to help free them from these cleverly designed traps.

The First Weapon of the Life-Takers. The first weapon they use is to attempt to deceive you by deliberately not telling you the truth so they can achieve their personal goals. They will use their guile or charm to trick you into believing something that is not true. They have become masters of deceit and double-signals because they know this causes the brain of others to short-circuit. This prevents them from seeing through the deceit and the twists in their logic or the arguments they are employing.

They also are able to confuse large segments of the population with their "Big Lies." They are counting on you to go along with their lies and not challenge them in any way. This is how they trap you. First, they have to manipulate you in some way to accept their version of the truth in order to get you to carry out their agenda.

The Second Main Weapon of the Life-Takers. The second weapon they use is to instill fear in you and others they want to con. They are good at understanding what "triggers" people into a trauma reaction and they manipulate the media to help them produce trauma reactions in the masses. For example, after 9-11 there was clearly widespread PTSD among the American people. This was heavily reinforced every time they showed pictures of the Twin Towers first being hit by an airplane and then crumbling to the ground. These images were shown over and over and had the calculated effect to cause widespread fear.

They triggered fear in millions of people who were already suffering from unhealed developmental trauma from unhealed experiences of being terrorized as a child. They knew what "buttons" to push to get unsuspecting victims to be afraid to act on their own behalf. Then they could manipulate them into believing their lies and helping them to advance their agenda.

The obvious objective was to convince the majority of Americans of the lie that Saddam Hussein was responsible for 9-11. When they had accomplished this objective, they were able to invade his country in order to seize the oil and gas resources of Iraq. In the meantime, they did not focus much attention on capturing Osama Bin Laden and his Al Qaeda terrorists who they knew were hiding in the mountains of Afghanistan.

The Third Main Weapon Of the Life-Takers. The third weapon they use is to operate in secret. They keep everything they do out of the light of day. This gives them the opportunity to plot surprise attacks on innocent and unsuspecting individuals or groups of individuals. They go to elaborate lengths to maintain their secrecy. They have secret meetings and secret locations from which they operate.

Our government funds many of these covert operations presumably to counter the other secret groups they deem as our enemy. Our government uses exactly the same tactics to spy on its citizens and attempts to control the flow of information to the general public that they use to presumably spy on the enemy. They get two for the price of one.

This also can raise the fears of the ordinary citizen, particularly since they have been able to operate in secret and now have powers to arrest people without charging them or granting them the right to an attorney. Of course, they claim they will only use this power to capture suspected terrorists, but it feeds widespread fears of the government.

Other Ways the Servant Leader Can Neutralize the Power of Predators. If a group of servant leaders is cleaver enough, they can get predators fighting among themselves. You need to remember that they are more afraid of each other than they are of you and me. So the cleaver servant leader helps find the cracks in their defenses, psychological or otherwise, and gets them fighting with each other. Leonard Cohen wrote in the lyrics to his song Anthem, "There is a crack in everything and that's how the light gets in."

There is nothing more powerful than to launch a campaign designed to find the cracks in their defenses and make sure that the light gets in. This often ends up with them fighting among themselves and totally distracting themselves from trying to deceive those outside their ranks. This strategy was how the major mafia organizations in this country were brought to justice.

Where there is a code of pride, as in many of the life-taking organizations, it hides a code of shame. The worst sin in this kind of organization is to betray someone who you have sworn to secrecy or feel betrayed by someone who violates one of the strict behavior codes of the organization.

Even floating a rumor that so-and-so might have betrayed someone in the organization can start a fear-based chain reaction. The typical response to a betrayal is to try to get even in some way or seek revenge on them. Revenge leads to counter-revenge and soon they are too busy plotting against each other to plot against you or the general public.

The other related strategy that currently is working is the one developed by Julian Assange and his associates, who managed to hack into the secret government emails and meeting notes of other secret organizations.

By then making them public, they are exposing their dirty little secrets. There is nothing worse for these people then to be exposed to the light of day in this way. It makes them look small, which is what they really are. However, they wish to appear larger than life is some ways, which they believe helps them achieve their fear and intimidation goals.

NOTES

1Byrd, R. (July 1988). *Positive Therapeutic Effects of Intercessory Prayer on Coronary Care Unit Population. Southern Medical Journal. Vol. 81, No. 7.*

2Sicher, F.; Targ, E.; Moore D.; and Smith, H. (December 1998). *A Randomized Double-Blind Study of the Effect of Distant Healing in a Population With Advanced AIDS. Western Journal of Medicine. Vol. 169, No. 6. pp. 356-363.*

3Sweet, B. (2004). *A journey into prayer: Pioneers of prayer in the laboratory agents of science or satan? Portland, OR: Xlibris.*

4Braden, G. (2001). *The Isaiah Effect: Decoding the lost science of prayer and prophesy. New York: Harmony Press.*

5Weinhold, B & Hendricks, G. (2004). *Transpersonal approaches to counseling and psychotherapy. Denver, CO: Love Publishing Co.*

CHAPTER 15

THE FUTURE OF A WORLD FILLED WITH SERVANT LEADERS

"In my dream, the Angel shrugged and
Said, if we fail
This time, it will be
A failure of imagination,
And then she placed the
World gently in the palm
Of my hand."

—*Brian Andreas*

THE SHIFT IS HAPPENING

We are in the middle of a huge shift in consciousness. This means that if this shift continues, and I see no reason to doubt that it will, we will create a new world that will be more life-giving. I have set the bar very high for the servant leader. This is a very important role, and we need to know that these people are serious about working to develop their ability to be a servant leader. I feel strongly that people who want to serve others need to take their role seriously. Having said that, even if people who wish to be servant leaders are able to do half of the work that I recommend, they will be well prepared to call themselves a servant leader. It is a process and as long as people are willing to work on themselves, they have the mind-set they need to become a servant leader.

In this chapter, I will describe projects and programs that I believe are possible in the future, if we have a world filled with servant leaders. Some of these programs have already proven to be effective and could easily be implemented and extended into the future. The shift in consciousness that is required to support these initiatives is currently happening.

HO'OPONOPONO: THE ULTIMATE HEALING
METHOD OF THE FUTURE.[1]

I read about a psychologist at a Hawaiian Mental Hospital who utilized an ancient Hawaiian healing process called ho'oponopono to completely cure the patients in the criminally insane unit of this hospital. He utilized the same Unconditional Surrender Process that I described in Chapter 11. This healing process involves repeating the following prayer: "I'm sorry, please forgive me, thank you and I love you."

This caught my attention and I found out more about how he did this. I immediately realized this may be the healing process of the future for servant leaders who wish to serve those who are mentally or physically ill or help heal the whole planet.

What I learned was that the psychologist would study an inmate's chart and then look within himself to see how he created that person's illness. As he improved himself, the patients improved. This seems unbelievable, but it was true.

Dr. Ikaleakala Hew Len, a staff psychologist, went to work in this hospital where other psychologists quit on a monthly basis and the staff regularly called in sick. He said that staff would walk through the ward with their backs against the wall, afraid of being attacked by patients.

Apparently, Dr. Len never saw the patients. He decided to just sit in his office and review their files. While he looked at these files, he would work on himself by repeating the four elements of the ho'oponopono healing prayer. As he worked on himself, the patients began to heal. After a few months, patients who had to be shackled because they were too dangerous, were being able to walk around freely. Others who had to be heavily medicated were getting off their medication. Even those who were thought to never have a chance of being released, were now being freed.

Not only that, but the staff began to enjoy coming to work. Absenteeism and turnover almost disappeared completely. They ended up with more staff than they needed because patients were now being released and all the staff were showing up for work.

Dr. Len explained that he believed total responsibility for your life means that everything in your life—simply because it is in your life, it is your responsibility. In a literal sense the entire world is your creation.

Wow! This is tough to swallow. Being responsible for what I say or do is one thing, and that is difficult enough, but being responsible for what everyone in my life says or does is quite another. Yet, the truth that Dr. Len discovered is if you take complete responsibility for your life, then everything you see, hear, taste, touch, or in any way experience is your responsibility because it is part of your life.

This means that any terrorist activity, the president, the economy or anything you experience while reading the newspaper, listening to the radio or watching television that you don't like, is up for you to heal. They don't exist, in a manner of speaking, except as projections from inside of you. The problem isn't with them, it's with you, and to change them, you have to change yourself.

This is a radical approach to healing that is tough to grasp at first, let alone accept or actually live. If you want to improve your life, you have to heal your life. If you want to cure anyone, even a mentally ill criminal, you have to do it by healing yourself.

Apparently all Dr. Len did as he reviewed the patient files was to keep repeating these four statements. In Hawaiian, ho'oponopono means loving yourself. Dr. Len says there is no out there. It would take a whole book to explain this advanced technique with the depth it deserves. Suffice it to say, if you want to improve anything in your life, there's only one place to look: inside yourself. In addition, when you look, do it with love.

As a servant leader, this is your ultimate challenge. If you take responsibility to help heal everything you see, you will first have to heal yourself and even more than that, you have to love yourself unconditionally. How can you expect to love someone else unconditionally, if you do not love yourself unconditionally?

Dr. Len's message may be quite hard to believe; yet, it's amazingly simple. He states that we are all responsible for everything that we see in our world. By taking full personal responsibility and then healing the wounded places within ourselves, we can literally heal ourselves and heal our world. This could be the future role of all servant leaders.

I urge you to experiment with this process. Go back and reread the section in Chapter Eleven on Unconditional Surrender. Then pick out something or someone in your life that you don't like for some reason. With this person or thing in mind, begin repeating the four statements: "I'm sorry, please forgive me, thank you and I love you." You may be surprised at the results you get.

THE SERVANT LEADER AS A SOCIAL/POLITICAL ACTIVIST

In Chapter Fourteen, I discussed my ideas of how a servant leader can utilize new tools for social/political activism. My hope for the servant leader is that he/she will become an effective social/political activist. This will take your imagination plus all you have learned about yourself along the way. Servant leaders will need to work closely with organizations that have a vision of a different world.

In the 60's, many people protested, but they basically fought against something and they were quick to point out the evils of what they were against. They had very few ideas of how the "system" they were protesting against should change and virtually no plans on how to make that happen.

The servant leader of the future must spend his/her time and energy promoting the benefits of the new system and not waste his/her energy just protesting the evils of the old system. The only way you can do that kind of work to serve humanity is by first doing your inner work to become fully individuated.

This enables the servant leader to give and receive unconditional love. This is the only way people and society evolve and that lasting social change can happen. This chapter provides several examples of servant leader programs and organizations that already exist to help show you where you might begin.

Where to Begin: Campaign Finance Reform. The most important political barrier facing elected servant leaders is to get special interest money out of politics. American democracy is based on the ideal of one person, one vote. However, it's harder and harder for that promise to be met with a political system increasingly dominated by self-serving millionaires, billionaires, lobbyists, and big money interest groups. The current system creates a political inequality that skews public policy toward those able to write big checks and away from ordinary Americans. This increasing reliance on large financial backers also creates increased opportunities for corruption.

It doesn't have to be this way, and with a collective effort, we can change it. We must increase political participation and raise the voices of everyday people in politics through various forms of public financing of elections that have worked in many cities and states across the country. Below is a list of principles and ways people working together under the leadership of strong servant leaders can develop a fair and equitable system of public funding of all elections.

THE PRINCIPLES FOR CREATING SERVANT LEADER-POWERED CAMPAIGN FINANCE REFORM:

1. We must empower ordinary citizens. These systems give ordinary Americans a more robust voice in the political process by incentivizing candidates to rely on a broad base of small donations to receive public funds. This is what Bernie Sanders did in the 2016 Presidential Primary elections. He took no PAC money or donations from the moneyed interests. His donations averaged about $27 each. He raised $207.7 million this way.

2. We must increase political participation. Public financing programs encourage candidates to build a large grassroots base of supporters and bring more people into the political process. Again, Bernie Sanders campaign attracted millions of young voters who never participated in political campaigns before this. They must reduce The influence of big donors. With public financing systems, candidates can focus on their constituents and small donor base, instead of wealthy donors and deep pocket interests that usually fund campaigns. If Sanders were nominated, this is exactly what he says he would do in the general election.

3. Americans want —and deserve— a government that's truly of, by, and for the people. One in which the men and women they elect to Congress are free to do what's best for their constituents and their country, what founding father James Madison called a government "dependent on the people alone." Unfortunately, today, the voices of everyday Americans aren't being heard because big money dominates the financing of campaigns. Big money campaign donors fill the bank accounts of the candidates from both parties, fund super PACs, and hire lobbyists to bend policy in their direction. We must break the dependence on big money so that Congress can focus on the people's priorities. In the 2016 presidential primary campaign, this was an important issue and, hopefully, this will help create momentum toward this goal.

4. We must return our government to one that is of, by, and for the people, not of, by, and for the big money donors. There are two bills currently in Congress that best embody the principles above. They are the Government By the People Act in the U.S. House and the Fair Elections Now Act in the U.S. Senate. These laws would amplify the voices of everyday Americans. I urge you to look up these bills currently in Congress and provide vocal support for them.

BARRY K. WEINHOLD, PhD

NEW FORMS OF POLITICAL SERVANT LEADERSHIP

Below are examples of successful life-giving violence prevention innovations for communities, schools and families. These examples will show you that when you practice servant leadership, it can shift your consciousness and the consciousness of others. For example, did you know that when you are doing something kind for someone, it is impossible to also be angry with him or her? Kindness and compassion overrides the wiring in the part of the brain where we feel angry and hostile toward ourselves or others.

The Kindness Campaign. Sam Keen in his book, Hymns to an Unknown God wrote, "Creating a political community based on kindness may seem like an impossibility." He adds that, "We are discovering lately in American society that we can't build a good society on the principles of self-interest and entitlement alone. Without generosity there can be no community. Without the kindness of strangers, a society is turned into an armed camp. The atmosphere of compassion that transforms a mass of alienated individuals into a caring community is created by countless acts of kindness and charitable foresight."[2]

This quote captured my eye as the possible intention of the Kindness Campaign. It had its beginning in Eastern Europe in 1992. My wife and I were on an assignment with the United Nations in Eastern Europe, during my sabbatical leave from the University of Colorado at Colorado Springs. We were living in Bratislava, Czechoslovakia and working out of the United Nations Center in Vienna, Austria some 45 miles away.

Our task was to help create an International Centre for Family Studies in Bratislava and get the centre affiliated with the United Nations. It was to be a training center for family life educators particularly from underdeveloped nations. This was part of the U.N. International Year of the Family in 1993, which was housed in the Center for Social Development and Humanitarian Affairs in the U.N. Center in Vienna, Austria.

During the fall of 1992, while we were working on this project and living in Bratislava, we saw news reports of the anti-gay rights legislation that was approved by the voters (Amendment Two) in Colorado, where we had lived, prior to our work in Czechoslovakia. When people in Bratislava and in Vienna wanted to know where we were from in the United States and we answered, "Colorado," they would immediately say, "Oh, that's the hate state, isn't it? When they asked where we were from in Colorado and we answered

320

"Colorado Springs", they would ask, "Isn't that where all this anti-gay hatred got started?"

Needless to say, this disturbed us very much. We had been long-time residents of Colorado Springs and felt defensive when people made these generalizations about our home state and our home city. We tried in vain, at first, to defend our home city with statements about its beauty and how not everyone there felt prejudiced toward gays. Later we just learned to smile and say, "Yes, we know and we don't like it either."

Before describing what I decided to do about this situation, I would like to give you a little background about Colorado Springs. It is the home of over 71 fundamentalist Christian organizations, over 100 thousand military personnel and dependents, the Olympic Training Center and The Air Force Academy. In 1992, Bill Moyers hosted a PBS documentary on Colorado Springs and after interviewing a number of its leaders, called it "Ground Zero of the Next Holy War."

When we returned to Colorado Springs in the spring of 1993, we found many people divided into two camps that were firing insults at each other through the media. The peaceful community of Colorado Springs and the state of Colorado we had left less than a year earlier now were polarized over gay rights issues. The law never was enacted because the U. S. Supreme Court eventually ruled that it was unconstitutional.

However, I saw how this law had created a lingering conflict in the community and state among members of two groups of citizens. One was for it and one was opposed to the amendment. I wondered what would be a heart-felt response to this kind of community conflict. I remembered reading Sam Keen's quote about the role to kindness in creating community.

The question I asked myself was, "What might happen if people paid more attention to the positive things, like kindness, that are happening in their lives?" "Would they pay less attention to the negative things, like anti-gay hatred, that was happening around them?"

My hypothesis was that if I could help citizens to re-focus their attention on positive events in the community rather than the negative events in their lives, they would significantly change their behavior. In addition, it would change how they feel about themselves, other people and the world around them. In other words, they could change their "internal working model of the world" that I described earlier in this book.

In short, I believed it could facilitate a paradigm shift in both their personal and collective lives. (Talk about grandiose fantasies of changing the world. What was I thinking?) However, I hypothesized that if I could get between 15-20% of the population of the Colorado Springs community or schools focusing on positive things that were happening every day in their lives instead of negative things, it would change their lives. It would change the way the community, or schools perceived themselves, other people and the world around them.

I decided to test my hypothesis to see if I could change the community's response to this heated community conflict. After approaching each of the leaders of the two polarized groups with my ideas and finding no interest in them, finally I approached the local CBS affiliate television station.

I personally knew the General Manager and the News Director of this television station. I actually had done both of them a personal favor. I sat down with the News Director one morning and discussed how through their news shows they might begin a change to this toxic environment.

I suggested that they might begin their news shows with the "good news" instead of the "bad news." That didn't go over very well with the News Director. He told me clearly that people wanted to see the bad news on his station, such as the accident on the Interstate. He added that if they didn't see it at the beginning of the news show when they turned on the news, they would just switch to another station. As I listened to this News Director, I became increasingly discouraged about my ideas for promoting kindness through the news media.

Finally, as a parting shot, I suggested that they might end the news show each night with the good news. He thought about that for a few moments and said, "That could be possible." He told me he would talk it over with the General Manager and get back to me. I left the station with very little hope that I would ever hear from him again about my ideas.

Well, I got lucky because that same afternoon on this same network television station, Oprah Winfrey devoted her whole show to the effects of random acts of kindness in a community. The next day, I got a call back from the News Director and we began a five-year partnership with this television station becoming a media sponsor of the Kindness Campaign.

They agreed to find ways to use the news media to report the good news as well as the bad news. Each news show at 5:30 p.m. and 10:30 p.m. ended with a story about something positive that happened in the community that day.

They also did news features on acts of kindness on their early morning and noon news shows. They also created a "kindness line" where viewers could call in and report acts of kindness that they had witnessed. In the first six months of the kindness line, they received over 22,000 calls. They played one of these calls each night on the evening news show.

This was the beginning of the Kindness Campaign in Colorado Springs. The news department at this CBS affiliate had been rated third behind the ABC and NBC affiliates in the viewing area. Largely as a result of their co-sponsorship of the Kindness Campaign, they eventually rose to be the top-rated news show in this viewing area.

One of the things the TV station agreed to do was to tape 30-second public service announcements (PSAs) on the Kindness Campaign, to be shown between regular shows. For one of them, they asked the leader of the group that promoted the anti-gay amendment to come to the station to tape a PSA, and without telling him, they also invited the leader of the opposition group that fought against the amendment.

These two men had never actually met in person, but they knew each other from being on the news. When they saw each other, they were both ready to leave, but the Station Manager, who knew both of them, convinced them to stay and shoot a 30 second PSA for the Kindness Campaign.

Can you imagine the effect of seeing these two men, perceived in the community as bitter enemies, standing side-by-side talking about the importance of being kind to each other? It was enormous. This PSA was played repeatedly at different times of the day ofn this station.

This led these two men to decide to get together for lunch regularly and discuss their differences. Finally, they decided to create a joint project called "Dialogue Dinners." This involved inviting very diverse groups of people to break bread together at three dinner meetings with a trained facilitator.

Ultimately, this project, along with Kindness Campaign activities, helped change the emotional climate in Colorado Springs. They held over 500 of these dinners over the next few years. Minorities and gays began to be treated better by the news media aided by the Kindness Campaign that helped people focus on the positive things happening in this community. It was reflected in many news shows and any local media efforts. Eventually, this project was called Food For Thought and is still operating today in many other cities as well.

The Kindness Campaign was eventually implemented in twelve other U. S. towns and cities. The main goal of this program is to recognize and reinforce pro-social behaviors in order to reduce the recognition given to family violence, gang activity, and other antisocial behaviors.

The currency of the Campaign was a button that read, "Spread Kindness---its Contagious." People were asked to wear the button and pass it on if they "caught" someone doing an act of kindness. Then this person was also asked to wear the button and pass it on when witnessing an act of kindness. Over a period of about two years we had about 80,000 buttons circulating in the community and schools in Colorado Springs.

The community-based component of the campaign enlisted the support of the media in promoting the campaign. Newspapers, radio stations, and the CBS affiliate television station all became part of a grassroots effort to generate positive human-interest stories for daily broadcast. Media sponsors made daily PSAs and helped sponsor and cover special kindness-related events.

Research by the local CBS television station indicated that, after only six months of sponsorship, more than 70% of its viewers were aware of the Kindness Campaign and its goals, and 75% of these people believed it was making a significant impact on reducing violence in the community.3

During Kindness Week each February, churches and neighborhoods organized special events such as Interfaith Celebrations of Kindness and Neighborhood Kindness Awards Ceremonies. Neighborhood associations created special kindness projects to involve different segments of the community.

School children nominated their teachers and others nominated adults they knew for Community of Kindness awards. Teachers also nominated the kindest students in their school. In addition, companies, churches, and non-profit organizations also received awards for spreading kindness in the community.

Such community events recognized the unsung heroes and heroines and reinforced pro-social behaviors throughout the community. We found that by enrolling a critical mass of community members (usually 15-20% of the population) we gave it enough momentum to make it effective.

As the community-based program took hold, I began to get requests for information from school officials on how they could implement the program. Actually the idea for the school-based program grew out of a need perceived by my students in one of my graduate classes in counseling at the University of Colorado at Colorado Springs. When I introduced the idea of focusing attention on acts of kindness as a way of shifting consciousness, some of my students immediately saw the application of this idea to the schools where they were teaching or counseling. There was a big concern with bullying behavior and student-to-student put-downs.

Therefore, I began offering Kindness Campaign materials to schools. After the first six-months of doing this, the teachers kept asking for more kindness activities they could do with kids. I decided to put it back on the teachers and I asked them to submit kindness activities that they had tried and were very successful.

After I got back lots of good kindness activities, I compiled them into a Program Guide for the Kindness Campaign in the Schools and sold it as a "cookbook" of proven successful kindness activities for the schools. Some of them were classroom activities, some were all-school activities and the rest were activities that counselors could use in a small counseling group at school.

Eventually, I produced three Program Guides for the schools and I changed the name of the school program to The Kind and Safe Schools Initiative (KASSI).[3] KASSI included the Kindness activities for the classroom keyed to various subject matter. I added classroom activities on Cooperative Education and Character Education. I included a Peer Mediation training module and a Conflict Resolution curriculum to teach CR to all the students. I also included a module on the prevention of bullying and put-downs. Finally, I included a module on how to add a restorative justice approach to the schools discipline practices.

Below is one of the over 350 activities in the KASSI Program Guides for Schools. This activity is designed to help students develop a heart-felt connection and to understand the impact that their bullying and put-downs are having on others.

KINDNESS ACTIVITY[4]

Name of Activity: "The Heart Exercise"
Type of Activity: Classroom or school assembly activity
Grade Level: K-12

Objective(s) of Activity: To sensitize students to the negative effects of bullying and put-downs on others. To show students how to repair any damage to someone's heart that bullying and put-downs can cause.

Materials Needed: A sheet of flip chart paper and a red marking pen

Procedures:

1. Draw a large heart on the flip chart paper with your red marking pen and then use the pen to shade it in.

2. Hold up the heart and talk about the fact that this is what we have in common with everybody else. Tell them that there are over 7 billion hearts beating at this moment.

3. Tell the audience that there are things that other people say and do that hurt our heart. If we are put-down, laughed at or ridiculed or hit, kicked or pushed around this can hurt our heart.

4. Ask the members of the class or assembly to give you examples of things that they heard other people say or do to someone that you know hurt that person's heart.

5. As students give you examples (i.e., called them fat, stupid, a fag, etc) and as you get each one begin to crumble up the paper with the heart on it until, if you get enough negative examples, you have a tight ball of paper in your hand. Say, "This heart is closed, full of anger and hurt. It is the heart of someone who has been bullied and it is the heart of a bully."

6. Now ask students for positive "put-ups" and other ways to help people open their hearts again after they are closed down. As students give positive examples, start opening up the paper until it is back the way it was. Point out, however, that even though it is open again, it still has wrinkles or scars from the previous hurts that may take longer to heal. Say, "That is why we must be very careful about what we say and do toward others, it can leave permanent scars on their heart."

7. If you do this in a classroom, you may want to tack it up on your bulletin board or frame it as a reminder.

Expected Outcomes: Fewer put-downs in the classroom or school.

Evaluation: Pre-post count the number of put-downs you observe among your students.

RETRIBUTIVE VS. RESTORATIVE JUSTICE.

As a servant leader, you will need new and effective ways to help people resolve conflicts and disputes. The resolution of conflicts that focus on win-

win solutions is needed to help restore the relationships that are damaged or disrupted in the conflict or dispute. Otherwise, you end up creating more problems than you solve. The restorative justice model of dispute resolution is designed to help heal and restore relationships. Servant leaders need to use this approach and support the efforts of others to utilize this approach to resolving conflicts and handling offenses.

Therefore, I want to share with you this life-giving, openhearted conflict resolution program called restorative justice. It is a quietly growing alternative in the criminal justice system and in other places like schools. In my opinion, the area that cries out the most for use of servant leadership principles is our current criminal justice system.

The current criminal justice system is based on retributive justice that focuses on discovering who violated a law and then to decide how they should be punished for their crime. It is based on a fear-based belief system that only finds what it is looking for: bad people. Once they get into the prison system they are not treated as individuals, but as a category and they are lost to society.

As a result of its prevailing self-serving beliefs, the criminal justice system in this country has incarcerated a record number of adolescents and adults. Currently, the U. S. has less than 5 percent of the world's population, but has almost 25 percent of the world's prisoners or over 6 million people who are under "correctional supervision."[5] Criminologists and scholars in other industrial nations say they are mystified and appalled by the number of people in prisons and length of prison sentences in this country.

Restorative justice actually frees people who commit crimes or other offenses to become more responsible citizens. It is a democratic approach to handling any violations of laws and resolving interpersonal conflicts. The approach is based on everybody answering the following questions related to any conflict or lawbreaking action:

1. How have others been harmed by this act?
2. Is there a need to repair the harm that was done?
3. Is the victim willing to face his/her offender?
4. Has the offender admitted the offense?
5. How can the relationship between the victim and the offender be repaired?

Restorative justice offers a whole process that helps find answers to these questions that, hopefully, leads to some level of restoration of the relationship and often involves some form of restitution if money is needed to repair the damages and restore the relationship. This process is growing in use in the current criminal justice system in many states and in some schools, although there is still much resistance to it.

Again, the retributive criminal justice system is based on a set of beliefs about, "What people are like?" Most people believe they are bad people because they broke the law and they deserve to be punished. In addition, it is not even worth spending much of society's money in any effort to rehabilitate them. The belief is that the best thing to do to protect society from their evil ways is to lock them up and throw away the key. Almost all those in prison feel anger and resentment about the way they are treated by the criminal justice system. There is no heart or love in the kind of treatment they have received.

Gandhi carefully stated the specific objections he had to the use of punishment as a way of correcting behavior. He said:
1. Punishment has the potential for abuse of power by authorities.
2. People often feel intimidated, humiliated and shamed when punished. This usually prevents them from learning the consequences of their behavior on others.
3. Punishment teaches people to fear rather than reflect on why they should not harm other.
4. Punishment can overshadow teaching people about their responsibility to others.
5.   Punishment causes people to focus on how the punishment is affecting them rather than how their behavior affected others.
6. Punishment often limits choices between obeying the rules or resisting them. This limits people's moral development so they follow rules only to avoid being punished rather than developing a personal moral and ethical code to regulate their own behavior.

The key to restorative justice is to get the offender to admit his offense, to take responsibility for repairing the damage that was caused by the offense, and to be willing to restore the relationship with the victim or victims by making amends and/or restitution for the harm that was done. In schools, this is a very practical approach to prevent repeated offenses. The offender and the victim are in close proximity to each other during the school day and the opportunities for repeated offenses are numerous, unless the relationship is restored.

When utilizing a restorative approach in schools, the key is to look for possible non-punitive and restorative interventions that either supplement or augment the traditional punitive sanctions such as filing detention, criminal charges, suspension from school, or expulsion. The non-punitive interventions include counseling, voluntary restitution and reconciliation with the victim of any offense.

Restorative justice interventions also include peer mediation, victim-offender mediation, and community group conferencing. In addition, under the restorative justice model it is possible to hold restorative class meetings, offender competency classes, victim impact panels, peacemaking circles, and talking circles. There are RJ programs all over the world and one web site contains many publications on the various applications of restorative justice. Check out this website at http://restorativejustice.org/rj-library/

I also recommend you check out the website of Marty Price JD, an expert on restorative justice at http://www.vorp.com. Marty has helped start restorative justice programs in many countries and is getting ready to teach restorative justice at a university in Mumbai, India.

THE FIRST VISITOR PROGRAM: A SERVANT LEADERSHIP PROGRAM FOR THE PRIMARY PREVENTION OF CHILD ABUSE AND NEGLECT

I would like to share with you my story of how I used my servant leadership skills to create a program to prevent child abuse and neglect in new families. One Sunday afternoon in the fall, Janae and I were driving thorough the high country in Colorado enjoying the fall colors. I got in touch with a deep need and told Janae about what I was thinking and feeling. I said that I realize that if I hadn't had the support of my extended family when I was an infant, I most likely would not have survived. I realize that most new parents do not have that kind of extended family support close by.

I was seriously neglected as an infant. My mother was only 20 years old when I was born. I was her first child and she suffered from a post-partum psychosis immediately after my birth and was unable to take care of me. Right after my birth, my mother tried unsuccessfully to nurse me. As a result, she felt like a failure and a week after I was born she hired a baby sitter to care for me and went back to work. In the first 2 months of my life I was passed among numerous other young baby sitters. When I was eight weeks old, she accidently tried to drown me while giving me a bath in the bathtub.

I weighed six pounds at birth and at eight weeks I weighed only five pounds. I was a "failure to thrive" baby.

At that point, my Dad intervened and arranged for me to live with his mother and sister. I was with my mother only on weekends where my Dad could watch her. My grandmother and aunt were very nurturing and that helped to bring me back from near-death.

I realized that today very few new parents have the support of their extended family nearby and I thought about how many infants do not survive as a result. I told Janae that one of my goals in my lifetime is to give back for what was given to me that saved my life. That is, I wanted to do something that gives new parents needed support to get over the shock of having to be totally responsible 24/7 for the life of a helpless infant.

I got my chance when I joined The Pikes Peak Coalition for Children in Colorado Springs, an advocacy group started to help promote programs and legislation to support the needs of children. I became the co-chair of the Program Committee, whose job it was to develop programs that would help support the needs of children and families.

I pitched the idea of a home visitation program to prevent child abuse and neglect to the committee. They liked my idea and recommended that the coalition start a home visitation program for new parents. We trained volunteers, who were mostly parents themselves, and who knew they would have benefitted from more support when they became new parents. We received funding for the program from some of the agencies that were part of the coalition.

The research on similar programs in other parts of the country showed that when new parents got needed support and information they were less likely to abuse or neglect their children. In fact, some research showed that this was the most effective way to eliminate child abuse and neglect and it did not cost very much to implement.

Actually, all the developed countries, except the U. S. and South Africa, offer universal, free home visitation services to all parents. As a result, have much less child abuse and neglect than does the U.S. It is a voluntary program and parents sign up to have a home visitor while the mother is in the hospital delivering their first child. Each home visitor is assigned to serve a family for three-years. Each home visitor is instructed to visit the home and bring a gift for the child in the first week after the mother is home from the hospital.

We had the help of a local church where the lady's auxiliary made baby blankets for us to give as a gift to the parents for the baby. The role of the home visitor is to be there to listen, to offer suggestions and information about any services available to the parents if they need them. We supervised them and met regularly with them to help them with any difficult situations.

I also had the opportunity to name the program. My co-chair, Sharon Littrell, called me one day and said, "We need a name for the home visitation program." It was around Christmas time and I thought about the story of the first visitors who came to visit baby Jesus. I suggested we call it the "First Visitor Program."

It has served the needs of thousands of new parents and eventually became part of a larger statewide home visitation program called the Colorado Bright Beginnings program. Most importantly, it did significantly reduce incidents of child abuse and neglect. Most states have created some kind of free home visitation services, but it is still not free and universal as it is in all other developed countries.

Voluntary home visiting programs that are designed to help young at-risk families, however, got a big boost with the new health reform legislation in 2010. The Patient Protection and Affordable Care Act invests $1.5 billion over five years in maternal and child health block grants for home visitation programs, according to Tom Birch, legislative council for the National Child Abuse Coalition.

These services are usually available for low-income, at-risk, families, including pregnant women under age 21, and living in communities in need of such services. Eligible families would also include those with:

- A history of child abuse or neglect,
- A history of substance abuse,
- Children with low student achievement,
- Children with disabilities or developmental delays, and
- Family members serving in the military, including those "who have had multiple deployments outside the United States."

Family members eligible for the home visitation services included a child's parents or primary caregivers, such as grandparents or other relatives of the child, foster parents, and a noncustodial parent with an ongoing relationship with the child.

COMMUNITIES THAT PRACTICE SERVANT LEADERSHIP: DAMANHUR[6]

As we transition into new ways to relate to each other using the principles of servant leadership, we need models of how to do this successfully. One such model is nestled in the alpine foothills north of Piedmont, Italy, between Turin and Aosta. It is a truly magical place on earth called Damanhur. In a 15-kilometer area surrounding the lush, green valley of Valchiusella lives a very active, multilingual community of 600 people.

Damanhur is a Federation of spiritual communities, with its own Constitution, culture, art, music, currency, schools and uses of science and technology. Its citizens are open to sharing their knowledge and research with other groups and cultures of the world, with anyone who is interested in exploring these themes.

Damanhur holds events at numerous centers, organizations and points of outreach in many cities around the world, and also hosts thousands of visitors each year who participate in tours, seminars, retreats and courses through Damanhur University. The community has attracted interest from scholars, educators and researchers in the fields of art, social sciences, spirituality, medicine and alternative health, economics and environmental sustainability.

When it was founded? Damanhur was founded in 1975 out of the imagination of Falco Tarassaco, né Oberto Airaudi (1950-2013). His enlightened and pragmatic vision created a fertile reality based on solidarity, sharing, love and respect for the environment.

Staying true to Falco's original vision of a community based upon ethical and spiritual values, Damanhur has captivated attention around the world as a laboratory for experimenting with sustainable ways of living, in harmony with nature and its elements and forces.

Damanhur is perhaps best known for its extraordinary subterranean work of art and architecture, a cathedral known as the Temples of Humankind. It has been profiled on international television as the "Eighth Wonder of The World." This complex was entirely dug by hand into the heart of the mountain. Decorated with mosaics, stained glass, sculptures, wall paintings and other works of art, it is dedicated to the awakening the divine spark present in every human being. Their website shows pictures of these wonderful temples.[7]

Where "con te" is a way of life. There is a spark on the faces and in the daily actions of those who live at Damanhur. It is where "con te" (or, "I am with you")...comes to life, where every encounter is an opportunity to remember our shared essential divine nature. Our citizens reside in 25 distinct "nucleo communities," inspired by Falco's original tenets of self-refinement through positive thinking, promoting diversity, embracing change and pursuing one's dreams with a sense of humor and adventure. Every day, Damanhurians experience these philosophies by taking action in every area...from art, culture, family life, labor and politics to research on the subtle energies that comprise the universe.

In fact, to emphasize the importance of change, humor and a respect for life, many Damanhur citizens choose to adopt an animal and plant name, which they use everyday. If you come visit us, you will encounter some of our beloved citizens such as Cigno Banano (Swan Banana), Piovra Caffè (Octopus Coffee), and Condor Girasole (Condor Sunflower).

While the pursuit of one's individual talents and "ways of service" are always encouraged, Damanhur residents agree that the community as a whole is equally important. The individual is both "I" and "we." As one community, Damanhurians (and any others who wish to join in) recognize themselves as a Popolo Spirituale (Spiritual People).

At Damanhur, the spiritual path...which they call the School of Meditation...leads every citizen through a lifelong process of self-exploration and search for the meaning of existence. This is facilitated through the study of ancient magical traditions and the celebration of the rhythms of nature. On this path, everyone learns to develop their talents and overcome their weak points (and helping others do the same).

Damanhur has created its own written Constitution, which contains the principles that are the basis for the social and spiritual experience. Damanhur also has a flag, which is yellow with a double square and an infinity sign, and the dandelion flower is a symbol of Damanhur.

A sustainable community in constant experimentation. In 2005, Damanhur received recognition from the United Nation's Global Forum on Human Settlements as a model for a sustainable society. The award was no accident. It was the result of Damanhur's deep respect for the environment as a conscious, sensitive entity and their citizens' commitment to co-existing with the plant and animal worlds (as well as intelligences that inhabit this universe) in a reverent and nurturing way.

One expression of this philosophy is Music of the Plants, in which communication with the plant world inspires concerts where the musicians are trees, and plants play music alongside human musicians. Damanhur citizens cultivate organic food and livestock, and restructure and build according to green building principles. Some citizens have created companies in the fields of renewable energy, eco-clothing, food production, and much more.

Damanhurians prefer natural healing methods and a holistic view of wellness, but not to the exclusion of science and medicine. The goal is to appreciate life in all its forms, while leaving the lowest possible impact on the environment. Where appropriate, leading-edge technologies are employed as a valuable ally in the defense of health and nature.

A powerful energy center on the planet. As you can see, what sets Damanhur apart from other intentional communities is that it actively utilizes the practical application of science, research and a spiritual philosophy in harmony with the planet. Yet, there is one more phenomenon that makes Damanhur truly unique: It's an axis point where four of the 18 worldwide synchronic lay lines intersect. The very ground breathes. Rocks, trees and plants resonate prana. Everything seems to be subtly energized. The effect, when you visit here, is an unmistakable lifting of the human spirit.

To walk in Damanhur is to walk through past, present and future. Ancient mysteries and the forgotten wisdom of great civilizations coalesce with a fresh, tech-infused vision of an evolving potential future. They encourage visitors, so go visit them and see for yourself the magic they have created.

The Damanhur Federation of Communities is a member of the Global Ecovillage Network (GEN), Italian Ecovillage Network (RIVE) and Conacreis (National Coordination of Associations and Communities of Ethical Spiritual Research).[8]

UBUNTU: THE SERVANT LEADERSHIP COMMUNITY OF THE FUTURE[9]

Albert Camus, one of the most unsentimental persons of the 20th century once wrote the following, "It would be completely Utopian to wish that men should no longer kill each other. Skeptical though we are, realism forces us to this Utopian alternative. When our Utopia has become part of history, men will find themselves unable to conceive of reality without it. For history is simply man's desperate attempt to give body to his most clairvoyant dreams."[10]

I would like to finish this book with a vision of a society of servant leaders that clearly is utopian in nature. I believe it is one that is entirely possible, if the cards fall the way I think they will. It is called Ubuntu. The old order is dying and we need visions of what will eventually replace the status quo. Ubuntu is one of those visions that is just coming into form and in my opinion holds tremendous promise.

What Is Ubuntu? Ubuntu is a vision of what we can create in a world filled with servant leaders. I wanted to introduce you to this concept at the end of this book, but actually it is more the beginning than the end. To learn more about Ubuntu go to several websites. The first one is all about the structure of an Ubuntu community: http://community.ubuntu.com Next go to Michael Tellinger's website to learn more about this worldwide movement: http://michaeltellinger.com. In addition, Michael Tellinger wrote a book I would highly recommend. The title is "Ubuntu: Contributionism, A Blueprint For Human Prosperity. It is available at Amazon.

An Interview With Corey Goode, A Whistleblower and Michael Tellinger, the Founder of Ubuntu. This interview took place on a show on the GAIA TV network out of Boulder, CO. It contains information that is very advanced for most people's minds, but points to the possibilities for a new direction for this planet. The interviewer is David Wilcox, the host of a show called Cosmic Disclosure. The guests on this particular show, are Michael Tellinger, the chief spokesperson for the Ubuntu Movement he calls "Contributionism," and Corey Goode, a whistleblower who was recruited and deeply involved in by the Secret Space Program. This particular show aired first on January 2016. FN.

It was a far-reaching interview, but I will quote only those parts that are relevant to Ubuntu. Hold on to your seats, this interview could knock your socks off.

DAVID: You have an advantage that Michael and I don't have, which is that you've met with a number of these people, you've looked them in the eye, and you've heard their arguments about why they think billions of people should be killed. The people who believe in that, how could they want that? What is their agenda? Why do they want so many people to die?

GOODE: It's not that much different from the Nazi-type of ideology. So many different of these non-terrestrial groups have a genetic purist kind of ideology or a genetic purist part of their experiment. That's why a lot of them, going back thousands of years, they did not want intertribal marriages

335

or mixing of tribes. They would have one tribe, if it came across another tribe, wipe out the entire bloodline of another tribe.

This is something that's gone back a long time. These are programs that compete with each other. And they, in more recent times, they've come together and found a way to work alongside each other a little bit better. But there are the syndicate groups, the occultist syndicate groups here on the planet that are humans that feel that they come from a bloodline that is non-terrestrial, and that we are all from a polluted worthless bloodline and that we should be wiped (out).

DAVID: So when they use terms like "useless eaters" and "sheeple," do they feel that they could control the planet better if there were fewer people here? Is that part of it?

GOODE: Part of it. Yes. And they put a lot of platitudes in that it would put the Earth more in balance with nature.

DAVID: Humans are bad for the environment.

GOODE: Right. When they know full well that we have the technologies that-- if the Secret Space Program wants to bring down technologies, such as replicators that would feed people, free energy, healing technologies that work off of light and sound frequency, a whole lot of different technologies that will improve the lives of people and help them live in balance with the planet. And this could be brought down, implemented with all of humanity immediately. And they don't want to bring it to the Americans and the British and then let it trickle down to the other members of the planet. They want to bring it to everyone on the planet all at the same time.

DAVID: All right. Let's start blending why we got Michael into the discussion here. And I'm going to ask you one question. And I want you to answer it, and then we'll open it up.

Some of the most controversial stuff that you and I have talked about in the show is the idea that we don't really need a financial system once these types of technologies come out. You've often dropped the term that the Space Program Alliance uses "the Babylonian money magic system." What's so bad about money? How is the financial system a tool for control by these secret Earth government syndicates that you've been describing? How do they use money against us?

GOODE: When you have money, you have debt. When you have debt, you have servitude and slavery. You have people that are of the "haves" lending money to the "have-nots." And the have-nots are the ones that end up carrying all of the burden. And that's the way that it's been set up to work from the very beginning.

And we've been so highly programmed for many thousands of years to believe that you have to have this paper folded up in your pocket. People have heard me talk, and they freak out. You want to take away our money. You want to move to a cashless society.

This is crazy. What are we going to do without money? How can you have a society without money? And--

GOODE: They can't fathom it. They're so highly programmed, they cannot fathom it.

DAVID: But how is what you're saying not communism? Aren't you going to have a group of oligarchs that absorb all the wealth, and then everybody gets paid the same, and therefore, nobody has any incentive to do anything?

GOODE: Or you're using the word paid. That would denote that there's money involved. When everyone has everything that they need-- I mean if you really want to have money or gold, the replicators have the ability.

You could synthesize a little bit of gold or synthesize an old 20th century $100 bill and carry that around in your pocket if that makes you feel more secure. But you're not going to need it because everything's going to be based off of bartering skills, people sharing their knowledge and abilities with each other as a community, and it's going-- and everyone's going to have what they need through these technologies. You're not going to need to work 9:00 to 5:00 to pay an electricity bill-- free energy. I mean you're not going to need to have to buy groceries-- replicator technology.

DAVID: Hold on right there. These people in space, these Space Program Alliance people, they mentioned to you before you even knew the name, Michael Tellinger and Ubuntu contributionism. What were they saying?

GOODE: To be clear, I had heard of Michael Tellinger and some of his work in ancient civilizations and some of the studies that he had done. And I had found a lot of that very interesting. I had no idea of the political movement thing that he was doing until it was brought up in a situation to where Lieutenant Colonel Gonzalez was there. And they were talking about Michael Tellinger in the Ubuntu-- did I say it right?

DAVID: That's It. Well done.

GOODE: Thank you. Movement, and how they said that this is the wave of the future and that this after there was going to be a catalyst event. There was going to be a full disclosure event. And after the monetary system is gone and capitalism, all the isms are gone, this is going to be the type of system that we're going to move into and use as we're a transitional civilization moving to be like a Star Trek civilization.

And as we're integrating and learning all of these new technologies exist and integrating them into our lives. And they said that they have been following this movement with great interest. And I thought it was very interesting. And I don't know what Mr. Tellinger has to say about that.

DAVID: Well, Michael, let's dive right into it here. Assume for the moment that whoever's watching this doesn't know you, hasn't seen your work before. Could you give us a short summary of Ubuntu contributionism, and what that is, and how it factors into our lives today.

TELLINGER: Thanks David. Sure. And there is an "ism" here, but it's a very different "ism" from all the other "isms" that we've ever heard of. And it's the "contributionism" part of Ubuntu.

First of all, Ubuntu is an African word. It's an ancient philosophy of sharing and caring. I've defined it as unity within community. And the often-used definition of it is: I am who I am because of who we all are. So, this is an ancient African philosophy, which is shared by all ancient cultures around the world. They have their own names for it and their own expressions for it, but it ultimately comes down to the same philosophy of unity consciousness-- sharing and caring for each other.

So, the Ubuntu movement was started with sharing knowledge, as Corey said, and information about the origins of money and how money is being used to control and enslave humanity. And then at the same time present a solution for the system because I think that the days of fear and just talking about how bad it is are over. We need to start presenting a solution. So that's really what this movement is all about-- presenting a solution that resonates with peoples, not only in their minds, but in their hearts, specifically.

And it seems to be that, for some reason, I've become the messenger of this. This is not my system. It's not my message. I'm just the messenger.

And it's interesting for me to hear that it's being spoken about in other areas that I wasn't even aware of. Because I've been getting some interesting e-mails from people around the world mentioning things to me about prophecy and all this, and how Ubuntu features into it, and how the work that we're doing features into it. And it's taken me by surprise, but I don't really want to go down that route. It's just interesting to note. Let's carry on with the task at hand.

There's a lot of work to be done, and we need to-- what we're doing is providing an alternative solution. The system we've had for the last 6,000, 12,000 years has not worked. It's been a system that was designed to enslave us, using what Corey calls a Babylonian magic money system.

Money is a tool of enslavement. That's all it is supposed to do. And I remind people all the time about the fact it's not about the money. It's about the use of money as a tool of control.

Those that control the money can create as much money as they want because there's nothing backing it. Its just money out of thin air. So, it's about keeping the control of the supply of money on the planet. And that's how you control the planet.

DAVID: Even in the biblical book of Genesis, it sets up right at the beginning explaining that the money system is this evil force.

TELLINGER: Yeah.

DAVID: If you actually read it carefully, it's right in there. If we had Jordan Maxwell right here to talk to us, one of the things he said that was so shocking was that these numbers that you see on the Federal Reserve note, the US Dollar, he calls them stock numbers. And he says, every person in America is given 10 different stock numbers. And you worked at the Federal Reserve, so I'm sure you know what I'm talking about.

And that these numbers on the money, each person has a certain number, a certain quantity of money issued to them-- I guess 3.4 million was, I think, one of the numbers I heard. So that when you see any given piece of money, it's somebody's soul. The number actually corresponds to somebody's soul. So when they're stealing the money--

TELLINGER: It's amazing.

DAVID: They want to be stealing our souls.

TELLINGER: Yeah.

DAVID: How do you see this-- what is the black magic of the financial system? What are they doing?

TELLINGER: You just described it, you know. The money system is somehow has been imbued in ancient times with some sort of a black magic component because look what it's done to our planet. Look what it's done to humanity. People go crazy.

As Corey said upfront, you know, when you say to people we're going to remove money from the system, they go-- start going crazy because they imagine we're going to take their money away. That's not what we're saying. We're saying we're going to create a new system that doesn't work with money. So, nobody needs money.

And this is where the whole introduction to a world transitioning from a world that's driven by money and greed, and corporate structure and control, and scarcity, move from the money driven system to a system that's driven by people and their passion for life. That's what the whole Ubuntu movement is about. And slowly but surely introducing people to the fact that we don't need money because money does nothing.

People do everything. It's about the people. We grow the food. We plant the seeds. We create the mathematical equations and develop the free energy devices.

And we do everything. Money does nothing. It just keeps getting in the way of people expressing their passion and living out beautiful lives.

DAVID: Well, if we had Darth Cheney sitting right here, he's-- and he was going to talk off the cuff--

TELLINGER: Yeah.

DAVID: He's going to say, as soon as you take away people's need to earn money, they're going to drink beer, and they're going to sit and watch TV all day.

TELLINGER: Yeah. That's in a capitalist-driven system. We're changing the system, changing a system where people live out their lives and express their talents that they are born with where they don't have to worry about money. What you mentioned there, David, is one of the, what I call, the 13 frequently asked questions. And out of 11 years of work of talking and exploring a new way, a new social structure that works without money, I've filtered it down to 13 frequently asked questions.

It's incredible. In a world with money, we have an insurmountable number of problems. In addition, our governments and our banking, financial guys can't solve the problems we have with all the money in the world. Moreover, in a proposed world without money, over a period of 11 years since 2005, it's filtered down to 13 problems we have to solve in order to live in paradise.

TELLINGER: Well, there you've just mentioned the big scam-- the reserve banks, the central banks of the world. Now for people that aren't aware of this, all the central banks of the world are private companies. They control our governments. It's like, our governments are indebted to these private companies, and they use all of us as their slaves.

So part of the teaching and the sharing of information with the Ubuntu movement and Ubuntu Party is first telling people about the origin-- firstly, the origins of money, as Corey calls it, the Babylonian magic money system, where money first appears. That it was maliciously introduced, that it's not the consequence of thousands of years of barter and trade. It is a maliciously introduced tool of enslavement that gives the people the illusion and the belief that they are free, but they still have to work for money so that they can live and pay their taxes.

So if you change this whole system-- and this is why I do the Ubuntu workshops, where after a day or two days of an Ubuntu workshop going through all these processes, it's turned out now that it's become like a group therapy session for people. And this is the last thing I expected because people are suddenly feeling the sense of release and relief.

Oh, my God. We don't need money. I see what you mean. And they not only understand it. They understand the origins of it, the reason how and why it was introduced, and how it was twisted as a tool of enslavement, and what we can do to get ourselves out of it.

And with this comes the good news. This is where people really start getting excited when they see how simple it is. How we have-- just by undoing some of the programming and the conditioning and the brainwashing that we've had to go through, that we've gone through for thousands of years, and especially the last 100 years or so with the current education system that was set up to do all this damage to us to turn us into a future labor force. Once people realize that how simple it is to get ourselves out of this mess, that's when you see the deep realization.

DAVID: So Michael, don't you think that-- let's say the dreaded global economic collapse occurred. The sun still rises. The sun still sets. There's tides. There's rain. There's crops that are going to grow. We have what we need here.

TELLINGER: Exactly.

DAVID: If these people are saying all the money is gone, where the f--- did it go? It's ridiculous. The resources are here. We're living in a very abundant world.

TELLINGER: Yeah. Well, this is one of the things that you need to re-mind people of many times and, sometimes, over and over again. That we live on a planet of abundance. We've been taught-- we have now been led to believe that we live in a planet of scarcity through the corporate hierarchical structure.

And this is all to do with the principle-- and this philosophy has been shoved into our heads since the earliest days, is that competition is what we need to have progress. You know that competition drives progress, competi-tion drives innovation, and competition drives people's desires to succeed in all that. That is the poison pill-- sugar-coated poison pill that we've been given, falsely believing that that's how things work.

No, no, no. Competition creates scarcity. Competition makes corpora-tions hide things, so they can benefit from the knowledge and information, the technology while the rest of the humanity suffers.

Competition prevents new technology from being released-- petroleum, electricity, cures for disease. You understand, well, this is why competition is so bad. So, the whole thing with Ubuntu and contributionism is just switch-ing that one little thing around, turning competition into cooperation and collaboration.

GOODE: And the idea of forgiving other people, becoming forgiving of ourselves. There's a lot of forgiveness that needs to happen between tribes and nations. We need to move past that and start working on projects like the one you're talking about in detail that will help us come together and solve these problems ourselves after doing the inner work and come up with the solutions ourselves, instead of waiting for it to be done for us, because it will never happen otherwise.

TELLINGER: Again, you took the words right out of my mouth. I always tell people in my workshops, in the Ubuntu workshops, that we are the ones we've been waiting for. We are the wave of the New Age. And we can't sit on our backsides and wait for somebody to come and save us.

And this is always a problem. People are waiting for some sort of a knight in shining armor, some external savior. We have everything encoded in our DNA.

We are co-creators of our own reality. So let's create this own reality. Let's focus on a positive outcome for humanity. Let's stop fear mongering. Let's stop talking about the dark, negative stuff.

Well, we can talk about it, but as a platform of knowledge and information that we then use to launch ourselves into this new utopian world. And I like to use the word utopian, specifically, because utopian is a good word. It's not a bad word. Oh, it's just a utopian idea.

Yeah, I like utopian. It's a good word, right. Let's use utopian more. And I just want to also add just because we mentioned the word like barter and all that stuff. So, I want to firstly say that the whole Ubuntu contributionism philosophy is not a philosophy about creating self-sustaining communities. It's creating communities of abundance because we live on a planet of abundance.

One apple tree creates 1,000 or thousands of apple trees, not one other apple tree. And this is what we are capable of. Each one of us is capable of creating infinite abundance if we are left to create and do-- express our natural talents that we are born with.

So, it's creating communities of abundance and not bartering or trading or replacing the money system with any form of exchange. As long as you've got any kind of form or exchange, it is open to exploitation. And somebody will find a way to use that against the people for their own benefit.

DAVID: All right. Well, I'm sorry to end it right now while it's just getting good, but that's all the time we have for in this particular episode. We're going to be back next time continuing this fascinating discussion with the insider's insider, Corey Goode, and with Michael Tellinger, the face behind the Ubuntu movement. As always, we want to thank you for watching. And we'll see you next time.[11]

THE CYBORG AGE: THE THREAT AND THE PROMISE

One of the biggest obstacles that the servant leader must face in the future is the threat of Artificial Intelligence and the trans-human Cyborg. It means the servant leader will have to find a way to serve organic humans while relating to non-human machines that some humans have chosen to become.

Perhaps I need to give a bit of the history on how we got here. It is highly unlikely that humanity could have achieved this technological milestone without some help. That help likely came in July 1947 when an alien spacecraft crashed about 75 miles north of Roswell, New Mexico. The U. S. government covered up this event since it happened, claiming it was a Weather Balloon that they found. Near Roswell.

What likely happened is that two aliens found at the crash scene were taken to a place outside of Las Vegas, Nevada known at Area 51. At this secret location, U. S. scientists and technicians retro-engineered the technology they found on this craft and on its alien inhabitants. The two aliens were actually Cyborgs and that gave us valuable information on how these non-human beings functioned. I happened to know one of the scientists who told me he took regular tissue samples from these beings at Area 51.

He also observed other things while at Area 51. He saw the development of our most advanced aircraft, such as the B-1 bomber and other aircraft. Other technologies involving lasers were developed there as well. It is possible that this is where we gained the knowledge to be able to build replicas of the Cyborgs, who they studied intensively.

In 2001, the U. S. government sponsored a conference in Hawaii titled, "Converging Technologies for Improving Human Performance." They gathered the leading edge scientists in nanotechnology, neuroscience, biotechnology, information Technology and Cognitive Sciences. At this conference, participants were told that the goal was to unite the research and technology in four different areas of science:

1. BITS from computer scientists
2. Atoms from nano-scientists
3. Neurons from brain scientists
4. Genes from genetic and biological scientists

Their goal was to bring all this research together to create the super human or trans-human by 2035. This project, funded mostly by the U. S. government, has accelerated so fast that they are now predicting that by 2020, they will have reached their goal. They claim they will be able by that time to produce a trans-human Cyborg with superior intelligence, strength, longevity and the ability to shape-shift.

On February 20, 2015, researchers announced that they successfully demonstrated materials, mechanics designs, and integration strategies for what is called near field communication (NFC) enabled electronics. This will allow seamless, conformal contact with human skin and wireless interfaces to a NFC smart phone. Using tiny gold particles and a kind of resin they discovered to make a new kind of flexible sensor or electronic skin that could be placed on or under the human skin and by operated remotely. It is designed to interface with what is known as the Planetary Skin or Internet of Things. This was all reported in the February 2015 issue of Manwerk News.[12]

This tells us how close they are already to actually creating a chip that they can place on the human skin that will eventually take over all human functions, except the feeling function and the soul. It will also leave the human being without free will. The devil is truly in the details. For example, by "smarter" they do not necessarily mean higher I.Q. "Smarter humans" means that the chipped people will be more watchable, programmable and controllable.

The digerati want you to see your smart phone as a symbiotic extension of your brain. It gives you access to billions of brains and them access to yours. They also want you to understand that your phone is your personal gateway to the Internet of Things and the Cloud. Since billions of people already have a "smart phone," it will be easy to put a chip in you that does the rest of the job. They will be able to control everything you do and say.

It is hard to predict what the impact of this new technology actually will be, but it will be an issue that servant leaders and others will have face in the near future. Beam me up Scotty!

NOTES

1   *Vitale, J. Simple Steps to Healing: H'oponopono I love You, I'm Sorry, please Forgive Me, Thank You. Want To Know, Info.*
http://www.wanttoknow.info/070701imsorryiloveyoujoevitale
Accessed June 10, 2016.

2   *Keen, S. (1994). Hymns To An Unknown God. New York: Bantam, pp. 236–237.*

3   *Weinhold, B. (2006). Spreading Kindness: A Program Guide for the Kind & Safe Schools Initiative, Volumes I, II and III. Colorado Springs, CO: CICRCL Press.*

4   *Ibid. p. 45.*

5   *Center For Justice & Reconcilation. http://restorativejustice.org/rj-library/*
Check out this web site to learn more about this heartful innovation. Accessed May 24, 2016.

6   *http://www.damanhur.org*
Accessed May 24, 2016.

7   *http://www.thetemples.org/*
Accessed may 24, 2016.

8   *http://www.damanhur.org/en/what-is-damanhur*
Accessed on 4/27/16.

9   *Tellinger, M. (2013). Ubuntu contributionism: A blueprint for human prosperity. South Africa: Zulu Planet Publishers*

10   *Camus, A. (1980). Neither victims nor executioners. New York: Continuum Publishing Co., 51.*

11   *Transcript of Cosmic Disclosure: Ubuntu and the Blue Avians Message (Part 2 Season 3, Episode 9)*
http://spherebeingalliance.com/blog/transcript-cosmic-disclosure-ubuntu-and-the-blue-avians-message-part-2.html
Accessed May 27, 2016.

12   *Electronic skin tattoos with advanced near-field communication capabilities. (February 20, 2015). Manwerk News.*
http://www.nanowerk.com/nanotechnologynews/newsid=39135.php

37308350R00201

Made in the USA
Middletown, DE
28 November 2016